VOICES OF THE PAST

by John R. Bennett

VOCAL RECORDINGS—1898-1925

VOLUME 2

THE GRAMOPHONE COMPANY LIMITED (HMV)

ITALIAN CATALOGUE

PRICE TWENTY SHILLINGS

VOICES OF THE PAST

VOL. 2.

A Catalogue of Vocal Recordings

from

The Italian Catalogues

of

The Gramophone Company Limited 1899—1900
The Gramophone Company (Italy) Limited 1899—1909
The Gramophone Company Limited 1909
Compagnia Italiana del Grammofono 1909—1912
Società Nazionale del Grammofono 1912—1925

by

John R. Bennett (F.R.C.O.)

THE OAKWOOD PRESS

PREFACE

- by -

ALAN KELLY

Unlike P.G.Hurst who wrote the introduction to Volume
One in this series, I cannot recall the days when Red G. & Ts. of the
original London issue were not rare collectors' pieces but could be
bought freely in the shops, when Fonotipias were advertised by the
Gramophone Exchange as being available in thousands, and when Melba was
not simply a controversial name and a few fragments of badly recorded
sound but an artist in her prime who could be heard and judged at first
hand for the price of a seat in the gallery. Nor can I ever hope to
possess a collection similar to his, probably the next best thing, but
at least I am fortunate in that, through the medium of the microgroove
and the tape recorder, I again have the chance of purchasing records of
all kinds and ages over the counter (or at least by post), and in perfect condition.

I remember feeling frustrated by a remark in "The Record
Collector" that the lovely "O mio babbino caro" by Frances Alda, "should
be in everybody's collection". To-day, although the record is still
unknown to me, I can sit back and wait complacently, knowing that soon-
er or later it will appear on LP. Considering the rarity of original
pressings of some records, surely LP and tape are the answer to a collector's dream. This is not to say, however, that all LPs are good;
some are frightful concoctions which make one wonder whether any collector takes them seriously. But in spite of this, we still have the
possibility that at least the specialists in our own field will endeav-
our to produce honest, unboosted reproductions. In this way old catalogues, complete discographies and books similar to the present series
take on a new interest and a value which would otherwise be severely
limited by mundane considerations of price alone.

Taken as a group, collectors of "old" gramophone records,
like collectors of other oddities, are somewhat biassed in their opinions. We each tend, naturally, to highlight the importance of our own
pet likes, and we often tend to minimise the opinions and tastes of
others. But one thing we do have in common. There is not one among
us who could honestly say his collection is complete, and who would not
at least be tempted by some choice specimen in particularly favourable
circumstances. For this reason we show interest when someone discovers
an unpublished Plancon, although we may have next to no chance of hear-
ing it, let alone of owning a copy. We wonder what exactly H.M.V. int-
ended to issue on DB 1472 in case it turns out to be by Vanni-Marcoux,
or we scan lists or turn over piles of records in the hope of finding

one by Jean de Reszke or by Angelica Pandolfini. Stranger things have happened before and no doubt will happen again.

However, these are no longer purely academic speculations. Tomorrow's post may bring details of still more re-issues to delight us and we can look through the discographies in "The Record Collector" with every hope of putting the opinions of the writers to the proof - on our own machines and in our own good time. The possibilities in record collecting have changed considerably in the past few years. Before the war, a simple request in the columns of "The Gramophone" would bring parcels of old catalogues and lists from people who regarded them as junk, but who had preserved them for years. Nowadays these same catalogues are objects of interest in their own right, and collected eagerly at considerable cost. Yet they offer a poor solution at the best to the problem of obtaining information on our favourite artists. Some records remained on sale for years, others disappeared shortly after publication, and some remained unpublished. Even a complete set of catalogues is no good guide, for many interesting records appeared only in flimsy supplements in relatively obscure countries, leaving the collector to wonder what artists and titles are concealed by the blank spaces in his lists.

Many people, myself included, have spent years trying to fill in these blanks, to obtain a complete record of issues or projected issues. Those who have not tried to do this may not appreciate the size and difficulty of the task. Since 1898, the number of records issued by The Gramophone Company (and Sister Companies) must top the million mark. Most of these are of little interest to us and few collectors would seek lists of recordings in Urdu or Tamil. A large proportion of the remainder is instrumental or orchestral and of secondary interest. Of the rest, opinions differ. Leo Riemens objects to the remark that one of his favourite tenors, Campagnola, is a mediocrity, and while agreeing with him, I take exception to what I consider his strictures on Alessandro Valente. One collector rejoices in a perfect Richard Temple; another would not give it house room. Examples could be found by the dozen.

In order to cater for these tastes, it is necessary and not just desirable to have a catalogue of all vocal records likely to appeal to collectors. This is what Bauer produced in 1947 - five hundred pages of fine print covering the first ten years of commercial recording - a tremendous piece of research, even in these days of overstrained adjectives. The present volume is one section of an even more remarkable piece of work containing about one half of all the collectors' pieces ever issued - the work of His Master's Voice. If I were asked to guess which single block of records attracts the attention of the largest number of collectors, I should have difficulty in choosing between H.M.V's double-sided Celebrity series and those in the present volume. With the co-operation of collectors and of The Gramophone Company itself, Mr. Bennett presents us with both and much more besides. I can only record my gratitude to him and I am sure a great number of others will have similar feelings as they turn these pages.

AUTHOR'S INTRODUCTION

This volume comprises the familiar 52000, 53000 and 54000 numerals for 10 inch discs, 052000, 053000 and 054000 for 12 inch, and, probably for the first time, the domestic Green Labels of the lesser lights of the singing world.

In March 1903 Black Label "Piccoli" (7") and "Concerto" (10") were catalogued at L.3.50 and L.6.25. In the same list were Red Labels of Pinto, Bruno, Sammarco, Caruso, De Lucia, De Luca, Garbin, Battistini and Giraldoni at L.12.50. In November "Monarch" (12") Black Label were priced at L.9.50, with some Celebrity Red Labels of Joachim, the famous violinist, at L.18.75.

It is interesting to note the Company's assessment of probable demand for an artist at a particular time by the prices fixed.   For example, in August 1904 a 10 inch Tamagno sold at L.25; other celebrities were "Monarch" L.18.75, "Concert" L.12.50 and "Piccoli" L.7.50. Ruffo "Monarch" were L.15.75 and "Concert" L.10.   In April 1905 a 12 inch Tamagno was listed at L.25; Caruso, Giorgini and Boninsegna at L.18.75; Melba slightly surpassed Tamagno at L.26.50. The following month Sembrich "Monarch" stood at L.12.75.   In December 1906 Ruffo was priced at L.18.75; Patti was placed a little below Melba at L.25. In May 1906 Caruso advanced to L.25; in October three Red Label artists - Cucini, Sembrich and Eames were sold at L.18.75; De Lucia "Concert" were L.12.50 and "Monarch" L.18.75.   In January 1907 Battistini, Ruffo and Galvany joined De Lucia at his level. Melba, Patti and Tamagno Red Labels were L.26.50, L.25 and L.25, but Caruso at L.25 was accorded Pink Label status, as was Patti a little later.

September 1907 witnessed the probable first appearance of the double-sided Black Label ("Concert" L.6.25; "Monarch" L.9.50). The name of Calvé was added to the Celebrity band at L.15.75 for 12 inch Pink Label. The previous month Caruso, Abott, Homer and Scotti appeared in the "Rigoletto" Quartette at L.31.25 (Pale Blue); Caruso duets on Pale Green Label at L.25; Battistini's Orange Label, Patti's Pink and Melba's Lilac all realised L.15.75, as distinct from the slightly lower Reds of De Lucia, Giorgini, Ruffo, Journet, Boronat, Galvany, Cucini, Frascani and De Tura at L.11.25. In 1908 Ruffo, De Tura and Tetrazzini were upgraded to Pink; Marconi, Scampini, Pareto and De Casas were Red. In August 1908 Caruso's list issued White at L.37.50, Blue L.31.25, Green L.25, Pink L.16.50 and L.11, whereas a year earlier his list had read Blue L.31.25, Green L.25 and Pink L.15.75 and L.10, there then being no White Label.

The Angel Trade Mark was still in use in February 1910; in March the Dog appeared on the back page of the catalogue, in November on the front page. In the following year the Angel and the Dog represented the official Trade Marks, both featured on the front page of the February list and finally, in November 1911, attention was drawn to the Dog as representing the principal Trade Mark of the Company.

In December 1916 all new Black Labels went over to double-sided form, and from the 15th. October 1917 new wartime prices came into effect with Red "Concert" advancing from L.8 to L.9 and "Monarch" from L.12 to L.13.50, Pink and Lilac from L.11 to L.12 and from L.16.50 to L.17.50, Violet from L.6 to L.7 and from L.8.50 to L.10. The new double-sided Black Label advanced from L.6.75 to L.8 and from L.10 to L.12. The prices of the dearer records remained unchanged - White (Sextette) 12 inch L.37.50, Pale Blue (Quartette) 12 inch L.31.25, Pale Green (Duet) 12 inch L.25 and Buff 10 inch L.16.50, 12 inch L.21. On the 1st. August 1919 Black Label rose to L.12.50 and L.19.50, but two years later, from the 1st. July 1921, the ceiling prices of the post-war years began to return to more normal levels, so that Black Label 10 inch and 12 inch fell from L.24 to L.20 and from L.36 to L.30; Pink, Red and Violet from L.30 to L.25 and from L.44 to L.35; Buff L.36 to L.27 and L.48 to L.38; Pale Green 12 inch from L.50 to L.40; Pale Blue 12 inch from L.55 to L.45; White 12 inch from L.58 to L.42. The high ranking Battistini, Chaliapin and Patti 12 inch at L.58 also fell to L.42, while the 10 inch Tamagno at L.63 were reduced to L.50.

In 1918 His Master's Voice records were issued through the Italian Catalogue for British and American troops in Italy under the well known "B" and "C" English series; both the Angel and the Dog marks made an appearance in these lists.

The name of Gigli appeared in a supplement dated the 1st. February 1919, Dragoni in August, Schipa in January 1920, Heifetz and Elman in March, Poli-Randacio in September, Besanzoni in May 1921, Zanelli in June.

On the 1st. August 1924 Celebrity records were first given DA and DB letters, together with the old single-sided numbers, but the General Catalogue of the 1st. June omits the old numbers altogether. Prices for these new issues on the 1st. December were L.35 for "DA", L.45 for "DB", L.35 for "DJ", L.45 for "DK", L.48 for "DM", L.53 for "DO", L.54 for "DQ".

The general scheme of the items detailed herein follows that enumerated in the English Catalogue : catalogue number, name of artist, title of work performed, name of opera, oratorio or other work to which belonging, composer's name, speed in brackets if other than 78 (if known), matrix number in brackets, actual dates of recording in Roman numerals, or date of issue (month and year) in ordinary figures, any double-sided version such as VA, VB, IRCC, HRS. Where only the year is mentioned (i.e. "1904") this refers to the date of recording. In the Green Label Section, the dates supplied are those of issue and not recording dates.

Jedburgh
March 1957

ACKNOWLEDGMENTS

I am indebted to The Gramophone Company Limited, Hayes, Middlesex, for their kind co-operation in the compilation of this catalogue, and in particular I am especially grateful to Miss L.A. Walton, Head of the Museum, The Gramophone Company Limited, without whose assistance this project would have been impossible of achievement; her advice and criticisms have been invaluable.

I accord grateful acknowledgments to Miss Valentine Britten, the Gramophone Librarian, B.B.C., London, for her kind permission to visit the Library; to Mr. Alan Kelly, who has contributed a great amount of valuable information and who has kindly undertaken to write the Preface; to Mr.H.Hugh Harvey, for his willingness to read the proofs, and whose corrections have been most welcome; to Mr.W.A.Maw, Templestowe, Victoria, Australia, for the matrix numbers in the Green Label Series.

To any others whose names I have unwittingly omitted, who have contributed in any way towards the furtherance of this work, I tender thanks.

```
52011 SAMMARCO  Canzone della pulce  "Dannazione di Faust" (Berlioz)pno.1903/4
52016 MARCONI   Dai campi, dai prati  "Mefistofele" (Boito)pno. 1903/4
52017 MARCONI   Stanze "Nerone" (Rubinstein) pno. 1903/4
52034 CARUSO    Mattinata (Leoncavallo)pno.acc.comp.(2181h)1904.DA546
52059 SCOTTI    Suo padre - anch'io pugnai  "Aida" (Verdi) (A1091) 1904
52061 SCOTTI    Bella siccome "Don Pasquale" (Donizetti)(A1092)1904.IRCC 75
52062 CARUSO    La donna è mobile "Rigoletto" (Verdi)pno. (A995) 1904
52063 CARUSO    E lucevan le stelle "Tosca" (Puccini) (A998) 1904.DA125.VA34
52064 CARUSO    Siciliana "Cavalleria Rusticana" (Mascagni)pno.(A1000) 1904
52065 CARUSO    Una furtiva lagrima (v.1) "L'Elisir d'Amore" (Donizetti)
                                                          (A996) 1904.VA12
52066 CARUSO    Vesti la giubba "Pagliacci" (Leoncavallo)pno. (A1002) 1904
52067 SCOTTI    Dio possente "Faust" (Gounod) (A878) 1903
52070 PLANÇON   Pro peccatis "Stabat Mater" (Rossini)pno. (A991) 1904
52072 ANCONA    Mattinata (Tosti) 1904
52073 ANCONA    Il sogno "Otello" (Verdi) 1904
52074 ANCONA    Lucia -(Ballata)1904
52077 DE LUCIA  Mia madre "Fedora" (Giordano)pno. 1904
52078 DE LUCIA  Vedi io piango "Fedora" (Giordano)pno. 1904
52079 DE LUCIA  Occhi di fata (Denza)pno. 1904
52080 DE LUCIA  Un dì felice "la Traviata" (Verdi) (2156 I) pno. 1904
52081 DE LUCIA  Una vergine, un angiol di Dio "La Favorita" (Donizetti)pno.04
52082 DE LUCIA  Serenata (Tosti) pno. 1904
52083 DE LUCIA  L'anima ho stanca "Adriana Lecouvreur" (Cilea)pno. 1904
52084 DE LUCIA  Lontananza (Cilea) pno.acc.comp.    1904
52128 ANCONA    Mattinata (Tosti) (2307 L) 1904
52129 ANCONA    Il sogno "Otello" (Verdi) 1904
52130 ANCONA    Serenata "Don Giovanni" (Mozart) (2320 L) 1904
52168 GIORGINI  Recondita armonia "Tosca" (Puccini) 1904
52170 GIORGINI  E lucevan le stelle "Tosca" (Puccini) 1904
52173 GIORGINI  La dolcissima effige "Adriana Lecouvreur" (Cilea)(2359L)1904
52174 GIORGINI  L'anima ho stanca "Adriana Lecouvreur" (Cilea) 1904
52175 GIORGINI  No più nobile "Adriana Lecouvreur" (Cilea) 1904
52176 GIORGINI  La donna è mobile "Rigoletto" (Verdi) pno. 1904
52177 GIORGINI  Vedi io piango "Fedora" (Giordano) 1904
52178 GIORGINI  Amor ti vieta "Fedora" (Giordano) 1904
52191 CARUSO    Recondita armonia "Tosca" (Puccini) pno. (A999) 1904. VA34
52193 CARUSO    Viva il vino "Cavalleria Rusticana" (Mascagni)(77)(A2344)
                                                   1905. DA545. VA33
52194 GIORGINI  Prendi l'anel "La Sonnambula" (Bellini)(6982b)pno. 1905
52195 GIORGINI  Stornelli marini (Mascagni) pno. 1905
52197 GIORGINI  Cercherò lontana "Don Pasquale" (Donizetti) pno. 1905
52199 GIORGINI  Parmi veder le lagrime "Rigoletto" (Verdi) pno. 1905
52342 GRAVINA   Evocazione "Roberto il Diavolo"(Meyerbeer) 1902
52343 GRAVINA   Aria d'Alvise "La Gioconda" (Ponchielli) 1902
52344 CARUSO    Questa o quella "Rigoletto" (Verdi) (1783b) 1902
52345 CARUSO    Il sogno "Manon" (Massenet)(75)(1785b) 1902 VA58
52346 CARUSO    Una furtiva lagrima "L'Elisir d'Amore" (Donizetti)(1786b)1902
52347 CARUSO    Giunto sul passo estremo "Mefistofele" (Boito)(74)(1787b)1902
                                                   DA550.VA 7
52348 CARUSO    Dai campi, dai prati "Mefistofele" (Boito) 1st.ed.(1789b)1902
52348 CARUSO    Dai campi, dai prati    do.   do. (2871b)(75)1902.DA550.VA 7
52349 CARUSO    E lucevan le stelle "Tosca" (Puccini)(72)(1790b)1902.DA547.VA29
52367 GRAVINA   Romanza "Simone Boccanegra" (Verdi) 1902
52368 CARUSO    Apri la tua finestra "Iris" (Mascagni) (1791b) 1902
```

```
52369 CARUSO   Celeste Aida (1st.ed) "Aida" (Verdi)(1784b) 1902
52369 CARUSO   Celeste Aida "Aida" (Verdi)(75)(2873b) 1902. DA549. VA12
52370 CARUSO   No,non chiuder "Germania" (Franchetti)(75)pno.(1788b)1902
                                                         DA544. VA37
52371 SAMMARCO  Ferito prigionier "Germania" (Franchetti) 1902
52372 SAMMARCO  Pari siamo "Rigoletto" (Verdi) 1902
52373 SAMMARCO  Zazà piccola zingara "Zazà" (Leoncavallo) 1902
52374 SAMMARCO  Prologo "Pagliacci" (Leoncavallo) 1902
52375 SAMMARCO  Credo "Otello" (Verdi) 1902
52378 CARUSO   Studenti,udite "Germania" (Franchetti)(75)pno. (1782b)DA544.VA37
52401 GIRALDONI  Notturno "Cristoforo Colombo" (Franchetti)pno. 1902
52402 GIRALDONI  Aria del demone "Demone" (Rubinstein) pno. 1902
52403 GIRALDONI  O tu, bell'astro "Tannhäuser" (Wagner) 1902
52404 GIRALDONI  Aria della morte "Don Carlos" (Verdi) pno. 1902
52405 GIRALDONI  Visione fuggitiva "Hérodiade" (Massenet) pno. 1902
52406 GIRALDONI  Quest'assisa "Aida" (Verdi) pno. 1902
52410 DE LUCIA  Ideale (Tosti) pno. 1902. IRCC 5003
52411 DE LUCIA  La donna è mobile "Rigoletto" (Verdi)pno. (2863b)1902.HRS2001
52412 DE LUCIA  Marechiare (Tosti) pno. 1902
 52413 DE LUCIA  Napulitanata (Costa) pno. 1902
52414 DE LUCIA  Recondita armonia "Tosca" (Puccini) pno. 1902. HRS2001
52415 DE LUCIA  Fenesta che lucive - Neapolitan. pno. 1902
52416 DE LUCIA  Il sogno "Manon" (Massenet) pno. 1902. IRCC 57
52417 CARUSO   Cielo e mar "La Gioconda" (Ponchielli)(74)(2874b)1902.DA547.VA29
52418 CARUSO   Siciliana "Cavalleria Rusticana" (Mascagni)(74)(2876b)1902
                                                         DA545. VA30
 52419 CARUSO   No, più nobile "Adriana Lecouvreur" (Cilèa)pno.acc.comp.
                                                         (2880b) 1902
 52420 DE LUCA  Monologo di Michonnet "Adriana Lecouvreur" (Cilèa)pno.comp.1902
 52421 DE LUCA  Caro mio ben (Giordani) pno. 1902
 52422 DE LUCA  O casto fior "Re di Lahore" (Massenet) pno. 1902
 52423 DE LUCA  Vien Leonora "La Favorita" (Donizetti) pno. 1902
 52424 DE LUCA  Eri tu "Ballo in Maschera" (Verdi) pno. (2886-R) 1902
 52425 DE LUCA  Come il romito fior "Amleto" (Thomas) pno. 1902
 52426 DE LUCA  Deh vieni alla finestra "Don Giovanni" (Mozart) pno. 1902
 52427 DE LUCIA  Ecco ridente "Il Barbiere di Siviglia" (Rossini) pno.(2864b)02
 52428 GARBIN  Un dì felice "La Traviata" (Verdi) pno. 1902
 52429 GARBIN  Donna non vidi mai "Manon Lescaut" (Puccini) pno. 1902
 52430 GARBIN  Guardate pazzo son "Manon Lescaut" (Puccini) pno. 1902
 52431 GARBIN  Aspetti signorina "La Bohème" (Puccini) pno. 1902
 52432 GARBIN  Mimì è una civetta "La Bohème" (Puccini) pno. 1902
 52433 GARBIN  Brindisi "Cavalleria Rusticana" (Mascagni) pno. 1902
 52434 GARBIN  Una vergine un angiol di Dio "La Favorita" (Donizetti)pno. 1902
 52435 DE LUCIA  Ah! non mi ridestar "Werther" (Massenet) pno. 1902
 52436 DE LUCIA  Amor ti vieta "Fedora" (Giordano) pno. (2865 W2) 1902
·52437 DE LUCIA  Il fior "Carmen" (Bizet) (2899b)(76) 1902. VA13
 52438 DE LUCIA  Tu sei morta nella vita mia (Costa) pno. 1902
 52439 CARUSO  Amor ti vieta "Fedora" (Giordano)(74)(2872b)1902.DA549.VA53/58
 52440 CARUSO  Vesti la giubba "Pagliacci" (Leoncavallo)pno. Cottone (75) 1902
                                                         (2875b)DA546.VA30
 52441 CARUSO  Non t'amo più (Denza)(75)(2877b) 1902. DA548. VA31
 52442 CARUSO  Luna fedel (Denza) (2882b) 1902. VA9
 52443 CARUSO  La mia canzone (Tosti)pno. (75)(2879b) 1902. DA548. VA31
 52444 DE LUCA  Bella siccome un angelo "Don Pasquale" (Donizetti)pno. 1902
·52650 DE LUCIA  Cigno gentil "Lohengrin" (Wagner)(74)pno.(2905b)1902.VA13
 52651 DE LUCIA  A suon di baci (Baldelli) pno. 1902
 52652 DE LUCIA  Siciliana "Cavalleria Rusticana" (Mascagni) pno. 1902
```

52663 BATTISTINI Finch'han del vino "Don Giovanni" (Mozart)(439z)02.HRS1007
52664 BATTISTINI O tu, bell'astro "Tannhäuser" (Wagner)(440z) 1902
52665 BATTISTINI Aria "Eugen Onegin" (Tchaikovsky) (441z) 1902. IRCC 143
52666 BATTISTINI Serenata "Don Giovanni" (Mozart)(442z) 1902. VA5
52667 BATTISTINI La mantilla (Alvarez) (443z) 1902
52668 BATTISTINI Occhi di fata (Denza) (444z) 1902
52669 BATTISTINI Ancora (Tosti) (445z) 1902. VA15
52670 BATTISTINI Deh non plorar "Demone" (Rubinstein)(446z) 1902. IRCC 143
52671 BATTISTINI Cavatina "Il Barbiere di Siviglia" (Rossini)(447z)02.IRCC77
52672 BATTISTINI Aria di Valentino "Faust" (Gounod)(448z) 1902
52673 TAMAGNO Esultate "Otello" (Verdi)(74)(3001b) 1903. DR100
52674 TAMAGNO Niun mi tema "Otello" (Verdi)(74) (3002b) 1903. DR100
52675 TAMAGNO Ora e per sempre addio "Otello" (Verdi)(75)(3004b)1903-DR105
                                                                     IRCC193
52676 TAMAGNO Un dì all'azzurro "Andrea Chenier" (Giordano)(75)(3008b)03.DR102
52677 TAMAGNO Re del cielo "Profeta" (Meyerbeer)(74)(3011b) 1903. DR104
52678 TAMAGNO Di quella pira "Il Trovatore" (Verdi)(75)(3013b) 1903. DR102
52679 TAMAGNO Sopra Berta l'amor "Profeta" (Meyerbeer)(75)(3014b) 1903.DR104
52680 TAMAGNO Adieu vains objets "Hérodiade" (Massenet)(75)(3016b)03.IRCC172
52681 TAMAGNO Figli miei v'arrestate "Sansone e Dalila" (Saint-Saëns)(75)
                                               (3019b) 1903.DR101.VA62
52682 TAMAGNO O muto asil "Guglielmo Tell" (Rossini)(75)(3020b) 1903. DR103
52683 TAMAGNO Corriam, corriamo "Guglielmo Tell" (Rossini)(75)(3026b)03.DR103
52684 TAMAGNO Quand nos jours "Hérodiade" (Massenet)(75)(3027b) 1903.DR101
52685 TAMAGNO Perchè? (Romanza di Fillippi)(75) (3023b) 1903
52716 VALERO Dormi pure (Scuderi) 1903
52717 VALERO Siciliana "Cavalleria Rusticana" (Mascagni) 1903
52718 VALERO Brindisi "Cavalleria Rusticana" (Mascagni) 1903
52719 VALERO El amor es la vida (de los Moteros) 1903
52764 ZENATELLO Orride steppe "Siberia" (Giordano) pno. 1904
52773 DE LUCA La conobbi quand'era fanciulla "Siberia" (Giordano) pno. 1904
52774 A.PINI-CORSI Cani ed avari "Siberia" (Giordano) pno. 1904
52775 ZENATELLO T'incontrai per via "Siberia" (Giordano) pno. 1904
52782 SAMMARCO Gia l'ignea colonna "Mosè" (Perosi) pno. 1904
52788 MARCONI Questa o quella "Rigoletto" (Verdi) pno. 1904

10" records : G. & T. BLACK LABEL

52003 LA PUMA Azzurro occhio di cielo "Andrea Chenier" (Giordano)pno. 1904
52006 VENTURA Una vergine, un angiol di Dio "La Favorita" (Donizetti) 1904
52008 VENTURA Vedi io piango "Fedora" (Giordano) 1904
52012 VENTURA Improvviso "Andrea Chenier" (Giordano) 1904
52019 SCHIAVAZZI Apri la tue finestra "Iris" (Mascagni) 1904
52022 MARTINEZ-PATTI O mia Polonia "Chopin" (Orefice) pno. 1904
52023 KAMIONSKY Giulia (Denza) pno. 1904
52024 KAMIONSKY La gondola nera (Rotoli) pno. 1904
52025 KAMIONSKY Rosa (Tosti) pno. 1904
52027 DIDUR Maledizione "L'Ebrea" (Halévy) pno. 1903/4
52035 MARTINEZ-PATTI Vesti la giubba "Pagliacci" (Leoncavallo) pno. 1904
52036 MARTINEZ-PATTI Si fui soldato "Andrea Chenier" (Giordano)pno. 1904
52037 MARTINEZ-PATTI Come un bel dì "Andrea Chenier" (Giordano)pno. 1904
52038 MARTINEZ-PATTI Mai più Zazà "Zazà" (Leoncavallo) pno. 1904
52039 MARTINEZ-PATTI Un tal gioco "Pagliacci" (Leoncavallo) 1904
52046 GIRAUD Come un bel dì "Andrea Chenier" (Giordano) pno. 1904
52047 GIRAUD Sie lode a te "Tannhäuser" (Wagner) pno. 1904
52048 GIRAUD Nel verno al pie "MaestriCantori" (Wagner) pno. 1904
52049 GIRAUD Oblio (Tosti) pno. 1904

52051 ROTA   Chi sa? (d'Atri) 1904
52052 ROTA   Comm' a neve (Canzone napoletana) 1904
52053 ROTA   Il tuo pensiero (Rotoli) 1904
52054 ROTA   Sogno (Tosti) 1904
52055 ROTA   Oje ma' damillo (Cannio) 1904
52056 ROTA   Muntagnola (Di Capua)1904
52057 ROTA   'I te vurria vasà (Canz. nap.) 1904
52058 ROTA   Munasterio (Canz. nap,) 1904
52060 CAMPANARI Di Provenza il mar "La Traviata" (Verdi) 1903
52068 ROTA   Pecundria (Canz. nap.) 1904
52085 MARTINEZ-PATTI Giovinottino...stornello toscano (pno.) 1904
52086 MARTINEZ-PATTI Avrei pensato..stornello toscano (pno.) 1904
52087 MARTINEZ-PATTI D'un alma "Poliuto" (Donizetti) pno. 1904
52088 CELLINI Il pianto della bruna (acc.chitarra) 1904
52089 CELLINI La splendida Maria (acc.chitarra) 1904
52090 CELLINI In trattoria (1904)
52091 CELLINI Passerot - Canzonetta piemontese (acc.chitarra) 1904
52092 CELLINI La serenata del Barbapedana 1904
52093 ROTA   Uocchie mariuole (Canz. nap.) 1904
52094 ROTA   O sole mio   do.   do. 1904
52095 ROTA   Pusilleco addiruso do.   do. 1904
52096 ROTA   'A sirena mia   do.   do. 1904
52097 ROTA   Sonno a tte   do.   do. 1904
52098 POLISSENI Sortita del Tenore "I coscritti" (Lombardo) 1904 (pno)
52099 POLISSENI Fanfaretta militare "I saltimbanchi" (Ganve)pno1904
52100 POLISSENI Marcia del tamburino "I coscritti" (Lombardo) pno. 1904
52101 POLISSENI Spagnola Atto I. "Dall'ago al milione" (Dall'Argine)pno. 1904
52102 POLISSENI Barcarola Atto II.   do.   do.   do. pno. 1904
52103 POLISSENI Sortita di S.André "Il piccolo caporale" (Englander)pno.1904
52104 POLISSENI Sortita di Odoardo "I Granatieri" (Valente) pno. 1904
52105 POLISSENI Romanza Atto II. "Aldu" (Lombardo e Graffigna) pno. 1904
52106 POLISSENI Couplet derisorio di S.André "Il piccolo caporale" (Englander)
                                                              pno. 1904
52107 POLISSENI Romanza Atto II."Il mulino delle rose" (Desorme) pno. 1904
52108 POLISSENI Notturno Atto II. "I Granatieri" (Valente) pno. 1904
52109 POLISSENI Romanza della scala "La Bella Stiratrice" (Vasseur) pno.1904
52110 ROTA   Teniteme presente (Canz. nap.) 1904
52111 ROTA   Serenatella nera   do.   do. 1904
52112 ROTA   'A Gelusia (Nutile)   1904
52113 ROTA   L'eco (Canz. nap.) 1904
52114 ROTA   Era turnato Abbrile (Canz. nap.) 1904
52115 ROTA   'A Lucianella   do. do. 1904
52116 ROTA   Serenata bella   do. do. 1904
52117 ROTA   Torna a Surriento   do. do. 1904
52118 BUCALO   Resta immobile "Guglielmo Tell" (Rossini) 1904
52119 BUCALO   Credo "Otello" (Verdi) 1904
52120 BUCALO   O monumento "La Gioconda" (Ponchielli) 1904
52121 BUCALO   Presentazione di Schaunard "La Bohème" (Puccini) 1904
52122 BUCALO   Ella verrà "Tosca" (Puccini) 1904
52123 BUCALO   Già mi dicon venal "Tosca" (Puccini) 1904
52124 ROTA   Mattinata (Leoncavallo) 1904
52125 ROTA   Santa Lucia - Neapolitan 1904
52126 ROTA   Funiculì, Funiculà (Denza) 1904
52127 BUCALO   Pari siamo "Rigoletto" (Verdi) 1904
52131 BUCALO   Racconto Atto I. "Germania" (Franchetti) 1904
52132 BUCALO   Di Provenza il mar "La Traviata" (Verdi) pno. 1904
52133 ROTA   'O core d' 'e femmene (Canz. nap.) 1904
52134 ROTA   'mbraccia a te   do. do. 1904
52135 ROTA   Affacciate   do. do. 1904

52136 ROTA Fronne' 'e rose (Ricciardi) 1904
52137 ROTA Una furtiva lagrima "L'Elisir d'Amore" (Donizetti) pno. 1904
52138 TEDESCHI Ecco ridenti "Il Barbiere di Siviglia" (Rossini)pno.1904
52139 BUCALO Cortigiani, vil razza "Rigoletto" (Verdi) 1904
52140 ISALBERTI O amore "L'Amico Fritz" (Mascagni) (2310L) 1904
52141 MALESCI Mimi è una civetta "La Bohème" (Puccini) pno. 1904
52142 MALESCI Deserto sulla terra "Il Trovatore" (Verdi) 1904
52143 MALESCI Vedi, son io che piango "Manon Lescaut" (Puccini) pno. 1904
52144 MALESCI Addio alla madre "Cavalleria Rusticana" (Mascagni)pno. 1904
52145 MALESCI Imprecazione "Faust" (Gounod) pno. 1904
52146 VALLS Di quella pira "Il Trovatore" (Verdi) 1904
52147 VALLS Esultate / Ora e per sempre addio "Otello" (Verdi) pno. 1904
52148 VALLS O tu che in seno "La Forza del Destino" (Verdi) pno. 1904
52149 GALPERNI Largo al factotum "Il Barbiere di Siviglia" (Rossini)pno.04
52150 RICCIO L'ordinanza (Cans. à diction) 1904
52151 ROTA Lamento di Federico "L'Arlesiana" (Cilea) pno. 1904
52152 ROTA Fammi morir con te (Cosentino) 1904
52153 GALPERNI Non è ver (Mattei) pno. 1904
52154 GALPERNI Penso (Tosti) pno. 1904
52155 BUCALO Brindisi "Otello" (Verdi) 1904
52156 BUCALO Toreador "Carmen" (Bizet) 1904
52157 BUCALO Siciliana "Cavalleria Rusticana" (Mascagni) 1904
52158 MALESCI Ah sì,ben mio "Il Trovatore" (Verdi)(76)(2314L) pno. 1904
52159 MALESCI Ah! Manon sempre la stessa "Manon Lescaut" (Puccini)pno. 1904
52160 MALESCI Dei miei bollenti spiriti "La Traviata" (Verdi) pno. 1904
52161 ISALBERTI Stelle d'oro (Denza) pno. 1904
52162 MALESCI Mi par d'udir "I Pescatori di Perle" (Bizet) pno. 1904
52163 CAZAURAN Ah! non mi ridestar "Werther "(Massenet) 1904
52164 CAZAURAN Ah! non credevi tu "Mignon" (Thomas) 1904
52165 CAZAURAN Salve dimora "Faust" (Gounod) 1904
52167 CAZAURAN Il veder Griselda "Griselda" (Massenet) 1904
52169 ISALBERTI Brindisi "Cavalleria Rusticana" (Mascagni) 1904
52171 TEDESCHI Salve dimora "Faust" (Gounod) pno. 1904
52172 TEDESCHI Una furtiva lagrima "L'Elisir d'Amore" (Donizetti) pno. 1904
52179 PEREA Lamento di Federico "L'Arlesiana" (Cilea) pno. 1905
52180 PEREA Seconda Mattinata (Tosti) pno. 1905
52181 PEREA E un riso "Zazà" (Leoncavallo) pno. 1905
52182 ARIMONDI Vecchia zimarra "La Bohème" (Puccini) pno. 1904
52183 ARIMONDI Serenata "Faust" (Gounod) 1904
52184 PEREA Serenata (Schubert) pno. 1905
52185 PEREA Addio Mignon "Mignon" (Thomas) pno. 1905
52186 PEREA Ideale (Tosti) pno. 1905
52188 PEREA Se tanto in ira "Linda di Chamounix" (Donizetti) pno. 1905
52189 PEREA La vita è un inferno "La Forza del Destino" (Verdi) pno. 1905
52190 PEREA E la voce "Linda di Chamounix" (Donizetti) pno. 1905
52266 CAFFETTO E lucevan le stelle "Tosca" (Puccini)(7") 1903
52267 GIRARDI Vieni la mia vendetta "Lucrezia Borgia" (Donizetti)(7") 1903
52268 CAFFETTO Me protegge e me difende "Norma" (Bellini)(7") 1903
52269 CAFFETTO Troppo tardi t'ho conosciuta "Norma" (Bellini)(7") 1903
52270 GIRARDI Il mio sangue la vita darei "Luisa Miller" (Verdi)(7") 1903
52271 DADDI O sole mio (Di Capua)(7") 1903
52272 DADDI Luna lù (Ricciardi)(7") 1903
52273 DADDI Che buò fa? - Neapolitan (7") 1903
52274 OXILIA Libiam nei lieti calici "La Traviata" (Verdi) (7") 1903
52275 OXILIA Parigi o cara "La Traviata" (Verdi) (7") 1903
52277 CAFFETTO Nel fiero anelito "Aida" (Verdi) (7") 1903
52278 CANTALAMESSA Muntevergene (Cantalamessa) - canz. nap. (7") 1903
52279 FROSINI Bella figlia dell'amore "Rigoletto" (Verdi) (7") 1903

52280 FROSINI Amaro, sol per te "Tosca" (Puccini) (7") 1903
52281 FROSINI Morir si pura "Aida" (Verdi) (7") 1903
52284 APOSTOLU Tra voi belle "Manon Lescaut" (Puccini) (7") 1903
52285 BALDASSARRE Aria della frusta "Cavalleria Rusticana" (Mascagni)(7")
                                                                  9/05
52286 ODDO Maledizione "Lucia di Lammermoor" (Donizetti) (7") 9/05
52287 ODDO Di pescatore ignobile "Lucrezia Borgia" (Donizetti)pno.(7") 9/05
52288 ODDO Sulla tomba "Lucia di Lammermoor" (Donizetti) (7") 9/05
52290 ODDO Come rugiada "Ernani" (Verdi) (7") 9/05
52301 CORRADETTI Alla vita "Un Ballo in Maschera" (Verdi) 1900
52302 CORRADETTI O santa medaglia "Faust" (Gounod) 1900
52303 CORRADETTI O dei verd'anni miei "Ernani" (Verdi) 1900
52304 CORRADETTI Sei vendicata assai "Dinorah" (Meyerbeer) 1900
52305 CORRADETTI Credo "Otello" (Verdi) 1900
52306 CESARANI Un grande spettacolo "Pagliacci" (Leoncavallo) 1901
52308 CESARANI Fra poco a me ricovero "Lucia di Lammermoor"(Donizetti)1901
52310 CORRADETTI Senza tetto "Guarany" (Gomez) 1901
52312 CORRADETTI Canzone del Toreador "Carmen" (Bizet) 1900/1
52314 CORRADETTI Canzone bacchica "Amleto" (Thomas) 1900/1
52315 FRANCHI Ella giammai m'amo "Don Carlos" (Verdi) 1901
52316 CESARANI Vesti la giubba "Pagliacci" (Leoncavallo) 1901
52317 OXILIA Morir si pura "Aida" (Verdi) 1902
52318 CORRADETTI La donna russa "Fedora" (Giordano) 1900/1
52320 CORRADETTI Visione fuggitiva "Erodiade" (Massenet) 1900/1
52321 OXILIA Fra poco a me ricovero "Lucia di Lammermoor" (Donizetti) 1901
52322 CESARANI Di pescator ignobile "Lucrezia Borgia" (Donizetti) 1901
52323 FRANCHI Infelice "Ernani" (Verdi) 1901
52324 OXILIA Cielo e mar "La Gioconda" (Ponchielli) 1901
52325 CORRADETTI Serenata "Don Giovanni" (Mozart) 1901
52326 PINTUCCI Recondita armonia "Tosca" (Puccini) 1901
52327 CORRADETTI Ella verrà "Tosca" (Puccini) 1901
52328 MONTECUCCHI Spirto gentil "La Favorita" (Donizetti) 1901
52329 BEN DAVIES Salve dimora "Faust" (Gounod) 1901
52330 OXILIA Niun mi tema "Otello" (Verdi) 1902
52331 OXILIA Vesti la giubba "Pagliacci" (Leoncavallo) 1902
52332 OXILIA La donna è mobile "Rigoletto" (Verdi) 1902
52333 OXILIA Questa o quella "Rigoletto" (Verdi) 1902
52334 OXILIA Una vergine, un angiol di Dio "La Favorita" (Donizetti) 1902
52336 CAFFETTO Racconto del Graal "Lohengrin" (Wagner) 1902
52337 CAFFETTO Mercè, mercè "Lohengrin" (Wagner) 1902
52338 CAFFETTO Esultate "Otello" (Verdi) 1902
52339 CAFFETTO E lucevan le stelle "Tosca" (Puccini) 1902
52340 CAFFETTO Nel fiero anelito "Aida" (Verdi) 1902
52350 MALESCI Salve dimora "Faust" (Gounod) pno. 1902
52351 MALESCI Aspetti signorina "La Bohème" (Puccini) pno. 1902
52352 MALESCI Vesti la giubba "Pagliacci" (Leoncavallo) 1902
52353 MALESCI Brindisi "Cavalleria Rusticana" (Mascagni) 1902
52355 MALESCI Un grande spettacolo "Pagliacci" (Leoncavallo) 1902
52356 OXILIA Quando le sere "Luisa Miller" (Verdi) 1902
52357 OXILIA Dai campi, dai prati "Mefistofele" (Boito) 1902
52358 OXILIA Fra poco a me ricovero "Lucia di Lammermoor" (Donizetti) 1902
52359 CAFFETTO Ah troppo tardi "Norma" (Bellini) 1902
52360 OXILIA Dei miei bollenti spiriti "La Traviata" (Verdi) 1902
52361 OXILIA O paradiso "L'Africana" (Meyerbeer) 1902
52362 CAFFETTO Se quel guerrier io fossi "Aida" (Verdi) 1902
52363 FELIX Non t'amo più (Denza) 1902
52364 CAFFETTO Vieni a Roma "Norma" (Bellini) 1902
52365 CAFFETTO Meco all'altar di Venere "Norma" (Bellini) 1902

52366 GIRARDI Il mio sangue la vita darei "Luisa Miller" (Verdi) 1902/3
52376 GAFFETTO Siciliana "Cavalleria Rusticana" (Mascagni) 1903
52377 SCHRODTER Serenata (Tosti) 1902
52381 BONALDI/FANTONI Cavaliere di grazia "La Gran Via" (Valverde)1902/3
52382 BONALDI/FANTONI Pozzo fa' o pièvete (Canz. nap.) 1902/3
52383 BONALDI/FANTONI L'Altalena (Canz. nap.) 1902/3
52384 BONALDI/FANTONI Aria del ladroni "La Gran Via" (Valverde) 1902/3
52385 BONALDI/FANTONI Frate Braciola (Canz. nap.) 1902/3
52386 GAFFETTO Cielo e mar "La Gioconda" (Ponchielli) 1902
52387 PAGNONI Eri tu "Un Ballo in Maschera" (Verdi) 1902
52388 SCATTOLA Infelice "Ernani" (Verdi) 1902
52389 QUERCIA Quest'assise "Aida" (Verdi) 1902
52390 PAGNONI Cortigiani, vil razza "Rigoletto" (Verdi) 1902
52391 MAURI Sulla tomba "Lucia di Lammermoor" (Donizetti) 1902
52392 MAURI Prendi l'enel "La Sonnambula" (Bellini) pno. 1902
52393 OTTAVIANI Deserto sulla terra "Il Trovatore" (Verdi) 1902
52395 PAGNONI Deh non parlar "Rigoletto" (Verdi) 1902
52396 OTTAVIANI La rivedrò "Un Ballo in Maschera" (Verdi) 1902
52397 MAURI Fra poco a me ricovero "Lucia di Lammermoor" (Donizetti) 1902
52399 SCATTOLA Dio dell'or "Faust" (Gounod) 1902
52400 SCATTOLA Le calunnia "Il Barbiere di Siviglia" (Rossini) 1902
52408 E.GALLI Miserere "Il Trovatore" (Verdi) 1902
52409 E.GALLI Esultate "Otello" (Verdi) 1902
52445 OXILIA Giunto sul passo estremo "Mefistofele" (Boito) 1903
52447 TESSARI L'eroico del I Atto "Germania" (Franchetti) 1903
52448 CANTALAMESSA 'A nepot'e Don Camillo (Canz.nap.) 1902/3
52449 CANTALAMESSA La ciociara do. do. 1902/3
52450 CANTALAMESSA 'A montagna do. do. 1902/3
52451 CANTALAMESSA 'A Buscia do. do. 1902/3
52452 CANTALAMESSA Gui, Gui do. do. 1902/3
52453 CANTALAMESSA 'E ccape nenne do. do. 1902/3
52454 CANTALAMESSA Ndinghetimbo! do. do. 1902/3
52455 CANTALAMESSA Professore di trombone a spasso do. do. 1902/3
52456 TESSARI Dio possente "Faust" (Gounod) 1903
52457 TESSARI O casto fior "Re di Lahore" (Massenet) 1902/3
52629 TESSARI Vien Leonora "La Favorita" (Donizetti) 1903
52630 BALDASSARE Ambo nati "Linda di Chamounix" (Donizetti) 1903
52631 TISCI-RUBINI Prologo "Mefistofele" (Boito) 1903
52632 FROSINI Amor ti vieta "Fedora" (Giordano) 1903
52633 DE SEGUROLA Dio dell'or "Faust" (Gounod) 1903
52634 DE SEGUROLA Preghiera "Gli Ugonotti" (Meyerbeer) 1903
52637 DE SEGUROLA Aria di bajo "I Puritani" (Bellini) 1903
52638 DE SEGUROLA Piff, paff, puff "Gli Ugonotti" (Meyerbeer) 1903
52639 DE SEGUROLA Vecchia zimarra "La Bohème" (Puccini) 1903
52640 DE SEGUROLA Evocazione "Roberto il Diavolo" (Meyerbeer) 1903
52643 DE SEGUROLA Serenata "Faust" (Gounod) 1903
52647 RUIS O paradiso "L'Africana" (Meyerbeer) 1903
52649 DE SOUSA Prologo "Pagliacci" (Leoncavallo) 1903
52653 TESSARI A tanto amor "La Favorita" (Donizetti) 1902/3
52654 CANTALAMESSA La Risata (Canz. nap.) 1902/3
52655 TISCI-RUBINI Ecco il mondo "Mefistofele" (Boito) 1903
52657 TISCI-RUBINI Ella giammai m'amo "Don Carlos" (Verdi) 1903
52661 TISCI-RUBINI Vecchia zimarra "La Bohème" (Puccini) pno. 1903
52687 FRANCISCO Largo al factotum "Il Barbiere di Siviglia" (Rossini)pno.
(A188) 1903

52688 MALESCI Celeste Aida "Aida" (Verdi) pno. 6/03
52689 BIEL Deserto sulla terra "Il Trovatore" (Verdi) 1903
52690 BIEL Vesti la giubba "Pagliacci" (Leoncavallo) 1903

```
52691 BIEL      O paradiso  "L'Africana" (Meyerbeer) 1903
52692 BIEL      Ah sì, ben mio  "Il Trovatore" (Verdi) 1903
52693 BIEL      Sopra Berta   "Profeta" (Meyerbeer) 1903
52694 BIEL      Un dì all'azzurro spazio  "Andrea Chenier" (Giordano) 1903
52695 BIEL      Di quella pira "Il Trovatore" (Verdi) 1903
52696 BIEL      Celeste Aida  "Aida" (Verdi) 1903
52697 BIEL      Rachele allor che Iddio  "L'Ebrea" (Halévy) 1903
52698 CROMBERG  Scena della Chiesa  "Faust" (Gounod) 6/03
52699 CROMBERG  Vi ravviso  "La Sonnambula" (Bellini) 6/03
52700 CROMBERG  Romanza  "Simone Boccanegra" (Verdi) 1903
52701 SABATANO  O begli occhi di fata (Denza) 6/03
52702 ZENATELLO Un dì all'azzurro spazio  "Andrea Chenier" (Giordano) 1903
52703 ZENATELLO Salve dimora  "Faust" (Gounod) pno. 1903
52704 MECHERINI O' scemo (Canz. nap.) 6/03
52705 MECHERINI La prima donna     6/03
52706 MECHERINI Don Pipetto (Canz. nap.) 6/03
52707 MECHERINI Il furbo     do.  do.   6/03
52710 SABATANO  Povera stanza mia (Brahms) 6/03
52711 ZENATELLO O natura  "Dannazione di Faust" (Berlioz) pno. 1903
52712 ZENATELLO Un dì felice  "La Traviata" (Verdi) pno. 1903
52713 ZENATELLO Nel verno al piè  "I Maestri Cantori" (Wagner) 1903
52714 BIEL      O tu che in seno  "La Forza del Destino" (Verdi) 1903
52715 FRANCISCO Prologo  "Pagliacci" (Leoncavallo) pno. (A189) 1903
52718 ZENATELLO Donna non vidi mai  "Manon Lescaut" (Puccini) 6/03
52720 FRANCISCO Toreador song  "Carmen" (Bizet) (A1105) 1904
52723 VENTURA   Ah dispar vision  "Manon" (Massenet) 1903
52724 VENTURA   Donna non vidi mai  "Manon Lescaut" (Puccini) 1903
52725 VENTURA   Brindisi  "Cavalleria Rusticana" (Mascagni) 1903
52726 VENTURA   Ah non v' avvicinate  "Manon Lescaut" (Puccini) 1903
52727 VENTURA   Amor ti vieta  "Fedora" (Giordano) 1903
52728 VENTURA   Scena della tomba  "Lucia di Lammermoor" (Donizetti) 1903
52729 VENTURA   Mia tu sei  "Carmen" (Bizet) 1903
52731 VENTURA   Sperai tanto il delirio  "Pagliacci" (Leoncavallo) 1903
52732 VENTURA   Io non ho che una povera stanzetta  "La Bohème" (Leoncavallo)03
52733 BALDASSARE Barcarola  "La Gioconda" (Ponchielli) 1904
52734 BALDASSARE Vien Leonora  "La Favorita" (Donizetti) 1904
52735 VIGNAS    Studenti udite  "Germania" (Franchetti) 1903
52736 VENTURA   Mercè, mercè  "Lohengrin" (Wagner) 1903
52737 VENTURA   Dai campi, dai prati  "Mefistofele" (Boito) 1903
52738 VENTURA   Magiche note  "Regina di Saba" (Goldmark) 1903
52739 VENTURA   E il sol dell'anima  "Rigoletto" (Verdi) 1903
52740 VENTURA   Il sogno  "Manon" (Massenet) 1903
52741 VENTURA   Scena della borsa  "La Traviata" (Verdi) 1903
52742 RIGUZZI   Aria  "L'Elisir d'amore" (Donizetti) 1904
52744 VENTURA   Dei miei bollenti spiriti  "La Traviata" (Verdi) 1903
52745 VENTURA   E lucevan le stelle  "Tosca" (Puccini) 1903
52746 VENTURA   Cantabile del Duca  "Rigoletto" (Verdi) 1903
52747 VENTURA   E questo il bacio  "Iris" (Mascagni) 1903
52749 RIGUZZI   Femmine, tutte femmine  "Columella" (Bauer) 1904
52750 VENTURA   Ah non credevi tu  "Mignon" (Thomas) 1903
52752 VENTURA   Vesti la giubba  "Pagliacci" (Leoncavallo) 1903
52753 BUCALO    Cruda funesta smania  "Lucia di Lammermoor" (Donizetti) 1903
52754 VENTURA   Della mia vita  "I Pescatori di Perle" (Bizet) 1903
52755 VENTURA   Parmi veder  "Rigoletto" (Verdi) 1903
52756 VENTURA   Giunto sul passo estremo  "Mefistofele" (Boito) 1903
52758 GIUSTI    Non t'amo più (Denza) 1904
52759 GIUSTI    Strofe  "Nerone" (Rubinstein) 3/04
52760 RIGUZZI   Aria di Trivella  "Donne Curiose" (Wolf-Ferrari) 1904
```

52761 RIGUZZI   Scena a soggetto musicale 1904
52762 RIGUZZI   L'opera del maestro Pastiza 1904
52763 RIGUZZI   Dottrina in musica 1904
52765 GIUSTI   Tu sei morta nella vita mia 3/04
52766 BUCALO   Monologo Atto III. "Andrea Chenier" (Giordano) 3/04
52767 BUCALO   Il progettista - stornello (Scontrino) 3/04
52768 GIUSTI   Sulla bocca amorosa 3/04
52769 GIUSTI   Napulitanata (Costa) 1904
52770 GIUSTI   Povera mamma 3/04
52771 GIUSTI   A Frangesa 3/04
52778 VENTURA   Apri la tua finestra "Iris" (Mascagni) 1904
52779 VENTURA   Recondita armonia "Tosca" (Puccini) 1904
52784 VENTURA   Mercè, diletti "Ernani" (Verdi) 1904
52787 LA PUMA   Alla vita che t'arride "Un Ballo in Maschera" (Verdi)pno.1904
52794 MARTINEZ-PATTI Gocce grosse "Chopin" (Orefice) pno.acc.comp. 1904
52795 BERRIEL   Anch'io pugnai "Aida" (Verdi) 1904
52796 BALDASSARE Il balen del suo sorriso "Il Trovatore" (Verdi) 1904
52800 ODDO   O Colombina "Pagliacci" (Leoncavallo) (7") 1904
52800 SABATANO Maria Marì (Canz. nap.) (7") 6/03
52801 SABATANO Feneste che lucivi (7") 6/03
52802 MECHERINI A sfugliatella (Canz. nap.) (7") 6/03
52803 MECHERINI Don farfallino do.   do. (7") 6/03
52804 SABATANO O canto de scugnizze (7") 6/03
52809 ODDO   Serenata di Arlecchino "Pagliacci" (Leoncavallo) (7") 9/05
52810 ODDO   Troppo tardi "Norma" (Bellini) (7") 9/05
52814 RIGUZZI Pover sciavatia (7") 3/04
52815 RIGUZZI Giulia (Denza) (7") 3/04
52819 VENTURA Solingo, errante, misero "Ernani" (Verdi) (7") 9/05
52820 CAPPONI Presentazione di Mimì "La Bohème" (Puccini) (7") 1904
52821 VENTURA Già ti veggo "La Gioconda" (Ponchielli) (7") 9/05
52825 LA PUMA Et paperit "Il Natale" (Perosi) (7") 9/05
52826 LA PUMA Abba pater "La Passione di Cristo" (Perosi) (7") 9/05
52831 LA PUMA Canzone della pulce "Dennazione di Faust" (Berlioz)(7")pno.1904
52832 VENTURA O tu che l'alma adora "Ernani" (Verdi) (7") 1904
52833 CORRADETTI Numero quindici "Il Barbiere di Siviglia" (Rossini)(7") 9/05
52834 CORRADETTI Io son, signore, un infelice "Fra Diavolo" (Auber)(7") 9/05
52837 LA PUMA Canzone del Toreador "Carmen" (Bizet) pno. (7") 1904
52842 LA PUMA Per me ora fatale "Il Trovatore" (Verdi) (7") 9/05
52843 ODDO   Deserto sulla terra "Il Trovatore" (Verdi) (7") 9/05
52845 ODDO   Già ti veggo "La Gioconda" (Ponchielli) (7") 1904
52848 BUCALO Deh non parlar al misero "Rigoletto" (Verdi) (7") 1904
52849 ODDO   Un grande spettacolo "Pagliacci" (Leoncavallo) (7") 9/05
52850 ODDO   Di quella pira "Il Trovatore" (Verdi) (7") 1904
52859 VENTURA Questa è Mimì "La Bohème" (Puccini) 9/05
52863 ISALBERTI Alto là "Carmen" (Bizet) pno. 1904 (7")
52864 MALESCI Un grande spettacolo "Pagliacci" (Leoncavallo) (7") pno. 4/05
52865 RICCIO Il cane (7") 4/05
52866 RICCIO Al veglione (7") 4/05
52867 RICCIO Lo sbadiglio (7") 4/05
52868 RICCIO Il tenentino (7") 4/05
52869 RICCIO La fissazione di mia moglie (7") 4/05
52870 RICCIO Le due code (7") 4/05
52871 RICCIO Mio fratello piccolo (7") 4/05
52872 RICCIO La risata (7") 4/05
52874 RICCIO Il fungo   (7") 4/05
52875 RICCIO Madama Lafù. La fine della canzonettista (7") 4/05
52876 RICCIO Martin Caproni (7") 10/05
52877 RICCIO L'avvocato (7") 10/05

```
52878 RICCIO  L'inventore  (7") 10/05
52879 RICCIO  Il marchese  (7") 10/05
52880 RICCIO  L'abitué del Caffè Calzone  (7") 10/05
52881 RICCIO  La serenata di Don Felice  (7") 10/05
52882 RICCIO  Sabella  (7") 10/05
52883 RICCIO  Il berretto da notte  (7") 10/05
52884 MARTINEZ-PATTI  T'incontrai per via  "Siberia" (Giordano) pno.(7") 9/05
52885 CELLINI  Il veglione (acc. chitarra) (7") 9/05
52887 RICCIO  Bebé  (7") 10/05
52889 COLAZZA  Qui sotto al ciel  "Gli Ugonotti" (Meyerbeer) (7") 1905
52890 COLAZZA  Sfolgorò divino raggio  "Poliuto" (Donizetti)Pno. (7") 1905
52891 CAFFO  Da quel dì  "Linda di Chamounix" (Donizetti)Pno. (7") 7/06
52892 CAFFO  Bella siccome un angelo  "Crispino e la comare" (Frat.Ricci)pno.
                                                                    (7") 7/06
52893 CAFFO  Il cor ferito a morte  "Vasiello Fantasma" (Wagner)pno.(7") 7/06
52894 CAFFO  Alma soave e cara  "Maria di Rohan" (Donizetti)pno.(7") 7/06
52895 CARONNA  Sei vendicata assai  "Dinorah" (Meyerbeer) (7") 1905
52896 PIGNATARO  Un dì quando le veneri  "La Traviata" (Verdi) pno. (7") 1906
52897 VALLS  Deserto sulla terra  "Il Trovatore" (Verdi) pno. (7") 1905
52898 MARTINEZ-PATTI  Nelle sue sale il re t'appella  "La Favorita" (Donizetti)
                                                                    (7") 1905
52899 SALA  Ballata di Rambaldo  "Roberto il Diavolo" (Meyerbeer) (7") 1905
52900 MARTINEZ-PATTI  Ribelle chi mi chiama così  "L'Africana" (Meyerbeer)
                                                                    (7") 1905
52901 DADDI  Pusilleco addiruso (pno) (7") 7/06
52902 DADDI  Uocchie c'arraggiunate  (pno) (7") 7/06
52903 DADDI  Carmela mia  (pno) (7") 7/06
52904 DADDI  Mena mè  (pno) (7") 7/06
52905 DADDI  Rosa Rusella (pno) (7") 7/06
52906 LARA  Mille grazie  "Il Barbiere di Siviglia" (Rossini) (7") 1906
52908 CIGADA  All'erta marinar  "L'Africana" (Meyerbeer) (7") 1905/6
```

7" records : BERLINER

```
52200 CESARANI  La rivedrò  "Un Ballo in Maschera" (Verdi) 1901
52201 CESARANI  Apri la tua finestra  "Iris" (Mascagni)  1901
52202 CORRADETTI  Barcarola  "La Gioconda" (Ponchielli)  1901
52204 CORRADETTI  Panis Angelicus (Franck)  1901
52205 CORRADETTI  Vien Leonora  "La Favorita" (Donizetti)  1901 (2nd. ed.)
52206 CORRADETTI  Toreador  "Carmen" (Bizet)  1901
52209 CORRADETTI  O casto fior  "Re di Lahore" (Massenet)  1901
52212 CORRADETTI  Cruda funesta smania  "Lucia di Lammermoor" (Donizetti) 1901
52213 FERRETTI  Santa Lucia - Neapolitan  1901
52214 CORRADETTI  La Paloma (Yradier)  1901
52215 CORRADETTI  Come il romito fior  "Amleto" (Thomas)  1901
52216 CESARANI  Già ti veggo  "La Gioconda" (Ponchielli)  1901
52217 CESARANI  Maledizione  "Lucia di Lammermoor" (Donizetti) 1901
52218 CORRADETTI  Il sogno  "Manon" (Massenet)  1901
52219 CORRADETTI  Ella verrà  "Tosca" (Puccini)  1901
52221 CORRADETTI  Non t'amo piu (Denza)  1901
52222 CORRADETTI  Alla vita  "Un Ballo in Maschera" (Verdi) 1901
52223 FRANCHI  Splendon piu belle  "La Favorita" (Donizetti) 1901
52224 CORRADETTI  Ricordo di Quisisana (Denza) w.mandoline 1901
52225 MONTECUCCHI  Serenata d'Arlecchino  "Pagliacci" (Leoncavallo) 1902
52227 CORRADETTI  E allor perchè di?  "Pagliacci" (Leoncavallo) 1901
52228 CORRADETTI  Serenata  "Don Giovanni" (Mozart)  1901
52230 CORRADETTI  Malià (Tosti)  1901
```

52231 CORRADETTI Mia sposa sarà (Rotoli)   1901
52232 MONTECUCCHI Questa o quella "Rigoletto" (Verdi) 1900
52233 MONTECUCCHI Se il mio nome "Il Barbiere di Siviglie" (Rossini) 1900
52234 MONTECUCCHI La donna è mobile "Rigoletto" (Verdi) 1900
52235 MONTECUCCHI Sulla tomba "Lucia di Lammermoor" (Donizetti) 1900
52237 CORRADETTI O sole mio (Di Capua)   1901
52239 CORRADETTI La donna russa "Fedora" (Giordano)   1901
52242 CORRADETTI Bella e di sol vestita "Maria di Rohan" (Donizetti) 1901
52243 CORRADETTI Occhi di fata (Denza)   1901
52244 CORRADETTI Lo scaociate, io bandite "Ruy Blas" (Marchetti) 1901
52245 MONTECUCCHI Dai campi, dei prati "Mefistofele" (Boito) 1900
52246 OXILIA Un grande spettacolo "Pagliacci" (Leoncavallo) 1901
52247 CORRADETTI Senza tetto e senza cuna "Guarany" (Gomez) 1901
52250 FERRETTI E' Spingole Fiencesi (Canz.nap.)   1901
52251 FERRETTI Pozzo fa o' prevete   do. do.   1901
52252 FERRETTI L'altalena (Canz. italiana)   1901
52253 CANTALAMESSA 'Cchio, 'Cchio, 'Cchio   1901
52254 FERRETTI Oje Caruli (Canz.nap.)   1901
52255 OXILIA È scherzo "Un Ballo in Maschera" (Verdi)   1901
52256 CORRADETTI Maria Marì (Di Capua)   1901
52257 PINTUCCI O paradiso "L'Africana" (Meyerbeer)   1901
52260 CANTALAMESSA La Risata di Cantalamessa   1901
52261 CANTALAMESSA A spasso di Cantalamessa   1901
52263 CANTALAMESSA A Montagna (Fragna)   1901
52458 CAFFETTO Mercè cigno gentil "Lohengrin" (Wagner)   1901
52459 D.GIANNINI N'dinghetinbo   1901
52460 FRANCHI Ballata del fischio "Mefistofele" (Boito)   1900
52461 CAFFETTO Io non ho che una povera stanzetta "La Bohème" (Leoncavallo)
                                                              1900/1
52462 CAFFETTO Mercè diletti amici "Ernani" (Verdi)   1900
52463 CAFFETTO Un dì felice "La Traviata" (Verdi)   1900
52464 CAFFETTO Spirto gentil "La Favorita" (Donizetti)   1900
52465 CAFFETTO Parmi veder "Rigoletto" (Verdi)   1900
52466 CAFFETTO Donna non vidi mai "Manon Lescaut" (Puccini) 1900
52467 CAFFETTO O Colombina "Pagliacci" (Leoncavallo)   1900
52468 CAFFETTO E il sol dell'anima "Rigoletto" (Verdi)   1900
52469 CAFFETTO Un tal gioco "Pagliacci" (Leoncavallo)   1900
52470 CAFFETTO Un grande spettacolo "Pagliacci" (Leoncavallo)1900
52471 CAFFETTO Tombe degli avi miei "Lucia di Lammermoor" (Donizetti) 1900
52472 CAFFETTO Di pescator ignobile "Lucrezia Borgia" (Donizetti) 1900
52473 CAFFETTO Sento una forza indomita "Guarany" (Gomez)   1900
52474 CAFFETTO Fra poco a me ricovero "Lucia di Lammermoor" (Donizetti) 1900
52475 CAFFETTO Tu che a Dio "Lucia di Lammermoor" (Donizetti) 1900
52476 VIALE Sei vendicata assai "Dinorah" (Meyerbeer)   1900
52477 PALUMBO Guarda una mare   1900
52478 MOREO O sommo Carlo "Ernani" (Verdi)   1900
52479 FRANCHI Vecchia zimarra "La Bohème" (Puccini)   1900
52480 FRANCHI La Ballera Terribile   1900
52481 CAFFETTO Il sogno "Valkiria" (Wagner)   1900
52483 CAFFETTO Romanza del Aprile "Valkiria" (Wagner)   1900
52484 CAFFETTO Esultate "Otello" (Verdi)   1900
52485 CAFFETTO Ah Manon sempre la stessa "Manon Lescaut" (Puccini) 1900
52486 CAFFETTO La rivedrò nell' estasi "Un Ballo in Maschera" (Verdi) 1900
52487 CAFFETTO Dai campi, dai prati "Mefistofele" (Boito)   1900
52488 CAFFETTO Ballata "Rigoletto" (Verdi)   1900
52489 CAFFETTO È scherzo "Un Ballo in Maschera" (Verdi)   1900
52490 CAFFETTO Che gelida manina "La Bohème" (Puccini)   1900
52491 CAFFETTO La donna è mobile "Rigoletto" (Verdi)   1900

```
52492 CAFFETTO  Parigi,o cara  "La Traviata" (Verdi)                          1900
52493 CAFFETTO  Giunto sul passo estremo  "Mefistofele" (Boito)1900
52494 CAFFETTO  Di quella pira  "Il Trovatore" (Verdi)                        1900
52495 CAFFETTO  Siciliana  "Cavalleria Rusticana " (Mascagni)  1900
52496 VIALE     Eri tu  "Un Ballo in Maschera" (Verdi)                        1900
52497 VIALE     Toreador  "Carmen" (Bizet)                                    1900
52498 PALUMBO   Luisella                                                      1900
52500 PALUMBO   E Marinare                                                    1900
52501 PALUMBO   O Pescatore                                                   1900
52502 D.GIANNINI  Filomena                                                    1900
52504 D.GIANNINI  Torna Caruli                                               1900
52505 D.GIANNINI  Ve Voglio Cene                                             1900
52506 D.GIANNINI  Serenata de Rose                                           1900
52507 D.GIANNINI  Maria Marì                                                 1900
52508 D.GIANNINI  Santa Lucia                                                1900
52509 D.GIANNINI  A Montagna                                                 1900
52510 VIALE     O monumento  "La Gioconda" (Ponchielli)                      1900
52511 VAITE     Mi par d'udir  "I Pescatori di Perle" (Bizet)  5.VII.1900
52512 CAFFETTO  Un dì all'azzurro spazio  "Andrea Chenier" (Giordano)1900
52513 CAFFETTO  Morir si pura  "Aida" (Verdi)                                1900
52515 CAFFETTO  Già ti veggo  "La Gioconda" (Ponchielli)                     1900
52516 CAFFETTO  Questa o quella  "Rigoletto" (Verdi)                         1900
52517 CAFFETTO  Addio alla madre  "Cavalleria Rusticana" (Mascagni)  1900
52518 CAFFETTO  Tra voi belle  "Manon Lescaut" (Puccini)                     1900
52519 CAFFETTO  Il fior  "Carmen" (Bizet)                                    1900
52521 PENZA  Canzone de mammurali                                            4/01
52523 D.GIANNINI  O Marenariello (de Curtis)                                 1900
52524 MAZZARA  Greek Hymn (Dua Niccele)                          issd.1902
52526 FRANCHI  Infelice  "Ernani" (Verdi)                                    1899
52527 FRANCHI  Vieni la mia vendetta  "Lucrezia Borgia" (Donizetti) 1899
52528 FRANCHI  Dio dell'or  "Faust" (Gounod)                                 1899
52529 FRANCHI  Serenata  "Faust" (Gounod)                                    1899
52530 MALESCI  Ah non credevi tu  "Mignon" (Thomas)                          1900
52531 MALESCI  O paradiso  "L'Africana" (Meyerbeer)                          1900
52532 MALESCI  Improvviso  "Andrea Chenier" (Giordano)                       1900
52533 MALESCI  Tra voi belle  "Manon Lescaut" (Puccini)                      1900
52534 VIALE    Bella donna  "La Bohème" (Leoncavallo)                        1900
52535 VIALE    Nozzo ma lieto in core  "Don Carlos" (Verdi)                  1900
52537 VIALE    O casto fior  "Re di Lahore" (Massenet)                       1900
52538 CAFFETTO  Cielo e mar  "La Gioconda" (Ponchielli)      ?   1900
52538 MALESCI  Un dì all'azzurro spazio  "Andrea Chenier" (Giordano) 1900
52539 VIALE    Romanza  "La Bohème" (Puccini)                                1900
52540 CAFFETTO  Da voi lontan  "Lohengrin" (Wagner)                          1900
52541 CAFFETTO  O paradiso  "L'Africana" (Meyerbeer)                         1900
52542 CAFFETTO  Se quel guerrier io fossi  "Aida" (Verdi)                    1900
52543 CORRADETTI  Sei vendicata assai  "Dinorah" (Meyerbeer)  1900
52544 MOREO    Toreador  "Carmen" (Bizet)                                    1900
52545 MOREO    All'erta marinar  "L'Africana" (Meyerbeer)                    1900
52546 MOREO    Pura siccome  "La Traviata" (Verdi)                           1900
52547 CORRADETTI  Pari siamo  "Rigoletto" (Verdi)                            1900
52548 MOREO    Prologo  "Pagliacci" (Leoncavallo)                            1900
52549 FANTONI  Da risa (laughing song)                                       1900
52550 CORRADETTI  Si vendetta  "Rigoletto" (Verdi)                           1900
52551 FANTONI  Lo studente in Medecina                                       1900
52552 FANTONI  Fiere tempete Valzer                                          1900
52553 CORRADETTI  Cortigiani, vil razza  "Rigoletto" (Verdi)  1900
52554 MOREO  Per una ora fatale  "Il Trovatore" (Verdi)                      1900
52555 MOREO  Di Provenza il mar  "La Traviata" (Verdi)                       1900
```

52556	MOREO	Il balen del suo sorriso "Il Trovatore" (Verdi)	1900
52557	FANTONI	Il vaglione "Frou-Frou"	1900
52558	CAFFETTO	Vesti la giubba "Pagliacci" (Leoncavallo)	1900
52559	MOREO	Andi quando de Veneri	1900
52560	MOREO	O dei verd'anni miei "Ernani"	1900
52561	MOREO	Strofe del Toreador "Carmen" (Bizet)	1900
52562	MOREO	O santa medaglia "Faust" (Gounod)	1900
52563	CORRADETTI	O tu, bell'astro "Tannhäuser" (Wagner)	1900
52564	NICOLETTI	Vecchia zimarra "La Bohème" (Puccini)	1900
52565	CESARANI	Il fior "Carmen" (Bizet)	1900
52566	CESARANI	Pery m'appella "Il Guarany" (Gomez)	1900
52567	CESARANI	Dei miei bollenti spiriti "La Traviata" (Verdi)	1900
52568	CESARANI	Spirto gentil "La Favorita" (Donizetti)	1900
52569	NICOLETTI	Infelice e tu credevi "Ernani" (Verdi)	1900
52570	CESARANI	Dai campi, dai prati "Mefistofele" (Boito)	1900
52571	NICOLETTI	Vieni la mia vendetta "Lucrezia Borgia" (Donizetti)	1900
52572	CORRADETTI	Duetto dei briganti "Fra Diavolo" (Auber)	1900
52573	MOREO	Barcarola	1900
52574	FANTONI	Tempi felice	1900
52575	CORRADETTI	Numero quindici "Il Barbiere di Siviglia" (Rossini)	1900
52576	CORRADETTI	Largo al factotum "Il Barbiere di Siviglia" (Rossini)	1900
52577	CESARANI	Esultate "Otello" (Verdi)	1900
52578	CESARANI	Cielo e mar "La Gioconda" (Ponchielli)	1900
52579	MOREO	Ai miei rivali cedere "Ruy Blas" (Marchetti)	1900
52580	NICOLETTI	Serenata "Faust" (Gounod)	1900
52581	FANTONI	Carme (de Curtis)	1900
52582	CESARANI	Morir si pura "Aida" (Verdi)	1900
52583	CESARANI	Apri la tua finestra "Iris" (Mascagni)	1900
52584	CESARANI	Amor ti vieta "Fedora" (Giordano)	1900
52585	CESARANI	Tra voi belle "Manon Lescaut" (Puccini)	1900
52586	CESARANI	O tu che in seno "La Forza del Destino" (Verdi)	1900
52587	CESARANI	Di pescator ignobile "Lucrezia Borgia" (Donizetti)	1900
52588	CESARANI	Deserto sulla terra "Il Trovatore" (Verdi)	1900
52589	CESARANI	Une vergine, un angiol di Dio "La Favorita" (Donizetti)	1900
52590	CESARANI	Che gelida manina "La Bohème" (Puccini)	1900
52591	CESARANI	Un dì felice eterea "La Traviata" (Verdi)	1900
52592	FRANCHI	Dio dell'or "Faust" (Gounod)	1899
52593	FRANCHI	Suore che riposate "Roberto il Diavolo" (Meyerbeer)	1899
52594	FRANCHI	Splendon piu belle "La Favorita" (Donizetti)	1899
52595	FRANCHI	Ella giammai m'amo "Don Carlos" (Verdi)	1899
52596	FRANCHI	E tempo alfin	1899
52597	FRANCHI	La calunnia "Il Barbiere di Siviglia" (Rossini)	1899
52598	FRANCHI	Vi ravviso "La Sonnambula" (Bellini)	1899
52599	MOREO	Quest'assisa ch'io visto "Aida" (Verdi)	1900
52600	MOREO	O monumento "La Gioconda" (Ponchielli)	1900
52601	MOREO	A tanto amor "La Favorita" (Donizetti)	1900
52602	MOREO	Eri tu "Un Ballo in Maschera" (Verdi)	1900
52603	MOREO	Vieni meco sol de rose	1900
52604	MOREO	Cruda funesta smania "Lucia di Lammermoor" (Donizetti)	1900
52605	MOREO	Quand'ero paggio "Falstaff" (Verdi)	1900
52606	FANTONI	Don Carluccio	1900
52607	FANTONI	Studente in Medecina	1900
52608	FANTONI	Funiculì, Funiculà (Denza)	1900
52609	FANTONI	Il Marchese	1900
52610	FANTONI	Fazzo fare Prevete	1900
52611	FANTONI	Il Presidente	1900
52612	FANTONI	Santa Lucia	1900
52613	MOREO	De non parlar al misero "Rigoletto" (Verdi)	1900

```
52614 FANTONI   Il gran Dottore                                      1900
52615 CESARANI  Di quella pira  "Il Trovatore" (Verdi)               1900
52616 MOREO  Da quel di che t'ho venduta                             1900
52617 MOREO  Vien Leonora  "La Favorita" (Donizetti)                 1900
52618 FRANCHI. Cinta di fiori "I Puritani" (Bellini)                 1900
52817 CORRADETTI/PINTUCCI  Duetto dei briganti  "Fra Diavolo" (Auber) 1901
```

10" records : G. & T. RED and PINK LABEL
PRE-DOG issued 1908. DOG LABEL 1909
DOG LABEL 1910 : "LA VOCE DEL PADRONE"

```
2-52421 GIORGINI  Sogno casto e soave "Don Pasquale"(Donizetti)(7293b)1905
2-52422 GIORGINI  Quando le sere "Luisa Miller" (Verdi)             1905
2-52423 GIORGINI  A te o cara  "I Puritani" (Bellini)               1905
2-52433 SCOTTI    Mandolinata (Paladilhe) pno. (A2236)              1905
2-52434 SCOTTI    O casto fior  "Re di Lahore" (Massenet)pno.(A2358)1905
2-52435 SCOTTI    Alla vita  "Un Ballo in Maschera" (Verdi)(A2360)05.IRCC 75
2-52472 DE LUCIA  Deh non t'incantan "Lohengrin" (Wagner) pno.      1906
2-52473 DE LUCIA  S'ei torna alfin "Lohengrin" (Wagner) pno.        1906
2-52474 DE LUCIA  Della mia vita "I Pescatori di Perle" (Bizet)pno.1906
2-52475 DE LUCIA  Le tua bell'alma "Mignon" (Thomas) pno.          1906
2-52479 CARUSO    Il sogno "Manon" (Massenet)pno. (A1001) 1904.DA125.VA32
2-52480 CARUSO    Questa o quella "Rigoletto" (Verdi) pno. (A994)   1904
2-52481 SCOTTI    Prologo "Pagliacci" (Leoncavallo)(76) (A876)      1903
2-52482 SCOTTI    Vi ravviso "La Sonnambula" (Bellini)(76) (A877)   1903
2-52483 SCOTTI    Inaffia l'ugola "Otello" (Verdi) (A2235)          1905
2-52489 CARUSO    Di quella pira "Il Trovatore" (Verdi)(A3103) 1906.DA113
2-52515 JOURNET   Canzone del porter "Marta" (Flotow) 1905. DA258
2-52516 JOURNET   Vecchia zimarra "La Boheme" (Puccini) (A3162) 1906.DA258
2-52518 DE LUCIA  Ah non credevi tu "Mignon" (Thomas)pno.(8054b) 1906.DA124
2-52519 DE LUCIA  Salve dimora "Faust" (Gounod) pno.               1906
2-52520 DE LUCIA  Mi par d'udir "I Pescatori di Perle" (Bizet)pno. 1906
2-52528 RUFFO     Il balen "Il Trovatore" (Verdi)(79) (9059b)       1907
2-52529 RUFFO     Di Provenza il mar "La Traviata" (Verdi)(79)(9060b)1907.DA165
2-52555 RUFFO     Miei signori "Rigoletto" (Verdi) (4733h) 1907. DA165
2-52564 GIORGINI  Quant'è bella "L'Elisir d'amore" (Donizetti)      1907
2-52565 GIORGINI  Una vergine, un angiol di Dio "La Favorita"(Donizetti)
                                                           (9075b)1907
2-52566 GIORGINI  Se il mio nome "Il Barbiere di Siviglia" (Rossini)1907
2-52585 PLANÇON   Canzone del porter "Marta" (Flotow)(A4346) 1907.IRCC 133
2-52593 DE TURA   Siciliana "Cavalleria Rusticana" (Mascagni)(77) 1907
2-52594 DE TURA   Brindisi "Cavalleria Rusticana" (Mascagni)(77)(10607b)1907
2-52595 PAOLI     Si, io t'amo "Mdlle. de Belle Isle" (Samara) 1907. DA415
2-52596 PAOLI     Deserto sulla terra "Il Trovatore" (Verdi)
2-52597 PAOLI     Figli miei "Sansone e Dalila" (Saint-Saëns)(10521b)1907.DA409
2-52598 PAOLI     Re del cielo "Profeta" (Meyerbeer)(10522b) 1907. DA409
2-52601 DE TURA   Romanza di Erik "Albatro" (Pacchierotti)          1907
2-52602 DE TURA   Serenata di Erik "Albatro" (Pacchierotti)         1907
2-52603 DE TURA   O sole mio tesoro "Jery & Betly" (Romano)         1907
2-52604 DE TURA   La lettera (Puccio) pno.                          1907
2-52607 DE LUCIA  Il sogno "Manon" (Massenet) pno.(10515b) 1907. IRCC 57
2-52608 DE LUCIA  Aria di chiesa (Stradella) pno.                   1907
2-52611 SCAMPINI  Come rugiada "Ernani" (Verdi)                     1908
2-52612 SCAMPINI  Ah si, ben mio "Il Trovatore" (Verdi)             1908
2-52613 SCAMPINI  O tu che in seno "La Forza del Destino" (Verdi) 1908
2-52614 SCAMPINI  La vita e un inferno "La Forza del Destino" (Verdi)1908
2-52615 SCAMPINI  La rivedrò "Un Ballo in Maschera" (Verdi)(10827b)1908
```

```
2-52616 SCAMPINI  Di tu se fedele  "Un Ballo in Maschera" (Verdi)    1908
2-52621 RUFFO     Spettro santo  "Amleto" (Thomas) 1908. DA352
2-52622 RUFFO     Spettro infernale  "Amleto" (Thomas) (10898½b) 1908. DA170
2-52623 RUFFO     Ma tu sfiorita di rugiada gentil  "Malena" (Titta)(10548b)1907
2-52624 RUFFO     Disse il saggio  "Malena" (Titta) (10549b) 1907. DA162
2-52625 RUFFO     Deh vieni  "Don Giovanni" (Mozart)(10914b) 1908. DA462
2-52631 MARCONI   Invan, invan  "Nerone" (Rubinstein) pno.           1908
2-52632 MARCONI   Questa o quella  "Rigoletto" (Verdi)pno.           1908
2-52639 DE TURA   O tu che in seno  "La Forza del Destino" (Verdi)   1908
2-52640 DE TURA   La vita è un inferno  "La Forza del Destino" (Verdi)1908
2-52641 CARUSO    La donna è mobile  "Rigoletto" (Verdi)(A6033)(82)1908.DA561
2-52642 CARUSO    Questa o quella  "Rigoletto" (Verdi)(80)(A6035) 1908.DA102
2-52655 SOBINOFF  Nella vostra casa  "Eugenio Onegin" (Tchaikovsky) 4/05
2-52660 DE LUCIA  Deh sorgi, o luce  "Romeo e Giulietta" (Gounod)pno.1908
2-52661 DE LUCIA  Il mio tesoro  "Don Giovanni" (Mozart) pno.(11166b) 1908
                                                             DA124. VA65
2-52662 MARCONI   Ed ei non  "Ruy Blas" (Marchetti)                  1908
2-52663 MARCONI   Una vergine, un angiol di Dio  "La Favorita" (Donizetti)1908
2-52664 GIORGINI  Della mia vita  "I Pescatori di Perle" (Bizet)     1908
2-52666 DE LUCIA  Dalla sua pace  "Don Giovanni" (Mozart) pno.       1908
2-52667 DE LUCIA  Si il mio nome  "Il Barbiere di Siviglia" (Rossini)(77)pno.
                                                      (11167b)1908.VA
2-52668 SIGNORINI Tu sola a me rimani  "Chatterton" (Leoncavallo)    1908
2-52669 SIGNORINI Ah si, ben mio  "Il Trovatore" (Verdi)             1908
2-52670 DE TURA   Dai campi, dai prati  "Mefistofele" (Boito)        1908
2-52671 DE TURA   Giunto sul passo estremo  "Mefistofele" (Boito)    1908
2-52672 MARCONI   Dai campi, dai prati  "Mefistofele" (Boito)        1908
2-52673 MARCONI   In questa sera (Denza)                             1908
2-52676 DE LUCIA  Ahi perche non posso  "La Sonnambula" (Bellini)    1908
2-52677 GIORGINI  Questa o quella  "Rigoletto" (Verdi)               1908
2-52678 RUFFO     E la mia dama - stornello toscano (80) 1908. DA169
2-52679 RUFFO     E canta il grillo (Billi)(80) 1908. DA169
2-52680 RUFFO     Non penso a lei (Ferradini)(80) 1908
2-52685 RUFFO     Meriggiata (Leoncavallo)(80) 1908. DA351
2-52686 RUFFO     Tu sola a me  "Chatterton" (Leoncavallo)(9228e) 1908. VA16
2-52687 RUFFO     Per me ora fatale  "Il Trovatore" (Verdi) 1908. HRS 2015
2-52689 SCAMPINI  Deserto sulla terra  "Il Trovatore" (Verdi)pno. 1908
2-52690 SCAMPINI  La mia letizia  "I Lombardi" (Verdi)               1908
2-52691 GIORGINI  A una fonte  "I Puritani" (Bellini)                1908
2-52692 GIORGINI  Il sogno  "Manon" (Massenet)                       1908
2-52695 DE TURA   Tombe degli avi miei  "Lucia di Lammermoor" (Donizetti)1908
2-52696 DE TURA   La donna è mobile  "Rigoletto" (Verdi)             1908
2-52697 DELLA TORRE  Te sol sublime  "Tannhäuser" (Wagner)           1908
2-52698 DE LUCIA  Sulla bocca amorosa (Barthélemy) 1908. IRCC 5001
2-52699 DE LUCIA  Era di maggio (Costa)             1908. IRCC 5003
2-52700 DE LUCIA  Triste ritorno (Barthélemy)      1908
2-52701 DE LUCIA  O sole mio (di Capua)(81) 1908. DA335
2-52708 GIOVANELLI  Ma come dopo  "Werther" (Massenet)               1908
2-52709 GIOVANELLI  Ah! non mi ridestar  "Werther" (Massenet)        1908
2-52710 PAOLI     Inno  "Cid" (Massenet)                             1909
2-52711 PAOLI     Questa o quella  "Rigoletto" (Verdi)               1909
2-52712 PAOLI     Di mi patria  "Roberto il Diavolo" (Meyerbeer)     1909
2-52721 PAOLI     Siciliana  "Roberto il Diavolo" (Meyerbeer)        1909
2-52722 DE LUCIA  Oili, oila (Costa)(77)(13335b) 1909. DA333
2-52723 DE LUCIA  Nun me guardate (Gambardella)(77)(13338b)1909.DA333
2-52724 DE LUCIA  Luna lu (Ricciardi) (13340b) 1909. DA335
2-52726 MACNEZ    Si, dannato  "Jana" (Virgilio)                     1909
2-52727 MACNEZ    L'alba nascente (Parelli)                          1909
```

```
2-52728 MACNEZ  L'alba nascente (Parelli)                                   1909
            NB. Il N.2-52727 e interpretato con prevalente dolcezza,
                il N.2-52728 con prevalente vigorio.
2-52772 DE LUCIA  Serenamente (Barthélemy)                                  1909
2-52773 DE LUCIA  Carmela mia (Cannio)                                      1909
2-52774 DE LUCIA  A Surrentina (de Curtis)                                  1909
2-52783 PAOLI  Sì, fui soldato "Andrea Chenier" (Giordano)                  1909
2-52787 CICCOLINI  Giunto sul passo estremo "Mefistofele" (Boito)          3/11
2-52789 CICCOLINI  Vesti la giubba "Pagliacci" (Leoncavallo)               3/11
2-52808 PAOLI  Epithalame "Dejanine" (Saint-Saëns)
                (Viens, ô toi dont le claire visage)     DA413           1913 ?
2-52809 PAOLI  La donna è mobile "Rigoletto" (Verdi) DA413               1913 ?
2-52811 PAOLI  Ora e per sempre addio "Otello" (Verdi)(1302AH)DA412.1913 ?
2-52813 PAOLI  Apri la tua finestra "Iris" (Mascagni) DA414                2/12
2-52814 PAOLI  Sì, fui soldato "Andrea Chenier" (Giordano) DA411        1913 ?
2-52815 PAOLI  Come un bel dì "Andrea Chenier" (Giordano) DA411            2/12
2-52817 PAOLI  Canzone guerresca (Giordano)                DA414          2/12
2-52826 SMIRNOV  Mattinata (Leoncavallo)                   DA463         1913 ?
2-52828 RUFFO  Torna a Surriento (de Curtis) (1911AH) 1913  DA353
2-52829 RUFFO  Maria, Marì (di Capua)        (1912AH) 1913  DA353
2-52831 JADLOWKER  E lucevan le stelle "Tosca" (Puccini)                    1913
2-52847 BATTISTINI  Deh vieni "Don Giovanni" (Mozart)(17569b)1913.Orange
2-52848 BATTISTINI  Vien Leonora "La Favorita" (Donizetti)(17570b)1913.Orange
2-52849 BATTISTINI  Dei nemici tuoi "La Favorita" (Donizetti)(17571b)13.Orange
2-52857 JADLOWKER  M'appari tutt'amor "Marta" (Flotow)(13200r) DA432
2-52858 CICCOLINI  Recondita armonia "Tosca" (Puccini)                     2/14
2-52859 CICCOLINI  Fra poco a me ricovero "Lucia di Lammermoor" (Donizetti)1/15
2-52860 CICCOLINI  Donna non vidi mai "Manon Lescaut" (Puccini)          12/16
2-52861 CICCOLINI  No! pazzo son!    "Manon Lescaut" (Puccini)           1/15
```

10" records : G. & T. BLACK LABEL
PRE-DOG issued 1908. DOG LABEL 1909
DOG LABEL 1910 : "LA VOCE DEL PADRONE"

```
2-52400 PEREA  Prendi l'anel "La Sonnambula" (Bellini)                      1905
2-52402 ACERBI  Cercherò lontana terra "Don Pasquale" (Donizetti)          1905
2-52403 CONSTANTINO  Spirto gentil "La Favorita" (Donizetti)               1905
2-52404 CONSTANTINO  Questa o quella "Rigoletto" (Verdi)                   1905
2-52405 CONSTANTINO  O paradiso "L'Africana" (Meyerbeer)                   1905
2-52406 CONSTANTINO  M'appari tutt'amor "Marta" (Flotow)                   1905
2-52407 CONSTANTINO  Celeste Aida "Aida" (Verdi)                           1905
2-52408 CONSTANTINO  E lucevan le stelle "Tosca" (Puccini)                 1905
2-52409 CONSTANTINO  Siciliana "Cavalleria Rusticana" (Mascagni)          1905
2-52410 CONSTANTINO  La donna è mobile "Rigoletto" (Verdi)                 1905
2-52411 CAFFO  Regna amor in ogni loco "Flauto Magico" (Mozart)pno. 1905
2-52412 DE LUNA  Abbietta zingara "Il Trovatore" (Verdi)(76) 1905. E129
2-52413 MARTINEZ-PATTI  O tu che l'alma "Ernani" (Verdi)                   1905
2-52414 CARONNA  Prologo "Pagliacci" (Leoncavallo) pno.                    1905
2-52415 COLAZZA  Re del cielo "Profeta" (Meyerbeer)                        1905
2-52416 COLAZZA  Pastorale "Profeta" (Meyerbeer)                           1905
2-52417 ACERBI  A te o cara "I Puritani" (Bellini)                         1905
2-52418 PEREA  A te o cara "I Puritani" (Bellini)                          1905
2-52419 PEREA  Quant'è bella "L'Elisir d'amore" (Donizetti)               1905
2-52420 ACERBI  Di pescator ignobile "Lucrezia Borgia" (Donizetti)pno. 1905
2-52424 COLAZZA  Barcarola "Un Ballo in Maschera" (Verdi)                  1905
2-52425 ACERBI  Questa o quella "Rigoletto" (Verdi) pno.                   1905
2-52426 VALLS  Brindisi "Jone" (Petrella)                                  1905
```

2-52427 MARTINEZ-PATTI Tu che a Dio "Lucia di Lammermoor" (Donizetti) 1905
2-52428 COLAZZA La mia letizia infondere "I Lombardi" (Verdi)pno.   1905
2-52429 DE LUNA Sull'orlo dei tetti "Il Trovatore" (Verdi)(76) 1905. E129
2-52430 VALLS O Jone di quest'anima "Jone" (Petrella)   1905
2-52431 CARONNA Per me ora fatale "Il Trovatore" (Verdi)(76) 1905. E132
2-52436 ACERBI Una vergine, un angiol di Dio "La Favorita" (Donizetti)1905
2-52437 CAFFO Ah si per sempre "Fra Diavolo" (Auber)   1905
2-52438 ACERBI Sogno casto e soave "Don Pasquale" (Donizetti)   1905
2-52439 CIGADA Figlia di regi "L'Africana" (Meyerbeer)   1905
2-52440 CIGADA Quando amor m'accende "L'Africana" (Meyerbeer)   1905
2-52441 CIGADA Averla tanto amata "L'Africana" (Meyerbeer)   3/06
2-52444 PREVE Ninna Nanna "Mignon" (Thomas)   1905
2-52445 PREVE Fuggitivo e tremante "Mignon" (Thomas)   1905
2-52446 PREVE Il lacerato spirito "Simone Boccanegra" (Verdi) pno.   1905
2-52467 CIGADA Il balen del suo sorriso "Il Trovatore" (Verdi)(76)1906
                                                (7310½b) E131
2-52468 PREVE Sull'orlo dei tetti "Il Trovatore" (Verdi)   1906
2-52469 CIGADA A tanto amor "La Favorita" (Donizetti)   1906
2-52470 PIGNATARO Come il romito fior "Amleto" (Thomas) pno.   1906
2-52471 PIGNATARO Di tua beltade "Poliuto" (Donizetti) pno.   1906
2-52476 VALLS Di quella pira "Il Trovatore" (Verdi)(76) 1905. E133
2-52477 PIGNATARO Cruda funesta smania "Lucia di Lammermoor" (Donizetti)1906
2-52484 PREVE Evocazione "Roberto il Diavolo" (Meyerbeer)   1906
2-52485 MINOLFI Son Pereda "La Forza del Destino" (Verdi)   1906
2-52486 PREVE Il santo speco "La Forza del Destino" (Verdi)   1906
2-52487 PREVE Invocazione "L'Africana" (Meyerbeer)   1906
2-52488 MARTINEZ-PATTI Rachele allor che Iddio "L'Ebrea" (Halévy)   1906
2-52490 REICH Caro mio ben (Giordani)   1906
2-52491 DADDI Marechiare (Tosti)   1906
2-52492 DADDI Santa Lucia   1906
2-52493 DADDI Serenatella nera   1906
2-52494 DADDI 'A core d'e femmena   1906
2-52495 DADDI Scétate (Costa)   1906
2-52496 DADDI Serenata 'a Maria   1906
2-52497 DADDI Torna a Surriento (Di Capua)   1906
2-52498 DADDI Funiculì, funiculà (Denza)   1906
2-52499 DADDI Ucchiuzulle Mariuncielle   1906
2-52500 DADDI Musica proibita - romanza (pno)   1906
2-52501 DADDI 'O sole mio (de Curtis)   1906
2-52502 DADDI Voce 'e notte (de Curtis)   1906
2-52503 MALDACEA Un cameriere filosofo   1906
2-52504 MALDACEA Il pompiere del teatro   1906
2-52505 MALDACEA Il tenore di grazia   1906
2-52506 MALDACEA Il benefattore moderno   1906
2-52507 MALDACEA Gilet e calzoni   1906
2-52508 MALDACEA Il parrucchiere moderno   1906
2-52509 MALDACEA Il capotreno   1906
2-52510 MALDACEA L'inventore   1906
2-52511 MALDACEA La risata   1906
2-52512 MALDACEA Echi del mondo   1906
2-52513 CIGADA Brindisi "Amleto" (Thomas)   1905
2-52514 LARA Agnese la zitella "Fra Diavolo" (Auber)   1906
2-52517 MINOLFI O dei verd'anni miei "Ernani" (Verdi)   1906
2-52521 G.ROSSI Vieni la mia vendetta "Lucrezia Borgia" (Donizetti)   1906
2-52522 LANZIROTTI La vaga pupilla "Faust" (Gounod)(77) 1906. E120
2-52525 LARA La rivedrò nell'estasi "Un Ballo in Maschera" (Verdi)   1906
2-52526 A.PINI-CORSI Tutta bella (Marino)   1906
2-52527 A.PINI-CORSI Tu non mi vuoi più bene (Falvo)   1906

```
2-52539 CIGADA   Figlia di regi  "L'Africana" (Meyerbeer)  ?            1907
2-52540 CIGADA   Quando amor m'accende  "L'Africana" (Meyerbeer) ?       1907
2-52541 CIGADA   Averla tanto amata  "L'Africana" (Meyerbeer)  ?         1907
2-52547 LARA  Piano, pianissimo  "Il Barbiere di Siviglia" (Rossini)    1907
2-52548 CIGADA  Adamastor, re dell'onde profonde  "L'Africana" (Meyerbeer)07
2-52549 LARA  Fra poco a me ricovero  "Lucia di Lammermoor" (Donizetti) 1907
2-52552 CAMPANARI  Il balen del suo sorriso  "Il Trovatore" (Verdi)     1905
2-52554 MINOLFI  Egli e salvo  "La Forza del Destino" (Verdi)           1907
2-52556 MINOLFI  Urna fatale  "La Forza del Destino" (Verdi)            1907
2-52557 A.PINI-CORSI  Predica di Fra Melitone"La Forza del Destino" (Verdi)07
2-52567 DE SEGUROLA  Dio dell'or  "Faust" (Gounod)(77) 1907. E121
2-52568 DE SEGUROLA  Serenata  "Faust" (Gounod)(77) 1907. E124
2-52569 CIGADA  Corale della spada "Faust" (Gounod)(77)                 1907
2-52570 SILLICH  Invocazione  "Faust" (Gounod)(77)                      1907
2-52571 DE SEGUROLA  Ah del Tebro  "Norma" (Bellini)                    1907
2-52572 SILLICH  Infelice, e tuo credevi  "Ernani" (Verdi)             1907
2-52574 SILLICH  O qual funesto avvenimento  "Lucia di Lammermoor" (Donizetti)0
2-52575 COLAZZA  Ah si, ben mio  "Il Trovatore" (Verdi)                 1907
2-52576 COLAZZA  Come rugiada  "Ernani" (Verdi)                         1907
2-52577 MINOLFI  Cortigiani, vil razza  "Rigoletto" (Verdi)             1907
2-52578 MINOLFI  Pura siccome un angelo  "La Traviata" (Verdi)          1907
2-52579 ACERBI  La donna è mobile  "Rigoletto" (Verdi)                  1907
2-52580 CIGADA  Ah se l'error t'ingombra  "Il Trovatore" (Verdi)        1907
2-52582 DE SEGUROLA  Splendon più belle  "La Favorita" (Donizetti)      1907
2-52583 DE SEGUROLA  Vieni la mia vendetta  "Lucrezia Borgia" (Donizetti) 07
2-52584 DE SEGUROLA  Vi ravviso  "La Sonnambula" (Bellini)              1907
2-52586 MINOLFI  O tu che piangi  "Jana" (Virgilio)                     1907
2-52587 TACCANI  Si dannato morrò  "Jana" (Virgilio)                    1907
2-52588 TACCANI  Miriam fa core  "Hermes" (Parelli)                     1907
2-52589 TACCANI  Se alcuna tregua avessi  "Hermes" (Parelli)            1907
2-52590 TACCANI  Serenata interna di Erik  "Albatro" (Pacchierotti)     1907
2-52591 TACCANI  Romanza di Erik  "Albatro" (Pacchierotti)              1907
2-52592 MINOLFI  Il cavallo scalpita  "Cavalleria Rusticana" (Mascagni)(77)1907
2-52606 SANCOVY  Deserto sulla terra  "Il Trovatore" (Verdi)            1907
2-52609 BADINI  Strofe di Hun-Ci  "Geisha" (Jones)                      1908
2-52610 G.PINI-CORSI  O mia Mimosa "Geisha" (Jones)                     1908
2-52617 CANCIELLO  Parola quinta (Mercadante)                           1908
2-52618 CANCIELLO  Ave Maria (Mercadante)                               1908
2-52619 CANCIELLO  Stabat Mater                                         1908
2-52620 CANCIELLO  Salutaris Ostia                                      1908
2-52627 G.PINI-CORSI  Ah per sempre  "Fra Diavolo" (Auber)              1908
2-52628 ARMENTANO  Urna fatale  "La Forza del Destino" (Verdi)          1908
2-52629 BADINI  Per me ora fatale  "Il Trovatore" (Verdi)               1908
2-52633 DE SEGUROLA  Evocazione  "Roberto il Diavolo" (Meyerbeer)       1908
2-52634 DE SEGUROLA  Corale di Marcello  "Gli Ugonotti" (Meyerbeer)     1908
2-52635 DE SEGUROLA  Cinta di or  "I Puritani" (Bellini)                1908
2-52636 ARMENTANO  Morrò, ma lieto in core  "Don Carlos" (Verdi)        1908
2-52637 A.PINI-CORSI  Madamina  "Don Giovanni" (Mozart)                 1908
2-52638 ISCHIERDO  Fra poco a me ricovero  "Lucia di Lammermoor" (Donizetti)08
2-52643 DAVIDOFF  Comme 'o zuccaro (Fonzo)                              1908
2-52644 DAVIDOFF  Maggio (Fonzo)                                        1908
2-52645 DAVIDOFF  Tu nun me vo' cchiù bene (Falvo)                      1908
2-52646 DAVIDOFF  Palomma 'e notte (Buongiovanni)                       1908
2-52649 BERNAL-RESKY  Aria  "Un Ballo in Maschera" (Verdi)              1908
2-52650 BERNAL-RESKY  Aria  "Amleto" (Thomas)                           1908
2-52652 MARAK  Una furtiva lagrima "L'Elisir d'amore" (Donizetti)       1908
2-52653 MARAK  Brindisi  "Cavalleria Rusticana" (Mascagni)              1908
2-52654 MARAK  Aria  "Tosca" (Puccini)                                  1908
```

```
2-52656 MARAK    Siciliana  "Cavalleria Rusticana" (Mascagni)                1908
2-52657 MARAK    Arioso  "Pagliacci" (Leoncavallo)                           1908
2-52658 MARAK    Romanza del fiore  "Carmen" (Bizet)                         1908
2-52659 MARAK    Che gelida manine  "La Bohème" (Puccini)                    1908
3-52665 DE SEGUROLA Piff, paff, puff  "Gli Ugonotti" (Meyerbeer)            1908
2-52674 TESSARI  La mia diletta  "Geisha" (Jones)                           1908
2-52675 TESSARI  Io son navigator  "Geisha" (Jones)                         1908
3-52682 TAMINI   Vesti la giubba  "Pagliacci" (Leoncavallo)                 1908
2-52684 DE SEGUROLA Pro peccatis  "Stabat Mater" (Rossini)                  1908
2-52688 GRANADOS Son certo  "Chatterton" (Leoncavallo)                      1908
2-52702 FEDERICI Come Paride vezzoso  "L'Elisir d'amore" (Donizetti)        1908
2-52703 A.PINI-CORSI Udite o rustici  "L'Elisir d'amore" (Donizetti)        1908
2-52704 BADINI   Cavaliere di grazia "La Gran Via" (Chueca y Valverde)      1908
2-52705 CICCOLINI Addio Mignon  "Mignon" (Thomas)                           1908
2-52706 DE GREGORIO Ah! non credevi tu  "Mignon" (Thomas)                   1908
2-52707 BADINI   Di Provenza il mar  "La Traviata" (Verdi)                  1908
2-52714 BARRERA  Ora e per sempre addio  "Otello" (Verdi)                   1909
2-52715 BADINI   Per me l'ora fatale  "Il Trovatore" (Verdi)                1909
2-52716 BADINI   Oh dei verd'anni miei  "Ernani" (Verdi)                    1909
2-52717 A.PINI-CORSI Don Gregorio il semicroma  "Tutti in Maschera"(Pedrotti)
                                                              Pt.I - 1909
2-52718 A.PINI-CORSI Don Gregorio il semicroma       do. do.  Pt.II. 1909
2-52719 GHELARDINI De' miei bollenti spiriti "La Traviata" (Verdi)          1909
2-52725 BADINI   Barcarola "La Gioconda" (Ponchielli)                       1909
2-52731 BADINI   Son sessant'anni  "Andrea Chenier" (Giordano)              1909
2-52732 CUNEGO   Sì, fui soldato "Andrea Chenier" (Giordano)                1909
2-52733 CUNEGO   Come un bel dì di maggio "Andrea Chenier" (Giordano)       1909
2-52734 CUNEGO   Celeste Aida "Aida" (Verdi)                                1909
2-52735 MOLINARI Vecchia zimarra  "La Bohème" (Puccini)                     1909
2-52736 CUNEGO   Brindisi  "Cavalleria Rusticana" (Mascagni)                1909
2-52737 RIMONDINI Sei vendicata assai  "Dinorah" (Meyerbeer)                1909
2-52738 LARA     Di pescator ignobile "Lucrezia Borgia" (Donizetti)         1909
2-52739 GALBIERO Spirto gentil  "La Favorita" (Donizetti)                   1909
2-52740 GALBIERO Salve dimora  "Faust" (Gounod)                             1909
2-52741 DE GREGORIO Amor ti vieta  "Fedora" (Giordano)                      1909
2-52742 GALBIERO O tu che in seno  "La Forza del Destino" (Verdi)           1909
2-52743 BADINI   La mia bandiera (Rotoli) pno.                              1909
2-52744 DE GREGORIO Cielo e mar  "La Gioconda" (Ponchielli)                 1909
2-52745 CUNEGO   Donna non vidi mai  "Manon Lescaut" (Puccini)              1909
2-52746 DE GREGORIO Tra voi belle  "Manon Lescaut" (Puccini)               1909
2-52747 DE GREGORIO Chiudo gli occhi  "Manon" (Massenet)                    1909
2-52748 DE GREGORIO Guardate, pazzo son  "Manon Lescaut" (Puccini)          1909
2-52749 DE GREGORIO Dai campi, dai prati  "Mefistofele" (Boito)            1909
2-52750 MOLINARI Son lo spirito  "Mefistofele" (Boito)                      1909
2-52751 CUNEGO   Ridi Pagliaccio  "Pagliacci" (Leoncavallo)                 1909
2-52752 DE GREGORIO Serenata d'Arlecchino  "Pagliacci" (Leoncavallo)        1909
2-52753 BADINI   Te Deum  "Tosca" (Puccini)                                 1909
2-52754 DE GREGORIO Recondita armonia  "Tosca" (Puccini)                   1909
2-52755 BADINI   Già mi struggea  "Tosca" (Puccini)                         1909
2-52756 DE GREGORIO E lucevan le stelle  "Tosca" (Puccini)                 1909
2-52757 GALBIERO Taci, la valle e azzurra  "Eidelberga mia" (Pacchierotti)09
2-52758 DE GREGORIO Ah! Manon mi tradisce!  "Manon Lescaut" (Puccini) 1909
2-52759 MOLINARI Ave Signor  "Mefistofele" (Boito)                          1909
2-52760 FEDERICI A tanto amor  "La Favorita" (Donizetti)                    1909
2-52761 DE GREGORIO Apri la tua finestra  "Iris" (Mascagni)                 1909
2-52762 DE GREGORIO Chi son?  "La Bohème" (Puccini)                         1909
2-52763 DE GREGORIO Il sogno  "Manon" (Massenet)                            1909
2-52764 DA GRADI Malìa (Tosti)                                              1909
```

```
2-52765 BADINI    Largo al factotum   "Il Barbiere di Siviglia" (Rossini)  1909
2-52766 MOLINARI  La calunnia         "Il Barbiere di Siviglia" (Rossini)  1909
2-52767 LARA    Amore, amore (Tirindelli)                                  1909
2-52768 LARA    Serenata (Cooper)                                          1909
2-52771 BADINI  Pari siamo  "Rigoletto" (Verdi)                            1909
2-52775 DE GREGORIO  La dolcissima effige  "Adriana Lecouvreur" (Cilea)   1909
2-52776 DE GREGORIO  L'anima ho stanca     "Adriana Lecouvreur" (Cilea)   1909
2-52777 CUNEGO  Studenti, udite  "Germania" (Franchetti)                   1909
2-52778 BADINI  Ferito, prigionier "Germania" (Franchetti)                 1909
2-52779 BLANCHARD  Figlia di regi  "L'Africana" (Meyerbeer)                1909
2-52780 BLANCHARD  All'erta marinar "L'Africana" (Meyerbeer)               1909
2-52781 BLANCHARD  Su queste rose  "Dannazione di Faust" (Berlioz)         1909
2-52782 BLANCHARD  Che fai tu qui  "Dannazione di Faust" (Berlioz)         1909
2-52784 DE GREGORIO  O amore, o bella luce del core  "L'Amico Fritz" (Mascagni)
                                                                           1909
2-52785 BADINI  Bella dama, da questi milionari "La Bohème" (Leoncavallo)09
2-52786 CUNEGO  Io non ho che una povera stanzetta "La Bohème" (Leoncavallo)3/11
2-52788 BADINI  Inaffia l'ugola "Otello" (Verdi)                           3/11
2-52790 DE GREGORIO  È un riso gentil  "Zazà" (Leoncavallo)               4/11
2-52791 BADINI  Buona Zazà "Zazà" (Leoncavallo)                            4/11
2-52792 DE GREGORIO  Mai piu Zazà "Zazà" (Leoncavallo)                    4/11
2-52793 BADINI  Zazà, piccola zingara "Zazà" (Leoncavallo)                 4/11
2-52794 PEZZUTI  Galoppa morello (Quaranta)                                4/11
2-52795 DE GREGORIO  Una furtiva lagrima "L'Elisir d'amore" (Donizetti)5/11
2-52796 DE GREGORIO  Tu che a Dio "Lucia di Lammermoor" (Donizetti)       5/11
2-52797 DE GREGORIO  Di non t'incantan "Lohengrin" (Wagner)               5/11
2-52799 BARRERA  La rivedrò nell'estasi "Un Ballo in Maschera" (Verdi)    6/11
2-52800 MAGGI    Eri tu "Un Ballo in Maschera" (Verdi)                     6/11
2-52801 FEDERICI  Dio possente "Faust" (Gounod)                            6/11
2-52802 MOLINARI  Tu che fai l'addormentata "Faust" (Gounod)              6/11
2-52803 BADINI  La donna russa "Fedora" (Giordano)                        6/11
2-52804 FEDERICI  Miei signori "Rigoletto" (Verdi)                         6/11
2-52805 FEDERICI  Corale della spada "Faust" (Gounod)                      10/11
2-52806 DE GREGORIO  O Lola "Cavalleria Rusticana" (Mascagni)             11/11
2-52807 BELLATTI  Buona Zazà "Zazà" (Leoncavallo)                          1/12
2-52810 CANALI  Allori e pampini "Educande di Sorrento"(Usiglio)          9/13
2-52812 TOMMASINI  Dichiarazione (Silver)                                 10/12
2-52819 GASINI  Vien Leonora "La Favorita" (Donizetti)                    1/12
2-52820 GALLI   Ecco il mondo "Mefistofele" (Boito)                       1/12
2-52821 LUSSARDI  Urna fatale "La Forza del Destino" (Verdi)              7/12
2-52823 LUSSARDI  Son Pereda  "La Forza del Destino" (Verdi)              7/12
2-52827 PEZZUTI  Lontananza (Cilea)                                       10/12
2-52834 TISCI-RUBINI  O re del ciel "Lohengrin" (Wagner)                  12/12
2-52835 DE GREGORIO  S'ei torna alfin "Lohengrin" (Wagner)               12/12
2-52836 BADINI  Era la notte "Otello" (Verdi)                             2/13
2-52837 CASTELLANI  Di quella pira "Il Trovatore" (Verdi)                 5/13
2-52838 SALVATI  Se il mio nome "Il Barbiere di Siviglia" (Rossini)       6/13
2-52839 BETTONI  Protetti dalla notte "Faust" (Gounod)                    6/13
2-52840 SALVATI  Cerchero lontana terra "Don Pasquale" (Donizetti)        9/13
2-52841 SALVATI  Sogno soave e casto   "Don Pasquale" (Donizetti)         9/13
```

10" records : RED & PINK LABEL

```
7-52000 SCOTTI    Vi ravviso "La Sonnambula" (Bellini) 1909. DA 377
7-52001 SCOTTI    Ei favella già con troppo bollor "Otello" (Verdi) 1909.DA377
7-52002 CARUSO    E lucevan le stelle "Tosca" (Puccini)(80)(A6346)1909. DA112
7-52003 CARUSO    Magiche note "Regina di Saba" (Goldmark)(82)(A6062)1908.DA122
7-52004 CARUSO    Recondita armonia "Tosca" (Puccini)(81)(A8347)1909. DA112.VA36.
7-52005 ZEROLA    La rivedrò nell'estasi "Un Ballo'in Maschera" (Verdi)(81)
7-52006 ZEROLA    Addio "Otello" (Verdi)
7-52007 ZEROLA    Di quella pira "Il Trovatore" (Verdi)(80)
7-52008 ZEROLA    Di' tu se fedele "Un Ballo in Maschera" (Verdi)
7-52011 ZEROLA    Figli miei v'arrestate "Sansone e Dalila" (Saint-Saëns)
7-52013 CARUSO    Studenti, udite "Germania" (Franchetti)(81)(A8710)1910.DA543.
                                                                          VA38
7-52014 CARUSO    No, non chiuder "Germania" (Franchetti)(81)(A8713)1910.DA543
                                                                          VA38
7-52015 DE GOGORZA  O sole mio (di Capua)(80)(A7099) 1909. DA185
7-52016 McCORMACK   Vieni al contento profondo "Lakmé" (Delibes)(81)1910.DA379
7-52017 CARUSO    Ora e per sempre addio "Otello" (Verdi)(81)(A9743)1910. DA561
7-52018 CARUSO    Siciliana "Cavalleria Rusticana" (Mascagni) w.harp (82)(A9745)
                                                                     1910. DA117
7-52019 SCOTTI    Scètate (Costa) 1911
7-52020 DE GOGORZA  Mandolinata (Paladilhe)(81) 1910. DA179
7-52023 AMATO     Il cavallo scalpita "Cavalleria Rusticana" (Mascagni)(A11282)
                                                                     1911. DA504
7-52024 AMATO     Pescator, affonda l'esca "La Gioconda" (Ponchielli)(81)(A11283)
                                                                     1911. DA126
7-52025 CARUSO    Di' tu se fedele "Un Ballo in Maschera" (Verdi)(81)(A11270)
                                                                     1911. DA102
7-52026 CARUSO    Canta pe' me (de Curtis) (A11306) 1911. DA104
7-52027 AMATO     Senza tetto "Il Guarany" (Gomez)
7-52028 SAMMARCO  Sono un demonio buono "I Gioielli della Madonna"
                                        (Wolf-Ferrari) (HO 116ae) 1912. VA6
7-52029 RUFFO     Suono e fantasia (Capolongo)(80) 1912. DA162
7-52030 RUFFO     Visione veneziana (Brogi) 1912. DA350
7-52031 RUFFO     Zazà, piccola zingara "Zazà" (Leoncavallo)(79)(A12660)1912.DA355
7-52032 McCORMACK Mi par d'udir "I Pescatori di Perle" (Bizet)(A12707)1912
                                                                     DA502. VA21
7-52033 McCORMACK Dai campi, dai prati "Mefistofele" (Boito)(80)(A12705)'12.DA498
7-52034 McCORMACK Giunto sul passo estremo "Mefistofele" (Boito) 1913
7-52035 RUFFO     Buona Zazà "Zazà" (Leoncavallo)(A12621) 1912. DA355
7-52036 RUFFO     Alla vita "Un Ballo in Maschera" (Verdi) (A12622) 1912. DA358
7-52037 RUFFO     Dei vieni "Don Giovanni" (Mozart) (A12620) 1912. DA357
7-52038 CARUSO    Pimpinella (Tchaikovsky)(80)(A12805) 1913. DA119. VA44
7-52039 CARUSO    Donna non vidi mai "Manon Lescaut" (Puccini)(A12945)1913
                                                                     DA106.VA33
7-52040 RUFFO     Non penso a lei (Ferradini)(A12623) 1912. DA348
7-52041 McCORMACK Sospiri miei, andate ove vi mando (Bimboni)(A13032)1913
                                                                     DA297.VA20
7-52042 CARUSO    Lasciati amar (Leoncavallo)(79)(A13104) 1913. DA113
7-52043 CARUSO    Guardann' a luna (de Crescenzo)(A13105) 1913. DA106. VA44
7-52044 McCORMACK Questa o quella "Rigoletto" (Verdi) 1913. DA498 (A13223)
7-52045 CICCOLINI E lucevan le stelle "Tosca" (Puccini) 1913
7-52046 CICCOLINI Amor ti vieta "Fedora" (Giordano)(80)(HO 750ak) 1913
7-52047 McCORMACK Chiudo gli occhi "Manon" (Massenet)(A12764)1913.DA297.VA21
7-52048 RUFFO     Ahimè! fanciulla ancora "Thaïs" (Massenet)(A14267) 1914. DA354
7-52049 RUFFO     E suonan le campane (Ruffo) 1914. DA356
7-52050 RUFFO     Ecco dunque "Thaïs" (Massenet)(A14268) 1914. DA354
```

7-52051 MARTINELLI E. lucevan le stelle "Tosca" (Puccini)(79)(A14277)1914.DA3Ω
7-52052 MARTINELLI Cielo e mar "La Gioconda" (Ponchielli)(79)(A14340)1914.DA33
7-52053 MARTINELLI La donna è mobile "Rigoletto" (Verdi)(A14238) 1914. DA325
7-52054 RUFFO Fin ch'han dal vino "Don Giovanni" (Mozart)(A14274)1914. DA357
. 7-52055 CARUSO Amor mio (Ricciardi)(79)(A14356) 1914. DA105. VA45
7-52056 MARTINELLI Donna non vidi mai "Manon Lescaut" (Puccini)(79)(A14341)
                                                              1914. DA331
7-52057 AMATO Torna a Surriento (de Curtis)(79)(A14367) 1914. DA504
• 7-52058 AMATO Aprila bella "I Gioielli della Madonna" (Wolf-Ferrari)(A14714)
                                                              1914. DA126
7-52060 MARTINELLI Recondita armonia "Tosca" (Puccini)(79)(A14276) 1914.DA285
7-52061 McCORMACK Funiculì, funiculà (Denza)(79)(A14679) 1914. DA310
7-52062 RUFFO Oh, che m'importa? (Ruffo)(80)(A14519) 1914. DA356
7-52063 RUFFO Tremin gl'insani del mio furore "Nabucco" (Verdi)(A14518)1914
                                                              DA358
7-52065 MARTINELLI Vesti la giubba "Pagliacci" (Leoncavallo)(A15546)1915.DA32
7-52066 MARTINELLI Di tu se fedele "Un Ballo In Maschera" (Verdi)(A15666)
                                                              1915.DA52
7-52067 MARTINELLI Ideale (Tosti)(80)(A15661) 1915. DA332
7-52068 CARUSO La mia canzone (Tosti)(A15481) 1915. DA116
7-52070 RUFFO Rammenta i lieti di quando "Faust" (Gounod)(A15889) 1915.DA360
7-52071 RUFFO Vous qui faites l'endormie "Faust" (Gounod) 1915. DA360
• 7-52072 RUFFO All'erta marinar "L'Africana" (Meyerbeer)(A15894) 1915. DA164
7-52073 CARUSO Cielo turchino (Ciociano)(A15569) 1915. DA105. VA45
7-52074 DE GOGORZA Comme se canta (Mario) 6/16. DA179
7-52075 McCORMACK Carmela (de Curtis)w.vl.obb.KREISLER 6/16. DA455
7-52076 MARTINELLI Come rugiada "Ernani" (Verdi)(A16021) 1915. DA330
7-52077 MARTINELLI Di quella pira "Il Trovatore" (Verdi)(A15943) 1915
7-52078 MARTINELLI Questa o quella "Rigoletto" (Verdi)(A16710) 1915. DA285
7-52079 MARTINELLI Siciliana "Cavalleria Rusticana" (Mascagni)(A16709)1915.
                                                              DA326
7-52080 CARUSO Luna d'estate (Tosti)(A17123) 1916. DA120
7-52081 GIRAUD Rosa (Tosti) 11/17
7-52082 GIRAUD Sogno (Tosti) 11/17
7-52083 GIRAUD Oblio (Tosti) 11/17
7-52084 GIRAUD Io ricordo (Tosti) 11/17
7-52085 GIRAUD Invano (Tosti) 11/17
7-52086 GIRAUD Non m'ama più (Tosti) 11/17
7-52087 MARTINELLI Mattinata (Leoncavallo) (A17385) 1916.
. 7-52088 GIRAUD Lungi (Tosti) 9/17
7-52089 GIRAUD Primavera (Tosti) 9/17
7-52090 GIRAUD Ave Maria (Grigoleto) 9/17
7-52091 GIRAUD Rimpianto (Toselli) - Serenata 9/17
7-52092 CARUSO O sole mio (di Capua) (A17124) 1916. DA103
7-52093 JOURNET Inno di Mameli (Novaro)(A17076) 1916. DA260
7-52094 CARUSO Come un bel dì di maggio "Andrea Chenier" (Giordano)(A18659)
                                                              1916. DA117
• 7-52095 DE LUCA Il balen del suo sorriso "Il Trovatore" (Verdi) 1917. DA190
7-52096 DE LUCA Se vuol ballare "Le Nozze di Figaro" (Mozart) 1917. DA192
7-52098 DE LUCA Nuttata 'e sentimento (Capolongo) 1917. DA191
7-52099 DE LUCA Pastorale (De Leva) 1918. DA527
7-52100 MARTINELLI Apri la tua finestra "Iris" (Mascagni)(A17613)1916. DA330
7-52101 PALET Siegmund's love song "Die Walkure" (Wagner)
• 7-52103 PALET Forging Song. "Siegfried" (Wagner)
ø 7-52104 CARUSO L'alba separa dalla luce l'ombra (Tosti)(A19484)1917.DA121.VA40
7-52105 DE GOGORZA Santa Lucia 1917. DA185
• 7-52106 SIMONETTA-RANGONI Com'è gentil "Don Pasquale" (Donizetti) .1/19

7-52107 MARTINELLI Com'è gentil "Don Pasquale" (Donizetti)(A19974)1917.DA326
7-52109 GIGLI Apri la tua finestra "Iris" (Mascagni)(20270b) XI/1918
7-52110 GIGLI Dai campi, dai prati "Mefistofele" (Boito)(20253b) XI/1918
7-52111 GIGLI/SCATTOLA Si tu mi doni "Mefistofele" (Boito)(20257b)X/18.DA223
7-52112 GIGLI Giunto sul passo estremo "Mefistofele" (Boito)(20275b) XI/1918
7-52113 GIGLI Canzone napoletana (Cannio) (20265b) XI/1918. DA224
7-52114 GIGLI Recondita armonia "Tosca" (Puccini)(20255b) X/1918. DA221
7-52115 GIGLI E lucevan le stelle "Tosca" (Puccini)(20256b) X/1918. DA223
7-52118 CARUSO Inno di Garibaldi (Olivieri)(A22260) 1918. DA116
7-52120 SIMONETTA-RANGONI Notturno d'amore "I Milioni d'Arlecchino"(Drigo)12/19
7-52121 SIMONETTA-RANGONI Caro mio ben (Giordani) 1/20
7-52122 SCHIPA Salve dimora "Faust" (Gounod) 1/20. DA365
7-52123 SCHIPA Tu che a Dio "Lucia di Lammermoor" (Donizetti) 1/20. DA365
7-52124 SCHIPA Parmi veder le lagrime "Rigoletto" (Verdi)(2902ah) 1/20.DA366
7-52125 SCHIPA Ella mi fu rapita "Rigoletto" (Verdi)(2901ah) 1/20. DA366
7-52126 SIMONETTA-RANGONI Ah! mai non cessate (Donaudy) pno. 12/19
7-52127 SIMONETTA-RANGONI Chanson bohemienne (Dworak) 12/19
7-52128 SIMONETTA-RANGONI La bambola infranta (Tate) 12/19
7-52129 SIMONETTA-RANGONI Nebbie (Respighi) pno. 12/19
7-52130 SIMONETTA-RANGONI Quando ti vidi/Io dei saluti ve ne mando mille
                                          (Wolf-Ferrari) pno. 12/19
7-52132 GIRAUD Berceuse de Jocelyn (Godard) 8/20
7-52133 GIRAUD Sérénade d'autrefois (Silvestri) 8/20
7-52136 BAKLANOV Dei vieni "Don Giovanni" (Mozart)(A22877)1919. DA464. VA51
7-52137 DE GOGORZA Prologo "Pagliacci" (Leoncavallo) 1916. DA485
7-52138 JOURNET Ave Signor "Mefistofele" (Boito) DA482
7-52139 JOURNET Pie Jesu "Requiem" (Fauré) DA482
7-52141 MARTINELLI O ben tornato amore (Roxas)(A21428) 1918. DA523
7-52143 RUFFO Se la giurata fede "Tosca" (Puccini) 1915. DA163
7-52144 SCOTTI La mandolinata (Paladilhe) 1905
7-52145 ZANELLI La spagnola (di Chiara)(A23163) 1919. DA526
7-52146 ZANELLI Buono Zazà "Zazà" (Leoncavallo)(A23156) 1919. DA399
7-52147 ZANELLI Prologo "Pagliacci" (Leoncavallo)(Si puo?)(A23161)1919.DA398
7-52148 ZANELLI Prologo   do.   do.   (Un nido)(A23162)1919.DA398
7-52149 JOHNSON Vesti la giubba "Pagliacci" (Leoncavallo) 12/20
7-52150 GIGLI Amor ti vieta "Fedora" (Giordano)(4233ah) XII/1919. DA225
7-52151 GIGLI Vedi, io piango "Fedora" (Giordano)(4234ah) XII/1919. DA225
7-52152 CARUSO Vieni sul mar (anon.)(A23139) 1919. DA119. VA41
7-52153 DE' MURO Ch'ella mi creda "La Fanciulla del West" (Puccini)(4316ah)
                                                          1919. DA171
7-52154 DE' MURO Come un bel dì di maggio "Andrea Chenier" (Giordano)1919
7-52156 JOHNSON Ch'ella mi creda "La Fanciulla del West" (Puccini)(A23461)
                                                          1919. DA166
7-52158 JOHNSON Amor ti vieta "Fedora" (Giordano) 1919. DA166
7-52159 CARUSO L'addio a Napoli (Cottrau) 1919. DA104
7-52160 DE LUCA Oi luna (Cordiferro-Cardillo) 1920. DA191
7-52161 ZANELLI Zazà piccola zingara "Zazà" (Leoncavallo)(A23157) 1919. DA399
7-52162 CARUSO 'A Vucchella (Tosti) (A23138) 1919. DA103
7-52166 ZANELLI O primavera (Tirindelli) 1920. DA397
7-52168 RUFFO Sei morta nella vita mia (Costa) (A24109) 1920
7-52170 GIGLI Dai campi, dai prati "Mefistofele" (Boito)(A24782-2)I/1921.DA222
7-52171 GIGLI Cielo e mar "La Gioconda" (Ponchielli)(A24922-3)II/1921.DA220
7-52172 SMIRNOV Marì, Marì! (di Capua) ?
7-52173 RUFFO Son sessant'anni "Andrea Chenier" (Giordano)(A24621)1920.DA351
7-52174 SMIRNOV Marì, Marì! (di Capua) 1921. DA463
7-52175 SMIRNOV La donna è mobile "Rigoletto" (Verdi)(Bb100) 1921.DA461.VA49
7-52176 GIGLI Recondita armonia "Tosca" (Puccini)(A24919-3) I/1921. DA221

- 7-52177 DE LUCA   O Carlo, ascolta "Don Carlos" (Verdi) 1921. DA190
  7-52179 SMIRNOV Hai ben ragione "Il Tabarro" (Puccini)(Bb304)1921.DA461.VA49
  7-52180 GIGLI   E lucevan le stelle "Tosca" (Puccini)(A24920-5) II/1921.DA223
  7-52192 BATTISTINI Vittoria, Vittoria! (Carissimi)(BA3) w.pno. 21.V.1921.DA127
- 7-52194 BATTISTINI Egli è salvo "La Forza del Destino" (Verdi)(BA13)
                                              21.V.1921. DA189.VA5
  7-52195 GIGLI   Santa Lucia luntana (Mario)(A25017-6)IV/1921.DA572.w.fl.,mand.,
                                                           vln.& guitar
  7-52198 GIGLI   Apri la tua finestra "Iris" (Mascagni)(A25110-2)III/1921.DA221
  7-52199 DE LUCA Mattinata (Carducci-Tatuo) 1921. DA527
  7-52200 GIGLI   Giunto sul passo estremo "Mefistofele" (Boito)(A24783-7)II/1921
                                                                         DA222
  7-52201 GIGLI   Tu sola (Genise-de Curtis)(A25141-2) IV/1921. DA224
  7-52202 ZANELLI Mariemina (Ferri) (A25123) 1921. DA397
  7-52203 DE LUCA Ultima rosa (Fogazzaro-Sibella) 3/23
  7-52204 SCHIPA Viva il vino "Cavalleria Rusticana" (Mascagni)(2907ah)4/23.
                                                                         DA364
  7-52205 SCHIPA O Lola "Cavalleria Rusticana" (Mascagni)(2903ah) DA364
  7-52207 CARUSO Crucifixus "Messe Solennelle" (Rossini) 1920. DJ100 (A24474)
  7-52209 DRAGONI In testa la cappellina "Gianni Schicchi" (Puccini)5/23.DA424
  7-52210 DRAGONI La Leggenda del Piave (Mario) 12/22
  7-52211 DRAGONI Scorri fiume eterno! "Il Tabarro" (Puccini) 5/23. DA424
  7-52212 DRAGONI La donna russa "Fedora" (Giordano) 5/23. DA425
  7-52214 DE GOGORZA Lasciali dir, tu m'ami! (Stecchetti-Quaranta) 3/23. DA359
  7-52215 MARTINELLI E un riso gentil "Zazà" (Leoncavallo)(A26164)1922.DA329
  7-52216 SCHIPA O Colombina "Pagliacci" (Leoncavallo)(A26109) 1922. DA363
  7-52217 SCHIPA Chiudo gli occhi "Manon" (Massenet)(A26140) 1922. DA363
  7-52218 DRAGONI Ascolta, io morrò "Germania" (Franchetti) 10/23. DA425
  7-52219 GIGLI   Vesti la giubba "Pagliacci" (Leoncavallo)(A26192-2)III/1922.
                                                                         DA220
  7-52220 GIGLI   Serenata (Toselli) (A26795-1) IX/1922. DA572
  7-52223 GIGLI   O dolci mani "Tosca" (Puccini)(A27010-2) X/1922. DA586
  7-52224 RUFFO   Quand'ero paggio "Falstaff" (Verdi)(A27022) 1922. DA396
  7-52225 RUFFO   Chi mi dira "Marta" (Flotow) (A27024) 1922. DA396
- 7-52226 RUFFO   E che fai tu qui all'uscio "Dannazione di Faust" (Berlioz)
                                              (A27026) 1922. DA164
  7-52227 CHALIAPIN Ave Signor "Mefistofele" (Boito)(A27089) 1922. DA101
  7-52228 SCHIPA Chi se'nne scorda cchiù (Marvasi-Barthelemy) 2/24
  7-52229 CHALIAPIN Vi ravviso "La Sonnambula" (Bellini)(A27088) 1922. DA101
  7-52234 CARUSO Nina (Pergolesi) (A23143) 1919. DA120. VA40
  7-52235 DE LUCA Resta immobile "Guglielmo Tell" (Rossini) 1923. DA192
  7-52236 FLETA   A te, o cara "I Puritani" (Bellini) 10/23. DA445
  7-52237 FLETA   La donna è mobile "Rigoletto" (Verdi)
  7-52238 ZANELLI T'amo ben io! "La Wally" (Catalani)(A23402) 1919. DA526
  7-52241 PINZA   Dio dell'or "Faust" (Gounod) 1924. DA695
  7-52242 PINZA   Il santo specco "La Forza del Destino" (Verdi) 1924. DA567
  7-52243 PINZA   Ah del Tebro "Norma" (Bellini)(BE1281) 1924. DA566
- 7-52244 GILLY   Vecchia zimarra "La Bohème" (Puccini)(Bb3341) 1924.DA559.VA66
- 7-52245 GILLY   Scorri fiume "Il Tabarro" (Puccini)(Bb3342) 1924.DA559.VA66
  7-52246 CHALIAPIN Madamina "Don Giovanni" (Mozart)(Bb3200) 1924. DA555
  7-52247 CHALIAPIN Nella bionda. "Don Giovanni" (Mozart)(Bb3201) 1924. DA555
  7-52250 CARUSO Tu ca nun chaigne (de Curtis)(A23131) 1919. DA574. VA41
  7-52251 CARUSO Noche feliz (Pasados) in Spanish (A24460) 1920. DA574
  7-52252 HISLOP Ella mi fu rapita "Rigoletto" (Verdi)(Bb3874) 1924. DA226
  7-52253 HISLOP Parmi veder le lagrime "Rigoletto" (Verdi)(Bb3880)1924.DA226
  7-52254 SCHIPA Ecco ridente "Il Barbiere di Siviglia" (Rossini)(A27993)
                                                                 1923.DA594
  7-52255 SCHIPA Se il mio nome "Il Barbiere di Siviglia" (Rossini)(A28050)
                                                                 1923.DA594

```
7-52257 GIGLI    Nel verde maggio  "Loreley" (Catalani)(A27533-1)II/1923.DA586
7-52258 RUFFO    Lolita (Buzzi-Peccia) 1923. DA687
7-52260 RUFFO    Santa Lucia  1923. DA687
7-52262 FLETA    E lucevan le stelle  "Tosca" (Puccini)(A29265) 1923. DA446
7-52263 RUFFO    Marechiare (Tosti)  1923. DA748
7-52264 BATTISTINI  Alla vita  "Un Ballo in Maschera" (Verdi)(Bk1422)1923.DA600
7-52265 BATTISTINI  Deh vieni  "Don Giovanni" (Mozart)(Bk1433) 1923. DA600
7-52268 CARUSO    Scordame (Fucito) (A23152) 1919. DA608. VA43
7-52269 CARUSO    Senza nisciuno (de Curtis) (A23149) 1919. DA608. VA43
7-52270 FLETA    La donna è mobile "Rigoletto" (Verdi) (A29266) 1923. DA446
7-52273 DE LUCA   Canta il mare (Mazzola-De Leva) 1924. DA651
7-52274 DE LUCA   Occhi di fata (Denza) 1924. DA651
7-52275 McCORMACK  Luoghi sereni e cari (Donaudy) pno. 1924. DA627(Bb 5033)
7-52276 McCORMACK  O del mio amato ben (Donaudy) pno. 1924. DA627(Bb 5035)
7-52277 TAMAGNO   Deserto sulla terra "Il Trovatore" (Verdi)(75)(3028b) 1903
                                                issd.1910 Dog Label
7-52284 SCHIPA    Serenata medioevale (Silvestri) 1925. DA705
7-52285 SCHIPA    Pesca d'amore (Barthelemy) 1925. DA705
7-52286 GIGLI    Funiculì, funiculà (Denza)(A31457-3) XI/1924. DA713
7-52287 GIGLI    Povero Pulcinello (Buzzi-Peccia)(A31477-2) XI/1924. DA713
7-52289 PINZA    Splendon più belle "La Favorita" (Donizetti) 1925. DA708
7-52290 PINZA    Del suo cor calmai "Mignon" (Thomas) 1925. DA708
7-52292 FLETA    Bimba, non t'avvicinar (Cortesi-Bettinelli)(A31578) 1925. DA714
7-52306 JOURNET   Vecchia zimarra  "La Bohème" (Puccini) 9/26. DA771
7-52307 CARUSO    Veghissime sembienza (Donaudy)(A24463) 1920. DA754
7-52310 CARUSO    Sultanto a te (Fucito)(A22515) 1919. DA754
7-52328 JOURNET   Chi mi dira  "Marta" (Flotow) 9/26. DA771
7-52332 RUFFO     Chitarrata abruzzese (Tosti) 1923. DA769
```

10" records : BLACK LABEL

```
7-52009 RICCARDO MARTIN  E lucevan le stelle  "Tosca" (Puccini)(81)
7-52064 VALLO(VALENTE)   A Trieste (Caromio) (HO 1118ak)
7-52181 TORRE    Voce 'e notte! (de Curtis) 11/23
7-52182 TORRE    Comme facette mammeta? (Gambardella) 11/23
7-52183 TORRE    Ngiuline (di Chiara) 11/23
7-52184 DADDI    Torna a Surriento (de Curtis) 11/23
7-52185 TORRE    'A tiene fresca (Mazzola) 11/23
7-52186 TORRE    Tarantella ciociara (Gambardella) 11/23
7-52187 DADDI    Palomma 'e notte (Buongiovanni) 11/23
7-52188 DADDI    Rusinella (Monaco) 11/23
7-52189 MILANO   'O guaglione 'e mala vita  9/22
7-52190 DADDI    Tarantelle malandrina (Galgani) 11/23
7-52191 QUARANTA  Voci di costumi napoletani  9/22
7-52197 MILANO   Totonno 'e Quagliarella (Capurro-Buongiovanni) 9/22
7-52230 DEL BOSCO  El Sindic Sant Buin (cantato in dialetto Piemontese) con
                                        acc.di flauto e chitarra 12/24
7-52231 DEL BOSCO  La Rusmunda 12/24
7-52281 PAPA RICCARDI  'A Canzone 'e Capo d'Anno  (Pt.II) 1/25
7-52282 PAPA RICCARDI  'A Canzone 'e Capo d'Anno  (Pt.IV) 1/25
7-52283 PAPA RICCARDI  'A Canzone 'e Capo d'Anno  (Pt.III)1/25
```

12" records : G.&T. RED & PINK LABEL. PRE-DOG issued 1908
DOG LABEL 1909. DOG LABEL 1910 : "LA VOCE del PADRONE"

052000 SANTLEY   Ehi capitano/Non più andrai "Le Nozze di Figaro" (Mozart)
                                                          (187 R) 1903
052010 GARBIN   Donna non vidi mai "Manon Lescaut" (Puccini) pno.   1903
052020 SAMMARCO   Racconto di Gerace "Lorenza" (Mascheroni) pno.   1903
052025 SAMMARCO   Ballata di Adamastor "L'Africana" (Meyerbeer) pno.   1903
052026 SAMMARCO   Monologo "Andrea Chenier" (Giordano) pno.   1903
052027 SAMMARCO   Racconto "Germania" (Franchetti)   pno.   1903
052031 KASCHMANN   Carlo che solo "Don Carlos" (Verdi) pno.   1903
052032 KASCHMANN   O dei verd'anni miei "Ernani" (Verdi) pno. 1903. IRCC 214
052033 SAMMARCO   O dei verd'anni miei "Ernani" (Verdi) pno.   1903
052034 SAMMARCO   Credo "Otello" (Verdi) pno.   1903
052036 KASCHMANN   Brindisi "Amleto" (Thomas) pno. 1903. IRCC 214
052037 KASCHMANN   Serenata "Meduca" (Leoncavallo) pno.   1903
052038 KASCHMANN   Credo "Otello" (Verdi) pno.   1903
052039 SAMMARCO   Il sogno "Otello" (Verdi) pno.   1904
052040 SAMMARCO   Arioso di Cascart "Zazà" (Leoncavallo) pno.   1904
052041 SAMMARCO   Prologo "Pagliacci" (Leoncavallo)   pno.   1904
052054 MARCONI   Romanza del duello "Eugen Onegin" (Tchaikovsky) pno. 1904
052055 MARCONI   O paradiso "L'Africana" (Meyerbeer)   pno.   1904
052056 MARCONI   Cielo e mar "La Gioconda" (Ponchielli) pno.   1904
052057 MARCONI   Ingemisco "Messa da Requiem" (Verdi)   pno.   1904
052058 MARCONI   Bella cantiam l'amore (Mascagni)   pno.   1904
052063 SAMMARCO   Canzone delle rose "Dannazione di Faust" (Berlioz)pno. 1904
052065 MARCONI   Non guardami così (Paloni)   pno.   1904
• 052066 CARUSO   Mi par d'udir "I Pescatori di Perle" (Bizet)(268)pno.03.VB44
• 052068 TAMAGNO   Niun mi tema "Otello" (74)(269b) 1903. DS100
• 052073 CARUSO   Un solo istante "L'Elisir d'amore" (Donizetti)(A996-1)1904
                                                         VB16.VB44
052074 CARUSO   Celeste Aida "Aida" (Verdi) pno. (A997)   1904
052075 ANCONA   Prologo "Pagliacci" (Leoncavallo)(76) 2 eds.   1904
052076 ANCONA   Serenata "Don Giovanni" (Mozart)   1904
052078 DE LUCIA   Ecco ridente "Il Barbiere di Siviglia" (Rossini)pno.1904
052080 ANCONA   Credo "Otello" (Verdi)   1904
052083 GIORGINI   Mia madre "Fedora" (Giordano)   1904
052084 GIORGINI   O paradiso "L'Africana" (Meyerbeer) pno.   1904
052085 GIORGINI   Che gelida manina "La Bohème" (Puccini)(239m)   1904
• 052086 CARUSO   Com'è gentil "Don Pasquale" (Donizetti)pno.(A2340)05.DB159.VB55
052087 CARUSO   Romanza del fiore "Carmen" (Bizet)pno.(A2341) 1905. VB57
• 052088 CARUSO   Bianca al par "Gli Ugonotti" (Meyerbeer)pno.(A2342)   1905
• 052089 CARUSO   Cielo e mar "La Gioconda" (Ponchielli)(A2343) 1905. DB113
052090 PLANCON   Possenti Numi "Flauto Magico" (Mozart)pno.(A2201) 1905.DB657
052091 SCOTTI   Eri tu "Un Ballo in Maschera" (Verdi)(77)(A2233)   1905
052092 SCOTTI   Credo "Otello" (Verdi) (A2234)   1905
• 052093 JOURNET   Infelice e tuo credevi "Ernani" (Verdi)(77)(A2309)   1905
052100 TAMAGNO   Un dì all'azzurro spazio "Andrea Chenier" (Giordano)(74)
                                            (270b) 1903. DS101
052101 TAMAGNO   Esultate "Otello" (Verdi)(75)(10b) 1903. DS101
• 052102 TAMAGNO   Ora e per sempre addio "Otello" (Verdi)(75)(12b) 1903.DS100
052103 TAMAGNO   O muto asil "Guglielmo Tell" (Rossini)(74)   1905
052105 GIORGINI   M'appari tutt'amor "Marta" (Flotow)(77)   1905
052106 GIORGINI   Spirto gentil "La Favorita" (Donizetti)(529c)   1905
052107 SCOTTI   Prologo "Pagliacci" (Leoncavallo) (A876)   1905
052108 SCOTTI   Per me giunto "Don Carlos" (Verdi)pno. (A2359)1905.IRCC 190
052109 SCOTTI   Come Paride vezzoso "L'Elisir d'amore" (Donizetti)pno.(A2361)
                                             1905. DB589. IRCC 190. VB
052110 SCOTTI   Triste aprile (de Lara) (A2362)   1905

052111 DE LUCIA Addio Mignon "Mignon" (Thomas)(77)pno.(549c)   1905
052112 SCOTTI Dio possente "Faust" (Gounod) (A878)   1903
052113 SCOTTI Serenade "Don Giovanni" (Mozart/Quand'ero paggio "Falstaff"
               (Verdi)(76)(A875) pno.   1903
052114 SCOTTI Morte di Valentino "Faust" (Gounod)pno.(A1093)   1904
052115 SCOTTI Deh non parlare "Rigoletto" (Verdi)/Finch'han dal vino
               "Don Giovanni" (Mozart)pno.(A1094)1904.IRCC 18
052116 SCOTTI Pari siamo "Rigoletto" (Verdi)pno.(A1095)   1904
052117 PLANÇON Qui sdegno "Flauto Magico" (Mozart)pno.(A2337) 1905.DB657
052120 CARUSO Spirto gentil "La Favorita" (Donizetti)(A3104) 1906. DB129
052121 CARUSO M'appari tutt'amor "Marta" (Flotow)(A3100) 1906. DB159
• 052122 CARUSO Che gelida manina "La Bohème" (Puccini)(A3101) 1906. DB113
052123 SCOTTI Pari siamo "Rigoletto" (Verdi) 1906. DB424
052128 SCOTTI Crede "Otello" (Verdi)(80)   1906
• 052129 DE LUCIA Dei miei bollenti spiriti "La Traviata" (Verdi)pno.(622c)06
052132 RUFFO Largo al factotum "Il Barbiere di Siviglia" (Rossini)(80)(76)
                                                               1907. DB502

052133 RUFFO Dio possente "Faust" (Gounod)(76)(792c)   1907
052139 SCOTTI Vi ravviso "La Sonnambula" (Bellini)(80)   1906
052140 BATTISTINI Per la patria (Cocchi)(866c) 1907. DB209. Orange Label.
052141 BATTISTINI Oh dei verd'anni miei "Ernani" (Verdi)(76)(874c)07.DB197.Or.
052142 BATTISTINI Alla vita "Un Ballo In Maschera" (Verdi)(877c)07.DB198.Or.
• 052143 BATTISTINI Il mio Lionel "Marta" (Flotow)(75)(883c)1907.DB209.Orange
• 052144 BATTISTINI A tanto amor "La Favorita" (Donizetti)(76)(884c)07.DB228.Or.
052145 BATTISTINI O Lisbona "Don Sebastiano" (Donizetti)(76)(885c)07.DB207.Or.
• 052146 BATTISTINI Eri tu "Un Ballo in Maschera" (Verdi)(76)(886c)07.DB200.Or.
052147 BATTISTINI Su queste rose "Dannazione di Faust" (Berlioz)(76)(888c)
                                                       1907.DB189.Orange
052148 BATTISTINI Perche tremar "Zampa" (Herold)(76)(889c)1907.IRCC202.Orange
052149 GIORGINI Serenata "Don Pasquale" (Donizetti)   1907
052153 CARUSO Triste ritorno (Barthélemy)(82)(A4159) 1906. DB140
052154 CARUSO Ideale (Tosti)(80)(A4162) 1906. DB129
052155 ANCONA Prologo "Pagliacci" (Leoncavallo)   1907
052156 ANCONA Dio possente "Faust" (Gounod)   1907
• 052157 CARUSO O paradiso "L'Africana" (Meyerbeer)(82)(A4160) 1907. DB117
052158 CARUSO Un dì all'azzurro spazio "Andrea Chenier" (Giordano)(82)(A4316)
                                                               1907. DB700
052159 CARUSO Vesti la giubba "Pagliacci" (Leoncavallo)(82)(A4317)1907.DB111
052160 SCOTTI Maria, Mari (di Capua)(81) 1907. DB422
052161 SCOTTI Inaffia l'ugola "Otello" (Verdi) (A4324)   1907
052166 PAOLI Vesti la giubba "Pagliacci? (Leoncavallo)(79) 1907. DB469
052167 PAOLI No, pagliaccio "Pagliacci" (Leoncavallo)(79) 1907. DB469
052168 PAOLI Un tal gioco "Pagliacci" (Leoncavallo)(77)   1907
052169 PAOLI Spezza i ceppi "Sansone e Dalila" (Saint-Saëns)   1907
• 052170 PAOLI Di quella pira "Il Trovatore" (Verdi)   1907
052171 PAOLI O paradiso "L'Africana" (Meyerbeer)   1907
052172 PAOLI Esultate "Otello" (Verdi)   1907
052173 PAOLI Dio mi potevi "Otello" (Verdi) 1907. HRS 1009
052177 DE GOGORZA Caro mio ben (Giordani)(80) 1907. DB323
052178 ANCONA O dei verd'anni miei "Ernani" (Verdi)   1907
052179 ANCONA A tanto amor "La Favorita" (Donizetti)   1907
052180 ANCONA Eri tu "Un Ballo in Maschera" (Verdi)   1907
052184 DE LUCIA Cigno fedel "Lohengrin" (Wagner)(1174c) 1907. DB605
052185 DE LUCIA Romanza del fiore "Carmen" (Bizet)(79)(1175c) 1907. DB359

052186 SCAMPINI Rachele allor che Iddio "L'Ebrea" (Halévy)   1908
052187 SCAMPINI Ricordanze (Vittadini)   1908
052188 RUFFO Brindisi "Amleto" (Thomas)(1315c) 1908. DB569
052189 RUFFO Essere o non essere "Amleto" (Thomas)   1908

- 052190 RUFFO Per me giunto "Don Carlos" (Verdi) 1908. DB178
- 052191 RUFFO Pari siamo "Rigoletto" (Verdi)(1330c) 1908. DB502
- 052192 RUFFO Prologo "Pagliacci" (Leoncavallo)(77)(1341c)   1908
- 052200 MARCONI Di pescator ignobile "Lucrezia Borgia" (Donizetti)pno.(77)
                                        (1417c) 1908. VB27
- 052206 DE TURA Dei miei bollenti spiriti "La Traviata" (Verdi)   1908
- 052207 DE TURA Tu che a Dio "Lucia di Lammermoor" (Donizetti)   1908
- 052208 GIORGINI Una furtiva lagrima "L'Elisir d'amore" (Donizetti)   1908
- 052209 CARUSO In terra solo "Don Sebastiano" (Donizetti)(82)(A5008)1908.DB700
- 052210 CARUSO Ah sì, ben mio "Il Trovatore" (Verdi)(82)(A5034) 1908. DB112
- 052212 DE GOGORZA Dio possente "Faust" (Gounod)(81)   1908
- 052214 JOURNET La calunnia "Il Barbiere di Siviglia" (Rossini)   1907/8
- 052215 DE GOGORZA Pari siamo "Rigoletto" (Verdi) 1908. DB323. IRCC 113
- 052216 DE GOGORZA O sole mio (de Capua) 1908. DB188
- 052217 PLANÇON Berceuse "Mignon" (Thomas)(81)(A6112) 1908. IRCC 94
- 052218 PLANÇON Pro peccatis "Stabat Mater" (Rossini)(81)(A6113) 1908.IRCC 81
- 052221 MARCONI Fra poco a me ricovero "Lucia di Lammermoor" (Donizetti)1908
- 052222 CHALIAPIN La calunnia "Il Barbiere di Siviglia" (Rossini)(614i) 1908
- 052224 CARUSO Celeste Aida "Aida" (Verdi)(82)(A3180) 1908. DB144
- 052225 SCOTTI Già mi dicon venal "Tosca" (Puccini)(81) 1908. DB423
- 052226 DELLA TORRE O casto fiore "Re di Lahore" (Massenet)   1908
- 052227 DELLA TORRE La lotta dei bardi "Tannhäuser" (Wagner)(76)   1908
- 052228 GIORGINI Mi par d'udir ancora "I Pescatori di Perle" (Bizet)(1483c)08
- 052229 SIGNORINI Pastorale "Profeta" (Meyerbeer)   1908
- 052230 SIGNORINI O muto asil "Guglielmo Tell" (Rossini)(80)   1908
- 052231 SIGNORINI Celeste Aida "Aida" (Verdi)   1908
- 052232 GIORGINI Che gelida manina "La Boheme" (Puccini)(1482½c)   1908
- 052233 MARCONI O paradiso "L'Africana" (Meyerbeer)   1908
- 052234 MARCONI Tu che a Dio "Lucia di Lammermoor" (Donizetti)   1908
- 052239 DE LUCIA Quando le sere "Luisa Miller" (Verdi)pno.   1908
- 052240 GIORGINI Dei miei bollenti spiriti "La Traviata" (Verdi)(1490c)08.VB16
- 052241 DELLA TORRE Quel ciglio "Lakmé" (Delibes)   1908
- 052242 DELLA TORRE O tu, bell'astro "Tannhäuser" (Wagner)   1908
- 052243 DELLA TORRE Accusa di Telramondo "Lohengrin" (Wagner)   1908
- 052244 GIORGINI Ma come dopo "Werther" (Massenet)   1908
- 052245 SCAMPINI O Jone di quest'anima "Jone" (Petrella)   1908
- 052248 RUFFO Come il romito fior "Amleto" (Thomas)(80) 1908. DB569
- 052249 RUFFO Canzone del Toreador "Carmen" (Bizet)(80)(2736f) 1908. DB406
- 052250 DE LUCIA Ecco ridente "Il Barbiere di Siviglia" (Rossini)pno.(214m)
                                                        1908. HRS 1053
- 052251 RUFFO Cortigiani, vil razza "Rigoletto" (Verdi)(2735f) 1908. DB175
- 052253 SIGNORINI Stanco, spossato, arresta! "Chatterton" (Leoncavallo)1908
- 052254 SIGNORINI E un pane mi chiedeva "Chatterton" (Leoncavallo)   1908
- 052255 SIGNORINI Di lagrime mio malgrado "Chatterton" (Leoncavallo)   1908
- 052256 DE TURA Come rugiada "Ernani" (Verdi)   1908
- 052257 GIORGINI Ah! dispar vision "Menon" (Massenet)   1908
- 052258 SCAMPINI O muto asil "Guglielmo Tell" (Rossini)   1908
- 052259 SCAMPINI Romanza del fiore "Carmen" (Bizet)   1908
- 052260 DE GOGORZA Il balen del suo sorriso "Il Trovatore"(Verdi)(81)1908.DB184
- 052261 DALMORES Ah sì, ben mio "Il Trovatore" (Verdi)(81) 1908. HRS 1001
- 052264 SCAMPINI Da voi lontan "Lohengrin" (Wagner)(1496c)   1908
- 052265 DE TURA Spirto gentil "La Favorita" (Donizetti)   1908
- 052266 DELLA TORRE Domo o ciel da un vil straniero "Guglielmo Tell" (Rossini)
                                                                            1908
- 052271 PAOLI Un dì all'azzurro spazio "Andrea Chenier" (Giordano)   1909
- 052272 PAOLI Tu? indietro! Fuggi "Otello" (Verdi)   1909
- 052274 MACNEZ Aspetta sempre "Eidelberga mia" (Pacchierotti)   1909
- 052275 MACNEZ Hanno gittato in mare un angioletto (Virgilio)   1909

```
052276 MACNEZ   Passar volli poc'anzi al cimitero  "Eidelberga mia"  (Pacchierotti)
                                                                              1909
052277 MACNEZ   Taci la valle e azzurra  "Eidelberga mia"  (Pacchierotti)   1909
052286 GIORGINI  Spirto gentil  "La Favorita"  (Donizetti)                  1909
052292 CHALIAPIN  Dormiro sol  "Don Carlos"  (Verdi)(2012c)  Orange Label    1909
• 022293 SMIRNOV  Giunto sul passo estremo  "Mefistofele"  (Boito)(2058e)09.VB38
052295 DE TURA  La vaga pupilla  "Faust"  (Gounod)                          1909
052296 SMIRNOV  Spirto gentil  "La Favorita"  (Donizetti)                   1909
052297 PAOLI   Preghiera  "Le Cid"  (Massenet)                              1910
• 052302 BATTISTINI  O vin  "Amleto"  (Thomas)(81)(272ai) 1911. DB202.Orange Label
052303 BATTISTINI  Allor che tu coll'estro  "Tannhäuser"  (Wagner)(81)(274ai)
                                                               1911. Orange. DB196
052304 BATTISTINI  O tu, bell'estro  "Tannhäuser"  (Wagner)(287ai)          1911
052305 BATTISTINI  Prologo  "Pagliacci"  (Leoncavallo)(260ai)Orange.1911.DB239
052306 BATTISTINI  Un nido di memorie  "Pagliacci"  (Leoncavallo)(261ai)Or.'11.
                                                                             DB239
052307 BATTISTINI  Ma come dopo  "Werther"  (Massenet)(262ai)1911.Or. DB194
052308 BATTISTINI  Ah! non mi ridestar  "Werther"  (Massenet)(263ai)Or.'11.DB149
052309 BATTISTINI  Come il romito fior  "Amleto"  (Thomas)(267ai)Or.1911.DB202
052310 BATTISTINI  Le Soir  (Gounod)(79)pno. in Fr.(268ai)Orange. 1911. DB214
052311 BATTISTINI  Amor,  amor  (Tosti) (269ai) 1911. DB213. Orange
• 052312 BATTISTINI  Te Deum  "Tosca"  (Puccini)(76)(270ai)Orange. 1911. DB212
052313 BATTISTINI  O santa medaglia  "Faust"  (Gounod)(79)(275ai)Or.'11.DB196
052314 BATTISTINI  Ah! per sempre  "I Puritani"  (Bellini)(276ai)Or.'11.DB195
052315 BATTISTINI  Bella è di sol vestita  "Maria di Rohan"  (Donizetti)(81)
                                              (281aj) 1911. Orange. DB147
052316 BATTISTINI  Bel sogno beato  "I Puritani"  (Bellini)(284ai)1911.Or.DB195
052317 BATTISTINI  Di Provenza il mar  "La Traviata"  (Verdi)(285ai)'11.Or.DB201
052318 BATTISTINI  La lotta dei bardi  "Tannhäuser"  (Wagner)(286ai)'11.Or.DB199
052319 BATTISTINI  Culto (Denza) (288ai)1911. Orange. DB190
052320 BATTISTINI  Ideale (Tosti)(289ai)1911. Orange. DB213
052321 BATTISTINI  O ma charmante (Quaranta)(80)(290ai) 1911. Orange. DB190
052322 BATTISTINI  Mia sposa sara la mia bandiera (Rotoli)(291ai)'11.Or.DB206
052323 BATTISTINI  Serenata (Tosti) pno.(292ai) 1911. Orange. DB208
052324 BATTISTINI  Ballata (Rotoli) (293ai) 1911. Orange. DB192
052325 BATTISTINI  Melodie (Tosti) (295ai) 1911. Orange. DB192
052328 PAOLI   Niun mi tema  "Otello"  (Verdi) DB468                        c.1911/2
052329 PAOLI   Ah sì, ben mio  "Il Trovatore"  (Verdi) DB466                c.1911/2
052330 PAOLI   Celeste Aida  "Aida"  (Verdi) DB466                          c.1911/2
052332 PAOLI   Bianca al par  "Gli Ugonotti"  (Meyerbeer) DB470             c.1911/2
052335 PAOLI   Preghiera  "Le Cid"  (Massenet)                             c.1911/2
052336 PAOLI   Dio mi potevi  "Otello"  (Verdi) DB468                       c.1911/2
052337 PAOLI   Cielo e mar  "La Gioconda"  (Ponchielli)                     c.1911/2
• 052338 DE' MURO  Un dì all'azzurro spazio  "Andrea Chenier"  (Giordano)
                                              (02323½v) 1912. DB553
052339 DE' MURO  Tu ch'odi  "Isabeau"  (Mascagni)(02347v) 1912. DB557
052340 DE' MURO  E passera  "Isabeau"  (Mascagni)(02348v) 1912. DB557
052341 DE' MURO  Fu vile  "Isabeau"  (Mascagni)(02353v) 1912. DB558
052342 DE' MURO  O paradiso  "L'Africana"  (Meyerbeer)(02361v) 1912. DB549
052343 DE' MURO  Il fior  "Carmen"  (Bizet)                                 1912
052353 CHALIAPIN  Ite sul colle  "Norma"  (Bellini)(80)(613m) 1912. DB106
052354 CHALIAPIN  La calunnia  "Il Barbiere di Siviglia"  (Rossini)(81)(614m)'12
052355 CHALIAPIN  Ave Signor  "Mefistofele"  (Boito)(80)(615m)              1912
052356 CHALIAPIN  Vi revviso  "La Sonnambula"  (Bellini)(80)(616m)          1912
052357 BATTISTINI  Figlia di regi  "L'Africana"  (Meyerbeer)(214af)1912.IRCC.Or.
052358 BATTISTINI  Quando amor  "L'Africana"  (Meyerbeer)(215af) 1912.Or.DB210
052359 BATTISTINI  Averla tanto  "L'Africana"  (Meyerbeer)(216af) 1912.Or.DB210
```

052360 BATTISTINI   Ambo nati   "Linda di Chamounix" (Donizetti)(217af) 1912
            Orange. DB204. VB49
052361 BATTISTINI   Errar sull'ampio   "Quo Vadis" (Nougues)(218af)1912.Or.VB14
052362 BATTISTINI   Invocazione   "Quo Vadis" (Nougues)(216af)1912.Or.DB211.VB63
052363 BATTISTINI   Cruda funesta smania   "Lucia di Lammermoor" (Donizetti)
            (220af)1912. Or. DB207
052364 BATTISTINI   Resta immobile   "Guglielmo Tell" (Rossini)(225af)'12.Or.DB189
052365 BATTISTINI   Amica, l'ora   "Quo Vadis" (Nougues)(227af)1912.Or.DB206.VB14
052366 BATTISTINI   Era la notte   "Otello" (Verdi)(228af) 1912. Orange. DB212
052367 BATTISTINI   Delizia (Beethoven) (229af) 1912. Orange. DB214
052368 BATTISTINI   Visione fuggitiva   "Erodiade" (Massenet)(233af)'12.Or.DB149
052369 BATTISTINI   Pieta, rispetto, amore   "Macbeth" (Verdi)(234af)1912.
            Orange. DB199. IRCC 202
052370 BATTISTINI   Epitalamio   "Nerone" (Rubinstein)(235af)1912.Or.DB211.VB63
052371 BATTISTINI   Occhi di fata (Denza) (236af) 1912. Orange. DB208
052372 SMIRNOV   E lucevan le stelle   "Tosca" (Puccini) 1912. DB595
052373 SMIRNOV   Una furtiva lagrima   "L'Elisir d'amore" (Donizetti) 1912
052374 JADLOWKER   Arioso   "Pagliacci" (Leoncavallo)
052375 JADLOWKER   Vesti la giubba   "Pagliacci" (Leoncavallo) 6/13
052376 RUFFO   O monumento   "La Gioconda" (Ponchielli)(459ai) 1912. DB180
052378 RUFFO   Pescator, affonda l'esca   "La Gioconda" (Ponchielli)(461ai)1912
            DB180
• 052379 RUFFO   Un nido di memorie   "Pagliacci" (Leoncavallo)(467aj)1912.DB464
• 052380 RUFFO   Largo al factotum   "Il Barbiere di Siviglia" (Rossini) 1912
• 052381 RUFFO   Si può? "Pagliacci" (Leoncavallo) (462aj) 1912. DB464
052382 RUFFO   Dai canti d'amore (Titta) 1912
052383 RUFFO   Marechiare (Tosti)(465aj)(79) 1912. DB404
052385 JADLOWKER   Ecco ridente   "Il Barbiere di Siviglia" (Rossini)(HO 253al)
            1912.VB54
052386 JADLOWKER   Celeste Aida   "Aida" (Verdi)(80)(287½al) 1912
• 052387 CHALIAPIN   Le rovine son queste   "Roberto il Diavolo" (Meyerbeer)(79)
            (2692c).1912. DB106
052388 CHALIAPIN   Vieni, la mia vendetta   "Lucrezia Borgia" (Donizetti)(80)
            (2693c) 1912. DB403.VB72
052389 CHALIAPIN   Infelice   "Ernani" (Verdi)(2694c) 1912. DB403. VB72
052403 BATTISTINI   Malìa (Tosti)(79)(2807c) Orange. 1913
052404 BATTISTINI   Per mi giunto   "Don Carlos" (Verdi)(2808c)Orange.1913.IRCC
052405 BATTISTINI   Morrò, ma listo in core   "Don Carlos" (Verdi)(2809½c)
            Orange.1913.IRCC
052406 BATTISTINI   Il balen del suo sorriso   "Il Trovatore" (Verdi)(2810c)
            Orange,1913.
052407 BATTISTINI   Voce fatal di morte   "Maria di Rohan" (Donizetti)(2811c)
            Orange. 1913
052410 SMIRNOV   Se il mio nome   "Il Barbiere di Siviglia" (Rossini)(79)
            (2846c) 1913. DB562
052417 SMIRNOV   Mi par d'udir ancora   "I Pescatori di Perle" (Bizet) 1913
052418 CICCOLINI   Cielo e mar   "La Gioconda" (Ponchielli)(79) 1913 (713aj)
052419 CICCOLINI   E lucevan le stelle   "Tosca" (Puccini)   1913
052421 SCHIPA   Ah! dispar vision   "Manon" (Massenet) (722aj)'13.DB969.2-052150
052422 SCHIPA   Che gelida manina   "La Boheme" (Puccini)(731aj)1913. DB969
052425 BAKLANOV   Eri tu   "Un Ballo in Maschera" (Verdi)
052426 JADLOWKER   O paradiso   "L'Africana" (Meyerbeer)
052428 JADLOWKER   Una furtiva lagrima   "L'Elisir d'amore" (Donizetti)
052429 DE' MURO   Io l'ho perduta   "Don Carlos" (Verdi) 1914. DB554
052430 DE' MURO   Or dammi il braccio tuo   "Iris" (Mascagni) 1914. DB555
052431 DE' MURO   Morte d'Otello   "Otello" (Verdi)(742m) 1914. DB560
052434 CICCOLINI   Da voi lontano   "Lohengrin" (Wagner)

12" records : G. & T. BLACK LABEL.   PRE-DOG issued 1908
DOG LABEL 1909. DOG LABEL 1910 : "LA VOCE del PADRONE"

052001	VIGNAS	Ben altra prova	"Lohengrin" (Wagner)	1903
052002	VIGNAS	Racconto del Graal	"Lohengrin" (Wagner)	1903
052003	VENTURA	Spirto gentil	"La Favorita" (Donizetti)	1903
052004	VIGNAS	O paradiso	"L'Africana" (Meyerbeer)	1903
052005	VIGNAS	Addio a Elsa	"Lohengrin" (Wagner)	1903
052006	VENTURA	Il fior	"Carmen" (Bizet)	1903
052007	VIGNAS	Celeste Aida	"Aida" (Verdi)	1903
052008	VIGNAS	Dall'alba tinto	"I Maestri Cantori" (Wagner)	1903
052009	BUCALO	Un organetto suona per la via (Scontrino)		1903
052013	COJONINI	Se il mio nome	"Il Barbiere di Siviglia" (Rossini)	1903
052013	VIGNAS	Canto della primavera	"Walkiria" (Wagner) 3/04	
052014	VENTURA	Che gelida menina	"La Boheme" (Puccini)	1903
052015	BERRIEL	Eri tu	"Un Ballo in Maschera" (Verdi)	1904
052016	BERRIEL	Dio possente	"Faust" (Gounod)	1904
052017	BUCALO	Mia sposa sarà la mia bandiera (Rotoli)		1903
052018	TISCI-RUBINI	La calunnia	"Il Barbiere di Siviglia" (Rossini)	1903
052021	VENTURA	Cielo e mar	"La Gioconda" (Ponchielli)	1903
052024	DIDUR	Prologo	"Mefistofele" (Boito) pno.	1903
052028	DIDUR	Serenata	"Faust" (Gounod) pno.	1903
052029	DIDUR	Dio dell'or	"Faust" (Gounod) pno.	1903
052030	DIDUR	Cavatina	"L'Ebrea" (Halévy) pno.	1903
052042	LA PUMA	Io t'aspettavo	"Andrea Chenier" (Giordano) pno.	1904
052043	CORRADETTI	Manca un foglio	"Il Barbiere di Siviglia" (Rossini)	1904
052044	LA PUMA	Credo	"Otello" (Verdi) pno.	1904
052046	CORRADETTI	Predica di Fra Melitone	"La Forza del Destino" (Verdi)	1904
052049	CORRADETTI	Torna		1904
052064	KAMIONSKI	Cavatina	"Un Ballo in Maschera" (Verdi) pno.	1904
052067	GIRAUD	Ancora (Tosti) pno.		1904
052069	GIRAUD	Il fior	"Carmen" (Bizet) pno.	1904
052070	GIRAUD	Quando le sere al placido	"Luisa Miller" (Verdi) pno.	1904
052071	GIRAUD	Appena il mite april	"I Maestri Cantori" (Wagner)pno.	1904
052072	ROTA	O specchio (d'Atri)		1904
052077	MARTINEZ-PATTI	Un dì all'azzurro spazio	"Andrea Chenier" (Giordano)	
			pno.	1904
052079	BUCALO	Io scacciato	"Ruy Blas" (Marchetti) pno.	1904
052094	PEREA	Una furtiva lagrima	"L'Elisir d'amore" (Donizetti)	1905
052095	CARONNA	Sei vendicata assai	"Dinorah" (Meyerbeer) pno.	1905
052096	DE LUNA	Splendon più belle	"La Favorita" (Donizetti)	1905
052097	PREVE	Ite sul colle	"Norma" (Bellini)	1905
052098	CIGADA	Vien Leonora	"La Favorita" (Donizetti)	1905
052099	A.PINI-CORSI	Manca un foglio	"Il Barbiere di Siviglia" (Rossini)1905	
052104	ACERBI	O paradiso	"L'Africana" (Meyerbeer) pno.	1905
052112	PEREA	Dei miei bollenti spiriti	"La Traviata" (Verdi)	1906
052118	ZACCARI	Com'è gentil	"Don Pasquale" (Donizetti) pno.	1906
052119	CIGADA	O tu, bell'astro	"Tannhäuser" (Wagner)	1906
052124	LARA	Prova maggior	"Lohengrin" (Wagner)	1906
052125	LARA	Racconto del Graal	"Lohengrin" (Wagner)	1906
052126	MINOLFI	O dei verd'anni miei	"Ernani" (Verdi)	1906
052130	A.PINI-CORSI	Udite o rustici	"L'Elisir d'amore" (Donizetti)	1906
052131	CIGADA	Eri tu	"Un Ballo in Maschera" (Verdi)	1907
052134	MINOLFI	Quasi vinto	"Lucia di Lammermoor" (Donizetti)	1907
052135	A.PINI-CORSI	Manca un foglio	"Il Barbiere di Siviglia" (Rossini)	
			(637c) 1907	
052136	CAMPANARI	Dio possente	"Faust" (Gounod)	1905
052137	CAMPANARI	Prologo	"Pagliacci" (Leoncavallo)	1905

052150 MINOLFI Morte di Valentino "Faust" (Gounod)(76)(857c) 1907. D313
052151 SANGIORGI Meco all'altar di Venere "Norma" (Bellini)   1907
052152 DE SEGUROLA La calunnia "Il Barbiere di Siviglia" (Rossini) 1907
052162 CIGADA Un nido di memorie "Pagliacci" (Leoncavallo)(77) 1907.D319
052163 CIGADA Si può? "Pagliacci" (Leoncavallo)(77) 1907. D319
052164 BARBAINI No, pagliaccio, non son "Pagliacci" (Leoncavallo) 1907
052165 BARBAINI Un tal gioco "Pagliacci" (Leoncavallo)   1907
052181 CIGADA Dio possente "Faust" (Gounod)(77)(1200c) 1907. D312
052182 A.PINI-CORSI Scena della minestra "La Forza del Destino" (Verdi)1907
052183 RICCOBONO Ave Maria (Leoncavallo) orch. cond.comp. 11/07
052193 ISCHIERDO Romanza del fiore "Carmen" (Bizet)   1908
052194 ISCHIERDO Bianca al par "Gli Ugonotti" (Meyerbeer)   1908
052195 DE SEGUROLA Ella giammai m'amo "Don Carlos" (Verdi)   1908
052196 DE SEGUROLA Dormiro sol "Don Carlos" (Verdi)   1908
052197 DE SEGUROLA Se oppressi ognor "L'Ebrea" (Halévy)   1908
052198 DE SEGUROLA Maledizione "L'Ebrea" (Halévy)   1908
052201 A.PINI-CORSI La povera Anastasia "Campanello" (Donizetti)   1908
052202 MANSUETO Ninna nanna "Mignon" (Thomas)   1908
052203 DE SEGUROLA Infelice "Ernani" (Verdi)   1908
052204 DE SEGUROLA Sorge la notte "I Puritani" (Bellini)   1908
052205 DE SEGUROLA Introduzione "Mignon" (Thomas)   1908
052219 COATES Cielo e mar "La Gioconda" (Ponchielli)   1908
052223 COATES Giunto sul passo estremo "Mefistofele" (Boito)   1908
052235 A.PINI-CORSI Nella bionda "Don Giovanni" (Mozart)   1908
052236 DE SEGUROLA Ite sul colle "Norma" (Bellini)(1289c)   1908
052237 MANSUETO Eja mater "Stabat Mater" (Rossini)   1908
052238 CICCOLINI Il fior "Carmen" (Bizet)   1908
052246 FEDERICI Coro d'introduzione "Manon" (Massenet)   1908
052247 GIOVANELLI Io son solo "Manon" (Massenet)   1908
052262 QUINZI-TAPERGI Ninna Nanna "Mignon" (Thomas)   1908
052263 A.PINI-CORSI Cavatina "Mignon" (Thomas)   1908
052267 BARRERA Dio mi potevi scagliar "Otello" (Verdi)   1908
052278 BADINI Credo "Otello" (Verdi)   1909
052279 BADINI O monumento "La Gioconda" (Ponchielli)   1909
052280 CUNEGO Un dì all'azzurro spazio "Andrea Chenier" (Giordano) 1909
052281 BADINI Un dì m'era di gioia "Andrea Chenier" (Giordano)   1909
052282 FEDERICI Compagni udite "Eidelberga mia" (Pacchierotti)   1909
052283 FEDERICI O mia vaga "Eidelberga mia" (Pacchierotti)   1909
052284 FEDERICI Parean mill'anni "Eidelberga mia" (Pacchierotti)   1909
052285 RIMONDINI Addio figliuol "Eidelberga mia" (Pacchierotti)   1909
052287 CUNEGO Se vedrete pallida "Jana" (Virgilio)   1909
052288 A.PINI-CORSI Approfittiam "Maestro di Cappella" (Paer)   1909
052289 A.PINI-CORSI Ella compar "Maestro di Cappella" (Paer)   1909
052290 BARRERA Morte d'Otello "Otello" (Verdi)   1909
052294 BADINI Addio di Wotan "Walkiria" (Wagner)   1909
052298 CICCOLINI Addio alla madre "Cavalleria Rusticana" (Mascagni)1910
052299 GALLI Sì, morir ella de' "La Gioconda" (Ponchielli)   1910
052301 DE GREGORIO Da voi lontano "Lohengrin" (Wagner)   1910
052331 GILBERTI Cominciate "I Maestri Cantori" (Wagner) 11/12
052333 GOETZEN L'ora e fissata "Falstaff" (Verdi)   10/12
052344 BETTONI Finestre cieche! "Isabeau" (Mascagni)   1912
052347 BADINI M'odi, l'estrema e questa "Cristoforo Colombo" (Franchetti)'12
052348 DI BERNARDO Celeste Aida "Aida" (Verdi)   1912
052349 BADINI L'onore, ladri "Falstaff" (Verdi)   1912
052350 BADINI Aman lassù le stelle "Cristoforo Colombo" (Franchetti)1912
052352 RIMONDINI Addio figliuol "Eidelberga mia" (Pacchierotti)   1912
052384 GILBERTI Dall'alba tinto "I Maestri Cantori" (Wagner)   1912
052390 BELLABARBA Resta immobile "Guglielmo Tell" (Rossini)   1912

```
052393 BETTONI  All'erta, all'erta!  "Il Trovatore" (Verdi) 5/13
052394 BETTONI  Sull'orlo dei tetti  "Il Trovatore" (Verdi) 5/13
052395 BADINI   Eri tu "Un Ballo in Maschera" (Verdi)     6/13
052396 SALVATI  Com'è gentil  "Don Pasquale" (Donizetti)    6/13
052397 BADINI   Cruda, funesta smania "Lucia di Lammermoor" (Donizetti) 11/13
052398 DE GREGORIO  Che gelida manina "La Bohème" (Puccini) 9/13
052399 DE GREGORIO  Or dammi il braccio tuo  "Iris" (Mascagni) 4/14
052400 DE GREGORIO  Salve dimora "Faust" (Gounod) 11/13
052401 BETTONI  Ecco una nuova preda "Roberto il Diavolo" (Meyerbeer) 11/13
052411 BETTONI  Suore che riposate   "Roberto il Diavolo" (Meyerbeer) 11/13
052412 BETTONI  Tuba mirum  "Messa da Requiem" (Verdi) 12/13
052413 PAROLA   Ingemisco  "Messa da Requiem" (Verdi) 12/13
052414 BETTONI  Confutatis maledictis  "Messa da Requiem" (Verdi) 12/13
052432 BETTONI  Oh, santa lancia "Parsifal" (Wagner) 7/14
052433 BETTONI  Potesti uccidere  "Parsifal" (Wagner) 7/14
```

12" records : G. & T. RED & PINK LABEL. PRE-DOG issd.1908
DOG LABEL 1909. DOG LABEL 1910 : "LA VOCE del PADRONE"

```
2-052000 SCOTTI   Deh vieni  "Don Giovanni" (Mozart)/Quand'ero paggio "Falstaff"
                                                      (Verdi) 1909. DB668
2-052001 SCOTTI   Prologo  "Pagliacci" (Leoncavallo) 1906. DB422
2-052002 SCOTTI   L'onore, ladri  "Falstaff" (Verdi) 1909. DB424
2-052003 SCOTTI   Dio possente  "Faust" (Gounod)(81) 1910. DB423
2-052004 SCOTTI   Pari siamo "Rigoletto" (Verdi)    1906. DB424
2-052005 CARUSO   Mamma mia, che vo' sape (Nutile)(82)(A8344) 1909. DB119
2-052006 CARUSO   Oh tu che in seno  "La Forza del Destino" (Verdi)(81)(A8345)
                                                         1909. DB112
2-052007 CARUSO   Il fior  "Carmen" (Bizet)(81) (A8349) 1909. DB117
2-052008 CARUSO   Bianca al par "Gli Ugonotti" (Meyerbeer)(82)(A8351)1909.DB115
2-052009 SAMMARCO  Il sogno  "Otello" (Verdi)(80) 5/10
2-052010 SAMMARCO  Credo  "Otello" (Verdi) 5/10. DB609
2-052011 SAMMARCO  Eri tu  "Un Ballo in Maschera" (Verdi) (3744f) 5/10
2-052012 SAMMARCO  Ballata Adamastor  "L'Africana" (Meyerbeer)(80)(3745f) 5/10
2-052013 SAMMARCO  Quand'ero paggio "Falstaff" (Verdi)/Serenata "Don Giovanni"
                                                          (Mozart) 5/10
2-052014 SAMMARCO  Largo al factotum  "Il Barbiere di Siviglia" (Rossini)
                                                          (374-f) 5/10
2-052015 SAMMARCO  Pari siamo  "Rigoletto" (Verdi)
2-052016 SAMMARCO  A tanto amor  "La Favorita" (Donizetti)
2-052017 SAMMARCO  Oje marena (Costa)(80) pno. 5/10
2-052018 SAMMARCO  L'ultima canzone (Tosti)(80) 1/11
2-052019 ZEROLA   Morte d'Otello" Otello" (Verdi)(80)
2-052021 McCORMACK  Che gelida manina "La Bohème" (Puccini)(80)(A8589)'10.DB343
2-052022 McCORMACK  Una furtiva lagrima  "L'Elisir d'amore" (Donizetti)(80-81)
                                                (A8536) 1910.DB324
2-052023 McCORMACK  Fra poco a me ricovero  "Lucia di Lammermoor" (Donizetti)
                                                (80-82) (A8535) 1910. DB345
2-052024 McCORMACK  Tu che a Dio  "Lucia di Lammermoor" (Donizetti)(80)
                                                (A8740) 1910. DB345
2-052025 McCORMACK  Dei miei bollenti spiriti "La Traviata" (Verdi)1910.DB631
2-052026 McCORMACK  Per viver vicino a Maria "La Figlia del Reggimento"(A8693
                                   (Donizetti)(80) (A8739) 1910. DB631
2-052027 McCORMACK  Il fior  "Carmen" (Bizet)(80)(A8538) 1910. DB343
2-052028 McCORMACK  Salve dimora "Faust" (Gounod)(80)(A8694) 1910. DB634
2-052029 ZEROLA   La fatal pietra/Morir si pura  "Aida" (Verdi) 1910
2-052030 ZEROLA   Un dì all'azzurro spazio "Andrea Chenier" (Giordano) 1910
```

2-052031 SAMMARCO Prologo "Pagliacci" (Leoncavallo) c.1910/11
2-052032 CARUSO Cielo e mar "La Gioconda" (Ponchielli)(81)(A8718)1910.DB696
2-052033 SAMMARCO Dio possente "Faust" (Gounod) c.1910/11
2-052034 CARUSO No, pagliaccio, non son "Pagliacci" (Leoncavallo)(81)(A9742)
1910.DB111
2-052035 CARUSO Addio (Tosti)(81) (A9747) 1910. DB131
2-052037 SCOTTI Luna nova (Costa) 1911
2-052039 JOURNET Son lo spirito "Mefistofele" (Boito)(80) 1911.DB615.DB897
2-052041 SAMMARCO Lo vedremo "Ernani" (Verdi) 1911. DB606
2-052D42 SAMMARCO Non più andrai "Le Nozze di Figaro" (Mozart)(81)(3189f)
1911.DB607
2-052043 SAMMARCO O sole mio (di Capua) c.1911
2-052044 SAMMARCO Cruda funesta smania "Lucia di Lammermoor" (Donizetti)(81)
1911.DB607
2-052045 LAZARO La donna è mobile "Rigoletto" (Verdi) 1911. Purple Label
2-052046 LAZARO Questa o quella "Rigoletto" (Verdi) 1911. Purple Label
2-052047 LAZARO O paradiso "L'Africana" (Meyerbeer) 1911. Purple Label
2-052049 LAZARO Recondita armonia "Tosca" (Puccini) 1911. Purple Label
2-052050 LAZARO Spirto gentil "La Favorita" (Donizetti)(79)(±5268f)1911.Purpl·
2-052051 AMATO Largo al factotum "Il Barbiere di Siviglia" (Rossini)1911.DB15·
2-052052 AMATO Credo "Otello" (Verdi) 1911. DB146 ((A11214)
2-052053 AMATO Di Provenza il mar "La Traviata" (Verdi)(A11211ᵛ)1914. DB146
2-052054 AMATO Prologo "Pagliacci" (Leoncavallo) 1911. DB156 (A11210)
2-052055 AMATO Con voi ber "Carmen" (Bizet)(A11213) 1911. DB157
2-052056 AMATO Cortigiani, vil razza "Rigoletto" (Verdi) 1911. DB158
2-052057 AMATO/SETTI/BADA Povero Rigoletto "Rigoletto" (Verdi) 1911. DB158
2-052058 CARUSO Eternamente (Mascheroni)(81)(A11271) 1911. DB121. VB60
• 2-052059 CARUSO Testa adorata "La Bohème" (Leoncavallo)(81)(A11272)1911.DB122
2-052060 CARUSO Core'ngrato (Cardillo)(81)(A11274) 1911. DB142
• 2-052061 CARUSO Io non ho che una povera st anzetta
"La Bohème" (Leoncavallo)(81)(A11276)1911. DB12·
2-052062 CARUSO Quando nascesti tu "Lo Schiavo" (Gomez)(80)(A11273)1911.DB13·
2-052064 CARUSO Una furtiva lagrima "L'Elisir d'amore" (Donizetti)(A996-2)
1911. DB12·
2-052065 CARUSO Ma se m'è forza perderti "Un Ballo in Maschere" (Verdi)(80)
(A11420)1911. DB13·
• 2-052066 CARUSO Celeste Aida "Aida" (Verdi) with Recit.(A11423) 1911. DK115
2-052067 CARUSO Terantella sincera (de Crescenzo)(81)(A11472) 1912. DB141
2-052068 CARUSO La Danza (Rossini)(81) (A11590) 1912. DB141
2-052070 JADLOWKER Che gelida manina "La Bohème" (Puccini) DB495
2-052071 JADLOWKER Dei miei bollenti spiriti "La Traviata" (Verdi) DB495
2-052072 SAMMARCO Bacio di lama "I Gioielli della Madonna" (Wolf-Ferrari)1912
2-052073 SAMMARCO Aprila,bella"I Gioielli della Madonna" (Wolf-Ferrari)1912.DB60·
(81)
2-052074 SAMMARCO Figlia di regi "L'Africana" (Meyerbeer) 1912. DB606
2-052075 RUFFO Vien, Leonora "La Favorita" (Donizetti) 1912
2-052076 CARUSO Parmi veder le lagrime "Rigoletto" (Verdi)(80)(A11421)1913.DB·
2-052077 CARUSO Fenesta che lucive (Bellini)(79)(A13107) 1913. DB140
2-052078 AMATO Ferito prigionier "Germania" (Franchetti)1913. DB
2-052079 AMATO O vecchio cor che batti "I due Foscari" (Verdi)(79)(A13124)
1913. DB636
2-052080 CICCOLINI Cielo e mar "La Gioconda" (Ponchielli)
2-052081 CICCOLINI Fra poco a me ricovero "Lucia di Lammermoor" (Donizetti)
2-052082 CICCOLINI Che gelida manina "La Bohème" (Puccini)(80)(HO 513ai)
2-052083 CARUSO Addio alla madre "Cavalleria Rusticana" (Mascagni)(A14202)
1913. DB118
2-052085 MARTINELLI Che gelida manina "La Bohème" (Puccini)(A14236)1914.DB335
2-052086 CARUSO Cujus Animam "Stabat Mater" (Rossini)(80)(A14200)1913.DB138

```
• 2-052088 RUFFO     Sei vendicata assai  "Dinorah" (Meyerbeer) 1914. DB178
• 2-052089 AMATO     Eri tu  "Un Ballo in Maschera" (Verdi)(A11605) 1912. DB157
  2-052090 RUFFO     Credo  "Otello" (Verdi) (A14278) 1914. DK114
  2-052091 CARUSO    Manella mia (Valente)(79)(A14358) 1914. DB121. VB61
  2-052092 AMATO     Sei vendicata assai  "Dinorah" (Meyerbeer) DB636
  2-052094 AMATO     Te Deum  "Tosca" (Puccini)                 DB637
  2-052096 RUFFO     Aman lassù  "Cristoforo Colombo" (Franchetti)pno.(A14517)
                                                                1914. DB179
  2-052098 CARUSO    Perchè? (Pennino) (A15568) 1915. DB119
  2-052099 MARTINELLI  Serenata (Mascagni) (A15665) 1915. DB337
  2-052100 MARTINELLI  Celeste Aida  "Aida" (Verdi) (A14237) 1914. DB335
  2-052101 CARUSO    Angelo casto e bel  "Il Duca d'Alba" (Donizetti)(A15572)
                                                                1915.DB640.VB56
  2-052102 MARTINELLI  Ah sì, ben mio  "Il Trovatore" (Verdi)(A15907)1915.DB333
  2-052103 RUFFO     I due Granatieri (Schumann)(79) 1915. DB242
  2-052104 RUFFO     Dio possente  "Faust" (A15893)  1915. DB405
  2-052105 MARTINELLI  M'appari tutt'amor  "Marta" (Flotow)(A17340) 1916. DB336
  2-052106 CARUSO    Mia sposa sarà la mia bandiera (Rotoli)(A17195)  1916. DB128
  2-052107 CARUSO    Santa Lucia - Neapolitan  (A17344) 1916. DB142
  2-052108 CARUSO    Tiempo antico (Caruso) (A17343) 1916. DB143. VB61
  2-052109 DE GOGORZA  Non è ver (Mattei) DB188
• 2-052110 McCORMACK  Il mio tesoro  "Don Giovanni" (Mozart)(A17647) 1916. DB324
  2-052111 McCORMACK  Non è ver (Mattei)c.1916. DB630
  2-052112 CARUSO    Ah! la paterna mano  "Macbeth" (Verdi)(A17197) 1916. DB118
  2-052114 MURRAY-DAVEY  Possenti Numi  "Flauto Magico" (Mozart)(79) c.1916
  2-052115 MARTINELLI  Fra poco a me ricovero  "Lucia di Lammermoor" (Donizetti)
                                                      (A17339) 1916. DB332
  2-052116 DE LUCA   Largo al factotum  "Il Barbiere di Siviglia" (Rossini)
                                                                1917. DB217
  2-052118 DE LUCA   Oh dei verd'anni miei  "Ernani" (Verdi)   1917. DB217
  2-052119 DE' MURO  Esultate  "Otello" (Verdi)(79)(3183c) 1917. DB559
  2-052120 DE' MURO  Dio mi potevi scagliar  "Otello" (Verdi)(3179c) 1917.DB560
  2-052121 DE' MURO  Di quella pira  "Il Trovatore" (Verdi) 1917. DB562 (3177c)
  2-052122 DE' MURO  Sì, fui soldato  "Andrea Chenier" (Giordano)(3176c)1917.DB553
  2-052123 DE' MURO  Ora e per sempre addio  "Otello" (Verdi) 1917. DB559
  2-052124 MARTINELLI  L'ultima canzone (Tosti) (A17614) 1917. DB338
  2-052125 PALET     Canzone del concorso  "I Maestri Cantori" (Wagner)
  2-052127 DE LUCA   Eri tu  "Un Ballo in Maschera" (Verdi) 1917. DB218
  2-052128 MARTINELLI  Dei miei bollenti spiriti  "La Traviata" (Verdi)(A19137)
                                                                1917. DB339
  2-052129 CARUSO    Musica proibita (Gastaldon) (A15480) 1917. DB131
  2-052130 DE LUCA   Di Provenza il mar  "La Traviata" (Verdi) 1917. DB219
  2-052132 DRAGONI   Un dì m'era di gioia  "Andrea Chenier" (Giordano) 1917
  2-052133 DRAGONI   Canzone del Toreador  "Carmen" (Bizet) c.1917
  2-052134 DRAGONI   Credo  "Otello" (Verdi) 1917. DB477
  2-052135 DRAGONI   Prologo  "Pagliacci" (Leoncavallo) 1917
  2-052136 DRAGONI   Pari siamo  "Rigoletto" (Verdi)   1917
  2-052140 GIGLI     Salve dimora  "Faust" (Gounod) (3332c) XI/1918
  2-052141 GIGLI     Spirto gentil  "La Favorita" (Donizetti) (3325c) XI/1918
  2-052142 GIGLI     Cielo e mar  "La Gioconda" (Ponchielli) (3324c)  XI/1918
  2-052143 GIGLI     Ah! ritrovarla  "Lodoletta" (Mascagni)(3323c)XI/1918. DB270
  2-052144 CARACCIOLO  Che corsa  "Lodoletta" (Mascagni) 2/19
  2-052145 CARACCIOLO  Flammen, perdonami  "Lodoletta" (Mascagni) 2/19
  2-052146 CARACCIOLO  Bimbi del mio villaggio  "Lodoletta" (Mascagni) 2/19
  2-052148 DE' MURO  Alla madre (Preghiera)  (G.de'Muro) 1917. DB549
  2-052149 CARUSO    Uocchi celesti  (de Crescenzo)(A19483)1917. DB115. VB59
  2-052150 SCHIPA    Ah! dispar vision  "Manon" (Massenet)(722aj)1913.052421.DB969
  2-052151 SIMONETTA-RANGONI  Ah! non mi ridestar  "Werther" (Massenet) 12/19
```

2-052152 MARTINELLI Tu che a Dio "Lucia di Lammermoor" (Donizetti)(A19073)
                                                                          1916.DB332
2-052153 CARUSO Le campane di San Giusto (Arona)(A22514) 1919. DB616
2-052154 CARUSO Pietà! Signore (Stradella) (A22121) 1918. DB134
• 2-052155 DE LUCA A tanto amor "La Favorita" (Donizetti) 1919. DB220
2-052156 DE LUCA Lascia ch'io pianga "Rinaldo" (Handel) 1918. DB221
2-052157 BAKLANOV Eri tu "Un Ballo in Maschera" (Verdi) 1919. DB584 (A22875)
2-052158 BAKLANOV Era la notte "Otello" (Verdi)   1919. DB584
2-052159 DE GOGORZA Serenata "Don Giovanni" (Mozart)
                     Serenata "Dannazione di Faust" (Berlioz) DB184
2-052160 DE GOGORZA Dormi pure (Scuderi)   DB626
2-052161 DE GOGORZA Eri tu "Un Ballo in Maschera" (Verdi)(A9677) 1910.DB183
2-052162 DE GOGORZA Largo al factotum "Il Barbiere di Siviglia" (Rossini)
                                                 DB163
• 2-052163 JOURNET Abbietta zingara "Il Trovatore" (Verdi)c.1910.DB310
2-052164 JOURNET La calunnia "Il Barbiere di Siviglia" (Rossini) DB308
2-052165 JOURNET Nella bionda "Don Giovanni" (Mozart)(A8549) 1910. DB313
2-052166 JOURNET O salutaris hostia (Luce) DB309
2-052167 JOURNET Splendon più belle "La Favorita" (Donizetti) DB615
2-052168 MARTINELLI O paradiso "L'Africana" (Meyerbeer)(A15944) 1915. DB336
2-052169 McCORMACK Adeste Fideles 1913-15. DB328
• 2-052170 RUFFO Eri tu "Un Ballo in Maschera" (Verdi) 1915. DB398
2-052171 SAMMARCO Di Provenza il mar "La Traviata" (Verdi)
2-052174 DE' MURO Un dì all'azzurro spazio "Andrea Chenier" (Giordano) 8/20
2-052175 GIGLI Mamma! quel vino è generoso "Cavalleria Rusticana" (Mascagni)
                                         (1049aj)XII/1919.DB270
2-052176 DE' MURO Sono Ramerrez "La Fanciulla del West" (Puccini)(1056aj)
                                             1919.DB551
2-052177 CARUSO   Campane a sera (Billi-Malfetti)(A22259) 1918. DB134
2-052178 ZANELLI Pari siamo "Rigoletto" (Verdi)(A23193) 1919. DB459
2-052180 CARUSO Ombra mai fu "Xerxes" (Handel)(A23714) 1920. DB133
2-052181 RUFFO Era la notte "Otello" (Verdi) 1920. DB404
2-052182 ZANELLI A tanto amor "La Favorita" (Donizetti)(A23401) 1919.DB459
2-052183 DE LUCA Dio possente "Faust" (Gounod)(A22647) 1920. DB219
2-052184 RUFFO Largo al factotum "Il Barbiere di Siviglia" (Rossini)1920.DB405
2-052185 RUFFO Pari siamo "Rigoletto" (Verdi) 1920. DB402   ((A23945)
2-052186 RUFFO Adamastor, rè dell'onde profonde "L'Africana" (Meyerbeer)
                                            (A23947) 1922. DB406
2-052187 RUFFO Nemico della patria "Andrea Chenier" (Giordano) 1920. DB242
2-052189 DRAGONI Urna fatal "La Forza del Destino" (Verdi) DB740
2-052190 RUFFO O casto fior "Re di Lahore" (Massenet) 1920. DB401
2-052191 CARUSO Serenata (Bracco) (A23151) 1919. DB143. VB62
2-052192 SMIRNOV O dolce incanto "Manon" (Massenet) DB583. c.1920/1
2-052193 SMIRNOV Giunto sul passo estremo "Mefistofele" (Boito) c.1920/1.DB582
2-052194 SMIRNOV Mi par d'udir ancora "I Pescatori di Perle" (Bizet) c.1920/1
                                             DB583
• 2-052195 CARUSO Domine Deus "Messe Solennelle" (Rossini)(A24473)1920.DB120
2-052196 MARTINELLI O mio piccolo tavolo "Zazà" (Leoncavallo)(A24930)1921
                                             DB337
2-052197 GIGLI Spirto gentil "La Favorita" (Donizetti)(A24921-2)III/1921.DB273
2-052198 CARUSO T' m'arricordo e Napule (Gioe)(A24462) 1920. DB640. VB62
2-052199 RUFFO Onore! ladri "Falstaff" (Verdi) 1921. DB402
2-052200 HISLOP Addio alla madre "Cavalleria Rusticana" (Mascagni)(Cc398)
                                          1921. DB522
2-052201 BATTISTINI O casto fior "Re di Lahore" (Massenet)(CA2)21.V.1921.DB150
2-052202 BATTISTINI A miei rivali "Ruy Blas" (Marchetti)(CA4) 21.V.1921. DB197
2-052203 BATTISTINI Per me giunto "Don Carlos" (Verdi)(CA5) 21.V.1921. DB148
2-052204 BATTISTINI O tu, bell'astro "Tannhäuser" (Wagner)(CA6)21.V.1921.DB194

2-052207 BATTISTINI Voce fatal "Maria di Rohan" (Donizetti)(CA10)21.V.1921.
DB147
• 2-052208 BATTISTINI Vien Leonora "La Favorita" (Donizetti)(CA11)21.V.1921.
DB148
2-052209 BATTISTINI Ah, non avea più lagrime "Maria di Rudenz" (Donizetti)
(CA27) 21.V.1921.DB150
2-052210 DE LUCA Per me giunto "Don Carlos" (Verdi) 1921. DB218
2-052212 CHALIAPIN In questa tomba oscura (Beethoven)(Cc551) 1921. DB107
2-052213 MARTINELLI Lontan, lontan "Eugen Onegin" (Tchaikovsky)(A24931)1921
DB338
2-052214 GIGLI Salve dimora "Faust" (Gounod)(A25109-2) III/1921. DB273
2-052215 FLETA Giulietta, son io "Giulietta e Romeo" (Zandonai)(CE393)1922.
DB524
2-052216 FLETA Il fior "Carmen" (Bizet) 1922. DB524
2-052218 CHALIAPIN La calunnia "Il Barbiere di Siviglia" (Rossini)(A26102)
1922.DB107
2-052219 GIGLI Notturno d'amore (Drigo)(A26061-4) III/1922. DB670
2-052220 CHALIAPIN Dormiro sol "Don Carlos" (Verdi)(A26102) 1922
2-052221 DRAGONI Grazie, Signor "Lohengrin" (Wagner) 10/23. DB476
2-052222 DRAGONI Anch'io la visione "Germania" (Franchetti) 10/23.DB740
2-052224 CARUSO Mia piccirella "Salvator Rosa" (Gomez)(A23150) 1919. DB144
• 2-052225 RUFFO O dei verd'anni miei "Ernani" (Verdi) 1921. DB398
2-052226 RUFFO Dunque ho sognato "Cristoforo Colombo" (Franchetti)(A25213)
1921.DB179
• 2-052232 HISLOP Che gelida manina "La Bohème" (Puccini)(Co1357) 1922.DB522
2-052233 GIGLI Un dì all'azzurro spazio "Andrea Chenier" (Giordano)(A27011-2)
X/1922. DB670
2-052235 GIGLI O paradiso "L'Africana" (Meyerbeer)(A27531-2) II/1923. DB109
2-052236 MARTINELLI O muto asil "Guglielmo Tell" (Rossini)(A27526)1923.DB339
2-052237 DE' MURO Il non ho amato ancor "Andrea Chenier" (Giordano)8/23.DB552
2-052238 MARTINELLI Inno dei Fascisti (Manni-Blanc) 1923
2-052239 MARDONES O tu Palermo "I Vespri Siciliani" (Verdi) 1922. DB726
2-052240 PINZA Il lacerato spirito "Simone Boccanegra" (Verdi)(CE1210)1924.
DB699
2-052241 PINZA Di due figli "Il Trovatore" (Verdi) 1924. DB828
2-052242 PINZA Dalle stanze "Lucia di Lammermoor" (Donizetti)1924.DB699.VB70
2-052243 PINZA Se oppressai ognor "L'Ebrea" (Halévy)(CE1282) 1924. DB698
2-052244 GIGLI M'appari tutt'amor "Marta" (Flotow)(A27995-1)VI/1923. DB109
2-052247 MARDONES Tu sul labbro de veggenti "Nabucco" (Verdi) 1923. DB726
2-052248 HISLOP Tombe degli avi miei "Lucia di Lammermoor" (Donizetti)12/24.
DB695
2-052249 HISLOP Fra poco a me ricovero "Lucia di Lammermoor" (Donizetti)12/24
DB695
2-052250 DE LUCA Sei vendicata assai "Dinorah" (Meyerbeer)(A29439)1924.VB6
2-052251 BATTISTINI Urna fatale "La Forza del Destino" (Verdi)(Ck1418) 1923
DB738
2-052252 BATTISTINI Per me giunto "Don Carlos" (Verdi)(Ck1419) 1923. DB737
2-052253 BATTISTINI A tanto amor "La Favorita" (Donizetti)(Ck1423)1923.DB736
2-052254 BATTISTINI Eri tu "Un Ballo in Maschera" (Verdi)(Ck1424)1923. DB738
2-052255 BATTISTINI Non più andrai "Le Nozze di Figaro" (Mozart)(Ck1427)1923
DB736
2-052256 BATTISTINI O del mio dolce ardor "Paride ed Elena" (Gluck)(Ck1428)
1923. DB731
2-052257 BATTISTINI Senza tetto"Il Guarany"(Gomez)(Ck1432) 1923. DB737
2-052268 HISLOP Ma.se m'è forza "Un Ballo in Maschera" (Verdi) 6/25.DB822
2-052269 HISLOP Ah non credevi tu "Mignon" (Thomas) 6/25. DB822
2-052270 JOURNET Gloria al tuo Dio "Nerone " (Boito) 1924. DB819
2-052271 LO GIUDICE Questa ad un lido fatal "Nerone" (Boito) 1924. DB819

2-052272 LO GIUDICE Oh! come viens ad errar "Nerone" (Boito) 3/25. DB820
2-052273 LO GIUDICE Scendi! scendi! "Nerone" (Boito) 3/25. DB820
2-052274 JOURNET Follia, follia delirio "I Maestri Cantori" (Wagner)7/25.DB827
2-052275 JOURNET La luccioletta "I Maestri Cantori" (Wagner) 7/25. DB827
2-052278 PINZA Voi che del Dio vivente "L'Ebrea" (Halévy) 1925. DB829
2-052279 PINZA Ave Signor "Mefistofele" (Boito) 1925. DB829
2-052280 PINZA Cinta di fiori "I Puritani" (Bellini)(Gk1817)1925.DB828.VB70
2-052281 SCHIPA Addio Mignon "Mignon" (Thomas)(A30080) 1924. DB843
2-052282 SCHIPA Ah non credevi tu "Mignon" (Thomas)(A30079) 1924. DB843
2-052284 GRANFORTE Largo al factotum "Il Barbiere di Siviglia" (Rossini)
                                                              10/25. DB834
2-052285 GRANFORTE O Lisbona "Don Sebastiano" (Donizetti)   10/25. DB834
2-052286 GRANFORTE Credo "Otello" (Verdi) 10/25. DB835
2-052287 GRANFORTE O monumento "La Gioconda" (Ponchielli) 10/25. DB835
2-052288 GRANFORTE Pari siamo "Rigoletto" (Verdi) 12/25. DB836
2-052289 GRANFORTE Cortigiani, vil razza "Rigoletto" (Verdi) 12/25. DB836

            12" records : G. & T. BLACK LABEL. PRE-DOG issued 1908
            DOG LABEL 1909. DOG LABEL 1910 : "LA VOCE del PADRONE"
2-052040 RADFORD Osmin's aria "Il Seraglio" (Mozart)(82)
2-052259 CIBELLI Regina coeli (in latino)

                    12" records : RED LABEL
5-052000 PALET Piu bianca "Gli Ugonotti" (Meyerbeer)
5-052001 PALET Il fior "Carmen" (Bizet)

            10" records : G. & T. RED & PINK LABEL. PRE-DOG issued 1908
            DOG LABEL 1909. DOG LABEL 1910 : "LA VOCE del PADRONE"
53132 BRUNO Giorni poveri vivea "Il Trovatore" (Verdi) (7")   1902
53133 BRUNO Cari luoghi "Linda di Chamounix" (Donizetti) pno. (7")   1902
53227 BRUNO Stride la vampa "Il Trovatore" (Verdi)   1902
53228 BRUNO Figlio mio "Profeta" (Meyerbeer)   1902
53229 BRUNO Racconto di Pierotto "Linda di Chamounix" (Donizetti)   1902
53232 PINTO Vissi d'arte "Tosca" (Puccini)   1902
53232 PINTO Vissi d'arte "Tosca" (Puccini) (1780b) 2nd. ed.   1902
53233 PINTO Voi lo sapete o mamma "Cavalleria Rusticana" (Mascagni)pno.1902
53234 PINTO Vissi d'arte "Tosca" (Puccini) (1782b) 3rd. ed.   1902
53238 PINTO Romanza di Ero "Ero e Leandro" (Bottesini)   1902
53239 PINTO Tu non sei buono "Germania" (Franchetti)   1902
53240 PINTO Suicidio! "La Gioconda" (Ponchielli)   1902
53241 BRUNO Cantabile di Dalila "Sansone e Dalila" (Saint-Saëns)   1902
53242 BRUNO O aprile foriero "Sansone e Dalila" (Saint-Saëns)   1902
53318 FABBRI Se Romeo t'uccise un figlio "Romeo e Giulietta" (Bellini)
                                                       pno. 1904. IRCC 236
53321 FABBRI Ah se tu dormi "Romeo e Giulietta" (Vaccai) pno.   1904
53322 FABBRI Brindisi "Lucrezia Borgia" (Donizetti) pno.   1904
53325 ALBANI Ombra mai fu "Serse" (Handel) (4760 L)   1904
53331 STORCHIO Non sol un pensier "Siberia" (Giordano)pno. 1904. IRCC 238
53332 STORCHIO Non odi la il martir "Siberia" (Giordano)pno.1904.IRCC 238
53333 PANDOLFINI Chanson de Florian (Godard) pno.   1904
53340 PANDOLFINI Sortita di Adriana "Adriana Lecouvreur" (Cilea)pno. 1904
53341 CARELLI Vissi d'arte "Tosca" (Puccini)   1904
53346 BORONAT Valse "La Traviata" (Verdi)(75) (1770 L)   1904

```
53347 BORONAT    Senza l'amore (Tosti) (1771 L)                                      1904
53348 BORONAT    Caro nome "Rigoletto" (Verdi) (1772 L)                              1904
53349 BORONAT    Valse "Mirella" (Gounod) (1773 L)                                   1904
53350 BORONAT    Air "Zabava" (Ivanow) (1774 L)                                      1904
53351 BORONAT    Andante "I Puritani" (Bellini) (1775 L) VA11                        1904
53352 BORONAT    Desiderio (Zardo) (1776 L)                                          1904
53353 BORONAT    Cavatina "I Pescatori di Perle" (Bizet) (1777L) VA11               1904
53354 BORONAT    Aria della rosa "Marta" (Flotow)(76) (1778 L)    VA19               1904
53372 BONINSEGNA In quelle trine morbide  "Manon Lescaut" (Puccini)
                                                        (2144 L)   VA4               1904
53373 BONINSEGNA Suicidio! "La Gioconda" (Ponchielli)                                1904
53374 BONINSEGNA Aria della lettera "Maschere" (Mascagni)                            1904
53375 BONINSEGNA D'amor sull'ali rosee "Il Trovatore" (Verdi)(81)
                                                        (2176 L)   VA10   1904
53376 BONINSEGNA Voi lo sapete o mamma "Cavalleria Rusticana" (Mascagni)1904
53392 BONINSEGNA Ninna Nanna (Leoncavallo) pno.                                      1904
53394 SEMBRICH   Ah non giunge "La Sonnambula" (Bellini) 1904. IRCC 8
53415 BONINSEGNA Morro, ma prima in grazia  "Un Ballo in Maschera" (Verdi)05
53416 BONINSEGNA La vergine "La Forza del Destino" (Verdi)(7309b)      1905
53417 BONINSEGNA Ernani involami "Ernani" (Verdi)(81)(7321b) 1905. DA430
53418 BONINSEGNA Quai celesti concenti "L'Africana" (Meyerbeer)pno.    1905
53419 BONINSEGNA Bolero "I Vespri Siciliani" (Verdi)pno. (7325b)       1905
53431 KURZ  Caro nome "Rigoletto" (Verdi)(76) (3981 H)                 1906
53465 ARNOLDSON  Bolero "I Vespri Siciliani" (Verdi)                   1906
53466 ARNOLDSON  Voi che sapete "Le Nozze di Figaro" (Mozart)          1906
53467 ARNOLDSON  Ah fors'è lui "La Traviata" (Verdi) (1298 R)          1906
53479 KURZ  Caro nome "Rigoletto" (Verdi)                              1907
53481 BONINSEGNA Ah! bello a me ritorna "Norma" (Bellini)(79) 1907. DA430
53482 GALVANY    Gli angui d'inferno "Flauto Magico" (Mozart)(4728H) 1907.DA426
53483 GALVANY    Oh d'amore - Valzer "Mirella" (Gounod) (4731 H) 1907.DA494.VA4
53484 GALVANY    Una voce poco fa "Il Barbiere di Siviglia" (Rossini)
                                                        (4732 H)1907.DA426
53485 GALVANY    Qui la voce  "I Puritani" (Bellini)                   1907
53486 KURZ  Il Pensieroso (Handel)                                     1907
53491 KURZ  Parla - Valse (Arditi)                                     1907
53492 BONINSEGNA Te solo (Sabaino)(81) pno.                            1907
53494 KURZ  Ah non giunge "La Sonnambula" (Bellini)(76)(9946u)         1907
53496 KURZ  Air de Mysoli "Perle du Bresil" (David)(9889u)             1907
53500 CUCINI Stride la vampa "Il Trovatore" (Verdi)                    1907
53501 CUCINI Habanera "Carmen" (Bizet)(77)                             1907
53502 CUCINI Il segreto per esser felici "Lucrezia Borgia" (Donizetti)1907
53503 CUCINI Canzone ignota (Ranzata) vln.obb.comp.                    1907
53515 ARNOLDSON  Batti, batti "Don Giovanni" (Mozart)                  1907
53516 GAY  Seguidilla "Carmen" (Bizet)(76-79) (7293 E)                 1908
53517 ARNOLDSON  Una voce poco fa "Il Barbiere di Siviglia" (Rossini)
                                                        (3579 R) 1907. VA56
53520 DONALDA    Vedrai carino "Don Giovanni" (Mozart)(80)             1908
53521 PARETO Sovra il sen "La Sonnambula" (Bellini)                    1908
53522 PARETO Ah non giunge "La Sonnambula" (Bellini)                   1908
53526 GALVANY    Variazioni (Proch)(80)(10894b) 1908. DA494. VA46
53527 GALVANY    Carceleras "Hijas de Zebedeo" (Chapi)(80)(10895b)     1908
53528 DE CASAS   Cari luoghi "Linda di Chamounix" (Donizetti)          1908
53529 DE CASAS   Seguidilla "Carmen" (Bizet)                           1908
53530 DE CASAS   La mia regina "Don Carlos" (Verdi)                    1908
53531 DE CASAS   Habanera "Carmen" (Bizet)                             1908
53535 KURZ  Ah fors'è lui "La Traviata" (Verdi) (13067u)               1908
53537 DONALDA    Ballatella "Pagliacci" (Leoncavallo)(80)              1908
```

53548 PIETRACEWSKA Quando a te lieta "Faust" (Gounod)   1908
52549 GALVANY O luce di quest'anima "Linda di Chamounix" (Donizetti)1908
                                                                        IRCC 92
53550 GALVANY Io non sono più l'Annetta "Crispino e la comare" (Ricci)08
53551 GALVANY Ah non giunge "La Sonnambula" (Bellini)(11192b)   1908
53558 GALVANY Ouvi dizar "Fado portuguez" (Neuparth) 1908. IRCC 92
53559 DE CASAS Mi patria (Alvarez)   1908
53560 DE CASAS Zortzico - stornello (Hernander)   1908
53561 DE CASAS Ballata di Senta "Vascello fantasma" (Wagner)   1908
53564 KURZ Sempre libera "La Traviata" (Verdi)   1908
53565 KURZ Addio del passato "La Traviata" (Verdi)(13069u)   1908
53568 RUSZKOWSKA Ernani involami "Ernani" (Verdi)   1908
53570 KURZ Una voce poco fa "Il Barbiere di Siviglia" (Rossini)(15284u)
                                                                 1908. DA408
53587 DOMAR Ei m'ama "Faust" (Gounod) 11/10
53601 DE CASAS Su crudeli "La Favorita" (Donizetti)   1908/9
53605 PASSERI Dopo! (Costa) 4/11
53606 ROCCHI Il libro santo (Pinsuti) 4/11
53607 LUFRANO Leggenda valacca (Braga) 4/11
53611 LUFRANO Su questa santa "Fedora" (Giordano) 6/11
53631 ARNOLDSON Addio del passato "La Traviata" (Verdi)   1908

                10" records : G. & T. BLACK LABEL. PRE-DOG issued 1908
                DOG LABEL 1909. DOG LABEL 1910 : "LA VOCE del PADRONE"
53134 TEBRO Suicidio! "La Gioconda" (Ponchielli) (7") issd.1903
53138 HUGUET Bolero "I Vespri Siciliani" (Verdi) (7")   1903
53139 HUGUET Addio del passato "La Traviata" (Verdi) (7")   1903
53140 HUGUET Rondo "Linda di Chamounix" (Donizetti) (7")   1903
53141 HUGUET Allegro "Linda di Chamounix" (Donizetti)(7") pno.   1903
53142 D'AVIGNY Palomma mia (Canz. nap.) (7") issd. 1903
53143 D'AVIGNY Nnuncetella do. do. (7") issd. 1903
53144 D'AVIGNY Trezza d'oro do. do. (7") issd. 1903
53146 D'AVIGNY Sciamma d'ammore do.do. (7") 8/03
53147 FERRANI L'ora, o Tirsi "Manon Lescaut" (Puccini) (7")   1903
53149 FERRANI Aria di Salome "Erodiade" (Massenet) (7")   1903
53150 FERRANI Sogno di Elsa "Lohengrin" (Wagner) (7")   1903
53151 HELENA Ah non giunge "La Sonnambula" (Bellini)(7")   1904
53152 TRENTINI Aria dell'atto terzo "Crispino e la comare" (Ricci)
                                                      (7") pno.   1904
53153 TRENTINI Saper vorreste "Un Ballo in Maschera" (Verdi)(7")pno.1904
53154 TRENTINI Mimi Pinson "La Bohème" (Leoncavallo)(7") pno. 7/06
53155 TRENTINI Volta laterrea fronte "Un Ballo in Maschera" (Verdi)(7")04
53208 CODOLINI Scritto in ciel "La Favorita" (Donizetti) (7")   1901
53212 ADAMI Sì, mi chiamano Mimi "La Bohème" (Puccini)   1901
53214 ADAMI Addio del passato "La Traviata" (Verdi)   1901
53217 R.CASINI O mio Fernando "La Favorita" (Donizetti)   1901
53218 R.CASINI Voce di donna "La Gioconda" (Ponchielli)   1901
53221 TEBRO Suicidio! "La Gioconda" (Ponchielli)   1901
53224 R.CASINI Seguidilla "Carmen" (Bizet)   1901
53225 ADAMI Non mi resta al pianta "L'Amico Fritz" (Mascagni)   1901
53230 TEBRO O cieli azzurri "Aida" (Verdi)   1902
53231 TEBRO Numi pieta "Aida" (Verdi)   1902
53235 TEBRO La vergine degli angeli "La Forza del Destino" (Verdi) 1902
53236 TEBRO Ma dall'arrido stelo "Un Ballo in Maschera" (Verdi)   1902
53237 TEBRO Pace, pace, mio Dio "La Forza del Destino" (Verdi)   1902
53244 VASQUEZ Ave Maria "Otello" (Verdi)   1903
53247 DE PASQUALI Caro nome "Rigoletto" (Verdi)   1901

```
53248 E.PALLISER  Largo in G.  "Serse" (Handel)                                      1903
53249 D'AVIGNY    A' sirena (Canz. nap.)                                             1903
53250 D'AVIGNY    Quant'è bella  do.do.                                             1903
53251 BRESONNIER  Lontano dalla patria (Alvarez)                                     1903
53252 BRESONNIER  Valzer di Musetta  "La Bohème" (Puccini)                           1903
53253 D'AVIGNY    Io te vurria vasa (Canz. nap.)(di Capua)                           1903
53254 CERESOLI    Giorni poveri vivea  "Il Trovatore" (Verdi )                       1903
53255 CERESOLI    O mio Fernando  "La Favorita" (Donizetti)                          1903
53256 CERESOLI    Habanera  "Carmen" (Bizet)                                         1903
53257 BRESONNIER  Ah fors'è lui  "La Traviata" (Verdi)                               1903
53258 BRESONNIER  Addio del passato  "La Traviata" (Verdi)                           1903
53259 BRESONNIER  Caro nome  "Rigoletto" (Verdi)                                     1903
53260 HUGUET      Ave Maria (Gounod) pno.                                            1903
53261 HUGUET      Polonaise  "Mignon" (Thomas)                                       1903
53262 HUGUET      Aria delle campanelle  "Lakmé" (Delibes)                           1903
53263 HUGUET      Strofe del 1º atto  "Lakmé" (Delibes) pno.                         1903
53264 HUGUET      Ombra leggera  "Dinorah" (Meyerbeer) pno.                          1903
53265 HUGUET      Non conosci il bel suol? "Mignon" (Thomas) pno.                    1903
53266 HUGUET      Styrienne  "Mignon" (Thomas) pno.                                  1903
53267 HUGUET      Recitativo cantabile  "Mignon" (Thomas)                            1903
53268 HUGUET      Casta diva  "Norma" (Bellini) pno.                                 1903
53269 HUGUET      Aria dei gioielli  "Faust" (Gounod)(7198 F) pno.                   1903
53270 HUGUET      Caro nome  "Rigoletto" (Verdi)                                     1903
53271 HUGUET      Son vergin vezzosa  "I Puritani" (Bellini)  pno.                   1903
53274 HUGUET      Grande aria del I Atto  "La Traviata" (Verdi)                      1903
53275 HUGUET      Rondo  "I Puritani" (Bellini)                                      1903
53276 HUGUET      Valse  "La Bohème" (Puccini)                                       1903
53277 GRASSOT     Gavotta  "Manon" (Massenet)                                        1903
53278 GRASSOT     Vissi d'arte  "Tosca" (Puccini) 9/05
53281 FERRANI     Racconto di Mimì  "La Bohème" (Puccini) pno. 1903. IRCC 234
53282 FERRANI     Addio senza rancor  "La Bohème" (Puccini)                          1903
53283 FERRANI     In quelle trine morbide  "Manon Lescaut" (Puccini)                 1903
53284 FERRANI     Addio picciol desco  "Manon" (Massenet)                            1903
53285 FERRANI     L'altra notte  "Mefistofele" (Boito) pno.                          1903
53286 FERRANI     Se tu m'ami (Pergolesi)                                            1903
53287 FERRANI     Serenata inutile (Brahms)                                          1903
53288 D'AVIGNY    'A frangesa napulitana (Canz. nap.)                         issd.1903
53289 D'AVIGNY    Oi 'ma dammillo        do.  do.                             issd.1903
53290 CERESOLI    Ah il di della vendetta  "Cristoforo Colombo" (Franchetti)1903
53291 OLITZKA     Voi lo sapete o mamma  "Cavalleria Rusticana" (Mascagni) 1903
53292 LINDEN      Largo  "Serse" (Handel)                                            1903
53293 GALVANY     Caro nome  "Rigoletto" (Verdi)                                     1903
53294 GALVANY     L'eco (Eckart)                                                     1903
53295 GALVANY     Rondo  "La Sonnambula" (Bellini)                                   1903
53296 GALVANY     Variazioni (Proch)                                                 1903
53297 GALVANY     Cavatina  "Il Barbiere di Siviglia" (Rossini)                      1903
53298 THEODORINI  Habanera  "Carmen" (Bizet)                                         1903
53299 THEODORINI  Rondo  "Lucrezia Borgia" (Donizetti)                               1903
53300 THEODORINI  M'odi, ah m'odi  "Lucrezia Borgia" (Donizetti)                     1903
53301 THEODORINI  Preghiera  "La Gioconda" (Ponchielli)                              1903
53302 THEODORINI  Parla-Valse (Arditi)                                               1903
53303 DRISTORA    O patria mia  "Aida" (Verdi) 6/03
53304 COLIVA      Ah non giunge  "La Sonnambula" (Bellini)                           1903
53305 COLIVA      Ah non credea mirarti  "La Sonnambula" (Bellini)                   1903
53306 COLIVA      Come per me sereno    "La Sonnambula" (Bellini)                    1903
53307 GALVANY     Ombra leggera  "Dinorah" (Meyerbeer)                               1903
53308 HUGUET      Bel raggio  "Semiramide" (Rossini)                                 1903
53309 HUGUET      La violetta (Mozart)                                               1903
```

```
53310 HUGUET    Gavotte "Mignon" (Thomas)                                      1903
53312 ARKEL     Spunta l'aurora pallida "Mefistofele" (Boito)                  1903
53313 DE MICHALSKA  In quelle trine morbide "Manon Lescaut" (Puccini)pno.1903
53314 LONGHI    Voi lo sapete o mamma "Cavalleria Rusticana" (Mascagni)1903
53315 LONGHI    Preghiera "Norma" (Bellini) pno.                               1903
53316 DE MICHALSKA  Ernani involami  "Ernani" (Verdi) pno.                     1903
53317 LONGHI    Voce di donna "La Gioconda" (Ponchielli)                       1904
53319 LONGHI    Stride la vampa "Il Trovatore" (Verdi)                         1904
53320 LONGHI    Evviva la guerra "La Forza del Destino" (Verdi)                1904
53323 CITTI-LIPPI  Il libro santo (Pinsuti)                                    1904
53324 CITTI-LIPPI  O patria mia "Aida" (Verdi)                                 1904
53326 CALIGARIS  Ernani involami "Ernani" (Verdi)                              1904
53327 CITTI-LIPPI  La mamma morta "Andrea Chenier" (Giordano)                  1904
53328 CITTI-LIPPI  Ave Maria (Bach-Gounod)                                     1904
53330 LONGHI    Aria delle carte "Carmen" (Bizet) 3/04
53334 HELENE    Caro nome "Rigoletto" (Verdi)                                  1904
53335 LONGHI    Voce di donna "La Gioconda" (Ponchielli)                       1904
53336 LONGHI    Stella del marinar "La Gioconda" (Ponchielli) 9/05
53337 LONGHI    O aprile foriero "Sansone e Dalila" (Saint-Saens)              1904
53338 LONGHI    Amor i miei fini "Sansone e Dalila" (Saint-Saens)              1904
53342 RUSS      In quelle trine morbide "Manon Lescaut" (Puccini)              1904
53343 FARRAR    Valse "Romeo e Giulietta" (Gounod)                             1904
53344 FARRAR    Sempre libera "La Traviata" (Verdi)                            1904
53345 FARRAR    Non conosci il bel suol? "Mignon" (Thomas) (2174 H)            1904
53358 HELENA    Ah non giunge "La Sonnambula" (Bellini) 9/05
53359 HELENA    Caro nome "Rigoletto" (Verdi)                      9/05
53360 HELENA    Non fu sogno "I Lombardi" (Verdi)                  9/05
53361 CROSSLEY  Caro mio ben (Giordani)                                        1903
53362 FRASCANI  Alla mia bambina (Giordani) pno.                               1904
53363 FARRAR    Mattinata (Tosti) 2 eds.                                       1904
53364 FARRAR    Valse "Romeo e Giulietta" (Gounod)     .                       1904
53366 GALAN     Romanza de la ciega "La Gioconda" (Ponchielli)                 1904
53367 GALAN     Cancion de la gitana "Il Trovatore" (Verdi)                    1904
53368 TRENTINI  Io sono come l'ape "Donne curiose" (Usiglio) pno.              1904
53369 TRENTINI  Son pochi fiori "L'Amico Fritz" (Mascagni)     pno.            1904
53370 TRENTINI  Aria d'Amelia "Papa Martin" (Cagnoni)          pno.            1904
53371 TRENTINI  Tutte le feste al tempio "Rigoletto" (Verdi) pno.              1904
53377 FINZI-MAGRINI  Quando rapita in estasi  "Lucia di Lammermoor" (Donizetti)
                                                               pno.            1904
53378 FINZI-MAGRINI  Regnava nel silenzio "Lucia di Lammermoor" (Donizetti)
                                                               pno.            1904
53379 FINZI-MAGRINI  Ballatella "Pagliacci" (Leoncavallo)     pno.            1904
53380 FINZI-MAGRINI  Brahma, Gran Dio "I Pescatori di Perle" (Bizet)pno.1904
53382 DE CASAS  S'apre per te "Sansone e Dalila" (Saint-Saens) pno. 1904
53383 FINZI-MAGRINI  Rondo "Lucia di Lammermoor" (Donizetti)fl.obb.& pno.1904
53385 ARKEL     Roberto, tu che adoro "Roberto il Diavolo" (Meyerbeer)pno.1904
53386 DE CASAS  Quando a te lieta "Faust" (Gounod)             pno.  1904
53387 DE CASAS  O mio Fernando "La Favorita" (Donizetti)       pno.  1904
53388 DE CASAS  Pallide memmole (Trimarchi) pno. 4/05
53389 DE CASAS  Scena delle carte "Carmen" (Bizet) pno. 4/05
53390 DE CASAS  Coro, Atto III con Coro "Voto" (Giordano) pno. 9/05
53391 LYCKSETH-SCHJERVEN  Ave Maria  "Cavalleria Rusticana" (Mascagni)1904
53395 TRENTINI  O luce di quest'anima "Linda di Chamounix" (Donizetti)1904
53396 POLLINI   Al dolce guidami "Anna Bolena" (Donizetti)     pno.  1904
53397 POLLINI   Addio terra natia "L'Africana" (Meyerbeer)           1904
53399 POLLINI   So anch'io la virtu magica "Don Pasquale" (Donizetti)(6984b)04
53400 MILERI    Vaga donna "Gli Ugonotti" (Meyerbeer)                          1904
53400 FASSIO    Selva opaca "Guglielmo Tell" (Rossini)                         1904
```

```
53401 FASSIO    Preghiera "I Lombardi" (Verdi) pno.                        1904
53402 FASSIO    Se vano e il pregare "I Lombardi" (Verdi)                  1904
53403 ESPOSITO  Rondo del paggio "Gli Ugonotti" (Meyerbeer)               1904
53405 ARKEL     Porgi amor "Le Nozze di Figaro" (Mozart)                   1904
53406 ARKEL     Toglietemi la vita ancor (Scarlatti) pno.                  1904
53407 FARELLI   La vergine degli angeli "La Forza del Destino" (Verdi) 1905
53408 CRESTANI  Pace, pace, mio Dio     "La Forza del Destino" (Verdi) 1905
53409 CRESTANI  Morrò, ma prima in grazia "Un Ballo in Maschera" (Verdi)1905
53410 CRESTANI  Tacea la notte placida "Il Trovatore" (Verdi)(76) 1905.E130
53411 CRESTANI  D'amor sull'ali rosee "Il Trovatore" (Verdi)(76) 1905. E133
53413 MILERI    Nel veder l'amata stanza "Mignon" (Thomas)               ·1905
53414 ZACCARIA  Le parlate d'amor "Faust" (Gounod)(77) 1905. E122
53420 MILERI    Stride la vampa "Il Trovatore" (Verdi)(76) 1905. E131
53421 MILERI    Vaga donna "Gli Ugonotti" (Meyerbeer) ·                    1905
53422 ZACCARIA  Il vecchietto cerca moglie "Il Barbiere di Siviglia" (Rossini)
                                                                           1905
53423 ZACCARIA  Re dell'abisso "Un Ballo in Maschera" (Verdi) pno.         1905
53424 PICCOLETTI Ei m'ama "Faust" (Gounod) 1906. E123
53425 FARRAR  ` L'altra notte "Mefistofele" (Boito) 1906. IRCC 30
53427 A.RIZZINI/MARTINEZ-PATTI/STOPPA  Alfredo, Alfredo  "La Traviata"(Verdi)06
53428 PICCOLETTI Addio del passato "La Traviata" (Verdi) pno.             1906
53429 GIACOMELLI Quante d'Iberia giovani "Ernani" (Verdi)                 1906
53430 FARRAR    Caro mio ben (Giordani)(76) 1906. IRCC 215
53435 FOERSTER  Il bacio (Arditi)                                          1906
53436 ROSELLI   Dolce zeffiro "La Favorita" (Donizetti)                    1906
53437 ROSELLI   Bei raggi  .  "La Favorita" (Donizetti)                    1906·
53438 FERRABINI Saria possibile "L'Elisir d'amore" (Donizetti)            1906
53439 MARCHESI  Se saran rose (Arditi)                                     1906
53440 MARCHESI  Vissi d'arte "Tosca" (Puccini)                             1906
53441 MARCHESI  Voi lo sapete o mamma "Cavalleria Rusticana" (Mascagni)1906
53442 MAMELI    E bella la guerra "La Forza del Destino" (Verdi)          1906
53444 SVICHER   Ah non credea mirarti "La Sonnambula" (Bellini)           1906
53445 SVICHER   Sovra il sen        "La Sonnambula" (Bellini)             1906
53446 SVICHER   Ah non giunge       "La Sonnambula" (Bellini) pno. 1906
53447 SVICHER   Come per me sereno  "La Sonnambula" (Bellini) pno. 1906
53449 PICCOLETTI Oh! quante volte "Capuleti e Montecchi" (Bellini)pno.1906
53450 PICCOLETTI Deh vieni "Le Nozze di Figaro" (Mozart)        pno. 1906
53451 CORSI     Ballata di Senta "Vascello fantasma" (Wagner)            1906
53452 HUGUET    Bolero "I Vespri Siciliani" (Verdi)                       1906
53453 DI LANDA  La Mattchiche                                             1906
53454 DI LANDA  'E rose gelose   9/06
53455 DI LANDA  .·La ciociara    9/06
53456 DI LANDA  La.zampognara    9/06
53457 DI LANDA  L'orticello      9/06
53458 DI LANDA  Canada           9/06
53459 DI LANDA  Tarentella d'b vase  9/06
53460 DI LANDA. Cinematografo    9/06
53461 DI LANDA· 'A vennegna      9/06
53462 DI LANDA  'O Sciammeria    9/06
53463 DI LANDA  E gira gi        9/06
53464 WEDEKIND  Ernani involami "Ernani" (Verdi) 24.VI.1905
53469 FARRAR    Sempre libera "La Traviata" (Verdi) 1906. IRCC 45
53470 CORSI     Temer non so per me "I Pescatori di Perle" (Bizet)       1906
53471 CORSI     Preghiera "Der Freischütz" (Weber) pno.                  1906
53472 CORSI     Della crudele Isotta "L'Elisir d'amore" (Donizetti) 10/06
53473 GRISI     Di tal amor "Il Trovatore" (Verdi)                        1906
53474 HUGUET    Ah fors'e lui "La Traviata" (Verdi)                       1906
53475 HUGUET    Arrivo del cigno "Lohengrin" (Wagner)       .             1906
```

```
53477 MILERI    Styrienne  "Mignon" (Thomas)                                      1906
53478 MILERI    Ella è là presso a lui  "Mignon" (Thomas)                        1906
53480 HUGUET    Tutte le feste al tempio  "Rigoletto" (Verdi)                    1906
53487 GRISI     Me pellegrina ed orfana  "La Forza del Destino" (Verdi)          1907
53488 ZACCARIA  Venite all'indovina  "La Forza del Destino" (Verdi)              1907
53489 ZACCARIA  Pane, pane  "La Forza del Destino" (Verdi)                       1907
53490 ZACCARIA  Rataplan  "La Forza del Destino" (Verdi)                         1907
53493 ZACCARIA  Deh! proteggimi o Dio  "Norma" (Bellini)                         1907
53495 GRISI     Ernani involami  "Ernani" (Verdi)                                1907
53497 GIACOMELLI Canto d'anime - Romanza (Puccini)                               1907
53498 ZACCARIA  E lui nei palpiti  "Un Ballo in Maschera" (Verdi)                1907
53504 GIACOMELLI Vago ricordo  "Hermes" (Parelli)                                1907
53505 GIACOMELLI Benche sia maschio  "Hermes" (Parelli)                          1907
53506 MELIS        Madonna ascolta  "Jana" (Virgilio)                            1907
53507 MELIS        Figlio del mar  "Hermes" (Parelli)                            1907
53508 MELIS     Resto così nel fascino  "Albatro" (Pacchierotti)                 1907
53510 HUGUET       Casta diva  "Norma" (Bellini)                                 1907
53511 HUGUET    Regnava nel silenzio  "Lucia di Lammermoor" (Donizetti)          1907
53512 HUGUET    Quando rapita in estasi "Lucia di Lammermoor"(Donizetti)1907
53513 HUGUET    O luce di quest'anima  "Linda di Chamounix" (Donizetti)          1907
53514 KOENEN    Vittoria mio core (Carissimi)                                    1907
53523 FOSCA     Me pellegrina ed orfana  "La Forza del Destino" (Verdi)          1908
53524 FOSCA     Tacea la notte placida  "Il Trovatore" (Verdi)                   1908
53525 PASSERI   La mia regina  "Don Carlos" (Verdi)                              1908
53532 DESTINN   Che tue madre  "Madama Butterfly" (Puccini) 1908 (3759 Eng.Cat.)
53533 DESTINN   Piccolo iddio  "Madama Butterfly" (Puccini)                      1908
53536 CIAPARELLI Quando m'en vo  "La Bohème" (Puccini)                           1908
53538 WEDEKIND  Un moto di gioia  "Le Nozze di Figaro" (Mozart)                  1908
53539 O.ROSALIN Aria del pesciolino  "Geisha" (Jones)                            1908
53540 O.ROSALIN La nostra vita è di piacer  "Geisha" (Jones)                     1908
53541 J.ROSALIN Canzone del papagallo  "Geisha" (Jones)                          1908
53542 J.ROSALIN Tcion Kina  "Geisha" (Jones)                                     1908
53543 MARCHETTI Un elisir io gli darò  "Geisha" (Jones)                          1908
53544 DIAZ      Canzone del papagallo  "Geisha" (Jones)                          1908
53545 DIAZ      Tcion Kina  "Geisha" (Jones)                                     1908
53546 D'ARCO    Se per un uom io sento  "Geisha" (Jones)                         1908
53547 SUTTER    Parla - Valse (Arditi)                                           1908
53552 DE FRATE  M'odi, ah m'odi  "Lucrezia Borgia" (Donizetti)                   1908
53553 DE FRATE  Ah bello a me ritorna  "Norma" (Bellini)                         1908
53554 DE FRATE  Anch'io dischiusa  "Nabucco" (Verdi)                             1908
53555 FRANCILLO-KAUFMANN  Parla - Valse (Arditi)                                 1908
53563 HUGUET    Aria della serva  "Gran Via" (Chueca y Valverde)                 1908
53566 HUGUET    Voi lo sapete o mamma  "Cavalleria Rusticana" (Mascagni)1908
53567 CASSANI   Addio del passato  "La Traviata" (Verdi)                         1908
53569 HUGUET    Ave Maria  "Otello" (Verdi)                                      1908
53571 ARDONI    Ascolta, ascolta  "La Bohème" (Puccini)                          1908
53573 BORELLI   Aria di Maddalena  "Andrea Chenier" (Giordano)                   1908
53574 RUBINO    I sacri nomi  "Aida" (Verdi) 5/10
53575 RUBINO    Ritorna vincitor  "Aida" (Verdi) 5/10
53576 FABRIS    Salve d'amor  "Tannhäuser" (Wagner) 5/10
53577 RUBINO    O grand'occhi lucenti di fede  "Fedora" (Giordano) 5/10
53578 BORELLI   Madre pietosa  "La Forza del Destino" (Verdi) 5/10
53579 LOPEZ-NUNES  Sulla vetta tu del monte  "Manon Lescaut" (Puccini) 5/10
53580 BRONZONI  In quelle trine morbide  "Manon Lescaut" (Puccini) 5/10
53581 BRONZONI  Vissi d'arte  "Tosca" (Puccini) 5/10
53582 MUSSINI   Stornello del pastore  "Tosca" (Puccini) 5/10
53583 MELLERIO  Penso (Tosti) 1/12
53584 FABRIS    La lettera  "Eidelberga mia" (Pacchierotti) 10/10
```

```
53585 RUBINO    In quelle trine morbide  "Manon Lescaut" (Puccini) 10/10
53586 RUBINO    Spunta l'aurora pallida  "Mefistofele" (Boito)      10/10
53588 MURINO    Ballata di Cecilia  "Il Guarany" (Gomez)            11/10
53589 HUGUET    Gavotta  "Manon" (Massenet)                         11/10
53590 LOPEZ-NUNES  Dopo! (Tosti)                                    11/10
53591 LOPEZ-NUNES  Il tuo pensieroso (Rotoli)                       11/10
53592 LOPEZ-NUNES  Non t'amo più (Tosti)                            11/10
53593 MELLERIO   Seconda mattinata (Tosti)                          11/10
53594 MELLERIO   La Serenata (Tosti)                                11/10
53595 MELLERIO   Sol (Tirindelli)                                   11/10
53596 MELLERIO   Serenata medioevale (Costa)                        11/10
53597 MELLERIO   Torna (Denza)                                      11/10
53598 MELLERIO   Rosa (Tosti)                                       11/10
53599 ADORNI     Sono innamorata del tuo corpo  "Salome"(R.Strauss)  1/11
53600 ADORNI     Il tuo corpo e dorica statua  "Salome"(R.Strauss)   1/11
53602 SANIPOLI   Poveri fiori  "Adriana Lecouvreur" (Cilea)          5/11
53603 BOCCOLINI  Son pochi fiori  "L'Amico Fritz" (Mascagni)         3/11
53604 BOCCOLINI  Oh! che volo d'augelli  "Pagliacci" (Leoncavallo)   3/11
53608 BESALÙ     Aurette a cui si spesso  "Lohengrin" (Wagner)       5/11
53610 CASSANI    Caro nome  "Rigoletto" (Verdi)                      6/11
53612 CASSANI    Ah non giunge  "La Sonnambula" (Bellini)           10/11
53613 HUGUET     Stella - Valzer cantato (Rico)                      1/12
53614 BOCCOLINI  Come vorrei sapere  "Faust" (Gounod)               10/11
53615 CHIESA     Inneggiano al Signore risorto  "Cavalleria Rusticana"
                                                     (Mascagni)     11/11
53616 GRAMAGNA   S'apre per te  "Sansone e Dalila" (Saint-Saëns)    11/11
53617 MANGINI    Ave Maria (Gounod)                                 11/11
53618 BOCCOLINI  Serenata (Gounod)                                  11/11
53622 BOCCOLINI  Ascolta, ascolta  "La Bohème" (Puccini)(1170ah)     1/12
53623 BONETTI    Mimi Pinson  "La Bohème" (Leoncavallo)              1/12
53626 MANGINI    Son vergin vezzosa  "I Puritani" (Bellini)          2/13
53627 BOCCOLINI  Perchè tanto severo?  "Thais" (Massenet)            8/13
53630 ROCCHI     Da quel suon soavemente  "La Bohème" (Leoncavallo)  1/12
53633 MARTINENGO  Stiriana  "Mignon" (Thomas)                       12/12
53634 MARTINENGO  Stella del marinar  "La Gioconda" (Ponchielli)    10/13
53636 CASINI     Ei m'ama  "Faust" (Gounod)                          6/13
53637 SARAH      Requiem  "Messa da Requiem" (Verdi)                12/13
```

7" records : BERLINER

```
53103 ADAMI   Ah fors'è lui  "La Traviata" (Verdi)                      1900
53105 ADAMI   Non sapete quale affetto  "La Traviata" (Verdi)           1900
53108 ADAMI   L'altra notte  "Mefistofele" (Boito)                      1900
53110 ADAMI   Voi lo sapete o mamma  "Cavalleria Rusticana" (Mascagni)  1900
53111 ADAMI   Sì, mi chiamano Mimi  "La Bohème" (Puccini)               1900
53112 ADAMI   Donde lieta uscì  "La Bohème" (Puccini)                   1900
53113 ADAMI   Or via Manon  "Manon" (Massenet)                          1900
53114 ADAMI   Son pochi fiori  "L'Amico Fritz" (Mascagni)               1900
53115 ADAMI   L'ora o Tirsi  Manon" (Massenet)                          1900
53117 ADAMI   Quando m'en vo  "La Bohème" (Puccini)                     1900
53118 ADAMI   Là tua non è la mano  "Manon" (Massenet)                  1900
53119 D'AVIGNY  Sciala tu e fa sciala'                                  1900
53121 CASINI  O mio Fernando  "La Favorita" (Donizetti)                 1901
53122 CASINI  Stride la vampa  "Il Trovatore" (Verdi)                   1901
53126 D'AVIGNY  Quant'è bello  "Lucrezia Borgia" (Donizetti)            1901
53127 D'AVIGNY  'A Sirena (Valente)                                     1901
53130 TEBRO   La vergine degli angeli  "La Forza del Destino" (Verdi)   1901
53131 TEBRO   Racconto  "Andrea Chenier" (Giordano)                     1901
```

```
53156 GRIPPA   Voi lo sapete o mamma  "Cavalleria Rusticana" (Mascagni)20.VII.00
53157 GRIPPA   L'altra notte  "Mefistofele" (Boito)              20.VII.1900
53158 GRIPPA   Ernani involami  "Ernani" (Verdi)                           1900
53159 GRIPPA   In quelle trine morbide  "Manon Lescaut" (Puccini)          1900
53160 GROSSI   A te questo Rosario  "La Gioconda" (Ponchielli)             1900
53161 GROSSI   O mia Regina  "Don Carlos" (Verdi)                          1900
53162 GROSSI.  Pace, pace, mio Dio  "La Forza del Destino" (Verdi)         1900
53163 ADAMI    Voi lo sapete o mamma  "Cavalleria Rusticana" (Mascagni)    1900
53164 ADAMI    Addio picciol desco  "Manon" (Massenet)                     1900
53165 ADAMI    Aria dei gioielli  "Faust" (Gounod)                         1900
53166 ADAMI    Aria di Micaela  "Carmen" (Bizet)                           1900
53167 ADAMI    Ave Maria  "Otello" (Verdi)                                 1900
53168 GALAN    Brindisi duorazia Borgia  "Lucrezia Borgia" (Donizetti)     1900
53169 GALAN    Rondo del paggio  "Gli Ugonotti" (Meyerbeer)                1900
53170 GALAN    Vaga donna  "Gli Ugonotti" (Meyerbeer)                      1900
53171 ADAMI    Sì, mi chiamano Mimì  "La Bohème" (Puccini)                 1900
53172 GALAN    Pace, pace, mio Dio  "La Forza del Destino" (Verdi)         1900
53173 GALAN    O mio Fernando  "La Favorita" (Donizetti)                   1900
53174 GALAN    Stride la vampa  "Il Trovatore" (Verdi)                     1900
53175 GALAN    Serenata d'Arlecchino  "Pagliacci" (Leoncavallo)           1900
53176 GALAN    Che farò?  "Orfeo ed Euridice" (Gluck)                      1900
53177 ADAMI    Se tu m'inassi                                              1900
53178 ADAMI    Io son la farfalla                                          1900
53179 ADAMI    Com'è bello  "Lucrezia Borgia" (Donizetti)                  1900
53180 GALAN    Stella del marinar  "La Gioconda" (Ponchielli)             1900
53181 GALAN    Habanera  "Carmen" (Bizet)                                  1900
53182 GALAN    Fior di giaggiolo  "Cavalleria Rusticana" (Mascagni)        1900
53183 GALAN    Su crudeli                                                  1900
53184 GALAN    Una voce poco fa  "Il Barbiere di Siviglia" (Rossini)       1900
53185 GALAN    Non conosci il bel suol?  "Mignon" (Thomas)                 1900
53186 GALAN    Addio Marcello  "La Bohème" (Puccini)                       1900
53187 GALAN    Valzer di Musetta  "La Bohème" (Puccini)                    1900
53188 GALAN    Scena del giudizio                                          1900
53189 GALAN    Seguidilla  "Carmen" (Bizet)                                1900
53190 GALAN    Le parlate d'amor  "Faust" (Gounod)                         1900
53192 SCOTTI   Luisella (w.mandoline & guitar)                             1900
53193 ANDREACE O re nuosto  (w.mandoline & guitar)                         1900
53194 ANDREACE Napule          do.        do.             16.VII.1900
53195 SCOTTI   A Campagnola                                                1900
53196 SCOTTI   'Ngiulina mia                                               1900
53199 ANDREACE Astrigne  (w.mandoline)                                     1900
53200 ANDREACE Quacchiariello                                              1900
53201 ANDREACE Reginella                                                   1900
53202 ANDREACE Gesummina mia                                               1900
53203 ANDREACE Ocanone                                                     1900
53204 ANDREACE Sott a fenesta - Serenata                                   1900
53205 GRIPPA   La vergine degli angeli  "La Forza del Destino" (Verdi)20.VII.1900
```

10" records : RED & PINK LABEL

```
7-53001 FARRAR   Ieri son salita  "Madama Butterfly" (Puccini)   1909. DA204
7-53002 FARRAR   Ancora un passo  "Madama Butterfly" (Puccini)
                                                2 eds. 1909 & 1916. DA204
7-53003 FARRAR   Piccolo Iddio   "Madama Butterfly" (Puccini)    1909. DA508
7-53004 FARRAR   Che tua madre   "Madama Butterfly" (Puccini)    1909. DA508
7-53005 HOMER    Stride la vampa  "Il Trovatore" (Verdi)                DA252
7-53008 GLUCK    La colomba - Tuscan folk song (A12100)          1912. DA236
7-53009 GLUCK    Serenata (Tosti) (A14261)                       1914. DA236
```

7-53010 BORI Addio del passato "La Traviata" (Verdi)(A14438) 1914. DA130
7-53011 BORI La Danza (Rossini) (A14439) 1914. DA133
• 7-53012 HEMPEL Qui la voce "I Puritani" (Bellini) (A14539) 1914. DA248
7-53018 BRASLAU Il segreto. "Lucrezia Borgia" (Donizetti) DA141
7-53019 BORI In pure stille "Iris" (Mascagni)(A15904) 1915. DA132. VA17
• 7-53021 GLUCK Quando m'en vo "La Bohème" (Puccini)(A17148) 1916. DA227
7-53022 DESTINN Con onor muore "Madama Butterfly" (Puccini) DA505
7-53023 GALLI-CURCI Non so più "Le Nozze di Figaro" (Mozart)(A20661)1917.DA214
• 7-53025 FARRAR Via! Così non mi lasciate "Segreto di Susanna" (Wolf-Ferrari)
                                                (A12923) 1913. DA 211. VA14
• 7-53026 HEMPEL Volta la terrea "Un Ballo in Maschera" (Verdi)(A13086)1916
                                                                        DA248
• 7-53027 GLUCK Donde lieta "La Bohème" (Puccini)(A10093) 1911. DA227
7-53028 HOMER Le parlate d'amor "Faust" (Gounod) DA252
7-53029 GALLI-CURCI La Capinera (Benedict)(A21961) 1918. DA217
7-53030 GALLI-CURCI Caro mio ben (Giordani)(A20041) 1917. DA217
7-53033 ALDA O mio babbino "Gianni Schicchi" (Puccini)(A22578)11.II.1919.DA136
7-53034 BRASLAU Villanella (Sibella) DA134
7-53038 POLI-RANDACIO Mezznotte! "Un Ballo in Maschera" (Verdi) 9/20. DA173
7-53039 BESANZONI S'apre per te il mio cor "Sansone e Dalila" (Saint-Saëns)5/21
7-53040 FARRAR Mamma usciva di casa "Zazà" (Leoncavallo) 1920. DA209
7-53041 BESANZONI Voce di donna "La Gioconda" (Ponchielli) 3/22. DA128
7-53042 BESANZONI Stride la vampa "Il Trovatore" (Verdi) 3/22. DA128
7-53044 GALLI-CURCI Addio del passato "La Traviata" (Verdi)(A24178)1920.DA216
7-53046 ALDA Ancora un passo "Madama Butterfly" (Puccini)(A13108)10.IV.1913.
                                                                        DA136
7-53047 GALLI-CURCI Sempre libera "La Traviata" (Verdi)(A22614) 1919. DA216
7-53049 BORI Villanella (Sibella) (A25321) 1921. DA133
• 7-53050 GALLI-CURCI Sovra il sen "La Sonnambula" (Bellini)(A23170)1919.DA213
7-53051 GALLI-CURCI Messaggero amoroso - Waltz (Chopin)(A23132) 1919. DA213
7-53052 BORI Vedrai carino "Don Giovanni" (Mozart)(A25145) 1921. DA130
7-53053 POLI-RANDACIO Laggiù nel Soledad "La Fanciulla del West" (Puccini)
                                                            2/23. DA173
7-53054 BORI In uomini, in soldati "Così fan tutte" (Mozart)(A26471) 1921
                                                            DA132. VA17
7-53055 JERITZA Vissi d'arte "Tosca" (Puccini) 11/25 ?
7-53056 GALLI-CURCI Spargi d'amaro "Lucia di Lammermoor" (Donizetti)
                                                (A26595) 1922. DA214
7-53057 ALDA Selva opaca "Guglielmo Tell" (Rossini)(A27368) 1923. DA123
7-53058 JERITZA Voi lo sapete o mamma "Cavalleria Rusticana" (Mascagni)
                                                11/25. DA565
7-53060 BORI Son pochi fiori "L'Amico Fritz" (Mascagni)(A28622)1923.DA649
7-53061 BORI Non mi resta "L'Amico Fritz" (Mascagni)(A28624)1923.DA649
7-53063 LASHANSKA Spiagge amati "Paride e Elena" (Gluck) 1/26. DA663
7-53064 LASHANSKA Lungi dal caro bene (Sarti, adatt.Secchi)1/26. DA663
7-53065 BORI Ciribiribin (Pestalozza) (A28643) 1923. DA585
7-53066 BORI Il bacio (Arditi) (A28619) 1923. DA585
7-53067 JERITZA Son gente risoluta "Fedora" (Giordano)(A29230) 1924.DA579
7-53068 JERITZA Dio di giustizia "Fedora" (Giordano)(A29231) 1924.DA579
7-53074 PONSELLE Maria, marì (di Capua)(A29411) 1924. DA637
7-53075 PONSELLE Carmela (de Curtis) (A29878) 1924. DA637
7-53077 CAPSIR Variazioni di Mozart (Adam) Part I. 1/25. DA681
7-53082 BORI Quando m'en vo "La Bohème" (Puccini)(A28620) 1923. DA709
7-53083 HEMPEL Voi che sapete "Le Nozze di Figaro" (Mozart)(Bb5432)1925.DA675
7-53084 DAL MONTE A Rosina (Fabris) 11/25. DA698
7-53085 DAL MONTE Magari (Filippi) 11/25. DA698
7-53086 CAPSIR Variazioni di Mozart (Adam) Part II. 5/25. DA681
                (some copies of 7-53077 were pressed on DA619)

7-53091 MELIUS Ah lo so "Il Flauto Magico" (Mozart)(Bb6476) 1925. DA723
7-53092 MELIUS Gli angui d'inferno "Il Flauto Magico"(Mozart)(Bb6477)1925.
                                                               DA723

10" records : BLACK LABEL

7-53000 VERLET Serenade a Laura (Ch.Pons)
7-53007 HELDER M'appari tutt'amor "Marta" (Flotow)(ab13858e¿81) c.1911
7-53093 MARINELLA Pascale a da parti (Rossi) 7/26
7-53094 SANTELIA   'O pescatore Napulitano (Sica-De Luca) 7/26

12" records : G. & T. RED & PINK LABEL. PRE-DOG issued 1908
DOG LABEL 1909. DOG LABEL 1910 : "LA VOCE del PADRONE"

053006	FABBRI	Cavatina di Arsace "Semiramide" (Rossini) pno.	1903
053007	FABBRI	Rondo "L'Italiana in Algeri" (Rossini) pno.	1903
053009	FABBRI	Cavatina "Romeo e Giulietta" (Bellini) pno.	1903
053014	BELLINCIONI	O grandi occhi lucenti "Fedora" (Giordano)	1903
053015	FABBRI	Una voce poco fa "Il Barbiere di Siviglia" (Rossini)pno.	1903
053017	BELLINCIONI	L'altra notte "Mefistofele" (Boito)	1903
053018	BELLINCIONI	Voi lo sapete o mamma "Cavalleria Rusticana" (Mascagni)	1903
053019	BELLINCIONI	Ah fors'è lui "La Traviata" (Verdi)(577R) 1903. VB11	
053028	CARELLI	Voi lo sapete o mamma "Cavalleria Rusticana" (Mascagni)1904	
053029	CARELLI	Addio senza rancor "La Bohème" (Puccini)	1904
053032	CARELLI	Addio piccol desco "Manon" (Massenet)	1904
053033	CARELLI	La piovra "Iris" (Mascagni)	1904
053034	CARELLI	La mamma morta "Andrea Chenier" (Giordano)	1904
053035	CARELLI	Dopo (Tosti)	1904
053036	CARELLI	Marechiare (Tosti)	1904
053037	PANDOLFINI	Deh vieni "Le Nozze di Figaro" (Mozart) pno.	1904
053038	PANDOLFINI	All'ombra di quel faggio (Taubert) pno.	1904
053041	FABBRI	Figlio mio "Profeta" (Meyerbeer) pno.	1904
053047	PANDOLFINI	Nenia di Margherita "Mefistofele" (Boito) pno.	1904
053048	FRASCANI	Crepuscolo triste (Giordano) pno. (312¿i)(76)pno. 1904.DB605	
053049	BONINSEGNA	O patria mia "Aida" (Verdi)	1904
053050	BONINSEGNA	Casta diva "Norma" (Bellini) (216m) 1904. VB28	
053054	SEMBRICH	Ah fors' è lui "La Traviata" (Verdi)(77)	1904
053055	SEMBRICH	Voce di primavera (Strauss)(77) (A1901)	1904
053056	SEMBRICH	Jewel song "Faust" (Gounod)	1904
053057	SEMBRICH	Batti, batti "Don Giovanni" (Mozart)	1904
053058	EAMES	Vissi d'arte "Tosca" (Puccini) 1st.ed.(A2401)pno. 1905.IRCC 32	
053063	BONINSEGNA	Tacea la notte placida "Il Trovatore" (Verdi)(537c) 1905	
053065	BONINSEGNA	Ma dall'arrido stelo "Un Ballo in Maschera" (Verdi) 1905	
053067	BONINSEGNA	Madre pietosa "La Forza del Destino" (Verdi)	1905
053068	BONINSEGNA	Gia l'odio m'abbandona "L'Africana" (Meyerbeer)	1905
053075	SEMBRICH	Parla - Valse (Arditi)(A3153) 1906. DB432	
053076	SEMBRICH	Scene de la folie "Lucia di Lammermoor" (Donizetti) 1906	
053077	SEMBRICH	Ernani involami "Ernani" (Verdi) 1906. DB434	
053078	SEMBRICH	Caro nome "Rigoletto" (Verdi)	1906. DB431
053079	CUCINI	Non conosci il bel suol? "Mignon" (Thomas)(76)	1906
053080	CUCINI	O mio Fernando "La Favorita" (Donizetti) (76)	1906
053088	BONINSEGNA	Pace, pace, mio Dio "La Forza del Destino" (Verdi)(76)	
		(793c) 1906. DB493	
053089	BONINSEGNA	Madre pietosa "La Forza del Destino" (Verdi)(76)	
		(800c) 1906. DB493	
053091	EAMES	Ave Maria "Otello" (Verdi) (A3385) 1906. IRCC 125	
053092	EAMES	Voi lo sapete o mamma "Cavalleria Rusticana" (Mascagni)	
		1st. ed.(A4034) 1906	

053096 SEMBRICH Ah fors'è lui   "La Traviata" (Verdi) (A3152) 1906. DB434
053097 SEMBRICH Voci di primavera (Strauss)   1906
053098 SEMBRICH Batti, batti "Don Giovanni" (Mozart) 1906. DB428
053099 SEMBRICH Deh vieni "Le Nozze di Figaro" (Mozart) 1906. DB433
053100 SEMBRICH Ah non giunge "La Sonnambula" (Bellini) 1906. DB428
053101 BONINSEGNA Notturno, Romanza (Cantoni)   1907
053103 SCHUMANN-HEINK Lascia ch'io pianga "Rinaldo" (Handel)(80) 1906
053104 DONALDA Sì, mi chiamano Mimi "La Bohème" (Puccini)(77)(687c)1907.VB10
053106 MELBA Sì, mi chiamano Mimi "La Bohème" (Puccini)(A4281)(82) 1907.Lilac
053107 MELBA Mattinata (Tosti) pno-acc.Melba (A4360) Lilac Label 1907
053108 MELBA Ah fors'è lui "La Traviata" (Verdi) (A4339) 1907. DB346.Lilac
053109 MELBA Se saran rose (Arditi) (A4356)   Lilac Label 1907
053110 MELBA Caro nome "Rigoletto" (Verdi) (A4283) 1907. DB346.Lilac Label
053111 MELBA Addio "La Bohème" (Puccini)(80) (A4341) Lilac Label 1907
053112 MELBA Mad Scene "Lucia di Lammermoor" (Donizetti)(A4349)w.fl.1907.Li.
053113 MELBA Voi che sapete "Le Nozze di Figaro" (Mozart)(A4353)   1907 Li.
053114 MELBA La Serenata (Tosti) w.harp (A4342) 1907. DB349. Lilac Label
053115 MELBA Vissi d'arte "Tosca" (Puccini) (A4282) 1907. Lilac Label
053117 CALVÉ Charmant oiseau "Perle du Brésil" (David) in Fr.(A6024) 1st.ed.
                                                                  1907
053118 CALVÉ Habanera "Carmen" (Bizet) in Fr. (A4427) 1st. ed. 1907. DB160
053119 CUCINI Scena delle Carte "Carmen" (Bizet)   1907
053120 CUCINI Condotta ell'era in ceppi "Il Trovatore" (Bizet)   1907
053121 CUCINI S'apre per te il mio cor "Sansone e Dalila" (Saint-Saëns)1907
053122 CUCINI O aprile foriero "Sansone e Dalila" (Saint-Saëns)   1907
053123 CUCINI Canzone boema "Carmen" (Bizet)(77)   1907
053124 CUCINI Crepuscolo triste (Giordano)   1907
053137 NIELSEN Una voce poco fa "Il Barbiere di Siviglia" (Rossini)1907
053140 GAY   Che faro? "Orfeo ed Euridice" (Gluck)(76)(2156f) 1908
053141 TETRAZZINI Caro nome "Rigoletto" (Verdi)(79)(2170f)   1908
053142 TETRAZZINI Io son Titania "Mignon" (Thomas)(2171f)   1908
053143 TETRAZZINI Ombra leggiera "Dinorah" (Meyerbeer)(2175f)   1908
053144 TETRAZZINI Splendon le sacre faci "Lucia di Lammermoor" (Donizetti)
                                                         (2176f)   1908
053145 TETRAZZINI Voi che sapete "Le Nozze di Figaro" (Mozart)(2177f)1908
053146 TETRAZZINI Una voce poco fa "Il Barbiere di Siviglia" (Rossini)
                                                         (2178f)1908
053147 TETRAZZINI Sempre libera "La Traviata" (Verdi)(2179f)   1908
053148 TETRAZZINI Batti, batti "Don Giovanni" (Mozart)(2180f)   1908
053150 TETRAZZINI Bell Song "Lakmé" (Delibes)(79)(2172f)   1908
053151 PARETO   Caro nome "Rigoletto" (Verdi)   1908
053152 PARETO   Quando rapita "Lucia di Lammermoor" (Donizetti)   1908
053153 PARETO   Aria di Lucia "Lucia di Lammermoor" (Donizetti)   1908
053154 PARETO   Spargi d'amaro pianto "Lucia di Lammermoor" (Donizetti)08
053155 PARETO   Voci di primavera (Strauss)   1908
053156 PARETO   Ah non credea mirarti "La Sonnambula" (Bellini) 1908
053157 PARETO   Aria delle Campanelle "Lakmé" (Delibes)   1908
053158 SCHUMANN-HEINK Bolero : Gitana (Arditi)(81)(A4701)   1907
053162 GALVANY Ballata d'Ofelia "Amleto" (Thomas)(80)1908.DB480.HRS 1010
053163 GALVANY Valzer "Romeo e Giulietta" (Gounod)(80)(1308c)1908.IRCC
053164 GALVANY O lieto suol "Gli Ugonotti" (Meyerbeer)(80)(1340c)
                                                        1908.DB481
053165 GALVANY L'Incantatrice (Arditi)(80)(1399½c) 1908. DB480. VB68
053166 SEMBRICH Una voce poco fa "Il Barbiere di Siviglia" (Rossini)
                                                        DB431. 1908
053168 DE CASAS Che faro? "Orfeo ed Euridice" (Gluck)   1908
053169 DE CASAS Figlio mio "Profeta" (Meyerbeer)   1908
053170 SEMBRICH Dolce amor - Waltz "Merry Widow" (Lehar)(80) 1908. DB432

053172 BONINSEGNA   Voi lo sapete o mamma   "Cavalleria Rusticana" (Mascagni)
                                            (1430½c) 1908. VB11
053174 SEMBRICH   Casta diva "Norma" (Bellini)   1908
053176 FARRAR Un bel dì vedremo "Madama Butterfly" (Puccini)(A5055) 1908
053177 FARRAR L'altra notte "Mefistofele" (Boito)(81) 1909. DB654
053179 KURZ   Ombra leggiera "Dinorah" (Meyerbeer)(0821v) 1908. DB330
053180 GALVANY Ombra leggiera "Dinorah" (Meyerbeer)(1451½c)1908. HRS 1010
053181 GALVANY Splendon le sacre face "Lucia di Lammermoor" (Donizetti)
                                            (1453½c) 1908. IRCC
053182 GALVANY Aria delle Campanelle "Lakmé" (Delibes)   1908
053183 CALVÉ   Voi lo sapete o mamma "Cavalleria Rusticana" (Mascagni)(033030)
                                            (A4426-2)(76-79)DB160
053184 PIETRACEWSKA Re dell'abisso "Un Ballo in Maschera" (Verdi)
                                            (1479¾c) 1908
053185 BORONAT So anch'io la virtù "Don Pasquale" (Donizetti)(1506½c)1908
053186 BORONAT Tutte le feste "Rigoletto" (Verdi) (1507c) 1908
053187 BORONAT La tenera parola "Gli Ugonotti" (Meyerbeer)(1517c)   1908
053188 BORONAT Come per me sereno "La Sonnambula" (Bellini)   1908
053189 BORONAT E lo sapevi "Olga" (Giannelli)   1908
053190 BORONAT Ave Maria (Bach-Gounod) (1544½c)   1908
053193 GALVANY Maggio Valzer (Dafeu) (1450c) 1908. VB68
053194 PIETRACEWSKA Scena delle Carte "Carmen" (Bizet)   1908
053195 TETRAZZINI Nella calma "Romeo e Giulietta" (Gounod)(80)(2524f)
                                            1908. DB542
053196 TETRAZZINI Ah fors'è lui. "La Traviata" (Verdi)(80)(2573f)   1908
053197 TETRAZZINI Voci di primavera (Strauss)(80)(2586f) 1908. IRCC 148
053200 GALVANY Spargi d'amaro pianto "Lucia di Lammermoor" (Donizetti)(80)
                                            (1454c) 1908. DB400
053201 PIETRACEWSKA O mio Fernando "La Favorita" (Donizetti)   1908
053202 PIETRACEWSKA S'apre per te "Sansone e Dalila" (Saint-Saëns) 1908
053203 DE CASAS Pietà "Profeta" (Meyerbeer)(76)   1908
053204 DE CASAS Crepuscolo triste (Giordano)   1908
053205 DE CASAS Per sua madre "Linda di Chamounix" (Donizetti)   1908
053206 DE CASAS O aprile foriero "Sansone e Dalila" (Saint-Saëns)   1908
053207 DE CASAS Amor i miei fini "Sansone e Dalila" (Saint-Saëns)(76)1908
053208 PARETO Aria di Micaela "Carmen" (Bizet)   1908
053211 MELBA   Salce, salce "Otello" (Verdi)(78-80)(A6704) 1909.Lilac Label
053212 MELBA   Ave Maria "Otello" (Verdi)(80) (A6705) 1909. Lilac Label
053213 SEMBRICH Bolero "I Vespri Siciliani" (Verdi)(81)   1908
053214 GADSKI Voi lo sapete o mamma "Cavalleria Rusticana" (Mascagni)1908
053215 FARRAR Voi che sapete "Le Nozze di Figaro" (Mozart)(81)   1908
                                            DB653. IRCC 68
053216 SEMBRICH O luce di quest'anima "Linda di Chamounix" (Donizetti)(81)
                                            1908. IRCC 48
053217 SEMBRICH Bel raggio "Semiramide" (Rossini)(81) 1908. DB433
053218 PIETRACEWSKA Canzone boema "Carmen" (Bizet)   1908
053222 TETRAZZINI Saper vorreste "Un Ballo in Maschera" (Verdi)(80)
                                            (3076f) 1908/9
053223 TETRAZZINI Regnava nel silenzio "Lucia di Lammermoor" (Donizetti)
                                            (80)(3077f) 1909. DB528
053224 TETRAZZINI Quando rapita in estasi "Lucia di Lammermoor"(Donizetti)
                                            (80)(3078f) 1909. DB528
053225 TETRAZZINI Carnevale di Venezia I. (Benedict)(80)(3079f)1909.
053226 TETRAZZINI Carnevale di Venezia II.(Benedict)(80)(3080f)1909
053227 TETRAZZINI Ah non credea mirarti "La Sonnambula" (Bellini)(80)
                                            (3101f)1909
053228 TETRAZZINI Siccome un dì "I Pescatori di Perle" (Bizet)(80)
                                            (3102f) 1909. DB544.

```
053229 TETRAZZINI   Aprile (Tosti)(80) (3103f) 1909. DB538
053230 TETRAZZINI   La Serenata (Tosti)(80) (3104f)                        1909
053231 BONINSEGNA   I sacri nomi "Aida" (Verdi) (1951c)                    1909
053232 BONINSEGNA   O cieli azzurri "Aida" (Verdi)                         1909
053235 BONINSEGNA   Ei m'ama  "Faust" (Gounod)                             1909
053237 RUSZKOWSKA   La vergine degli angeli  "La Forza del Destino" (Verdi)12/09
053238 PIETRACEWSKA Voce di donna "La Gioconda" (Ponchielli) 6/11
053242 DE CASAS     Canzone medioevale (Costa) 2/11
053243 RUSZKOWSKA   Vissi d'arte  "Tosca" (Puccini) 10/10
053250 RUSZKOWSKA   Inflammatus "Stabat Mater" (Rossini)                   1910
053253 BONINSEGNA   Ritorna vincitor "Aida" (Verdi) 11/10
053254 KURZ         Ernani involami  "Ernani" (Verdi) (2070c)              1910
053260 HEMPEL       Infelice, sconsolata "Flauto Magico" (Mozart)(545m)1911.DB331
                                                                           VB21
053261 HEMPEL       Il bacio (Arditi) (543m) 1911. DB298
053262 HEMPEL       Follie! Follie! Sempre libera  "La Traviata" (Verdi)(542m)1911
                                                                           DB272
053263 HEMPEL       Deh vieni  "Le Nozze di Figaro" (Mozart)(544m) 1911. DB353
053265 HEMPEL       Surta e la notte  "Ernani" (Verdi)(81) (2229c) 1911. DB296
053273 KURZ         Ah non credea mirarti  "La Sonnambula" (Bellini) (564m)   1911
053274 KURZ         Deh vieni  "Le Nozze di Figaro" (Mozart) (568m)  1911. DB500
053275 KURZ         Saper vorreste  "Un Ballo in Maschera" (Verdi)(81)(570m)1911.DB498
053276 KURZ         Merce diletti amici  "I Vespri Siciliani" (Verdi)(572m)1911.VB48
053277 KURZ         Qui la voce  "I Puritani" (Bellini)(81) (573m) 1911. DB777
053278 KURZ         Vien diletto "I Puritani" (Bellini)(80) (574m) 1911. DB777
053279 KURZ         D'amor sull'ali rosee "Il Trovatore" (Verdi)              1911
053280 KURZ         L'estasi valse (Arditi) (576m) 1911. DB499
053283 KURZ         Il bacio (Arditi)      (566m) 1911. DB499
053289 HEMPEL       Vien diletto  "I Puritani" (Bellini) (610½m) 1912. DB296
053290 HEMPEL       Oh d'amore  "Mirella" (Gounod)(81) (609m) 1912. DB373
053300 FRASCANI     Dopo! (Tosti) 8/13
053301 FRASCANI     Carmela (Tosti) 7/12
053303 CAPRILE      Ebben? "La Wally" (Catalani) 6/12
053304 CAPRILE      Addio del passato "La Traviata" (Verdi) 6/12
053306 CASINI       Hoe la, le guardie "La Bohème" (Puccini) 10/12
053313 CAPRILE      Sì, mi chiamano Mimì "La Bohème" (Puccini) 6/13
053326 HEMPEL       Che pur aspro al cuore "Il Seraglio" (Mozart)(719m)1913.DB331
                                                                           VB22
053327 HEMPEL       Sì, mi chiamano Mimì  "La Bohème" (Puccini)(1173s) 1913. DB353
053329 HEMPEL       Parla! Valse (Arditi) (1175s)                          1913
```

<u>12" records : G. & T. BLACK LABEL. PRE-DOG issued 1908</u>
<u>DOG LABEL 1909. DOG LABEL : "LA VOCE del PADRONE" 1910</u>

```
053000 SOBRINO     Ernani involami  "Ernani" (Verdi) (221 R)               1903
053001 HUGUET      Gli angui dell'inferno "Flauto Magico" (Mozart)         1903
053004 ARKEL       Tacea la notte "Il Trovatore" (Verdi)                   1903
053005 ARKEL       Salve d'emor "Tannhäuser" (Wagner)                      1903
053008 RUSS        Voi che sapete "Le Nozze di Figaro" (Mozart)            1903
053011 CALIGARIS   Madre pietosa "La Forza del Destino" (Verdi) pno.       1903
053012 CALIGARIS   Tacea la notte "Il Trovatore" (Verdi)        pno.       1903
053013 CALIGARIS   Ritorna vincitor "Aida" (Verdi)              pno.       1903
053016 CALIGARIS   Voi lo sapete o mamma "Cavalleria Rusticana" (Mascagni)1903
053020 CALIGARIS   D'amor sull'ali rosee "Il Trovatore" (Verdi)           1904
053021 GITTI-LIPPI Inflammatus "Stabat Mater" (Rossini) 3/04
053022 GITTI-LIPPI D'amor sull'ali rosee "Il Trovatore" (Verdi) 3/04
053023 LONGHI      Vaga donna "Gli Ugonotti" (Meyerbeer)                   1904
053025 RUSS        Sì, mi chiamano Mimì  "La Bohème" (Puccini)             1904
```

```
053039 ARKEL    Cieli azzurri   "Aida" (Verdi)                                    1904
053043 DE CISNEROS  Prologo  "Ero e Leandro" (Mancinelli) pno.S.Cottone 1904
053053 EXMAN    Largo  "Serse" (Handel)                                           1905
053059 ARKEL    Canto di Venere   "Tannhäuser"(Wagner)                            1905
053060 ARKEL    Aria del sonno  "L'Africana" (Meyerbeer)                          1905
053061 ARKEL    Casta diva  "Norma" (Bellini)                                     1905
053062 ARKEL    Quant'è bello  "Lucrezia Borgia" (Donizetti)   pno.               1905
053064 MILERI   Condotta ell'era in ceppi  "Il Trovatore" (Verdi)(76) 1905.D317
053066 CRESTANI Ma dall'arrido stelo  "Un Ballo in Maschera" (Verdi)    1905
053070 PICCOLETTI  Siccome un dì  "I Pescatori di Perle" (Bizet) pno.   1906
053071 PICCOLETTI  Sola nei miei prim'anni  "Lohengrin" (Wagner)        1906
053072 HUGUET   O lieto suol  "Gli Ugonotti" (Meyerbeer)                1906
053073 HUGUET   Ombra leggiera "Dinorah" (Meyerbeer)                    1906
053074 HUGUET   Ballata d'Ofelia  "Amleto" (Thomas)                     1906
053081 HUGUET   Aria dei gioielli  "Faust" (Gounod) 1906. D313
053082 HUGUET   Si carina caprettina  "Dinorah" (Meyerbeer)            1906
053083 CORSI    Sola nei miei prim'anni  "Lohengrin" (Wagner)          1906
053084 MILERI   Non conosci il bel suol? "Mignon" (Thomas)             1906
053085 HUGUET   Polonese  "Mignon" (Thomas)                            1906
053086 HUGUET   Non conosci il bel suol? "Mignon" (Thomas)             1906
053087 ZACCARIA Re dell'abisso  "Un Ballo in Maschera" (Verdi)         1907
053090 HUGUET   Una voce poco fa  "Il Barbiere di Siviglia" (Rossini)  1907
053093 CAVALIERI  Suicidio!  "La Gioconda" (Ponchielli)                1906
053094 CAVALIERI  L'altra notte  "Mefistofele" (Boito)                 1906
053095 CAVALIERI  Pace, pace, mio Dio  "La Forza del Destino" (Verdi)  1906
053102 GIACOMELLI  Preludio e scena Atto II.  "Norma" (Bellini)        1907
053105 BRAMBILLA  Brahma gran Dio  "I Pescatori di Perle" (Bizet)      1907
053116 BRAMBILLA  Ah non credea mirarti  "La Sonnambula" (Bellini)     1907
053125 VAN BRANDT  Ah fors'è lui  "La Traviata" (Verdi)                1907
053128 THORNTON   Flower Song  "Faust" (Gounod)                        1907
053129 JOANNA     Entrata di Santuzza  "Cavalleria Rusticana" (Mascagni)1907
053130 HUGUET     Stridono lassù  "Pagliacci" (Leoncavallo)(77) 1907. D320
053132 HUGUET   D'un sguardo un sorrisetto  "Don Pasquale" (Donizetti)  1907
053133 JOANNA     Romanza di Elisabetta  "Tannhäuser" (Wagner)         1907
053135 SALVADOR   Canzone boema  "Carmen" (Bizet)                      1907
053136 HUGUET     Aria di Micaela  "Carmen" (Bizet)                    1907
053149 BUTTI      Entrata di Micaela  "Carmen" (Bizet)(77) 1908. D310
053159 DAVID      Morte d'Isotta  "Tristano ed Isotta" (Wagner)        1908
053160 BALLIÈRES  Salve d'amor  "Tannhäuser" (Wagner) 4/08
053161 ALEXINA    Preghiera d'Elisabetta  "Tannhäuser" (Wagner) 4/08
053171 DESTINN  Un bel dì vedremo  "Madama Butterfly" (Puccini)(0801v)  1908
                                            (03110 Eng.Cat.)
053173 DAVID    Voi lo sapete o mamma  "Cavalleria Rusticana" (Mascagni)1908
053191 DE FRATE  Casta diva  "Norma" (Bellini) (1349c)                  1908
053192 DE FRATE  Inflammatus  "Stabat Mater" (Rossini)                  1908
053198 MARCHETTI  La nostra vita  "Geisha" (Jones)                      1908
053199 MARCHETTI  Orsu dal marchese si vada "Geisha" (Jones)            1908
053209 PICCOLETTI  Inflammatus  "Stabat Mater" (Rossini)                1908
053219 FRANCILLO-KAUFMANN  Voci di primavera (Strauss)
053220 FRANCILLO-KAUFMANN  O che assorta (Grande Valse)  (Venzano)
053221 VAN RAPPE  Dove sono  "Le Nozze di Figaro" (Mozart) (3003f)      1908
053233 CAPPIELLO  Chi mai fia  "Aida" (Verdi)                           1909
053234 CAPPIELLO  O tu che sei d'Osiride  "Aida" (Verdi)                1909
053236 HUGUET   Il bacio (Arditi)                                       1908
053240 DESTINN  Vissi d'arte  "Tosca" (Puccini)                         1908-10
053244 RUBINO   L'altra notte  "Mefistofele" (Boito) 5/10
053245 MURINO   Suicidio!  "La Gioconda" (Ponchielli)5/10
053246 MURINO   Inneggiamo al Signore risorto "Cavalleria Rusticana" (Mascagni)
                                                                       5/10
```

053247 MURINO   Voi lo sapete o mamma "Cavalleria Rusticana" (Mascagni) 5/10
053248 RUBINO   Addio senza rancor "La Bohème" (Puccini) 5/10
053249 MELLERIO Son pochi fiori "L'Amico Fritz" (Mascagni) 5/10
053251 FABRIS   Tu che invoco "La Vestale" (Spontini) 10/10
053252 FABRIS   Aria dei fiori "Eidelberga mia" (Pacchierotti) 10/10
053255 MELLERIO Un dì, verso il Murzoli "La Wally" (Catalani) 3/11
053256 MELLERIO Ebben? Andrò.. "La Wally" (Catalani) 3/11
053257 MARCELL   Gebet "Tosca" (Puccini)
053258 RUBINO   Un bel dì vedremo "Madama Butterfly" (Puccini) 4/11
053259 LUFRANO   Sola ne' miei primi anni "Lohengrin" (Wagner) 6/11
053264 MUZIO   Sì, mi chiamano Mimì "La Bohème" (Puccini)   1911
053266 RUBINO   O cieli azzurri "Aida" (Verdi) 11/11
053270 MANGINI   Oh! che volo d'augelli "Pagliacci" (Leoncavallo) 2/12
053271 MANGINI   Siccome un dì "I Pescatori di Perle" (Bizet)   4/13
053281 LOTTI   Salce, salce "Otello" (Verdi)
053284 GRAMAGNA Ohimè! morir mi sento "Aida" (Verdi) 3/12
053291 BARTOLOMASI Mio padre .. e Re! "Isabeau" (Mascagni) 5/12
053292 BARTOLOMASI Questo mio bianco manto "Isabeau" (Mascagni) 5/12
053293 BARTOLOMASI Venne una vecchierella "Isabeau" (Mascagni) 5/12
053297 CASINI N.   Addio, o nostro picciol desco "Manon" (Massenet) 4/13(Red)
053302 SANTOLIVA-VILLANI Un dì (ero piccina) "Iris" (Mascagni) 4/14
053307 LIPKOWSKAYA Cavatina I. "Semiramide" (Rossini)   c.1913/4
053308 LIPKOWSKAYA Cavatina II. "Semiramide" (Rossini)   c.1913/4
053314 PEREIRA   Splendon le sacre face "Lucia di Lammermoor" (Donizetti) 6/13
053315 ZIZOLFI   O mio Fernando "La Favorita" (Donizetti) 10/13
053316 BARBIERI Suicidio! "La Gioconda" (Ponchielli)   8/13
053317 BARBIERI Madre pietosa vergine "La Forza del Destino" (Verdi) 10/13
053320 ZIZOLFI   Venite all'indovina "La Forza del Destino" (Verdi)   8/13
053322 BARBIERI Pace, pace, mio Dio "La Forza del Destino" (Verdi)   8/13
053323 BARBIERI Ernani involami "Ernani" (Verdi)   9/13
053328 PONZANO   Liber scriptus "Messa da Requiem" (Verdi)   12/13
053332 SOLARI   Cibate il pan "Parsifal" (Wagner)   7/14

12" records : RED & PINK LABEL

* 2-053000 LUNN   O Don fatale "Don Carlos" (Verdi)(80) (3197f)   1909
  2-053001 LUNN   Non più di fiori "La Clemenza di Tito" (Mozart)   1909
  2-053009 FARRAR Vissi d'arte "Tosca" (Puccini)(A8264) 1909. DB246 1st.ed.
  2-053010 FARRAR Un bel dì vedremo "Madama Butterfly" (Puccini)(A5055)1909
                                                DB246 (also on 053176) 2nd. ed.
  2-053011 GAY   Giorni poveri "Il Trovatore" (Verdi)(81) 11/10
  2-053012 TETRAZZINI Brahma gran Dio "I Pescatori di Perle" (Bizet)(80)
                                                (3423f) 1909. DB544
  2-053013 TETRAZZINI Valse "Mirella" (Gounod)   (3426f) 1909. DB703
  2-053014 SCHUMANN-HEINK Lascia ch'io pianga "Rinaldo" (Handel)
  2-053016 GAY   Vedrai carino "Don Giovanni" (Mozart)   1909
  2-053017 GAY   Che farò? "Orfeo ed Euridice" (Gluck)   1909
  2-053018 GAY   Stride la vampa "Il Trovatore" (Verdi)(3803f) 1909. VB31
  2-053019 MELBA   Sola ne'miei "Lohengrin" (Wagner)(80)(4185f)1910.DB366.VB53.Li.
  2-053020 MELBA   Vissi d'arte "Tosca" (Puccini)(80)(4183f)1910.DB702.Lilac
  2-053021 MELBA   Ave Maria "Otello" (Verdi)(80)(A6705)1910.DB355.DM118.Lilac
  2-053022 MELBA   Salce, salce "Otello" (Verdi) (A6704)1910.DB366.Lilac Label
  2-053023 MELBA   Se saran rose (Arditi)(81) (A4356) 1910.   DB349.Lilac Label
  2-053024 MELBA   Vissi d'arte "Tosca" (Puccini) (A4282) 1910. Lilac Label
* 2-053025 MELBA   Sì, mi chiamano Mimì "La Bohème" (Puccini)(80)(A4281)
                                                1910. DB356. Lilac Label
  2-053026 MELBA   Mad Scene "Lucia di Lammermoor" (Donizetti)fl.Lemmone (A4349)
                                                1910. DB364. Lilac Label

2-053027 MELBA Voi che sapete "Le Nozze di Figaro" (Mozart)(80)(A4353)
                                           1910. DB367. Lilac Label
2-053028 MELBA Addio "La Bohème" (Puccini)(80)(A4341) 1910.DB356.Lilac Label
2-053029 MELBA Ah fors'è lui   "La Traviata" (Verdi)1910.(A4339) Lilac Label
                                           also 053108
2-053031 TETRAZZINI Solveig's Song "Peer Gynt" (Grieg) 1910. (4580f)
2-053033 TETRAZZINI Merce dilette amiche "I Vespri Siciliani" (Verdi)(4577f)
                                           1910
2-053034 TETRAZZINI Bel raggio "Semiramide" (Rossini)(4578f)1910.DB537.VB15
2-053035 TETRAZZINI O luce di quest'anima "Linda di Chamounix" (Donizetti)
                                           (4576f) 1910
2-053036 TETRAZZINI Splendon le sacre face "Lucia di Lammermoor" (Donizetti)
                                           (4579f) 1910
2-053037 FARRAR Ora stammi "Tosca" (Puccini) 1911. DB653
2-053038 TETRAZZINI Ah fors'è lui /Sempre libera "La Traviata" (Verdi)
                                           (A10065) 1911
2-053040 TETRAZZINI L'Eco (Eckert) (A10070) 1911. DB530
2-053041 TETRAZZINI Ah non giunge "La Sonnambula" (Bellini)(A10076)1911.DB533
2-053042 TETRAZZINI Io son Titania "Mignon" (Thomas) (A10073) 1911
2-053043 TETRAZZINI Carnevale di Venezia I. (Benedict)(A10066) 1911. DB689
2-053044 TETRAZZINI Carnevale di Venezia II.(Benedict)(A10067) 1911. DB689
2-053045 TETRAZZINI Variazioni (Proch)   (A10077) 1911
2-053046 TETRAZZINI Una voce poco fa "Il Barbiere di Siviglia" (Rossini)
                                           (A10071) 1911. DB690
2-053047 TETRAZZINI Ardon gli incensi "Lucia di Lammermoor" (Donizetti)
                                           (A10068) 1911. DB535
2-053048 TETRAZZINI Saper vorreste "Un Ballo in Maschera" (Verdi)
                                           (A10059) 1911. DB539
2-053049 TETRAZZINI Ah non credea mirarti "La Sonnambula" (Bellini)
                                           (A10064) 1911. DB533
2-053050 TETRAZZINI Caro nome "Rigoletto" (Verdi)   (A10074) 1911. DB536
2-053052 DESTINN   Un bel dì vedremo "Madama Butterfly" (Puccini)(81)(5133f)
                                           1911
2-053053 DESTINN   Vissi d'arte "Tosca" (Puccini)(80)(5134f) 1911.
2-053054 DESTINN   Ritorna vincitor "Aida" (Verdi)(81)   1911. DB646
2-053055 TETRAZZINI Candida Durga "Lakmé" (Delibes)(ac5166f) 1911. DB532
2-053056 TETRAZZINI Bell Song "Lakmé" (Delibes)(ac5167f) 1911. DB532.IRCC 27
2-053057 TETRAZZINI Batti, batti "Don Giovanni" (Mozart)(ac5168f) 1911.DB537
2-053058 TETRAZZINI Io son Titania "Mignon" (Thomas)(ai5181f) 1911. DB540
2-053059 TETRAZZINI Ah fors'è lui   "La Traviata" (Verdi)(ac5164f)1911.DB531
2-053060 TETRAZZINI Aria di Micaela "Carmen" (Bizet) (ac5163f) 1911
2-053061 TETRAZZINI O luce di quest'anima "Linda di Chamounix" (Donizetti)
                                           (ac5179f) 1911
2-053062 TETRAZZINI Sempre libera "La Traviata" (Verdi)(ac5169f) 1911.DB531
2-053063 TETRAZZINI Mad Scene "Amleto" (Thomas) (ai5180f) 1911. DB543
2-053064 TETRAZZINI Ritorna vincitor "Aida" (Verdi)(ac5170f)1911.DB529.IRCC27
2-053065 TETRAZZINI Variazioni (Proch) (ai5182f) 1911. DB523
2-053066 GLUCK O che volo "Pagliacci" (Leoncavallo)(80)(A10091)1911.DB282
2-053067 LUNN Stride la vampa "Il Trovatore" (Verdi)(80)(z5494f)
2-053068 LUNN Non più di fiori "La Clemenza di Tito" (Mozart)(80)w.clar.obb.
                                           DB517
2-053069 FARRAR Tutto per te mio bene "Le Donne Curiose" (Wolf-Ferrari) 2/13
2-053070 TETRAZZINI Come per me sereno "La Sonnambula" (Bellini)(ac188HO)
                                           1912.IRCC 148
2-053071 TETRAZZINI O vago suol "Gli Ugonotti" (Meyerbeer)(ac191HO) 1912
                                           VB41.IRCC 1015
2-053072 TETRAZZINI Vien diletto "I Puritani" (Bellini)(ac193HO)1912.IRCC 116
2-053073 TETRAZZINI Grande Valse (Venzano) (ac194HO) 1912

2-053074 LUNN   Voce di donna "La Gioconda" (Ponchielli)(81)
2-053075 LUNN   Lascia ch'io pianga "Rinaldo" (Handel)(81)(z6320f)1912.DB505
2-053076 BUTT   Lusinghe piu care (Handel)(80) (6381f) Dark Blue Label
2-053077 KURZ   Ballade "Jolie Fille de Perth" (Bizet)(HO 680m) 1913. VB48
2-053078 KURZ   So anch'io la vision "Don Pasquale" (Donizetti)(HO681m)1913.
                                                                    DB776
2-053079 KURZ   Batti, batti "Don Giovanni" (Mozart) (HO 684m)   1913
2-053080 KURZ   Vissi d'arte "Tosca" (Puccini)   (HO 683m)   1913
2-053081 FARRAR   Sì, mi chiamano Mimi "La Bohème" (Puccini)   1914
2-053082 FARRAR   Addio "La Bohème" (Puccini) w.harp   1914
2-053083 MELBA L'amero sarò costante "Il Re Pastore" (Mozart)w.Kubelik (vln)
                                         (z7322f) DK112. 1913.Buff Label
2-053084 TETRAZZINI   Tacea la notte "Il Trovatore" (Verdi)(A12918)1913.DB540
2-053085 TETRAZZINI   D'amor sull'ali rosee "Il Trovatore" (Verdi)(A12928)
                                                          1913.DB536
2-053086 TETRAZZINI   Rhapsody & Serenata Inutile (De Koven) (A12929) 1913
2-053087 TETRAZZINI   Grande Valse (Venzano) (A12930) 1913. DB530
2-053088 BUTT   Rendi'l sereno al ciglio "Sosarme" (Handel)(80)(ac6382f)Dk.Blue
2-053089 GLUCK Air de Micaela "Carmen" (Bizet) in Fr.(A10181) 1911. DB279
2-053090 GLUCK Ah non credea mirarti "La Sonnambula" (Bellini)(A10813)1911
                                                                    DB663
2-053091 GLUCK Parla - Valse (Arditi) (A12831) 1913. DB663
2-053092 TETRAZZINI   Pastorale "Rosalinda" (Veracini) (A12917) 1913. DB690
2-053093 TETRAZZINI   Io non sono "Crispino e la comare" (Ricci)(af520HO)
                                                  1913. DB535.VB41
2-053094 TETRAZZINI   La-la-la "L'Etoile du Nord".(Meyerbeer)(af522HO)
                                                  1913. DB542.VB15
2-053096 TETRAZZINI   Addio del passato "La Traviata" (Verdi)(af519HO)
                                                  1913.DB539.IRCC116
2-053098 HEMPEL   Parla! (Arditi) (A14365) 1914. DB298
2-053099 HEMPEL   Vien diletto "I Puritani" (Bellini) (A14540) 1914
2-053100 HEMPEL   Ah fors'è lui. "La Traviata" (Verdi)(A14364) 1914. DB294
2-053101 DESTINN   Un bel dì vedremo "Madama Butterfly" (Puccini) 1916. DB647
2-053102 BORI   Oh! che volo "Pagliacci" (Leoncavallo)(A14437) 1914. DB603
2-053103 BORI   Sì, mi chiamano Mimi "La Bohème" (Puccini)(A14477)1914.DB152
2-053104 DESTINN   Suicidio! "La Gioconda" (Ponchielli)(A14509) 1918.DB223
2-053111 DESTINN   O patria mia "Aida" (Verdi) (A14512) 1914   DB222
2-053112 DESTINN   Vissi d'arte "Tosca" (Puccini)(A14508) 1914. DB223
2-053113 TETRAZZINI   Aria di Micaela "Carmen" (Bizet)(80) (A14819) 1914. DB703
2-053114 TETRAZZINI   Pace mio Dio "La Forza del Destino" (Verdi)(77)(A14821)
                                                  1914. DB538
2-053115 TETRAZZINI   O luce di quest'anima "Linda di Chamounix" (Donizetti)
                                         (A14817) 1914. DB543
2-053116 TETRAZZINI   Solveig's Song "Peer Gynt" (Grieg) (A14820) 1914. DB534
2-053117 TETRAZZINI   Tre giorni son che Nina (Ciampi)(A14815)   1914
2-053118 TETRAZZINI   Merce dilette amiche "I Vespri Siciliani" (Verdi)
                                         (A14822)   1914. DB529
2-053120 BORI   Un dì al tempio "Iris" (Mascagni)(A15824) 1915. DB152. IRCC 70
2-053121 LUNN   Che farò? "Orfeo ed Euridice" (Gluck) (HO 1222ac) DB505
2-053126 GALLI-CURCI   Caro nome "Rigoletto" (Verdi) (A18596) 1916. DB257
2-053128 GALLI-CURCI   Il dolce suono "Lucia di Lammermoor" (Donizetti)
                                         (A18587) 1916. DB260
2-053130 GALLI-CURCI   Dov'è l'Indiana "Lakmé" (Delibes)(A18595) 1916. DB263
2-053131 BOSINI   Ebben, ne andrò lontana "La Wally" (Catalani) 2/19
2-053133 GALLI-CURCI   Variazioni (Proch) (A20663) 1917. DB265
2-053134 GALLI-CURCI   Ombra leggiera "Dinorah" (Meyerbeer)(A20047) 1917.DB260
2-053135 GALLI-CURCI   Ah non credea mirarti "La Sonnambula" (Bellini)
                                         (A20048) 1917.DB256

2-053136 BONINSEGNA Lascia per or che libera "Loreley" (Catalani)(3197c)
                                                   1917. DB491
2-053137 GALLI-CURCI Qui la voce "I Puritani" (Bellini)(A20669) 1917. DB259
2-053138 HOMER   Largo (Handel) 5/20. DB300
• 2-053139 DESTINN D'amor sull'ali rosee "Il Trovatore" (Verdi) 1914. DB646
2-053140 DESTINN L'ultima canzone (Tosti)   .   1916. DB645
2-053141 DESTINN Ave Maria (Bach-Gounod) (A17498) 1916. DB647
• 2-053142 GALLI-CURCI Una voce poco fa "Il Barbiere di Siviglia"(Rossini)
                                                   (A20045) 1917. DB261

2-053144 GADSKI Ave Maria (Bach-Gounod) w.vln. obb.
• 2-053145 GADSKI Ma dall'arido stelo "Un Ballo in Maschera" (Verdi)(A14805)
                                                   1914. DB661. VB52
• 2-053146 GADSKI Morrò, ma prima "Un Ballo in Maschera" (Verdi)(A14806)
                                                   1914. DB661. VB52
2-053147 GADSKI O patria mia "Aida" (Verdi) (A4128) 1906
2-053148 GADSKI Ritorna vincitor "Aida" (Verdi)
2-053149 GARRISON Voci di primavera (Strauss)
• 2-053150 EDVINA Vissi d'arte "Tosca" (Puccini)(HO 4089af) 1919. DB548
2-053151 HEMPEL Ernani involami "Ernani" (Verdi) (A16041) 1915. DB294
2-053152 HEMPEL Wine, Women & Song (Strauss) (A19858) 1917. DB293
2-053153 HOMER Che farò? "Orfeo ed Euridice" (Gluck) DB300
2-053154 HOMER Fac ut portem "Stabat Mater" (Rossini)
• 2-053155 HOMER Nobil signori "Gli Ugonotti" (Meyerbeer) DB665
2-053156 HOMER Voce di donna "La Gioconda" (Ponchielli) DB665
2-053157 HOMER Quando a te lieta "Faust" (Gounod) 1908. DB667
2-053158 SCHUMANN-HEINK Agnus Dei (Bizet) (A12803) 1913. DB412
2-053159 SCHUMANN-HEINK Leggiera invisibile : Bolero (Arditi) DB414
2-053160 SEMBRICH Qui la voce "I Puritani" (Bellini)
2-053161 GALLI-CURCI Quel guardo il cavaliere "Don Pasquale" (Donizetti)
                                                   (A23169) 1919. DB259
2-053162 POLI-RANDACIO I sacri nomi "Aida" (Verdi) 9/20. DB568
2-053164 POLI-RANDACIO Ebben? "La Wally" (Catalani)(919aj) 1919. DB182
2-053172 PARETO Caro nome "Rigoletto" (Verdi) 10/19
2-053173 PARETO Quel guardo il cavaliere "Don Pasquale" (Donizetti)12/20.
                                                   DB567
2-053174 PARETO O bimba bimbetta (Sibella) (HO 4432af) 1919. DB564
2-053175 PARETO Sempre libera "La Traviata" (Verdi)(HO 4431af) 1919. DB565
2-053176 PARETO Deh vieni "Le Nozze di Figaro" (Mozart)(HO 4430af)1919.DB567
2-053177 PARETO E strano... Ah fors'è lui "La Traviata" (Verdi)(HO 4429af)
                                                   1919. DB565
2-053178 PARETO Siccome un dì "I Pescatori di Perle" (Bizet)(HO 4411af) 1919
2-053179 PARETO Il bacio (Arditi) (HO 4415af) 1919. DB564
2-053181 BESANZONI Habanera "Carmen" (Bizet) 5/21. DB151
2-053182 ALDA Sì, mi chiamano Mimì "La Bohème" (Puccini)(A8885)15.VII.1915
                                                   DB155
2-053183 GALLI-CURCI Ah fors' è lui "La Traviata" (Verdi)(A22613)1919.DB257
2-053184 HEMPEL Sull'onde del Danubio (J.Strauss)(A16028) 1915. DB293
2-053185 ALDA L'altra notte "Mefistofele" (Boito)(A24609)4.X.1920. DB635
2-053186 GALLI-CURCI Io son Titania "Mignon" (Thomas) (A22615) 1919. DB264
2-053190 POLI-RANDACIO Ave Maria "Otello" (Verdi) (1148aj) 1919. DB182
2-053191 POLI-RANDACIO Un bel dì vedremo "Madama Butterfly" (Puccini)3/22
                                                   DB181
2-053192 POLI-RANDACIO Senza mamma "Suor Angelica" (Puccini) 3/22. DB181
2-053195 BESANZONI O mio Fernando "La Favorita" (Donizetti) 3/22. DB151
2-053196 BORI Deh vieni "Le Nozze di Figaro" (Mozart) (A25146) 1921.DB153
2-053198 GALLI-CURCI Come per me sereno "La Sonnambula" (Bellini)(A24177)
                                                   1920.DB256
2-053199 DESTINN Morrò, ma prima "Un Ballo in Maschera" (Verdi). 1914. .DB222

2-053200 ALDA Un bel dì vedremo "Madama Butterfly" (Puccini)(A13109)1913.DB596
2-053201 BESANZONI O aprile foriero "Sansone e Dalila" (Saint-Saëns) 3/22
2-053203 BORI O gioia! "Segreto di Susanna" (Wolf-Ferrari)(A25301) 1921
                                                DB603. IRCC 70
2-053205 POLI-RANDACIO Leggenda valacca (Braga) 2/23
2-053207 TETRAZZINI Ombra leggiera "Dinorah" (A12931)1912. DB534
• 2-053208 GALLI-CURCI Un bel dì vedremo "Madama Butterfly" (Puccini)(A26598)
                                                1922. DB261
• 2-053209 BUTT Il segreto per esser felice "Lucrezia Borgia" (Donizetti)Dk.Bl.
2-053210 BUTT Caro mio ben (Giordani) Dark Blue Label
2-053211 GALLI-CURCI O luce di quest'anima "Linda di Chamounix" (Donizetti)
                                                (A26889) 1922.DB597
2-053213 JERITZA Suicidio! "La Gioconda" (Ponchielli) (A27763) 1923.DB355
• 2-053214 GALLI-CURCI Polonaise "I Puritani" (Bellini) (A28466) 1923.DB641
• 2-053216 PONSELLE O patria mia "Aida" (Verdi) (A29061) 1923.DB854
• 2-053217 GALLI-CURCI Tutte le feste "Rigoletto" (Verdi) (A28470) 1923.DB641
2-053218 POLI-RANDACIO Voi lo sapete o mamma "Cavalleria Rusticana" (Mascagni)
                                                (Ck1255)10/24.DB729
2-053219 DAL MONTE Splendon le sacre face "Lucia di Lammermoor" (Donizetti)
                                                8/24.DB712
2-053220 DAL MONTE Spargi d'amaro pianto "Lucia di Lammermoor" (Donizetti)
                                                8/24.DB712
2-053222 PONSELLE Pace, pace, mio Dio "La Forza del Destino" (Verdi)
                                                (A29060) 1924.DB746
2-053223 PONSELLE Ernani involami "Ernani" (Verdi) (A29062) 1924.DB746
2-053226 OFFERS Condotta all'era in ceppi "Il Trovatore" (Verdi) 3/25-DB754
2-053227 OFFERS Non conosci il bel suol? "Mignon" (Thomas) 10/25.DB847
2-053230 GALLI-CURCI Si carina "Dinorah"(Meyerbeer) (A30291) 1924.DB798
2-053231 PONSELLE Salce, salce "Otello" (Verdi) (A29410) 1924.DB807
2-053232 PONSELLE Ave Maria "Otello" (Verdi) (A29409) 1924.DB807
· 2-053233 GALLI-CURCI Tacea la notte "Il Trovatore" (Verdi)(A28469) 1923.DB813
2-053234 GALLI-CURCI D'amor sull'ali rosee "Il Trovatore" (Verdi)
                                                (A30297) 1924.DB813
2-053235 GALLI-CURCI Bel raggio "Semiramide" (Rossini)(A30905) 1924.DB812.VB5
2-053236 GALLI-CURCI Ah non giunge "La Sonnambula" (Bellini)
                                                (A30906) 1924.DB812.VB5
2-053238 DAL MONTE Deh vieni "Le Nozze di Figaro" (Mozart)(A31272) 1924.DB831
2-053239 DAL MONTE Selva opaca "Guglielmo Tell" (Rossini) (A31271) 1924.DB831
2-053240 DAL MONTE Una voce poco fa "Il Barbiere di Siviglia" (Rossini)
                                                (A31280) 1924.DB830
2-053241 DAL MONTE Caro nome "Rigoletto" (Verdi) (A31281) 1924.DB830
2-053242 DAL MONTE Carnevale di Venezia (Benedict) I. (A31274) 1924.DB821
2-053243 DAL MONTE Carnevale di Venezia (Benedict) II. (A31273) 1924.DB821
2-053244 OFFERS O mio Fernando "La Favorita" (Donizetti) 10/25.DB847
2-053245 CAPSIR Vien diletto "I Puritani" (Bellini) 7/25.DB823
2-053246 CAPSIR Qui la voce "I Puritani" (Bellini) 7/25.DB823
• 2-053247 PONSELLE Suicidio! "La Gioconda" (Ponchielli) (A31709) 1925.DB854
2-053263 MELBA Salce, salce "Otello" (Verdi) Pt.I.(CR417)1926.DB1500.IRCC2.Li.
. 2-053264 MELBA Addio "La Bohème" (Puccini)(CR412)1926.DB943 & DB1500.Lilac

                          12" records : BLACK LABEL

2-053002 VERLET Voci di primavera (Strauss) (3118f) 1909
2-053003 VERLET Mad Scene "Lucia di Lammermoor" (Donizetti) 1909
2-053006 CASTLES Bel raggio "Semiramide" (Rossini) 1906
2-053051 THORNTON Ombra mai fu "Serse" (Handel)(80) 1911. D275
2-053122 LICETTE Ah fors'è lui "La Traviata" (Verdi) Pt.I.(79)
2-053123 LICETTE Ah fors'è lui "La Traviata" (Verdi) Pt.II.(79)

2-053124 VINCENT   Il bacio (Arditi)
2-053125 WOODMAN   Parla - Valse (Arditi)(79)
2-053127 WOODMAN   Ah, che assorta (Forest Fairy) (Venzano)
2-053132 BOCCOLINI Un bel dì vedremo "Madama Butterfly" (Puccini) 1/19
2-053167 POWER   Voi che sapete "Le Nozze di Figaro" (Mozart)   D55
2-053168 POWER   Ah lo so "Flauto Magico" (Mozart)   D55

10" records : G. & T. RED & PINK LABEL
PRE-DOG issued 1908. DOG LABEL 1909
DOG LABEL 1910 : "LA VOCE del PADRONE"

54021 CERESOLI/DE LUCA   Ah l'alto ardor "La Favorita" (Donizetti)   1903
54034 GAROTINI/BATTISTINI Ah l'alto ardor "La Favorita" (Donizetti)(449z) 03
54048 STORCHIO/DE LUCA   Quest'orgoglio non a noi "Siberia" (Giordano)pno. 1904
54056 BONINSEGNA/VALLS   Miserere "Il Trovatore" (Verdi) pno.   1904
54264 BONINSEGNA/CIGADA Mira d'acerbe lagrime "Il Trovatore" (Verdi)(77) 1905
54266 BONINSEGNA/CIGADA Vivra contende il giubilo "Il Trovatore" (Verdi)(77)05
54293 DE LUCIA/A.PINI-CORSI Numero quindici "Il Barbiere di Siviglia"(Rossini)
                                                                    pno.06
54315 GALVANY/RUFFO   Veglia o donna "Rigoletto" (Verdi)(4727h) 1907. DA564
54332 CUCINI/SANCOVY Ai nostri monti "Il Trovatore" (Verdi)   1907
54334 JOANNA/SALVADOR/DE.TURA Fior di giaggiolo "Cavalleria Rusticana"
                                                       (Mascagni)(77) 1907.E126
54340 JOANNA/PAOLI/CIGADA Di geloso amor "Il Trovatore" (Verdi)(80)   1907
54341 HUGUET/DE TURA   Verranno a te "Lucia di Lammermoor" (Donizetti)(79)1907
54342 SIEBANECH/DE TURA Dal rio che va "Jery & Betly" (Romano)   1907
54343 SIEBANECH/DE TURA Jery negli occhi miei "Jery & Betly" (Romano) 1907
54344 PICCOLETTI/DE TURA/CIGADA Prendi quest'è l'imagine "La Traviata"(Verdi)07
54357 DE LUCIA/BADINI Obbligato,obbligato "L'Elisir d'amore"(Donizetti)pno.07
54359 FOSCA/ISCHIERDO/RUFFO Di geloso amor "Il Trovatore"(Verdi)(10900#b)07.DA462
54360 RUFFO/DE SEGUROLA Suoni la tromba "I Puritani" (Bellini)(10906b)07.VA16
54370 GALVANY/DE SEGUROLA Piangi o figlia "I Puritani" (Bellini)   1908
54371 GALVANY/DE SEGUROLA Duetto Annina-Rodolfo "La Sonnambula" (Bellini)1908
54372 ABOTT/ANCONA Si vendetta "Rigoletto" (Verdi)   1908
54373 MARCONI/COTOGNI Duetto "I Mulattieri" (Masini) pno.   1908
54374 DE FRATE/SIGNORINI Nei piedi "Chatterton" (Leoncavallo)   1908
54375 PASSERI/DE TURA Fior di giaggiolo "Cavalleria Rusticana"(Mascagni)1908
54384 GALVANY/DE LUCIA Ah qual colpo in aspettato."Il Barbiere di Siviglia"
                                                          (Rossini) pno.1908
54385 TROMBEN/DE TURA Brindisi "La Traviata" (Verdi)   1908
54386 SIGNORINI/CIGADA Scrissa una lettera "Chatterton" (Leoncavallo)   1908
54398 DE TURA/BADINI O Mimi tu più "La Bohème" (Puccini)   1908
54399 HUGUET/DE TURA Lontan, lontan "Mefistofele" (Boito)   1908
54404 BATTAGLIOLI/BADINI Pura siccome un angelo "La Traviata" (Verdi)   1908
54405 MELLERIO/BADINI Si vendetta "Rigoletto" (Verdi)   1908
54406 MELLERIO/BADINI Tutte le feste "Rigoletto" (Verdi)   1908
54407 PAOLI/POPOVICI Al suon dell'arpe "Poliuto" (Donizetti)   1908
54408 DE TURA/MANSUETO Folletto, Folletto "Mefistofele" (Boito)   1908
54410 PIETRACEWSKA/ZEROLA Perigliarti ancora languente "Il Trovatore"(Verdi)08
54411 PIETRACEWSKA/BADINI Passa il sommo "Sansone e Dalila" (Saint-Saëns)08
54412 DE CASAS/ARDONI/G.PINI-CORSI Serenata "Mefistofele" (Boito)   1908
54413 RUSZKOWSKA/CUNEGO Trionfal di nuova speme "Tosca" (Puccini)   1908
54423 DE CASAS/RIZZO Sofferto hai tu "Mignon" (Thomas)   1908
54424 DE CASAS/CUNEGO Scena della danza "Carmen" (Bizet)   1908
54427 BATTAGLIOLI/BADINI Non sapete "La Traviata" (Verdi)   1908
54428 DOMAR/GIOVANELLI Sono andati "La Bohème" (Puccini)   1908
54429 GIORGINI/SANTORO/NICOLICCHIA O dolor "Manon" (Massenet)   1908
54430 BATTAGLIOLI/GHELARDINI Tardi si fa "Faust" (Gounod)   1908

54451 GOETZEN/PAOLI/SALVATI Questa è una ragna "Otello"(Verdi)(79)(1291AH)DA412
54757 VITTI Cantantibus orgius I. (Capocci) (7")   1902
54758 VITTI Cantantibus orgius II.(Capocci) (7")   1902
54760 COMANDINI Laudate pueri dominum I. (Capocci)   1902
54761 COMANDINI Laudate pueri dominum II.(Capocci)   1902
54763 VITTI Mi par d'udir ancora "I Pescatori di Perle" (Bizet)   1902
54764 MORESCHI Crucifixus (Rossini)   1902
54766 MORESCHI Domine, Domine   1902
54770 MORESCHI Et incarnatus est, et crucifixus   1902
54771 COMANDINI Laudate pueri dominum III. (Capocci)   1902
54773 MORESCHI Crucifixus (Rossini)   1902
54774 MORESCHI Pie Jesu (Laibach)   1902
54775 MORESCHI Hostias et preces (Terziani)   1902
54776 MORESCHI Preghiera (Tosti)   1902
54777 MORESCHI Ave Maria (Bach-Gounod)   1902
54780 MORESCHI/BOEZI/DADO/Cappella Sistina: Laudamus   1902

                  10" records : G. & T. BLACK LABEL. PRE-DOG issued 1908
                  DOG LABEL 1909. DOG LABEL 1910 : "LA VOCE del PADRONE"

54000 CESARANI/CORRADETTI Ah Mimi tu più "La Bohème" (Puccini)   1901
54001 ADAMI/CESARANI Sempre amar "Faust" (Gounod)   1901
54002 ADAMI/MONTECUCCHI Ci lasceremo "La Bohème" (Puccini)   1901
54003 MONTECUCCHI/CORRADETTI T'abborro "La Gioconda" (Ponchielli)   1901
54004 COLOMBATI/R.CASINI/PINTUCCI/CORRADETTI Bella figlia dell'amore
                                          "Rigoletto" (Verdi) 1901
54005 TEBRO/CESARANI/CORRADETTI Di geloso amor "Il Trovatore" (Verdi) 1901
54006 COLOMBATI/R.CASINI/CESARANI/CORRADETTI Chi mi frena
                              "Lucia di Lammermoor" (Donizetti)(7") 1901
54007 ADAMI/PINTUCCI/CORRADETTI Prendi, quest'è l'imagine "La Traviata"
                                                      (Verdi) 1901
54009 ADAMI/MONTECUCCHI Tardi si fa "Faust" (Gounod)   1901
54010 B.DE PASQUALI/P.DE PASQUALI Duetto "Ruy Blas" (Marchetti)   1901
54011 BONALDI/FANTONI Duetto dei piccioni "Mascotte" (Audran)   1903
54012 BONALDI/FANTONI Carme (duetto nap.)   issd.1903
54013 BONALDI/FANTONI Funiculì, Funiculà (Denza)   1903
54014 BONALDI/FANTONI La reale   issd.1903
54015 BONALDI/FANTONI Serenata "Boccaccio" (von Suppé)   issd.1903
54016 BONALDI/FANTONI Zigue   issd.1903
54017 BONALDI/FANTONI I cuochi   issd.1903
54018 HUGUET/DE SEGUROLA Leggiadre rondinelle "Mignon" (Thomas) pno. 1903
54019 HUGUET/MARISTANY/DE SEGUROLA Trio finale "Faust" (Gounod)   1903
54022 D'AVIGNY/CANTALAMESSA 'E tre d'a chiazza (canz.nap.)   issd.1903
54023 D'AVIGNY/CANTALAMESSA Il fischio   do.   issd.1903
54024 D'AVIGNY/CANTALAMESSA Purichi, purichia do.   issd.1903
54025 HUGUET/MARISTANY Duetto Atto III. "La Traviata" (Verdi)   1903
54026 HUGUET/MARISTANY Duetto Atto I. "La Bohème" (Puccini)   1903
54027 HUGUET/MARISTANY Duetto "Rigoletto" (Verdi)   1903
54028 HUGUET/MARISTANY Duetto Atto III. "La Bohème" (Puccini)   1903
54029 HUGUET/MARISTANY Duetto Atto II. "Gli Ugonotti" (Meyerbeer)   1903
54030 GRASSOT/DE SEGUROLA Duetto Valentina-Marcello I. "Gli Ugonotti"
                                                    (Meyerbeer) 1903
54031 GRASSOT/DE SEGUROLA Duetto Valentina-Marcello II. "Gli Ugonotti"
                                                    (Meyerbeer) 1903
54033 FERRANI/CERESOLI Duetto "Lohengrin" (Wagner) 8/03
54035 FERRANI/APOSTOLU Tardi si fa "Faust" (Gounod)   1903
54036 Coppia MECHERINI Duetto "La Società"   1903
54037 A.MECHERINI Tarantella (canz. nap.) 6/03

54038 A.MECHERINI Gli eleganti (canz. nap.) 6/03
54039 Coppia MECHERINI I campanari (duetto nap.) 6/03
54040 HUGUET/DE SEGUROLA Là ci darem la mano "Don Giovanni" (Mozart) pno.1903
54042 VENTURA/DE MICHALSKA Duetto Atto I. "Tosca" (Puccini) 9/05
54043 VENTURA/QUERCIA Ah Mimì tu più "La Bohème" (Puccini) pno.   1904
54044 LONGHI/VENTURA   Vieni, deh vieni "La Favorita" (Donizetti)   1904
54045 CITTI-LIPPI/BUCALO Duetto Nedda-Silvio "Pagliacci" (Leoncavallo) 1904
54046 RUSS/LONGHI/VENTURA Serenata (Terzetto) "Mefistofele" (Boito) 3/04
54047 TISCI-RUBINI/BUCALO Duetto "Ernani" (Verdi)   1904
54049 PINTUCCI/CORRADETTI Che invenzione "Il Barbiere di Siviglia" (Rossini)
                                                                 pno.1901
54050 PINTUCCI/CORRADETTI Pace, gioia "Il Barbiere di Siviglia" (Rossini)1901
54054 TRENTINI/TEDESCHI Noi sosteremo "Papa Martin" (Cagnoni)   pno.1904
54055 FINZI-MAGRINI/MATROIANI Ah dunque amiamoci "Rigoletto" (Verdi) pno.1904
54057 DEMHARTER/ISALBERTI Duetto delle ciliege "L'Amico Fritz" (Mascagni)
                                                                 pno.1904
54059 POLLINI/ACERBI Duetto d'amore "Lohengrin" (Wagner)   1904
54060 COLAZZA/CARONNA Solenne in quest'ora "La Forza del Destino" (Verdi)1905
54061 TRENTINI/CARONNA Duetto "Lucia di Lammermoor" (Donizetti)   1905
54062 TRENTINI/CAFFO Quell'uom dal fiero aspetto "Fra Diavolo" (Auber) 1905
54063 BERNACCHI/CARONNA Mira d'acerbe lagrime "Il Trovatore" (Verdi)(76) 1905
                                                                 (E134
54064 DE LUNA/CARONNA La vedremo "Ernani" (Verdi)   1905
54065 TRENTINI/MARTINEZ-PATTI Verranno a te "Lucia di Lammermoor"(Donizetti)
                                                                 pno.1905
54066 TRENTINI/CAFFO A consolarmi "Linda di Chamounix" (Donizetti)   1905
54068 MARTINEZ-PATTI/CARONNA Duetto della sfida "La Forza del Destino" (Verdi)
                                                                 1905
54069 D'AVIGNY/CANTALAMESSA La bella Maria (duetto nap.) (7")   1903
54073 D'AVIGNY/CANTALAMESSA Oje piccere (duetto nap.) (7")   issd.1903
54080 D'AVIGNY/CANTALAMESSA 'A cartolina (duetto nap.) (7")   issd.1903
54082 D'AVIGNY/CANTALAMESSA I vurria   (duetto nap.) (7")   issd.1903
54131 D'AVIGNY/CANTALAMESSA Voglio sisca (duetto nap.) (7")   issd.1903
54144 PINTUCCI/CORRADETTI Ah! che d'amore "Il Barbiere di Siviglia" (Rossini)
                                                                 (7") 9/05
54145 SALA/PREVE In arcion, cavalieri "Ernani" (Verdi) (7")   1906
54146 GIACOMELLI/MILERI Sì, fino all'ore estreme "Norma" (Bellini)(7") 1906
54147 MINOLFI/PREVE Suoni la tromba "I Puritani" (Bellini) (7")   1906
54150 MILERI/SANGIORGI Perigliarti ancor languente "Il Trovatore" (Verdi)(7")06
54151 ZACCARIA/LANZIROTTI Partite crudele "Rigoletto" (Verdi) (7")   1906
54152 GIACOMELLI/CIGADA/SILLICH Dunque l'onta di tutti "Un Ballo in Maschera"
                                                                 (Verdi)1906
54250 ESPOSITO/MARTINEZ-PATTI Pietoso al par del nume "La Favorita"
                                                  (Donizetti) pno. 1905
54251 FARELLI/MARTINEZ-PATTI Al suon dell'arpa angelica "Poliuto"(Donizetti)05
54252 FARELLI/MARTINEZ-PATTI Se l'angiol diletto "L'Africana" (Meyerbeer)1905
54253 TRENTINI/PEREA Esulti pure la barbara "L'Elisir d'amore" (Donizetti)1905
54254 TRENTINI/MARTINEZ-PATTI Sulla tomba "Lucia di Lammermoor" (Donizetti)05
54255 BERNACCHI/COLAZZA/CARONNA Odi tu "Un Ballo in Maschera" (Verdi)(79)1905
54256 TRENTINI/MARTINEZ-PATTI/STOPPA Prendi quest'è l'imagine "La Traviata"
                                                  (Verdi)   1905
54257 TRENTINI/MARTINEZ-PATTI Un dì felice eterea "La Traviata" (Verdi) 1905
54258 TRENTINI/STOPPA Morrò la mia memoria "La Traviata" (Verdi)   1905
54259 ESPOSITO/COLAZZA Ai nostri monti "Il Trovatore" (Verdi)(76) 1905. E119
54260 BERNACCHI/DE LUNA/COLAZZA Oro quant'oro "Ernani" (Verdi)(79)   1905
54261 BERNACCHI/COLAZZA/CARONNA Di geloso amor "Il Trovatore" (Verdi)(76)1905
54262 TRENTINI/ACERBI Tornami dir "Don Pasquale" (Donizetti)   1905

54263 ESPOSITO/COLAZZA Mal reggendo "Il Trovatore" (Verdi)(75)   1905
54265 DE ANGELIS/CIGADA Vivra contende il giubilo "Il Trovatore" (Verdi)
                                                            (76) 1905. E134
54267 BOVI/MARTINEZ-PATTI Mal reggendo "Il Trovatore" (Verdi)   1905
54268 GIACOMELLI/MARTINEZ-PATTI/PIGNATARO Tu sei Ernani "Ernani" (Verdi)(79)
                                                                         1906
54269 RIZZINI/TORRE Amami Alfredo "La Traviata" (Verdi)   1906
54270 RIZZINI/PEREA Parigi o cara "La Traviata" (Verdi)   1906
54271 RIZZINI/MINOLFI Si vendetta "Rigoletto" (Verdi)   1906
54272 RIZZINI/PEREA Brindisi "La Traviata" (Verdi)   1906
54273 RIZZINI/PEREA Un dì felice eterea "La Traviata" (Verdi)   1906
54274 GIACOMELLI/MARTINEZ-PATTI/PREVE Deh non volerli vittime "Norma"
                                                              (Bellini) 1906
54278 MARTINEZ-PATTI/PREVE Non sai tu che d'un giusto "La Favorita"
                                                            (Donizetti) 1906
54279 PEREA/A.PINI-CORSI Pace e gioia "Il Barbiere di Siviglia" (Rossini) 06
54280 POLESE/A.PINI-CORSI Aspetta, aspetta cara sposina "Don Pasquale"
                                                            (Donizetti) 1906
54281 PASSERI/A.PINI-CORSI Io son ricco "L'Elisir d'amore" (Donizetti) 1906
54282 PASSERI/A.PINI-CORSI Quanto amore "L'Elisir d'amore" (Donizetti) 1906
54283 MARTINEZ-PATTI/PIGNATARO Solenne in quest'ora "La Forza del Destino"
                                                              (Verdi)   1906
54284 GIACOMELLI/MARTINEZ-PATTI Non sai tu "Un Ballo in Maschera" (Verdi) 06
54285 MINOLFI/PREVE Esaltiam la tua potenza "Linda di Chamounix" (Donizetti)
                                                              pno. 1906
54286 A.PINI-CORSI/PREVE Del mondo i disinganni "La Forza del Destino"
                                                              (Verdi) 06
54287 MARTINEZ-PATTI/PIGNATARO/PREVE Terzetto "Faust" (Gounod) 1906. E125
54288 MARTINEZ-PATTI/PREVE Io voglio il piacer "Faust" (Gounod)   1906
54289 RIZZINI/ZACCARI/PREVE O del ciel "Faust" (Gounod)   1906
54290 GIACOMELLI/MILERI Mira o Norma "Norma" (Bellini)   1906
54291 GRISI/SANGIORGI/OTTOBONI/SALA Finale Atto primo "Ernani" (Verdi)(80)06
54292 GRISI/CIGADA/OTTOBONI Vieni meco "Ernani" (Verdi)   1906
54295 LARA/MILERI Vieni, ah vieni "La Favorita" (Donizetti)   1906
54296 HUGUET/LARA Sempre libera "La Traviata" (Verdi)   1906
54297 MILERI/MINOLFI Ah l'alto ardor "La Favorita" (Donizetti)   1906
54298 HUGUET/LARA/DE LUNA Trio finale "Faust" (Gounod)   1906. E125
54299 CORSI/A.PINI-CORSI Vieni cara sposina "Don Pasquale" (Donizetti) 1906
54300 MILERI/LARA Io ti chiedea "Mignon" (Thomas)   1906
54301 BADINI/A.PINI-CORSI Un fuoco insolito "Don Pasquale" (Donizetti) 1906
54302 HUGUET/CIGADA/GRISI/OTTOBONI Di che fulgor "Un Ballo in Maschera"
                                                        (Verdi)(80) 1906
54303 GRISI/LARA T'amo, sì t'amo "Un Ballo in Maschera" (Verdi)   1906
54304 CORSI/BADINI Vado, corro "Don Pasquale" (Donizetti)   1906
54305 CORSI/BADINI Bravo, bravo "Don Pasquale" (Donizetti)   1906
54306 HUGUET/MINOLFI Veglia o donna. "Rigoletto" (Verdi)   1906
54307 HUGUET/MINOLFI Piangi fanciulla "Rigoletto" (Verdi)   1906
54308 MINOLFI/NICCOLINI Della vendetta "Rigoletto" (Verdi)   1906
54309 HUGUET/LANZIROTTI Addio, addio "Rigoletto" (Verdi)   1906
54310 HUGUET/LANZIROTTI Dunque amiamoci "Rigoletto" (Verdi)   1906
54311 FARRAR/JORN E il sol dell'anima "Rigoletto" (Verdi)(4720h)   1907
54312 LARA/BADINI All'idea di quel metallo "Il Barbiere di Siviglia"
                                                            (Rossini)   1907
54313 LARA/BADINI Numero quindici "Il Barbiere di Siviglia" (Rossini) 1907
54314 HUGUET/BADINI Dunque io son "Il Barbiere di Siviglia" (Rossini) 1907
54317 GRISI/LARA Pronti i destrieri "La Forza del Destino" (Verdi)   1907
54318 GRISI/DE SEGUROLA Se voi scacciate "La Forza del Destino" (Verdi) 1907
54319 GRISI/DE SEGUROLA Sull'alba il piede "La Forza del Destino"(Verdi)1907

54320 BRAMBILLA/CODOLINI/ACERBI/SILLICH Permettereste a me "Faust" (Gounod)
(77) 1907. E122
54321 GRISI/MILERI Deh con te li prendi "Norma" (Bellini)   1907
54322 DE ANGELIS/SANGIORGI Ah! crudele! "Norma" (Bellini)   1907
54323 GIACOMELLI/CODOLINI/COLAZZA Ah non tremar "Norma" (Bellini)   1907
54324 ACERBI/MINOLFI O sole più rapido "Lucia di Lammermoor" (Donizetti) 07
54325 BRAMBILLA/CIGADA Il pallor funesto "Lucia di Lammermoor" (Donizetti)07
54326 BRAMBILLA/ACERBI/CIGADA/SILLICH Maledizione "Lucia di Lammermoor"
(Donizetti)1907
54327 CODOLINI/CIGADA/SILLICH Ah parenta il furore "La Favorita"(Donizetti)07
54328 CAPPIELLO/ACERBI/CIGADA Orsù Fernando "La Favorita" (Donizetti) 1907
54329 BRAMBILLA/A.& G.PINI-CORSI/SCIPIONI E rimasto là "Don Pasquale"
(Donizetti)1907
54330 SCIPIONI/A.PINI-CORSI Cheti, cheti "Don Pasquale" (Donizetti)   1907
54331 GRISI/DE SEGUROLA Duetto Valentina-Marcello "Gli Ugonotti" (Meyerbeer)
1907
54333 MELIS/MINOLFI Or se l'antico palito "Jana" (Virgilio)   1907
54335 JOANNA/MINOLFI Compar Alfio "Cavalleria Rusticana" (Mascagni)1907.E127
54336 JOANNA/MINOLFI Ad essi non perdono "Cavalleria Rusticana" (Mascagni)
(77) 1907.E127
54337 JOANNA/RAMBELLI Finale dell'Opera "Cavalleria Rusticana" (Mascagni) 07
54338 HUGUET/CIGADA/G.PINI-CORSI Arlecchino-Colombina "Pagliacci"
(Leoncavallo)(77)1907. E128
54345 SALVADOR/MINOLFI Duetto Ortruda-Telramondo "Lohengrin" (Wagner) 1907
54346 HUGUET/CIGADA Se tradirmi tu potrai "Lucia di Lammermoor" (Donizetti)
1907
54347 HUGUET/SALVADOR/SILLICH/CIGADA O figlio d'Inghilterra
"Un Ballo in Maschera" (Verdi)1907
54348 HUGUET/BADINI Vado, corro "Don Pasquale" (Donizetti)   1907
54349 JOANNA/A.PINI-CORSI Scena della finestra "La Forza del Destino"(Verdi)
1907
54350 HUGUET/A.& G.PINI-CORSI/BADINI Guarda Don Bartolo
"Il Barbiere di Siviglia" (Rossini) 1907
54351 HUGUET/A.& G.PINI-CORSI/BADINI Son tradito "Don Pasquale" (Donizetti)
1907
54352 G.PINI-CORSI/SILLICH Io voglio il piacer "Faust" (Gounod)(77)1907.E120
54353 SALVADOR/ISCHIERDO Lassù nella montagna "Carmen" (Bizet) 1907. E115
54354 SALVADOR/CIGADA Se tu m'ami "Carmen" (Bizet)   1907. E118
54355 ISCHIERDO/CIGADA Ho nome Escamillo "Carmen" (Bizet)(80) 1907. E117
54356 HUGUET/SALVADOR/CIGADA Canzone del Toreador "Carmen" (Bizet)(10516b)
1907. E115
54361 BUTTI/PASSERI/ALEXINA Un buon consiglio "Carmen" (Bizet) 1908. E119
54362 BUTTI/PASSERI/ALEXINA E nostro affar "Carmen" (Bizet)   1908. E117
54363 BADINI/A.PINI-CORSI Grazie al ciel "Fra Diavolo" (Auber)   1908
54364 PASSERI/A.PINI-CORSI Vedi o cara "Crispino e la comare" (Ricci) 1908
54365 PASSERI/A.PINI-CORSI Se trovasti una comare "Crispino e la comare"
(Ricci) 1908
54366 MALATESTA/A.PINI-CORSI Or che in ciel "Campanello" (Donizetti)   1908
54367 MALATESTA/A.PINI-CORSI Ho una bella "Campanello" (Donizetti)   1908
54368 PASSERI/ARMENTANO Morro la mie memoria "La Traviata" (Verdi)   1908
54369 PASSERI/G.PINI-CORSI A consolarmi "Linda di Chamounix" (Donizetti)1908
54376 MARCHETTI/TESSARI Duetto dei baci "Geisha" (Jones)   1908
54377 D'ARCO/ASCENZI Di Molly qual fia la sorte "Geisha" (Jones)   1908
54378 MARCHETTI/TESSARI/TANI Al vedere tal sorpresa "Geisha" (Jones)   1908
54379 ASCENZI/FAVI Vendita all'asta di Mimosa "Geisha" (Jones)   1908
54380 HUGUET/MINOLFI Piangi fanciulla "Rigoletto" (Verdi)   1908
54381 CIOTTI/TESSARI Quand'ero bambinella "Geisha" (Jones)   1908
54382 PASSERI/G.PINI-CORSI/BADINI Quest'opera ascondi "Fra Diavolo" (Auber)08

54383 PASSERI/G.PINI-CORSI Mio buon Lorenzo "Fra Diavolo" (Auber) 1908
54387 CIGADA/QUINZI-TAPERGI Charley! Olger! "Chatterton" (Leoncavallo)1908
54388 SANTORO/GRANADOS/CIGADA Uh! l'orso s'allontana "Chatterton"
                                              (Leoncavallo) 1908
54389 DE FRATE/CIGADA/QUINZI-TAPERGI Lord Clifford qui desidera
                                      "Chatterton" (Leoncavallo) 1908
54390 GRANADOS/CIGADA/FEDERICI/QUINZI-TAPERGI Vedeste Mistress Clark?
                                      "Chatterton" (Leoncavallo) 1908
54391 DE FRATE/SANTORO/G.PINI-CORSI/QUINZI-TAPERGI John, dite che ci
                              apprestino "Chatterton" (Leoncavallo) 1908
54392 SANTORO/GRANADOS Son certo ch'ei dorme "Chatterton" (Leoncavallo)
                                                            1908
54393 SANTORO/GRANADOS La, la presso quel tavolo "Chatterton" (Leoncavallo)
                                                            1908
54394 GRANADOS/CIGADA E finita mio Dio "Chatterton" (Leoncavallo) 1908
54395 GRANADOS/CIGADA Che parli mai "Chatterton" (Leoncavallo) 1908
54396 GRANADOS/CIGADA Ah! mistress! "Chatterton" (Leoncavallo) 1908
54400 DOMAR/BADINI/GIOVANELLI/NICOLICCHIA/MANSUETO Quintetto Atto II.
                                      "La Bohème" (Puccini) 1908
54402 BADINI/NICOLICCHIA Serenata "Boccaccio" (von Suppé) 1908
54403 NUVOLERI/BADINI/NICOLICCHIA Terzetto dei ladroni "La Gran Via"
                                      (Valverde) 1908
54409 RAKOWSKY/BADINI Mira d'acerbe lagrime "Il Trovatore" (Verdi) 1908
54415 MURINO/CUNEGO Pur ti riveggo "Aida" (Verdi) 1908
54416 NULLI/DE GREGORIO/SALA Questa è Mimi "La Bohème" (Puccini) 1908
54417 BRONZONI/DE GREGORIO Sono andati? "La Bohème" (Puccini) 1908
54418 DA GRADI/BADINI O Mimi, tu più "La Bohème" (Puccini) 1908
54419 FREZZI/LARA Verranno a te "Lucia di Lammermoor" (Donizetti) 1908
54420 FREZZI/LARA Un dì felice eterea "La Traviata" (Verdi) 1908
54421 FREZZI/LARA Parigi o cara "La Traviata" (Verdi) 1908
54422 MUSSINI/MOLINARI Padre nostro "Guglielmo Ratcliff" 1908
54425 GALBIERO/FABRIS Apri un poco "Eidelberga mia "(Pacchierotti) 1908
54426 DE GREGORIO/MOLINARI Folletto, Folletto "Mefistofele" (Boito) 1908
54431 GIOVANELLI/FEDERICI/QUINZI-TAPERGI Che fate qui? "Faust" (Gounod)
                                                            1908
54432 MURINO/CUNEGO Morir, o ciel, non dirmelo "Il Guareny" (Gomez) 1908
54433 CASSANI/FEDERICI Piangi fanciulla "Rigoletto" (Verdi) 1/11
54434 SANIPOLI/LARA Prendi l'anel "La Sonnambula" (Bellini) 2/11
54435 BOCCOLINI/DE GREGORIO No, più nobil tu sei "Adriana Lecouvreur"
                                      (Cilea) 3/11
54436 DE GREGORIO/MOLINARI Fin da stanotte "Mefistofele" (Boito) 3/11
54437 LOTTI/CONTI Già nella notte densa "Otello" (Verdi) 3/11
54438 CONTI/BADINI Enzo Grimaldo "La Gioconda" (Ponchielli) 4/11
54439 CONTI/BADINI O grido di quest'anima "La Gioconda" (Ponchielli) 4/11
54440 BADINI/MANSUETO La vedremo "Ernani" (Verdi) 5/11
54441 GRAMAGNA/GALLI Qui chiamata m'avete "La Gioconda" (Ponchielli) 5/11
54442 GRAMAGNA/GALLI Morir...morir...è troppo orribile "La Gioconda"
                                      (Ponchielli) 5/11
54443 POPOVICI/DAVI/MAGGI Tu sei Ernani "Ernani" (Verdi) 10/11
54444 CUNEGO/MOLINARI Solingo, errante misero "Ernani" (Verdi) 10/11
54445 HUGUET/GIOVANELLI Sulla tomba "Lucia di Lammermoor" (Donizetti)10/11
54446 CHIESA/GILBERTI/GOETZEN Introduzione al Quadro II. "La Bohème"
                                      (Puccini) 11/11
54447 BOCCOLINI/COMIDA Quando me'n vo "La Bohème" (Puccini) 11/11
54449 SALVATI/CANALI Giovinotto ehi! "L'Elisir d'amore" (Donizetti) 2/12

54450 MANGINI/CANALI Una tenera occhiatina "L'Elisir d'amore" (Donizetti)2/12
54454 PAVONI/TOMMASINI Sei l'angiol diletto "L'Africana" (Meyerbeer)
54455 BONETTI/SALVATI Vieni, ah vieni "La Favorita" (Donizetti) 1/12
54457 SALVATI/CANALI/MANGINI Adina credimi, te ne scongiuro
                                        "L'Elisir d'amore"(Donizetti) 2/13
54459 PAVONI/PASSERI/GILBERTI Fior di giaggiolo "Cavalleria Rusticana"
                                             (Mascagni) 1/12
54460 PASSERI/DE GREGORIO Dimmi se credi, Enrico "Mefistofele" (Boito) 1/12
54461 LOTTI/CONTI Pur ti riveggo "Aida" (Verdi) 3/12
54462 LOTTI/CONTI Sì, fuggiam da queste mura "Aida" (Verdi) 3/12
54467 CUNEGO/BETTONI Sì: corre voce "Aida" (Verdi) 10/12
54468 BESALÙ/CONTI Vicino a te "Andrea Chenier" (Giordano) 6/12
54469 LOTTI/GRAMAGNA Fu la sorte dell'armi "Aida" (Verdi) 10/12
54470 MARTINENGO/TISCI-RUBINI Leggiadre rondinello "Mignon" (Thomas) 12/12
54471 SOLLOHUB/BOTTA Amaro sol per te "Tosca" (Puccini) 5/13
54473 DE GREGORIO O dolci mani "Tosca" (Puccini) 5/13
54474 ZIZOLFI/CASTELLANI Ai nostri monti "Il Trovatore" (Verdi) 5/13
54475 SALVATI/FERRETTI Numero quindici "Il Barbiere di Siviglia" (Rossini)6/13
54476 BARBIERI/BADINI Mira d'acerbe lagrime "Il Trovatore" (Verdi) 11/13
54478 ZIZOLFI Stride la vampa "Il Trovatore" (Verdi) 11/13
54479 CASINI/BADINI D'acqua aspergimi "Thaïs" (Massenet) 8/13
54481 DE GREGORIO/PEREIRA E il sol dell'anima "Rigoletto"(Verdi) 8/13
54482 PEREIRA/MAGGI Deh non parlare al misero "Rigoletto" (Verdi) 8/13
54483 FERRETTI/SCALFARO Un bacio rendimi "Educande di Sorrento" (Usiglio)9/13
54521 ADAMI/CESARANI Miserere "Il Trovatore" (Verdi) 1900/1
54526 CESARANI Per te d'immenso giubilo "Lucia di Lammermoor" (Donizetti)1901
54653 SALA Per te d'immenso giubilo "Lucia di Lammermoor" (Donizetti) 2/06
54687 TANI Di gioia e di contento "Geisha" (Jones)

                              7" records : BERLINER
54070 CORRADETTI/FRANCHI Duetto dei briganti "Fra Diavolo" (Auber) 1901
54075 ADAMI/MONTECUCCHI Sempre amar "Faust" (Gounod) 1900
54077 ADAMI/MONTECUCCHI Parigi o cara "La Traviata" (Verdi) 1900
54081 D'AVIGNY/CANTALAMESSA Storia Naturale 1900
54084 GRIPPA/CAFFETTO Tardi si fa "Faust" (Gounod) 20/VII/1900
54085 MOREO/GRIPPA Fiero sangue d'Aragona "Ernani" (Verdi) 1900
54086 VIALE/CAFFETTO O Mimi tu più "La Bohème" (Puccini) 1900
54087 VIALE/CAFFETTO Quando la soglie saterne 1900
54088 VIALE/CAFFETTO Il fischio (The Whistler) 1900
54089 VIALE/CAFFETTO Verbena. Parodea "Carmen" 1900
54090 VIALE/CAFFETTO Do, re, mi 1900
54091 VIALE/CAFFETTO Carme (Napolitana) (De Curtis) 1900
54092 VIALE/CAFFETTO Caccurteillo (Napolitana) 1900
54093 VIALE/CAFFETTO Il cuschi do. 1900
54094 VIALE/CAFFETTO Pura siccome "Don Pasquale" (Donizetti) 1900
54095 ADAMI/CORRADETTI Bella voi siete "La Traviata" (Verdi) 1900
54096 ADAMI/CORRADETTI Duetto "Zigne" 1900
54097 ADAMI/CORRADETTI Mira d'acerbe "Ernani" (Verdi) 1900
54098 GALAN/MOREO Se tu m'ami "Carmen" (Bizet) 1900
54099 GALAN/MOREO Ah l'alto ardor "La Favorita" (Donizetti) 1900
54100 CESARANI/CORRADETTI Ho nome Escamillo "Carmen" (Bizet) 1900
54101 ADAMI/CORRADETTI Dite alla giovine "La Traviata" (Verdi) 1900
54102 CESARANI/CORRADETTI Una suora mi lasciasti "La Forza del Destino"
                                             (Verdi) 1900
54103 CESARANI/CORRADETTI Chi mi frena "Lucia di Lammermoor" (Donizetti)1900
54104 CESARANI/CORRADETTI Ah Mimi tu più "La Bohème" (Puccini) 1900
54105 CESARANI/CORRADETTI Solenne in quest'ora "La Forza del Destino"(Verdi)00

```
54106 CESARANI/FRANCHI     Cara luce soave  "La Favorita" (Donizetti)        1900
54107 CESARANI/FRANCHI     Ho nome Escamillo  "Carmen" (Bizet)              1900
54108 GALAN/CESARANI       Pur ti riveggo  "Aida" (Verdi)                   1900
54109 GALAN/CESARANI       Ah tu devi rivere                                1900
54110 GALAN/CESARANI       Fia vero lasciarti                               1900
54111 GALAN/CESARANI       Mal reggendo  "Il Trovatore" (Verdi)             1900
54112 GALASSI/CESARANI     Vieni, vieni  "La Favorita" (Donizetti)          1900
54113 GALASSI/CESARANI     Miserere  "Il Trovatore" (Verdi)                 1900
54114 CESARANI/CORRADETTI  T'abborro  "La Gioconda" (Ponchielli)            1900
54115 CESARANI/ADAMI       Sempre amar  "Faust" (Gounod)                    1900
54116 CESARANI/ADAMI       La tua Santuzza  "Cavalleria Rusticana" (Mascagni)1900
54117 CESARANI/ADAMI       Tardi si fa  "Faust" (Gounod)                    1900
54118 ADAMI/FRANCHI        Scena della chiesa  "Faust" (Gounod)             1900
54119 ADAMI/CORRADETTI     Ad essi non perdono                              1900
54120 ADAMI/CORRADETTI     Un bacio rendimi  "Educande di Sorrento" (Usiglio)1900
54121 ADAMI/CORRADETTI     T'arresta  "La Gioconda" (Ponchielli)            1900
54122 GALAN/FRANCHI        Invan tu piangi  "La Gioconda" (Ponchielli)      1900
54123 CORRADETTI/FRANCHI   Suoni la tromba  "I Puritani" (Bellini)          1900
54124 GALAN/MOREO          Rivedrai le foreste  "Aida" (Verdi)              1900
54125 ADAMI/CESARANI/CORRADETTI  Su una pudica vergine                      1900
54126 ADAMI/CESARANI/CORRADETTI  Di geloso amor  "Il Trovatore" (Verdi) 1900
54127 GALAN/CESARANI       Ai nostri monti  "Il Trovatore" (Verdi)          1900
54132 D'AVIGNY/CANTALAMESSA  Votete a Cca Votete a Lla                      1900
54133 D'AVIGNY/CANTALAMESSA  Donna Fifi (Napolitana)                        1900
54134 D'AVIGNY/CANTALAMESSA  'A cura 'E mamma   do.                         1900
54135 D'AVIGNY/CANTALAMESSA  Coccotte e studente (Napolitana)               1900
54136 D'AVIGNY/CANTALAMESSA  Il Clarinetto                                  1900
54137 ADAMI/CORRADETTI     L'ho lasciato al gioco  "Manon" (Massenet)       1900
54139 D'AVIGNY/CANTALAMESSA  I viveurs                                      1900
54140 GROSSI/CAFFETTO      Vieni, vieni  "La Favorita" (Donizetti)  28/VIII/1900
54141 D'AVIGNY/CANTALAMESSA  Ammore e mo (Napolitana)                       1900
54142 D'AVIGNY/CANTALAMESSA  Botta e risposta   do.                         1900
54143 D'AVIGNY/CANTALAMESSA  Bella e tutta core (Napolitana)                1900
54500 MALESCI  Brindisi  "Cavalleria Rusticana" (Mascagni)                  1900
54508 MOREO   Tu puoi la spada infrangere  "Faust" (Gounod)                 1900
54515 CORRADETTI  Ademastor  "L'Africana" (Meyerbeer)                       1901
54525 ADAMI/CESARANI/CORRADETTI  O sommo Carlo  "Ernani" (Verdi)       1900/1
```

10" records : RED & PINK LABEL

```
7-54000 DESTINN/GILLY  My Homeland - Folk song (Czech) 1914. DJ101 ?
7-54003 BORI/McCORMACK  O soave fanciulla  "La Bohème" (Puccini)(A14658) 1914
                                                         DA379. Buff
7-54005 DESTINN/GILLY  My Homeland - Folk song (Czech)(A14756) 1914. DJ101.Buff
7-54006 GLUCK/CARUSO  Brindisi; Libismo "La Traviata" (Verdi)(79)(A14729)
                                                      1914. DJ100.Buff
7-54007 DESTINN/GILLY  The Wedding - Folk song (Czech)(A14754) 1914.DJ101.Buff
7-54011 GALLI-CURCI/DE LUCA  Piangi fanciulla  "Rigoletto" (Verdi)(A21975)
                                                         1918. DA381
7-54012 FARRAR/DE LUCA  Il bacio  "Zazà" (Leoncavallo)(A23586) 1920. DA209.Buff
7-54014 BARTOLOMASI/DE TURA  Pur ti riveggo  "Aida" (Verdi)
7-54015 GARRISON/WERRENRATH  Là ci darem  "Don Giovanni" (Mozart)(80)(A23741)
                                                         1920. DA513
7-54018 HAYES/BATTISTINI  Sì vendetta  "Rigoletto" (Verdi)(BA8)21.V.1921.DA189
                                                         VA65
7-54020 GARELLI/SCHIPA  Un dì felice eterea  "La Traviata" (Verdi) 4/23
7-54023 DE' MURO/VIGANO  Pur ti riveggo  "Aida" (Verdi)(BE434) 1923. DA171
```

7-54026 DE' MURO/OLTRABELLA Ora soave "Andrea Chenier" (Giordano)(BE978)
                                             1923. DA495. VA52
7-54027 DE' MURO/OLTRABELLA Vicino a te "Andrea Chenier"(Giordano)(BE979)
                                             1923. DA495. VA52
7-54028 PINZA/D'ALESSIO Non sai tu "La Favorita" (Donizetti)(BE1216)
                                             1924. DA566. VA70
7-54029 CAPSIR/LULLI Soffriva nel pianto - I. "Lucia di Lammermoor"
                                  (Donizetti) 1925. DA679
7-54030 CAPSIR/CINISELLI Addio, addio, speranza ed anima "Rigoletto" (Verdi)
                                             1925. DA619
7-54034 GALLI-CURCI/SCHIPA Un dì felice eterea "La Traviata" (Verdi)
                                      (A30907) 1924. DA711
7-54035 GALLI-CURCI/SCHIPA Parigi o cara "La Traviata" (Verdi)
                                      (A30908) 1924. DA711
7-54036 PINZA/GIORGINI Ebben? Che ti pare "Faust" (Gounod) 11/25-DA695.VA70
7-54037 CAPSIR/NOTO Soffriva nel pianto - II. "Lucia di Lammermoor"
                                  (Donizetti) 1925. DA679

10" records : BLACK LABEL

7-54004 MURPHY/WERRENRATH Ah Mimì tu più "La Bohème" (Puccini)(80)(A14037)
                                             1913. E105
7-54008 Coppia LES SCALA Carmela'a Luciana (Califano-Segre)   8/21
7-54009 Coppia LES SCALA La mietitura (Mirelli)   8/21
7-54019 ARDITO/TORRE La Spagnola (Di Chiara)   9/22
7-54021 Duetto AMAULI Avventure al buio (Amauli)   4/24
7-54022 Coppia VOCCIA Stornelli al vento (Mario)   4/24
7-54024 Coppia DE NUNZIO Pacchianella (De Nunzio)   4/24
7-54025 DE NUNZIO/GENTILE Miez'e grade (Di Palma-Falvo)   4/24
7-54033 Papa RICCARDI e Compagnia 'A Canzone 'e Capo d'Anno (in Napoletano)
                                    acc.di mandolino e chitarra 1/25
                (Duetto con DE LAURENTIIS e Compagnia) Pt.I.

12" records : G. & T. RED & PINK LABEL. PRE-DOG issued 1908
DOG LABEL 1909. DOG LABEL 1910 : "LA VOCE del PADRONE"

054026 CARELLI/SAMMARCO Scena della Susanna al bagno "Lorenza" (Mascheroni)
                                             pno. 1904
054027 STORCHIO/ZENATELLO E qui con te il mio destin "Siberia" (Giordano)04
054028 CARELLI/SAMMARCO Già mi dicon venal "Tosca" (Puccini) pno. 1904
054034 CARELLI/VENTURA Morte di Fedora "Fedora" (Giordano) 1904
054039 DE LUCA/G.PINI-CORSI/GENNARI/POZZI-CAMOLLA Mattinata "Siberia"
                                      (Giordano) pno.1904
054043 BONINSEGNA/DE LUCIA Tardi si fa "Faust" (Gounod)(213m)(77) pno.1904
054044 BONINSEGNA/VALLS Il ciel dei nostri amori "Aida" (Verdi)(77)(215m)1904
054062 BONINSEGNA/CIGADA Da quel dì "Ernani" (Verdi)   1905
054070 CARUSO/SCOTTI Solenne in quest'ora "La Forza del Destino" (Verdi)(82)
                                    (A3179) 1906.DM105.Pale Gn.
054071 DE GOGORZA/EAMES Là ci darem "Don Giovanni" (Mozart)(A3173)   1906
                                           IRCC 20. Buff
054072 DE GOGORZA/EAMES Dove prende. "Flauto Magico" (Mozart)(A3171-3) 1906
                                           DK 121 Buff
054074 SEMBRICH/SCOTTI Vado, corro "Don Pasquale" (Donizetti)(77-78)(A3181)Bf.
                                      1906. DB589   VB29
054080 DE LUCIA/A.PINI-CORSI All'idea di quel metallo "Il Barbiere di Siviglia"
                                  (Rossini)(77)(619c) 1906. DB388
054081 DE LUCIA/HUGUET Parigi o cara "La Traviata" (Verdi)(77)(620c)1906.DB368
054082 DE LUCIA/HUGUET Non hai compreso "I Pescatori di Perle" (Bizet)(621c)
                                     1906.DB570.VB34.IRCC64

054083 DE LUCIA/HUGUET/A.PINI-CORSI Ah quel colpo in aspettato   (pno)
                "Il Barbiere di Siviglia" (Rossini)(77)(630c) 1906. DB388.VB1
• 054084 DE LUCIA/HUGUET E il sol dell'anima "Rigoletto" (Verdi)(77)pno.1906
                                                        (638c) DB368
054085 CUCINI/ROSSI Leggiadre rondinelle "Mignon" (Thomas)   1906
054086 CUCINI/CORSI Vieni al mio castel "Lohengrin" (Wagner)   1906
054097 BONINSEGNA/COLAZZA/DE SEGUROLA Deh non volerli vittime
                                                "Norma" (Bellini) 1906
054098 BONINSEGNA/ISCHIERDO Non sei tu "Un Ballo in Maschera" (Verdi) 1906
• 054100 RUFFO/GALVANY Piangi fanciulla "Rigoletto" (Verdi)   1907 DB177
054101 RUFFO/GALVANY Dite alla giovine "La Traviata" (Verdi)(79) 1907.DB176
◦ 054102 RUFFO/ISCHIERDO Le minaccie "La Forza del Destino" (Verdi)(79)07.DB177
054103 BATTISTINI/CORSI Da quel dì "Ernani" (Verdi)(876c)1907.DB205.Orange
• 054104 BATTISTINI/CORSI Là ci darem "Don Giovanni" (Mozart)(882c)   1907
                                                DB228.VB18.Orange
054105 BATTISTINI/SILLICH La vedremo o veglio audace "Ernani" (Verdi)(879½c)
                                                1907.DB200.VB23.Orange
054106 BATTISTINI/CORSI Vieni meco sol di rose "Ernani" (Verdi)(880c) 1907
                                                DB198.VB23.Orange
• 054107 BATTISTINI/CORSI/COLAZZA/SILLICH O sommo Carlo "Ernani" (Verdi)(881c)
                                                1907.DB205.Orange
054109 BONINSEGNA/COLAZZA O dolce volutta "Ruy Blas" (Marchetti)(854c)07.VB28
054110 GALVANY/GIORGINI Chiedi all'aura lusinghiera "L'Elisir d'amore"
                                                (Donizetti) 1907.IRCC
• 054111 GALVANY/GIORGINI Tornami dir che m'ami "Don Pasquale" (Donizetti)
                                                (549i) 1907 VB26
◦ 054112 GALVANY/GIORGINI Son geloso dello zeffiro "La Sonnambula" (Bellini)
                                                (548i) 1907 VB26
› 054117 ABOTT/HOMER/CARUSO/SCOTTI Bella figlia "Rigoletto" (Verdi)(80)(A4259)
                                                1907. DO100. Pale Blue
054126 FARRAR/HOMER Tutti i fior "Madama Butterfly" (Puccini)(81)(A4260)
                                                1907. DK125. Buff
054127 CARUSO/SCOTTI Ah Mimi tu più "La Bohème" (Puccini)(82)(A4315)1907
                                                DM105.Pale Green
054128 MELBA/GILIBERT Per valli, per boschi (Blangini)(80)(A4347) 1907.DM117
                                                Pale Green
054129 MELBA/CARUSO O soave fanciulla "La Bohème" (Puccini)(82)(A4326-1)
                                                1907. Pale Green
054134 CARUSO/ANCONA Del tempio al limitar "I Pescatori di Perle" (Bizet)(82)?
                                                (A4327)1907.DK116.Pale Gn.
054135 ANCONA/JOURNET Suoni la tromba "I Puritani" (Bellini) 1907. HRS 1003
054141 RAMBELLI/DE TURA Addio alla madre "Cavalleria Rusticana" (Mascagni)
                                                (77)(1185c)1907
054142 JOANNA/DE TURA Duetto I. "Cavalleria Rusticana" (Mascagni)   1907
054143 JOANNA/DE TURA Duetto II."Cavalleria Rusticana" (Mascagni)   1907
054144 DE TURA/CIGADA A voi tutti salute "Cavalleria Rusticana" (Mascagni)
                                                (77) 1907
054156 PAOLI/G.PINI-CORSI/CIGADA/ROSCI Un grande spettacolo "Pagliacci"
                                                (Leoncavallo)(76)   1907
054157 PAOLI/HUGUET/G.PINI-CORSI/CIGADA Aitalo Signore! "Pagliacci"
                                                (Leoncavallo)(76)   1907
054158 PAOLI/HUGUET/G.PINI-CORSI/BADINI/CIGADA Finale "Pagliacci"
                                                (Leoncavallo)(77)   1907
054159 JOANNA/PAOLI Miserere "Il Trovatore" (Verdi)   1907
054160 PAOLI/CIGADA Che finger tento "Guglielmo Tell" (Rossini)   1907
054161 PAOLI/CIGADA/SILLICH Troncar suoi   "Guglielmo Tell" (Rossini)1907
054162 PAOLI/HUGUET/SALVADOR/CIGADA· Mia tu sei "Carmen" (Bizet)   1907
054164 NIELSEN/CONSTANTINO E il sol dell'anima "Rigoletto" (Verdi)   1907

054169 PICCOLETTI/DE TURA Invitato a qui seguirmi "La Traviata" (Verdi) 1907
054171 HUGUET/DE LUCIA Cessaron i canti alfin "Lohengrin" (Wagner)(1170¼c)
                                                    1907. DB237
• 054172 HUGUET/DE LUCIA La tua madre "Carmen" (Bizet)(77)(1172c)07.DB359.VB34
054173 HUGUET/DE LUCIA Tardi si fa "Faust" (Gounod)(1173c)pno. 1907. DB570
054174 PASSERI/PAOLI Duetto finale "Carmen" (Bizet)   1907
054175 HUGUET/DE LUCIA Mai devi domandarmi "Lohengrin" (Wagner)1907.IRCC 104
                                                    (1171c)DB237
054178 DAVID/SCAMPINI Chi mi svela un tal mistero "L'Ebrea" (Halévy)   1908
054179 DAVID/SCAMPINI Dillo ancor "Gli Ugonotti" (Meyerbeer)   1908
054180 GALVANY/RUFFO Nega se puoi la luce "Amleto" (Thomas)   1908
054181 GALVANY/RUFFO Dunque io son "Il Barbiere di Siviglia" (Rossini)
                                        (1328½c)   1908   DB400
054181 GALVANY/RUFFO Dunque io son "Il Barbiere di Siviglia" (Rossini)
                                        (02190f)
054186 MILILOTTI/MARCONI Madrigale a due voci "Romeo e Giulietta" (Gounod)08
054187 MILILOTTI/MARCONI O mia Mimosa "Geisha" (Jones) pno.1908   (pno.
054188 MILILOTTI/MARCONI Duetto della rosa "Marta" (Flotow) pno.   1908
054189 MILILOTTI/MARCONI Sento una forza indomita   1908
054190 MILILOTTI/MARCONI Madre se ognor lontano "Lucrezia Borgia" (Donizetti)
                                                                         1908
054195 DE TURA/SEGUROLA Non sei tu "La Favorita" (Donizetti)   1908
054196 DE CASAS/GIORGINI Pietoso al per d'un nume "La Favorita" (Donizetti)
                                                                         1908
054197 DE CASAS/GIORGINI Fia vero lasciarti "La Favorita" (Donizetti) 1908
054198 HOMER/CARUSO Ai nostri monti "Il Trovatore" (Verdi)(82)(A6036-1) 1908
                                        (final note down)   Pale Green
054198 HOMER/CARUSO Ai nostri monti(final note UP)(82)1910.(A6036-2)DM112.P.Gn.
054199 SEMBRICH/SEVERINA/CARUSO/SCOTTI Bella figlia "Rigoletto" (Verdi)
                                        (A5053)1908.DQ101.P.Gn.
• 054200 SEMBRICH/EAMES Che soave "Le Nozze di Figaro" (Mozart)(A5040-3) 1908
                                        (81) DK 121   Buff
• 054201 FARRAR/CARUSO O quanti occhi fisi "Madama Butterfly" (Puccini)(79)
                                        (A6026) 1908.DM110.P.Gn.
054202 FARRAR/SCOTTI Ora a noi "Madama Butterfly" (Puccini)(80) 1909. DK 118
                                        (1st.ed) Buff
054203 FARRAR/SCOTTI Mimi è ver "La Bohème" (Puccini)(80)(76)?1908.DK111.Bf.
054203 FARRAR/SCOTTI Mimi è ver "La Bohème" (Puccini)(A5087) 1909 (2nd.ed.)
• 054204 FARRAR/VIAFORA/CARUSO/SCOTTI Addio, dolce svegliare "La Bohème"
                                        (Puccini)(80)(A6025) 1908. DO 101.P.Blue
054205 SEMBRICH/SEVERINA/CARUSO/DADDI/SCOTTI/JOURNET Chi mi frena   1908
                    "Lucia di Lammermoor" (Donizetti)(78-82)(A5052)DQ101
                                                    White Label
054206 FARRAR/SCOTTI Là ci darem "Don Giovanni" (Mozart)(76)(A5014)08.Buff
054206 FARRAR/SCOTTI Là ci darem "Don Giovanni" (Mozart)(81)(A5014)09.Buff
                                                    DK 111
054207 ABOTT/ANCONA Tutte le feste "Rigoletto" (Verdi)   1908
054208 GALVANY/MARCONI Vieni fra queste "I Puritani" (Bellini)(1446c)   1908
                                                    DB481. VB4
054209 GALVANY/ANDREINI Sempre libera "La Traviata" (Verdi)(1456c)   1908
054210 PIETRACEWSKA/SIGNORINI Ai nostri monti "Il Trovatore" (Verdi)   1908
054211 PIETRACEWSKA/SCAMPINI Mal reggendo "Il Trovatore" (Verdi)   1908
054212 PIETRACEWSKA/TROMBEN Al bel destin "Linda di Chamounix" (Donizetti)
                                                                         1908
054213 DE FRATE/SIGNORINI Il ciel dei nostri amori "Aida" (Verdi)   1908
054214 MARCONI/DELLA TORRE Solenne in quest'ora "La Forza del Destino"
                                        (Verdi)   1908
054215 GALVANY/DE LUCIA Son geloso del zeffiro "La Sonnambula"(Bellini) 1908
                                        pno. IRCC 104

054217 GALVANY/DE LUCIA Prendi l'anel "La Sonnambula" (Bellini)pno.08.IRCC64
054218 BUTTI/PIETRACEWSKA Canzone boema "Carmen" (Bizet)   1908
054219 PICCOLETTI/DELLA TORRE Non sapete quale affetto "La Traviata" (Verdi)
                                                                              1908
054228 PARETO/RUFFO Lassù in cielo "Rigoletto" (Verdi)(80)(2733f) 1908.DB176
054229 PARETO/RUFFO Là ci darem "Don Giovanni" (Mozart)(80)(2728f)1908.DB875
054231 DE FRATE/SIGNORINI Ah! Patria infame "Chatterton" (Leoncavallo) 1908
054232 DE FRATE/SIGNORINI Sui vanni suoi "Chatterton" (Leoncavallo)   1908
054240 SCAMPINI/QUINZI-TAPERGI Ribelle chi mi chiama così "L'Africana"
                                                            (Meyerbeer) 1909
054241 DE TURA/BADINI Assassini "La Gioconda" (Ponchielli)   1909
054242 DE TURA/MELLERIO/BADINI Mimì è una civetta "La Bohème" (Puccini) 1909
054243 DE TURA/BADINI Questo Mar Rosso "La Bohème" (Puccini)   1909
054248 DOMAR/MANSUETO Scena della chiesa - I. "Faust" (Gounod)   1909
054249 DOMAR/MANSUETO Scena della chiesa - II."Faust" (Gounod)   1909
054250 HUGUET/GIORGINI D'un pensiero "La Sonnambula" (Bellini)   1909
054251 SANTORO/BATTAGLIOLI Duettino delle carte "Carmen" (Bizet)   1909
054252 SANTORO/BARRERA/BADINI/BATTAGLIOLI Mia tu sei "Carmen" (Bizet)   1909
054254 RUSZKOWSKA/BARRERA Tra le foreste "Aida" (Verdi)   1909
054255 RUSZKOWSKA/BARRERA Morir si pura "Aida" (Verdi)   1909
054256 RUSZKOWSKA/MAGGI Rivedrai le foreste "Aida" (Verdi)   1909
054257 RUSZKOWSKA/MAGGI Su dunque sorgete "Aida" (Verdi)   1909
054258 PIETRACEWSKA/BARRERA Già i sacerdoti "Aida" (Verdi)   1909
054260 RUSZKOWSKA/QUINZI-TAPERGI/CAPPIELLO/DAVI Su del Nilo "Aida"(Verdi) 09
054261 RUSZKOWSKA/BARRERA O terra addio "Aida" (Verdi)   1909
054262 PAOLI/DE SEGUROLA Nume custode "Aida" (Verdi)   1909
054263 PIETRACEWSKA/FEDERICI/QUINZI-TAPERGI Giorni poveri vivea
                                              "Il Trovatore" (Verdi)   1909
054265 HUGUET/DE TURA Amore o mistero "Mefistofele" (Boito)   1909
054267 DE CASAS/RIZZO Ohimè! Morir mi sento "Aida" (Verdi)   1909
054268 RUSZKOWSKA/CUNEGO Non la sospiri la nostra casetta "Tosca"(Puccini)09
054269 RUSZKOWSKA/CUNEGO Quale occhio al mondo "Tosca" (Puccini)   1909
054270 RUSZKOWSKA/CUNEGO Amaro sol per te "Tosca" (Puccini)   1909
054271 DE CASAS/RUSZKOWSKA L'amo come il fulgor "La Gioconda" (Ponchielli)1909
054272 DE CASAS/RUSZKOWSKA Fu la sorte "Aida" (Verdi)   1909
054273 DE CASAS/RUSZKOWSKA Ebben qual nuovo "Aida" (Verdi)   1909
054274 RUSZKOWSKA/DE CASAS/CUNEGO Ahime di guerra fremere "Aida" (Verdi)1909
054276 DE CASAS/RUSZKOWSKA Pietà ti prenda "Aida" (Verdi)   1909
054277 DE CASAS/CUNEGO Quale insolita "Aida" (Verdi)   1909
054278 DE CASAS/RIZZO Radames, tu rivelasti "Aida" (Verdi)   1909
054289 GIORGINI/FEDERICI Del tempio al limitar "I Pescatori di Perle"
                                                      (Bizet) 11/10
054296 DE CASAS/RIZZO Sacerdoti, compiste "Aida" (Verdi) 2/11
054317 JANNI/BATTISTINI D'acqua aspergimi "Thais" (Massenet)(278ai)1911.DB215
                                                              Orange
054330 GOETZEN/PAOLI/SALVATI Vieni, l'aula è deserta "Otello" (Verdi)2/12.DB470
054331 PAOLI/GOETZEN/SALA Una vela! Uragano "Otello" (Verdi)(79)(360aj)DB467
054337 PAOLI/GOETZEN Ah! mille vite "Otello" (Verdi) (370aj) DB467
054346 BARTOLOMASI/DE' MURO Dormivi? Sognavo! "Isabeau" (Mascagni)(79)
                                              (02352v)   1912   DB556
054347 BARTOLOMASI/DE' MURO I tuoi occhi! "Isabeau" (Mascagni)(79)
                                              (02354v)   1912   DB556
054376 FRASCANI/DI BERNARDO Laggiù nelle nebbie remote "La Gioconda"
                                              (Ponchielli) 7/12
054381 CAPRILE/CONFORTI Morir si giovane "La Traviata" (Verdi)   6/12
054383 CAPRILE/BADINI In quelle trine morbide "Manon Lescaut" (Puccini) 6/12
054384 CAPRILE/BADINI Dite alla giovine "La Traviata" (Verdi)   10/12
054385 CAPRILE/BETTONI Spunto l'aurora pallida "Mefistofele" (Boito) 2/15

054076 CIGADA/HUGUET Nega se puoi "Amleto" (Thomas)   1906
054077 GRISI/LARA   O dolce voluttà "Ruy Blas" (Marchetti)   1906
054078 CIGADA/GRISI/SANGIORGI O sommo Carlo "Ernani" (Verdi)   1906
054079 CIGADA/GRISI/SANGIORGI/SALA/OTTOBONI Vedi come il buon vegliardo
                                              "Ernani" (Verdi)(80)   1906
054087 HUGUET/DE LUNA Church Scene - I. "Faust" (Gounod)(76)(611½c)1906.D314
054088 HUGUET/DE LUNA Church Scene - II."Faust" (Gounod)(76)(612c) 1906.D314
054089 CIGADA/GRISI/SANGIORGI E degg'io e posso crederlo "Il Trovatore"
                                                              (Verdi) 1906
054090 MILERI/MINOLFI Quando le soglie "La Favorita" (Donizetti)   1906
054091 BADINI/A.PINI-CORSI Son nov'ore "Don Pasquale" (Donizetti)   1906
054093 BADINI/CORSI Pronta io son "Don Pasquale" (Donizetti)   1906
054094 CORSI/A.PINI-CORSI Signorina in tanta fretta "Don Pasquale"
                                                              (Donizetti)   1906
054095 HUGUET/MINOLFI Lassù nel ciel "Rigoletto" (Verdi)   1906
054096 HUGUET/ZACCARIA/LANZIROTTI/CIGADA Bella figlia "Rigoletto"(Verdi) 06
054099 DADO/HUGUET/LANZIROTTI/MINOLFI Chi mi frena "Lucia di Lammermoor"
                                                              (Donizetti)   1907
054108 COLAZZA/MINOLFI Uniti in vita "La Forza del Destino" (Verdi)   1907
054113 ACERBI/CORSI   Duetto finale "Faust" (Gounod)   1907-D315
054114 ACERBI/BRAMBILLA/SILLICH Terzetto finale "Faust" (Gounod)(895c)
                                                              1907-D315
054115 CAPPIELLO/GIACOMELLI/COLAZZA Ah di qual sei tu vittima "Norma"
                                                              (Bellini) 1907
054116 CAPPIELLO/GIACOMELLI Sola furtiva al tempio "Norma" (Bellini) 1907
054118 ACERBI/MINOLFI Del tempio al limitar "I Pescatori di Perle" (Bizet)07
054119 CIGADA/CODOLINI/SILLICH Finale Atto II.- I. "La Favorita"(Donizetti)07
054120 CIGADA/CODOLINI/SILLICH Finale Atto II.-II. "La Favorita"(Donizetti)07
054121 BRAMBILLA/CODOLINI/SILLICH La tempesta "Rigoletto" (Verdi)(77) 1907
054122 ACERBI/CODOLINI/CIGADA/SILLICH O ciel di quest'alma "La Favorita"
                                                              (Donizetti)1907
054123 CIGADA/SILLICH Ch'io gli parli "Rigoletto" (Verdi)   1907
054124 BRAMBILLA/ACERBI/CIGADA Terzetto "I Pescatori di Perle" (Bizet) 1907
054125 BRAMBILLA/A.PINI-CORSI/SCIPIONI Via da brava "Don Pasquale"
                                                              (Donizetti) 1907
054130 CIGADA/COLAZZA La congiura "Guglielmo Tell" (Rossini)   1907
054132 BRAMBILLA/ACERBI/BORGHETTI Scena della borsa "La Traviata"(Verdi) 07
054133 GIACOMELLI/CIGADA/SILLICH Ve' se di notte "Un Ballo in Maschera"
                                                              (Verdi) 1907
054136 MELIS/TACCANI L'albatro è teco "Albatro" (Pacchierotti)   1907
054137 MELIS/TACCANI La fata sei   "Albatro" (Pacchierotti)   1907
054138 MELIS/TACCANI S'io t'amo   "Hermes" (Perelli)   1907
054139 MELIS/TACCANI Gaddu alla triste casa "Jana" (Virgilio)   1907
054140 GIACOMELLI/TACCANI/CIGADA Finale ultimo "Hermes" (Virgilio)   1907
054145 RAMBELLI/MINOLFI Regina coeli "Cavalleria Rusticana" (Mascagni)07.D316
054146 HUGUET/BADINI/CIGADA Introduzione Atto II."Pagliacci"(Leoncavallo)
                                                              (77) 1907.D322
054147 HUGUET/BADINI/CIGADA Decidi il mio destin "Pagliacci"(Leoncavallo) 07
054148 HUGUET/BADINI E allor perchè "Pagliacci" (Leoncavallo)(76) 1907.D321
054149 HUGUET/BADINI Nulla scordai "Pagliacci" (Leoncavallo)(76) 1907.D322
054150 HUGUET/CIGADA So ben che di forme "Pagliacci" (Leoncavallo)(77)07.D321
054151 HUGUET/CIGADA/G.PINI-CORSI Commedia - I. "Pagliacci" (Leoncavallo)(77)
                                                              1907.D323
054152 HUGUET/CIGADA/G.PINI-CORSI Commedia - II."Pagliacci" (Leoncavallo)(77)
                                                              1907.D323
054153 BARBAINI/CIGADA/G.PINI-CORSI/ROSCI Un grande spettacolo
                                              "Pagliacci" (Leoncavallo) 1907

```
054154 HUGUET/BARBAINI/G.PINI-CORSI/CIGADA/BADINI  Finale  "Pagliacci"
                                              (Leoncavallo)  1907
054155 HUGUET/BARBAINI/G.PINI-CORSI/CIGADA  Versa il filtro "Pagliacci"
                                              (Leoncavallo)  1907
054165 HUGUET/JOANNA/ISCHIERDO/ROSCI  Finale ultimo  "Un Ballo in Maschera"
                                                   (Verdi)  1907
054166 HUGUET/BADINI  Pronta io son  "Don Pasquale" (Donizetti)    1907
054167 HUGUET/G.PINI-CORSI/BADINI  Alfredo di questo cuore  "La Traviata"
                                                   (Verdi)  1907
054168 JOANNA/G.PINI-CORSI/SILLICH  Ferma crudele  "Ernani" (Verdi)  1907
054170 SALVADOR/ISCHIERDO  Duetto finale  "Carmen" (Bizet)          1907
054182 PASSERI/ISCHIERDO  Duetto finale  "Carmen" (Bizet)           1908
054183 DAVID/ISCHIERDO  Duetto d'amore  "Tristano e Isotta" (Wagner)  1908
054184 DAVID/DE SEGUROLA  Duetto  "Gli Ugonotti" (Meyerbeer)        1908
054185 ALEXINA/MANSUETO  Preghiera  "Mosè" (Rossini)                1908
054191 PASSERI/A.PINI-CORSI  Non fuggir  "Il Campanello" (Donizetti)  1908
054192 A.PINI-CORSI/BADINI  Io son, signore, un infelice "Fra Diavolo"(Auber)08
054193 A.PINI-CORSI/BADINI  Del capitan alla salute "Fra Diavolo" (Auber)1908
054216 PASSERI/A.PINI-CORSI  Vieni qui  "Pipele" (De Ferrari)       1908
054220 MARCHETTI/TESSARI/VOLTA  O mia Mimosa  "Geisha" (Jones)      10/10
054221 TROMBEN/GIOVANELLI  A Parigi andrem  "Manon" (Massenet)      1908
054222 TROMBEN/FEDERICI  Ancor son io  "Manon" (Massenet)           1908
054223 TROMBEN/FEDERICI  Mi raccomando  "Manon" (Massenet)          1908
054224 ANDREINI/TEGANI  La catena       "Manon" (Massenet)          1908
054225 BALLIÈRES/AMADI  Lettura della lettera  "Manon" (Massenet)   1908
054226 BALLIÈRES/AMADI  Scena della chiesa "Manon" (Massenet)       1908
054227 TROMBEN/TEGANI/FEDERICI/G.PINI-CORSI  Restate qua "Manon"(Massenet)'08
054230 BUTTI/LOPEZ-NUNEZ/CICCOLINI/BARDI  Chiusura dell'introduzione
                                  "Stabat Mater" (Rossini)  1908
054233 DE FRATE/CIGADA/QUINZI-TAPERGI  Lord Clifford qui desidera
                                  "Chatterton" (Leoncavallo)    1908
054234 DE FRATE/GRANADOS/FEDERICI/QUINZI-TAPERGI  Signori vi presento
                                  "Chatterton" (Leoncavallo)    1908
054235 GRANADOS/CIGADA/QUINZI-TAPERGI  Dacche sei giunto "Chatterton" do.1908
054236 DE FRATE/GRANADOS/CIGADA  Gli amici suoi perchè "Chatterton" do.1908
054237 DE FRATE/SANTORO/CIGADA  Toni, di' che hai?    "Chatterton" do.1908
054238 DE FRATE/CIGADA  Un angiol sei "Chatterton" (Leoncavallo)    1908
054239 GRANADOS/CIGADA/Qui! voi stesso! "Chatterton" do.1908
054244 DOMAR/BADINI  Mimi io son  "La Bohème" (Puccini)             1909
054245 BARRERA/BADINI  Giuramento  "Otello" (Verdi)                 1909
054246 BARRERA/MAGGI  Solenne in quest'ora "La Forza del Destino"(Verdi)'09
054247 BARRERA/MAGGI  Solenne in quest'ora "La Forza del Destino"(Verdi)'09
054253 DOMAR/SANTORO/BADINI/GIOVANELLI  Che facevi, che dicevi
                                  "La Bohème" (Puccini)  1909
054264 HUGUET/GIOVANELLI/FEDERICI  Alfredo, Alfredo "La Traviata"(Verdi)1909
054279 LOPEZ-NUNES/ROSSI-MURINO  Voce di donna "La Gioconda"(Ponchielli)5/10
054280 LOPEZ-NUNES/ROSSI-MURINO  L'amo come il fulgor"La Gioconda"(Ponchielli)
                                                              5/10
054281 LOPEZ-NUNES/DE GREGORIO  Laggiù nelle nebbie remote
                                  "La Gioconda" (Ponchielli) 5/10
054282 ROSSI-MURINO/LOPEZ-NUNES/DE GREGORIO  Quest'ultimo bacio
                                  "La Gioconda" (Ponchielli) 5/10
054283 BRONZONI/DE GREGORIO  O soave fanciulla "La Bohème" (Puccini)  10/10
054284 BRONZONI/DE GREGORIO  Tutto tace "L'Amico Fritz" (Mascagni)   10/10
054285 BORELLI/FABRIS  Alma Vesta "La Vestale" (Spontini)            10/10
054286 ROSSI-MURINO/BADINI  Vo' farmi più gaia "La Gioconda"(Ponchielli) 6/12
054287 POPOVICI/DAVI/FEDERICI  O sommo Carlo  "Ernani" (Verdi)       10/10
```

```
054288 PASSERI/BARRERA  Sei tu?...son io  "Carmen" (Bizet)            10/10
054290 DA GRADI/BADINI  O grido di quest'anima "La Gioconda"(Ponchielli)11/10
054291 ROSSI-MURINO/LOPEZ-NUNES/BADINI  Figlia che reggi
                                    "La Gioconda" (Ponchielli)11/10
054292 SANTA-MARINA/CUNEGO  Gaddu, alla triste casa  "Jana" (Virgilio) 11/10
054293 SANTA-MARINA/CUNEGO  Gaddu, mio Gaddu          "Jana" (Virgilio) 11/10
054294 DA GRADI/BADINI/SALA  Uragano  "Otello" (Verdi)                11/10
054295 BOCCOLINI/BADINI  C'è Rodolfo?  "La Bohème" (Puccini)           3/11
054297 BESALÙ/CICCOLINI  Tu qui Santuzza "Cavalleria Rusticana"(Mascagni)2/11
054298 BESALÙ/CICCOLINI  Ah! no, Turiddu!"Cavalleria Rusticana"(Mascagni)2/11
054299 SANIPOLI/PASSERI/CICCOLINI/BADINI  Quartetto  "La Bohème" (Puccini)3/11
054300 BESALÙ/BADINI  Turiddu mi tolse l'onore "Cavalleria Rusticana"
                                             (Mascagni)  3/11
054301 LOTTI/CONTI  Quando narravi  "Otello" (Verdi)                   3/11
054302 GALLI/CONTI  Nume custode  "Aida" (Verdi)                       4/11
054303 LOTTI/DE GREGORIO/BADINI  Già ti veggo "La Gioconda"(Ponchielli)4/11
054304 DE GREGORIO/BOCCOLINI  Via dall'anima in pena  "Madama Butterfly"
                                             (Puccini)  4/11
054305 LOTTI/BADINI  Rivedrai le foreste  "Aida" (Verdi)               5/11
054306 LOTTI/BADINI  Su dunque sorgete  "Aida" (Verdi)                 5/11
054307 PEZZUTI/CONTI/BADINI  Uragano  "Otello" (Verdi)                 5/11
054308 CONTI/LOTTI  Venga la morte  "Otello" (Verdi)                   5/11
054309 CONTI/LOTTI  Morir si pura  "Aida" (Verdi)                      6/11
054310 CONTI/LOTTI  O terra addio  "Aida" (Verdi)                      6/11
054311 SALVATI/CANALI  Venti scudi  "L'Elisir d'amore" (Donizetti)    10/11
054312 SALVATI/CANALI  Qua la mano giovinotto  "L'Elisir d'amore"
                                             (Donizetti)  10/11
054313 BOCCOLINI/GILBERTI  Sono andati?  "La Bohème" (Puccini)        10/11
054314 CHIESA/GOETZEN/GILBERTI  Quest'assisa ch'io vesto "Aida" (Verdi)11/11
054315 PAVONI/GOETZEN  Alfin t'ho colto  "Falstaff" (Verdi)           11/11
054316 PASSERI/TOMMASINI  Dal labbro il canto  "Falstaff" (Verdi)     11/11
054321 MANGINI/BELLATTI  Decidi il mio destin  "Pagliacci"(Leoncavallo) 2/12
054322 MANGINI/GOETZEN  Il pallor funesto  "Lucia di Lammermoor"
                                             (Donizetti) 11/12
054323 MANGINI/U.CANNETTI/PASSERI  Somiglia un Apollo  "Rigoletto"(Verdi)10/12
054324 SALVATI/CANALI  Voglio dire  "L'Elisir d'amore" (Donizetti)
054325 MANGINI/CANALI  Quanto amore!  "L'Elisir d'amore" (Donizetti)   1/12
054326 PAVONI/GILBERTI/GOETZEN/U.CANNETTI  La sacrilega parola
                                    "Poliuto" (Donizetti)  5/13
054328 SALVATI/MANGINI/GOETZEN/U.CANNETTI  A te o cara  "I Puritani"
                                             (Bellini)  2/13
054329 BONETTI/SALVATI/SALA/GOETZEN  L'oltraggio che scende
                                    "La Favorita" (Donizetti)  7/12
054332 PAVONI/TOMMASINI  Di te più bella immagine  "L'Africana" (Meyerbeer)2/12
054333 PAVONI/GOETZEN  Andrem raminghi e poveri  "Luisa Miller" (Verdi)11/12
054334 PAVONI/TOMMASINI  O mia Selika  "L'Africana" (Meyerbeer)        2/12
054336 MANGINI/SALVATI/CANALI  Qual trionfo  "Il Barbiere di Siviglia"
                                             (Rossini)  1/12
054339 BOCCOLINI/PASSERI/SALVATI  Sento ohime  "Il Matrimonio Segreto"
                                             (Cimarosa)  9/13
054340 BOCCOLINI/PASSERI/GILBERTI/U.CANNETTI  Dimmi in casa sei sola sovente?
                                    "Mefistofele" (Boito)  2/12
054342 LOTTI/GRAMAGNA  Ebben qual nuovo fremito  "Aida" (Verdi)        3/12
054343 LOTTI/GRAMAGNA  Pietà ti prenda          "Aida" (Verdi)        3/12
054344 MANGINI/SALVATI/CANALI/U.CANNETTI/N.N.(bs)  O mia Selika
                                    "L'Africana" (Meyerbeer)
054345 GRAMAGNA/GALLI  Radames, Radames: tu rivelasti "Aida" (Verdi)  3/12
```

```
054348 CASINI/PRINCIPE  O Reginotta, gli angioli dal cielo  "Isabeau"
                                              (Mascagni)   5/12
054349 MARCHINI/PRINCIPE  A te umile mente preghiam "Isabeau"(Mascagni)  5/12
054350 LEBRUN/PRINCIPE/CUNEGO/BETTONI/NEUMARKER  Finale Atto.II."Aida"
                                              (Verdi)    7/12
054351 PRINCIPE/CUNEGO/BETTONI  Alta cagion  "Aida" (Verdi)     10/13
054352 PRINCIPE/BETTONI  O tu che sei d'Osiride "Aida" (Verdi)  11/12
054353 MARCHINI/PRINCIPE/CASINI/GIOVANELLI/LUSSARDI
             Abbiamo in vista un bell'affar "Carmen" (Bizet)    4/12
054354 CASINI/GIOVANELLI  Vedi, io piango "Fedora" (Giordano)   7/12
054356 CASINI/GIOVANELLI  Fedora, io t'amo "Fedora" (Giordano)  7/12
054359 GIOVANELLI/LUSSARDI/BETTONI/DI ANNA  Chi mi frena
                      "Lucia di Lammermoor" (Donizetti)   11/12
054361 GIOVANELLI/LUSSARDI/MARIANI/BETTONI  Eccoci.Ebben?"La Bohème"
                                              (Puccini)   6/12
054362 LEBRUN/PRINCIPE/CUNEGO/NEUMARKER  Ma dimmi per qual via "Aida"
                                              (Verdi)   11/12
054363 CASINI/MARCHINI/GIOVANELLI/LUSSARDI/MARIANI/BETTONI
             C'è Mimi che mi segue "La Bohème" (Puccini)  6/12
054366 GIOVANELLI/BADINI/BETTONI  Questo Mar Rosso "La Bohème"(Puccini) 6/12
054368 GIOVANELLI/BETTONI/LUSSARDI  Ch'io gli parli "Rigoletto"(Verdi) 10/12
054370 PRINCIPE/BETTONI/SALA/NEUMARKER  Ah! paventa il furor
                      "La Favorita" (Donizetti)          7/12
054371 GIOVANELLI/BADINI/LUSSARDI/MARIANI/BETTONI  Si può?
                      "La Bohème" (Puccini) 6/12
054373 MARCHINI/GIOVANELLI/BADINI/LUSSARDI/BETTONI
             La giovinezza mia  "La Bohème" (Puccini)10/12
054377 DI BERNARDO/BADINI  Uniti in vita è in morte
                      "La Forza del Destino" (Verdi) 10/13
054379 SANTOLIVA/CUNEGO/BADINI  Vittoria, Vittoria "Tosca" (Puccini)  6/12
054380 SANTOLIVA/BADINI  Già mi dicon venal      "Tosca" (Puccini)  6/12
054386 CASINI/PRINCIPE/BETTONI  Angele Dei "La Gioconda" (Ponchielli) 6/12
054387 LOTTI/BADINI  Più presso al ciel "Amica" (Mascagni)        7/12
054388 BOCCOLINI/CICCOLINI  Han della porpora  "L'Amico Frits"(Mascagni) 7/12
054397 BOCCOLINI/BOTTA  Vedete io son fedele "Manon Lescaut" (Puccini) 12/12
054398 BOCCOLINI/BOTTA  O tentatrice      "Manon Lescaut" (Puccini) 12/12
054402 BOCCOLINI/MARTINENGO/BOTTA/TISCI-RUBINI
             Cavaliero illustre e saggio "Mefistofele" (Boito)  2/13
054403 BOCCOLINI/MARTINENGO/BOTTA  La luna immobile "Mefistofele"(Boito) 2/13
054404 BELLABARBA/TISCI-RUBINI  Suoni la tromba "I Puritani" (Bellini) 2/13
054406 BOCCOLINI/BOTTA  Mia madre "Carmen" (Bizet)               4/13
054407 BOTTA/TISCI-RUBINI  Giunto sul passo estremo "Mefistofele" (Boito)4/14
054408 BOTTA/TISCI-RUBINI  Stupor, stupor "Mefistofele" (Boito) 11/13
054409 SOLLOHUB/BOTTA  Amore! mistero!    "Mefistofele" (Boito) 11/13
054410 BOTTA/TISCI-RUBINI  Ecco la nuova turba "Mefistofele" (Boito)  4/14
054414 BOCCOLINI/BOTTA/BADINI  Prendi, quest'è l'immagine "La Traviata"
                                              (Verdi)    4/13
054415 BARBIERI/CASTELLANI  Qual cor tradisti "Norma" (Bellini)   5/13
054416 BARBIERI/CASTELLANI/BETTONI  Deh! non volerli vittime "Norma"
                                              (Bellini)   5/13
054417 BARBIERI/CASTELLANI  Il suon dell'arpa angeliche "Poliuto"
                                              (Donizetti)   5/13
054420 SCALFARO/FERRETTI  Saper vorreste "Un Ballo in Maschera" (Verdi) 6/13
054421 SCALFARO/SALVATI  Tornami a dir che m'ami "Don Pasquale"
                                              (Donizetti)   6/13
054422 PEREIRA/MAGGI  Soffriva nel pianto "Don Pasquale" (Donizetti)  6/13
054424 DE GREGORIO/BETTONI  Io voglio il piacere "Faust" (Gounod)  11/13
```

054428 BARBIERI/CASTELLANI In mia mano "Norma" (Bellini) 10/13
054432 BARBIERI/BADINI/BETTONI Vieni meco "Ernani" (Verdi) 9/13
054433 DE GREGORIO/SCALFARO/BETTONI Permettereste a me "Faust" (Gounod) 8/13
054438 BARBIERI/ZIZOLFI Mira o Norma "Norma" (Bellini) 10/13
054442 DE GREGORIO/PEREIRA/MAGGI/BETTONI T'allontana sciagurato
                         "Lucia di Lammermoor" (Donizetti) 11/13
054444 CASINI/SCALFARO/ZIZOLFI Le faccio un inchino
                         "Il Matrimonio Segreto" (Cimarosa) 9/13
054446 DE GREGORIO/CASINI Tardi si fa "Faust" (Gounod) 8/13
054447 DE GREGORIO/CASINI/FERRETTI Mimì è una civetta "La Bohème"(Puccini)9/13
054457 SARAH/PONZANO/PAROLA/BETTONI Rex tremendae "Messa da Requiem"(Verdi)
                                                               12/13
054458 SARAH/PONZANO Recordare Jesu "Messa da Requiem" (Verdi) 12/13
054459 SARAH/PONZANO/PAROLA/BETTONI Lacrymosa dies illa - I. do. do. 12/13
054460 SARAH/PONZANO/PAROLA/BETTONI Lacrymosa dies illa - II. do. do. 12/13
054461 BADINI/LUSSARDI C'è in Windsor una dama "Falstaff" (Verdi) 1/14
054462 BADINI/LUSSARDI Quella crudel belta "Falstaff" (Verdi) 1/14
054463 LLOPART/COSENTINO Dio ti giocondi, o sposo "Otello" (Verdi) 1/14
054464 LLOPART/COSENTINO Esterrefata fisso lo sguardo tuo "Otello"(Verdi)1/14
054473 PAVONI/COSENTINO/BETTONI Qual volutta trascorrere "I Lombardi"
                                                               (Verdi) 1/15
054474 LLOPART/BENDINELLI · Tu! voi...! tu qui? "Manon" (Massenet) 4/14
054475 LLOPART/BENDINELLI La tua non è la mano che mi tocca? "Manon"
                                                      (Massenet) 4/14
054480 CICCOLINI/SOLARI/BETTONI Forma ideal purissima "Mefistofele"(Boito)1/15
054481 SOLARI/DE GREGORIO Tu qui Santuzza? "Cavalleria Rusticana"
                                                      (Mascagni) 1/15
054482 SOLARI/DE GREGORIO No, No, Turiddu "Cavalleria Rusticana"(Mascagni)1/15

12" records : RED & PINK LABEL

2-054000 FARRAR/SCOTTI Ed ora a noi "Madama Butterfly" (Puccini) 1908
2-054001 FARRAR/SCOTTI Là ci darem "Don Giovanni" (Mozart)(A5014) 1908
2-054002 FARRAR/SCOTTI Mimì è ver "La Bohème" (Puccini)(A5087)054203. 1908
2-054003 FARRAR/SCOTTI Crudel! Perchè finora "Le Nozze di Figaro" (Mozart)
                                                         DK118 1909
2-054004 FARRAR/JACOBY Tutti i fior "Madama Butterfly" (Puccini) 1909
2-054005 GADSKI/CARUSO La fatal pietra "Aida" (Verdi)(81) DM114.1909.Pale Gn.
                                                         (A8353)
2-054006 GADSKI/CARUSO O terra addio "Aida" (Verdi)(81)(A8348)1909.DM114.P.Gn.
2-054007 ALDA/CARUSO Miserere "Il Trovatore" (Verdi)(82)(A8506)1910.DK119.P.Gn.
2-054010 CARUSO/JOURNET Solo, profugo "Marta" (Flotow)(82)(A8546)1910.
                                                         DM115.Pale.Gn.
2-054011 McCORMACK/SAMMARCO Ah Mimi, tu più "La Bohème" (Puccini) (A8737)1910.Bf.
2-054012 SEMBRICH/SAMMARCO Tutte le feste "Rigoletto" (Verdi) 1910   (DB630
2-054013 CARUSO/SCOTTI Ve lo dissi? "Madama Butterfly" (Puccini)(80) 1910
                                                         (A8712) DM113.P.Gn.
2-054014 CARUSO/SCOTTI Amore o grillo "Madama Butterfly" (Puccini)(80) 1910
                                                         (A8711) DM113.P.Gn.
2-054015 HOMER/CARUSO Già i sacerdoti "Aida" (Verdi)(80)(A9748)1910.DK115.P.Gn.
2-054016 HOMER/CARUSO Aida a me togliesti "Aida" (Verdi)(A9749)1910.DM111.P.Gn.
2-054017 HOMER/CARUSO Mal reggendo "Il Trovatore" (Verdi)(81)(A6682) 1910
                                                         DM112.P.Gn.
2-054018 McCORMACK/SAMMARCO Del tempio al limitar "I Pescatori di Perle"
                                                         (Bizet) 1910
2-054019 DESTINN/McCORMACK Mira la bianca luna (Rossini)(5203f)1911.DK123.Buff
2-054020 DESTINN/LUNN L'amo come il fulgor "La Gioconda" (Ponchielli)(80)Buff
                                                         (5143f)1911.DB517

2-054021 McCORMACK/SAMMARCO All'idea di quel metallo "Il Barbiere di Siviglia"
(Rossini)(5205f) 1911.Buff.DB608
VB33
2-054022 McCORMACK/SAMMARCO O grido di quest'anima "La Gioconda" (Ponchielli)
(5206f) 1911. Buff. DB608.VB33
2-054023 DESTINN/LUNN Ebben, qual nuovo fremito "Aida"(Verdi)(5145f)1911.Buff
2-054025 MELBA/THORNTON/McCORMACK/SAMMARCO Bella figlia "Rigoletto" (Verdi)
(4189f) 1910. DM118. Pale Green
2-054026 AMATO/SETTI Inaffia l'ugola "Otello" (Verdi)(A11284) 1911.DK110.Buff
2-054027 CARUSO/AMATO Invano, Alvaro "La Forza del Destino" (Verdi)(81)
(A11286) 1911.DM106.P.Gn.
2-054028 CARUSO/AMATO Le minaccie "La Forza del Destino" (Verdi)(81)
(A11286½) 1911.DM106.P.Gn.
2-054029 ALDA/CARUSO/JOURNET Qual volutta "I Lombardi" (Verdi)
(A11441) 7.I.1912.DM126.P.Green
2-054030 ALDA/JACOBY/CARUSO/JOURNET Siam giunte "Marta" (Flotow)(80)
(A11437) 7.I.1912.DM100.P.Green
2-054031 ALDA/JACOBY/CARUSO/JOURNET Che vuol dir cio? "Marta" (Flotow)(80)
(A11438) 7.I.1912.DM100.P.Green
2-054032 ALDA/JACOBY/CARUSO/JOURNET Presto, presto "Marta" (Flotow)
(A11439) 7.I.1912.DM101.P.Green
2-054033 AMATO/JOURNET Suoni la tromba "I Puritani" (Bellini)
(A11461) 1912. DK110. Buff
2-054034 TETRAZZINI/JACOBY/CARUSO/AMATO/BADA/JOURNET Chi mi frena
"Lucia di Lammermoor" (Donizetti) (A11446) 1912.White
2-054035 FARRAR/JADLOWKER Il cor nel contento "Le Donne Curiose"(Wolf-Ferrari)
(81)(A11607) 1912. DK124. Buff
2-054037 ALDA/JACOBY/CARUSO/JOURNET Dormi pur   "Marta" (Flotow)
(A11440) 7.I.1912.DM101.P.Gn.
2-054038 TETRAZZINI/CARUSO/AMATO/JOURNET Bella figlia "Rigoletto" (Verdi)
(A11447) 1912. Pale Green
2-054039 FARRAR/AMATO Il dolce idillio "Il Segreto di Susanna"(Wolf-Ferrari)
(A11606) 1912.DK124.Buff
2-054040 LUNN/McCORMACK T'ieri un giorno ammalato "I Gioielli della Madonna"
(Wolf-Ferrari)(80)(HO201af)1912.DK123.Buff
2-054041 LUNN/McCORMACK Il dolce idillio "Il Segreto di Susanna"   ?
(Wolf-Ferrari) 1912   ?
2-054042 SCHUMANN-HEINK/CARUSO Ai nostri monti "Il Trovatore" (Verdi)
(A12804) 1913. DK119. Buff
2-054043 CARUSO/SCOTTI Dio, che nell'alma "Don Carlo" (Verdi)(79)(2-054095)
(A12752) 1912. DM111.Pale Gn.
2-054044 FARRAR/HOMER Alla capanna andiamo (Campana)(A13127)1913.DK125.Buff
2-054045 GADSKI/AMATO Cieli mio padre "Aida" (Verdi)(A13120)1913.DK126.Buff
2-054046 GADSKI/AMATO Su dunque! "Aida" (Verdi)(A13119) 1913. DK126. Buff
2-054049 CARUSO/RUFFO Si pel ciel "Otello" (Verdi)(79)(A14272)1914.DK114.P.Gn.
2-054050 HEMPEL/DUCHENE/CARUSO/ROTHIER/DE SEGUROLA E scherzo od è follia
"Un Ballo in Maschera" (Verdi)(80)(A14660)1914.DM103.P.Bl.
2-054052 HEMPEL/ROTHIER/CARUSO/DE SEGUROLA La rivedro nell'estasi
"Un Ballo in Maschera" (Verdi)(80)(A14659)1914.DM103.P.Gn.
2-054053 DESTINN/CARUSO Sento una forza indomita "Il Guarany" (Verdi)(79)
(A14730) 1914. DB616. Pale Gn.
2-054055 BORI/McCORMACK Parigi o cara "La Traviata" (Verdi)(A14686) 1914
DM104. Buff
2-054056 JANNI/DE' MURO Ho nome Escamillo "Carmen" (Bizet)(743m)1914.DB554
2-054057 BALDINI/JANNI/BETTONI/DE' MURO E deggio "Il Trovatore" (Verdi)
(746m)1914.
2-054059 MARSH/McCORMACK O terra addio "Aida" (Verdi)(80)(A14694)1914.DB579

2-054060 HEMPEL/AMATO Figlia! mio padre "Rigoletto" (Verdi)(A14718)1914.Buff
2-054061 BORI/JACOBY/McCORMACK/WERRENRATH Bella figlia "Rigoletto" (Verdi)
         (A14657) 1914. DM104.P.Green
2-054062 DESTINN/GILLY Dobrou noc (Pisek) (Good-Night : Folk song)   Buff
         (A14765) 1914. DB593
2-054063 DESTINN/MARTINELLI Miserere "Il Trovatore" (Verdi) (A15906)1915.Bf.
              DB333
2-054066 GALLI-CURCI/PERINI/CARUSO/DE LUCA Bella figlia "Rigoletto" (Verdi)
         (A19132) 1917. DQ100   Buff
2-054067 GALLI-CURCI/EGENER/CARUSO/BADA/DE LUCA/JOURNET Chi mi frena
    "Lucia di Lammermoor" (Donizetti)(A19133)1917. DQ100   White
2-054068 MARTINELLI/JOURNET Ah! Matilde, io t'amo e amore "Guglielmo Tell"
      (Rossini) (A19136) 1917. DK120   Red & Bf.
2-054069 HOMER/GLUCK Mira, o Norma "Norma" (Bellini)(A12847) 1913.DB478
2-054070 RUGGERO/DE' MURO Miserere "Il Trovatore" (Verdi)(3172c) 1917.DB644
2-054071 BONINSEGNA/BOLIS M'ami, m'ami "Un Ballo in Maschera" (Verdi)   VB27
         (3204c) 1917.DB492.
2-054072 CASAZZA/DE' MURO Ai nostri monti "Il Trovatore" (Verdi)
         (3175c) 1917.DB562
2-054073 CASAZZA/DE' MURO Mal reggendo "Il Trovatore" (Verdi)(3174c)1917.DB561
2-054074 BONINSEGNA/BOLIS O qual soave brivido "Un Ballo in Maschera" (Verdi)
         (3203c) 1917
2-054075 BONINSEGNA/BOLIS Vicino a te s'acqueta "Andrea Chenier" (Giordano)
    (79) (3205c) 1917.DB492.VB4
2-054076 RUGGERO/BADINI/DE' MURO Prima que d'altri vivere "Il Trovatore"
        (Verdi)(79) 1917
2-054077 CASAZZA/DE' MURO Perigliarti ancor languente "Il Trovatore" (Verdi)
         1917. DB561
2-054079 PARETO/BERGAMINI E il sol dell'anima "Rigoletto" (Verdi)   1918
2-054080 PARETO/DRAGONI Sì, vendetta "Rigoletto" (Verdi)(3281c) 1918. DB875
2-054081 PARETO/BERGAMINI Libiam ne' lieti calici "La Traviata" (Verdi) 10/19
2-054082 PARETO/DRAGONI Dite alla giovine "La Traviata" (Verdi) 1918
2-054083 CASAZZA/GIGLI Addio! fuggir mi lascia "La Favorita" (Donizetti)
         (3314c) X/1918.DB269
2-054084 ZANI/GIGLI Enzo Grimaldo "La Gioconda" (Ponchielli)(3331c) XI/1918
           DB267
2-054085 CASAZZA/GIGLI Laggiù nelle nebbie "La Gioconda" (Ponchielli)
         (3316c) X/1918.DB267
2-054086 BOSINI/GIGLI Lontano, lontano "Mefistofele" (Boito)(3310c)X/'18.DB271
2-054087 BONINSEGNA/BOLIS Sento duo "Il Guarany" (Gomez)(3198c) VI/1917.DB491
2-054088 DE' MURO/BADINI Deserto sulla terra "Il Trovatore" (Verdi)
         (3171c) 1917. DB644
2-054089 GALLI-CURCI/DE LUCA Imponete "La Traviata" (Verdi)(A21976)1918.DB174
2-054090 ALDA/BRASLAU Tutti i fior "Madama Butterfly" (Puccini)(79)
        (A22244) 20.IX.1918.DB596
2-054091 ALDA/MARTINELLI O soave fanciulla "La Bohème" (Puccini)(79)
        (A22245) 20.IX.1918.DK100.Bf.
2-054092 CARUSO/DE LUCA Venti scudi "L'Elisir d'amore" (Donizetti)
        (A22576) 1919.DM107.P.Gn.
2-054093 CARUSO/DE LUCA Sleale! il segreto "La Forza del Destino" (Verdi)
        (A22123) 1918. DM107.P.Green
2-054094 HOMER/CARUSO Aida, a me togliesti "Aida" (Verdi)(A9749)1910.DM111.P.Gn.
2-054095 CARUSO/SCOTTI Dio, che nell'alma infondere "Don Carlo" (Verdi)
        (A12752) 1912. DM111 P.Gn.
2-054096 CARUSO/SCOTTI Ve lo dissi? "Madama Butterfly" (Puccini) 2-054013
2-054097 HOMER/CARUSO Mal reggendo "Il Trovatore" (Verdi)(A6682) 1910.DM112 ?
2-054098 FARRAR/CLEMENT Lontano, lontano "Mefistofele" (Boito)(A12913) 1913
              DB172

2-054099 GALLI-CURCI/DE LUCA Dite alla giovine "La Traviata" (Verdi)
                                           (A21974) 1918. DB174
2-054100 SEMBRICH/EAMES Che soave "Le Nozze di Figaro" (Mozart)
                                           (A5040) 1908. DK121.Buff
2-054101 GADSKI/HOMER Alla pompa "Aida" (Verdi)(79)(A7034)1908.P.Gn.DB666
2-054102 GADSKI/HOMER Fu la sorte "Aida" (Verdi)(79)(A7033)1908.P.Gn.DB666
2-054103 GLUCK/HOMER Quis est homo "Stabat Mater" (Rossini)(A11867)1912.DB575
2-054104 VAN HOOSE/DE GOGORZA Solo, profugo "Marta" (Flotow) 1906. DB169
2-054105 ZAMBONI/GIGLI Demmi ancor "Faust" (Gounod)(1046aj) XII/1919.DB268
2-054106 ZAMBONI/GIGLI O soave fanciulla "La Bohème" (Puccini)
                                           (1048aj) XII/1919.DB271
2-054107 BALDISSERI/GIGLI Suzel, buon dì "L'Amico Fritz" (Mascagni)
                                           (1051aj) XII/1919.VB46
2-054108 BALDISSERI/GIGLI Tutto tace "L'Amico Fritz" (Mascagni)
                                           (1052aj) XII/1919.VB46
2-054109 PACINI/GIGLI Del tempio al limitar "I Pescatori di Perle" (Bizet)
                                           (1055aj) XII/1919.DB269
2-054110 BARTOLOMASI/DE TURA Fuggiam gli ardori "Aida" (Verdi)
2-054111 BARTOLOMASI/DE TURA/DRAGONI Sì, fuggiam da queste "Aida" (Verdi)
2-054112 BARTOLOMASI/DRAGONI Rivedrai le foreste "Aida" (Verdi) DB477
2-054113 DRAGONI/GARGIULO So ben che difforme "Pagliacci" (Leoncavallo)
                                           2/25. DB741
2-054114 ZAMBONI/GIGLI Sempre amar! "Faust" (Gounod)(1053aj) XII/1919.DB268
2-054116 DRAGONI/IMPALLOMENI Turiddu mi tolse l'onore
                              "Cavalleria Rusticana" (Mascagni) 2/25. DB741
2-054117 MARTINELLI/DE LUCA Dio, che nell'alma "Don Carlo" (Verdi)
                                           (A25179) 1921.DK127.Bf.
2-054118 DE WITT/BATTISTINI/TACCANI O sommo Carlo "Ernani" (Verdi)
                                           (CA 7) 21.V.1921.DB216
2-054119 DE WITT/BATTISTINI Ebbrezza, delirio "La Gioconda" (Ponchielli)
                                           (CA 9) 1921. DB216
2-054120 BORI/DE LUCA Pronta io son "Don Pasquale" (Donizetti)
                                           (A25297) 1921.DK102.Bf.
2-054121 BORI/DE LUCA Vado, corro "Don Pasquale" (Donizetti)
                                           (A25296) 1921.DK102.Bf.
2-054122 DRAGONI/TURIGLIA Se ancor di me "Andrea Chenier" (Giordano)
                                           5/23. DB476
2-054123 ALDA/MARTINELLI O quanti occhi "Madama Butterfly" (Puccini)
                                           (A22246) 20.IX.1918.DK100.Bf.
2-054126 DE' MURO/GRAMAGNA Di lei non più "Aida" (Verdi)(CE432) 1922.DB551
2-054127 DE' MURO/VIGANO Fuggiam gli adori "Aida" (Verdi) 1/23. DB550
2-054128 DE' MURO/VIGANO/GRAMAGNA/BARACCHI Si fuggiam "Aida" (Verdi)1/23
                                           DB550
2-054129 DE' MURO/VIGANO Va nella tua stanzetta "Il Piccolo Marat" (Mascagni)
                                           (CE439) 1922.DB558
2-054130 MARTINELLI/DE LUCA/MARDONES Troncar suoi di "Guglielmo Tell"
                              (Rossini) (A27392) 1923.DK120.Bf.
2-054131 AUSTRAL/FLETA Presago il core "Aida" (Verdi)(Cc2849) 1923.DB580
2-054132 THORNTON/AUSTRAL/FLETA O terra addio "Aida" (Verdi)(Cc2848) 1923
                                           DB580
2-054133 AUSTRAL/FLETA Amaro sol per te "Tosca" (Puccini) 10/23. DB956
2-054134 DE' MURO/OLTRABELLA Vedi? la luce incerta "Andrea Chenier"(Giordano)
                                           8/23. DB552
2-054135 DE' MURO/BADINI/TONINELLO/QUINZI-TAPERGI Già ti vedo
                              "La Gioconda" (Ponchielli) 8/23.DB555
2-054136 PINZA/TURCHETTI Dal tuo stellato soglio "Mosè in Egitto" (Rossini)
                                           (CE1280) 1924.DB698

2-054137 POLI-RANDACIO/OFFERS Fu la sorte "Aida" (Verdi)(Ckl125) 8/24. DB728
2-054138 POLI-RANDACIO/OFFERS Pietà ti prenda "Aida" (Verdi)(Ckl125-)8/24.DB728
2-054139 POLI-RANDACIO/PINZA/BOSCACCI Deh! non volerli vittime "Norma"(Bellini)
                                            (Ckl254) 10/24.DB729
2-054140 PARNIS/GILLY/HISLOP Dovunque al mondo "Madama Butterfly" (Puccini)
                                            (Cc4006) 12/24.DB743
2-054141 HISLOP/GILLY Amore o grillo "Madama Butterfly" (Puccini)
                                            (Cc4007) 12/24.DB743
2-054144 LJUNGBERG/MUMMERY Ora stammi "Tosca" (Puccini)(Cc4661)   DB752
2-054145 LJUNGBERG/MUMMERY Chi e quella donna "Tosca" (Puccini)(Cc4662)DB752
2-054146 OFFERS/PINZA/MARTORANO Giorni poveri "Il Trovatore" (Verdi)3/25.DB754
2-054147 CAPSIR/CINISELLI Sulla tomba "Lucia di Lammermoor" (Donizetti)
                                            1/25.DB755
2-054148 CAPSIR/CINISELLI Verranno a te sull'aure
                         "Lucia di Lammermoor" (Donizetti) 1/25.DB755
2-054149 PARETO/MANURITTA D'un pensiero "La Sonnambula" (Bellini)12/24.DB762
2-054150 PARETO/CINISELLI Non hai compreso un cor fedele   12/24
                         "I Pescatori di Perle" (Bizet) DB762
• 2-054151 GALLI-CURCI/SCHIPA Son geloso "La Sonnambula" (Bellini)
                         (A27994) 1923. DB811. DB2397
• 2-054152 GALLI-CURCI/SCHIPA Finale Act.1. "Lucia di Lammermoor" (Donizetti)
                         (A30910) 1924. DB811

12" records : BLACK LABEL

2-054024 Grand Opera Company Sextette "Lucia di Lammermoor" (Donizetti)(81)1911
2-054051 MURPHY/WERRENRATH Solenne in quest'ora "La Forza del Destino"
                                            (Verdi) 1914
2-054064 ARNDT-OBER/ALTHOUSE Garden Scene "Simone Boccanegra" (Verdi)
2-054078 BOCCOLINI/BROCCARDI Via dall'anima in pena "Madama Butterfly"
                                            (Puccini) 1/19

INDEX TO ARTISTS

CELEBRITY SECTION

(PART I)

ABOTT Bessie, s.   54372
                         054117
                         054207

ACERBI Giuseppe, t.
  2-52402   54320
  2-52417   54324
  2-52420   54326
  2-52425   54328
  2-52436   054113/4
  2-52438   054118
  2-52579   054122
  052104   054124
  54059   054132
  54262

ADAMI Bice, s.
  53103   54007
  53105   54009
  53108   54075
  53110-5   54077
  53117/8   054095-7
  53163-7   54101
  53171   54115-21
  53177-9   54125/6
  53212   54137
  53214   54521
  53225   54525
  54001/2

ALBANI Emma, s.   53325

ALDA Francés, s.
  7-53033   2-054007
  7-53046   2-054029-32
  7-53057   2-054037
  2-053182   2-054090/1
  2-053185   2-054123
  2-053200

ALEXINA Maria, s.   053161
                        54361/2
                        054185

ALTHOUSE Paul, t.   2-054064

AMADI Alberto, t.   054225/6

AMATO Gennaro   7-52318

AMATO Pasquale, b.
  7-52023/4   2-052094
  7-52027   054401
  7-52057/8   2-054026-8
  2-052051-7   2-054033/4
  2-052078/9   2-054038/9
  2-052089   2-054045/6
  2-052092   2-054060

AMAULI Duetto   7-54021

ANCONA Mario, b.
  52072-4   052178-80
  52128-30   54372
  052075/6   054134/5
  052080   054207
  052155/6

ANDREACE   53193-4
                    53199-204

ANDREINI Remo, t.   054209
                     054224

APOSTOLU Giovanni, t. 52284
                     54035

ARDITO, s.   7-54019

ARDONI, s.   53571
                 53599/600
                 54412

ARIMONDI Vittorio, bs. 52182/3

ARKEL Teresa, s.
  53312   053004/5
  53315   053039
  53385   053059-62
  53405/6

ARMENTANO Antonio, b. 2-52628
                     2-52636
                     54368

ARNDT-OBER Margarethe, ms.
                     2-054064

ARNOLDSON Sigrid, s.
  53465-7   53517
  53515   53631

ASCENZI   54377
                     54379

AUSTRAL Florence, s. 2-054131-3

         .....

BADA Angelo, t.   2-054034
                   2-054067

BADINI Ernesto, b.
  2-52609   2-52715/6
  2-52629   2-52725
  2-52704   2-52731
  2-52707   2-52743

Badini (contd.)

2-52753	54427		
2-52755	54438-40		
2-52765	54476		
2-52771	54479		
2-52778	054091		
2-52785	054093		
2-52788	054146-9		
2-52791	054154		
2-52793	054158		
2-52803	054166/7		
2-52836	054192/3		
052278/9	054241-5		
052281	054252/3		
052294	054286		
052347	054290/1		
052349/50	054294/5		
052395	054299/300		
052397	054303		
54301	054305-7		
54304/5	054366		
54312-4	054371		
54348	054373		
54350/1	054377		
54357	054379/80		
54363	054383/4		
54382	054387		
54398	054414		
54400	054432		
54402-6	054461/2		
54409	2-054076		
54411	2-054088		
54418	2-054135		

BAKLANOV George, b.   7-52136
                        052425
                        2-052157/8

BALDASSARE Luigi, b.
    52285   054006/7
    52630   054010
    52733/4   054012
    52796

BALDINI   054477
                        2-054057

BALDISSERI Nerina, s.   2-054107/8

BALLIÈRES Maria, s.   053160
                        054225/6

BARACCHI Aristide, b.   2-054128

BARBAINI Augusto, t.   052164/5
                        054153-5

BARBIERI E., s.
    053316/7   054432
    053322/3   054438
    54476   054449/50
    054415-7   054452-5
    054428

BARDI Giovanni, bs.   054230

BARRERA Carlo, t.
    2-52714   054252
    2-52799   054254/5
    052267   054258
    052290   054261
    054245-7   054288

BARTOLOMASI Valentine, s.
    053291-3   054346/7
    7-54014   2-054110-2

BATTAGLIOLI Giulia, s. ms.
    54404   54430
    54427   054251/2

BATTISTINI Mattia, b.
    52663-72   2-052251-7
    2-52847-9   54034
    7-52192   7-54018
    7-52194   054103-7
    7-52264/5   054317
    052140-8   054389/90
    052302-26   054392/3
    052357-71   054395
    052403-7   054449-55
    2-052201-4   2-054118/9
    2-052207-9

BELLABARBA V., b.   052390
                        054404

BELLATTI Virgilio, b.   2-52807
                        054321

BELLINCIONI Gemma, s.   053014
                        053017-9

BENDINELLI A., t.   054474/5

BERGAMIMI, t.   2-054079
                        2-054081

BERNACCHI Maria, s.
    54063   054046
    54255   054053
    54260/1

BERNAL-RESKY Gustavo, b. 2-52649/50

BERRIEL Enrique, b.   52795
    052015/6

BESALÙ B., s.
    53608   054297/8
    54468   054300

BESANZONI Gabriella, ms.
    7-53039   2-053195
    7-53041/2   2-053201
    2-053181

BETTONI Vincenzo, bs.
    2-52839   054370/1
    052344   054373
    052393/4   054385/6
    052401   054416
    052411/2   054424
    052414   054432/3
    052432/3   054442
    54467   054449/50
    054350-2   054457
    054359   054459/60
    054361   054473
    054363   054477
    054366   054480
    054368   2-054057

BIEL Julien, t.   52689-97
    52714

BLANCHARD Ramon, b.   2-52779-82

BOCCOLINI Ebe, s.
    53603/4   054313
    53614   054339/40
    53618   054388
    53622   054397/8
    53627   054402/3
    053264   054406
    2-053132   054414
    54435   2-054078
    54447
    054295
    054304

BOEZI C., t.   54780

BOLIS Luigi, t.   2-054071
    2-054074/5
    2-054087

BONALDI   52381-5
    54011-7

BONETTI G., s.   53623
    54455
    054329

BONINSEGNA Celestina, s.
    53372-6   053235
    53392   053253
    53415-9   2-053136
    53481   54056
    53492   54264
    053049/50   54266
    053063   054043/4
    053065   054062
    053067/8   054097/8
    053088/9   054109
    053101   2-054071
    053172   2-054074/5
    053231/2   2-054087

BORGHETTI, ms.   054132

BORELLI T., s.   53573
    53578
    054285

BORI Lucrezia, s.
    7-53010/1   2-053102/3
    7-53019   2-053120
    7-53049   2-053196
    7-53052   2-053203
    7-53054   7-54003
    7-53060/1   2-054055
    7-53065/6   2-054061
    7-53082   2-054120/1

BORONAT Olympia, s.   53346-54
    053185-90

BOSCACCI, t.   2-054139

BOSINI Gemma, s.   2-053131
    2-054086

BOTTA Luca, t.
    54471
    054397/8   054406-10
    054402/3   054414

BOVI Tina, s.   54267

BRAMBILLA Linda, s.
    053105
    053116   054114
    54320   054121
    54325/6   054124/5
    54329   054132

BRASLAU Sophie, c.   7-53018
    7-53034
    2-054090

BRESONNIER Luisa, s.   53251/2
    53257-9

BROCCARDI   2-054078

BRONZONI, s.   53580/1
53580/1
54417
054283/4

BRUNO Elisa, ms.   53132
53227-9
53241/2

BUCALO Emanuele, b.
52118-23   052009
52127   052017
52131/2   052079
52139   054014-6
52155-7   054018/9
52753   054045
52766/7   54045
52848   54047

BUTT Clara, c.   2-053076
2-053088
2-053209/10

BUTTI Gilda, s.   053149
54361/2
054218
054230

.....

CAFFETTO Carlo, t.
52266   52461-75
52268/9   52512/3
52277   52515-9
52336-40   52538
52359   52540-2
52362   52558
52364-5   54084
52376   54086-94
52386   54140
52458

CAFFO Alberto, t.
52891   2-52437
52894   54062
2-52411   54066

CALIGARIS Rosa, s.
53326   053016
053011-3   053020

CALVÉ Emma, ms.   053117/8
053183

CAMPANARI Giuseppe, b.   52060
2-52552
052136/7

CANALI F., b.
2-52810   054324/5
54449/50   054336
54457   054344
054311/2

CANCIELLO Padre   2-52617-20

CANNETTI U.,bs.
054323   054340
054326   054344
054328

CANTALAMESSA Berardo
52253   54069
52260/1   54073
52263   54080-2
52278   54131-6
52448-55   54139
52654   54141-3
54022-4

CAPPIELLO Maria, ms.
053233/4   054115/6
54328   054260

CAPPONI Lorenzo, t.   52820

CAPRILE Giorgina, s.
053303/4   054418/9
053313   054465-8
054381   054470
054383-5

CAPSIR Mercedes, s.
7-53077   7-54030
7-53086   7-54037
2-053245/6   2-054147/8

CARACCIOLO I., s.   2-052144-6

CARELLI Emma, s.   7-54020
53341   054026
053028/9   054028
053032-6   054034

CARONNA Ernesto, b.
52895   54063/4
2-52414   54068
2-52431   54255
052095   54261
54060/1   054049

CAROTINI Tilde, ms.   54034

CARUSO Enrico, t.
52034   52193
52062-6   52344-9
52191   52368-70

Caruso, Enrico (contd.)

52378	2-05205B-62	CASSANI Albertina, s.	
52417-9	2-052064-8	53567	53612
52439-43	2-052076/7	53610	54433
2-52479/80	2-052083		
2-52489	2-052086	CASTELLANI F., t.	
2-52641/2	2-052091	2-52837	054415-7
7-52002-4	2-052098	54474	054428
7-52013/4	2-052101		
7-52017/8	2-052106-8	CASTLES Amy, s.	2-053006
7-52025/6	2-052112		
7-52038/9	2-052129	CAVALIERI Elda, s.	053093-5
7-52042/3	2-052149		
7-52055	2-052153/4	CAZAURAN Leone, t.	52163-5
7-52068	2-052177		52167
7-52073	2-052180		
7-52080	2-052191	CELLINI Enzo	52088-92
7-52092	2-052195		52885
7-52094	2-052198		
7-52104	2-052224	CERESOLI Elvira, ms.	
7-52118	7-54006	53254-6	54021
7-52152	054070	53290	54033
7-52159	054117		
7-52162	054127	CESARANI Giovanni, t.	
7-52207	054129	52200/1	52615
7-52234	054134	52216/7	54000/1
7-52250/1	054198/9	52306	54005/6
7-52268/9	054201	52308	54100
7-52307	054204/5	52316	54102-17
7-52310	2-054005-7	52322	54125-7
052066	2-054010	52565-8	54521
052073/4	2-054013-7	52570	54525/6
052086-9	2-054027-32	52577-8	
052120-2	2-054034	52582-91	
052153/4	2-054037/8		
052157-9	2-054042/3	CHALIAPIN Feodor, bs.	
052209/10	2-054049/50	7-52227	052353-6
052224	2-054052/3	7-52229	052387-9
2-052005-8	2-054066/7	7-52246/7	2-052212
2-052032	2-054092-7	052222	2-052218
2-052034/5		052292	2-052220
			2-052302

CASAZZA, s.

2-054072/3	2-054083	CHIESA Fernanda, s.	
2-054077	2-054085	53615	054314
		54446	054399

CASINI Rita, c.

53121/2	054348	CIAPARELLI Gina, s.	53536
53217/8	054353/4		
53224	054356	CIBELLI Eugenio, t.	7-52322
53636	054363		7-52327
053297	054386		2-052259
053305/6	054444		
54006	054446/7	CICCOLINI Guido, t.	
54479		2-52705	7-52045/6
		2-52787	052238
		2-52789	052298
		2-52658-61	052418/9

Ciccolini, Guido (contd.)

052434	054388
2-052080-2	054465-8
054230	054470
054297-9	054480

CIGADA Francesco, b.

52908	54354-6
2-52439-41	54386-90
2-52467	54394-6
2-52469	054057
2-52513	054062
2-52539-41	054076
2-52548	054078/9
2-52569	054089
2-52580	054096
052098	054119/20
052119	054122-4
052131	054130
052162/3	054133
052181	054140
54152	054144
54264-6	054146/7
54292	054150-8
54302	054160-2
54325-8	054233
54338-40	054235-8
54344	
54346/7	

CINISELLI, t.

7-54030
2-054147/8
2-054150

CIOTTI P.   54381

CITTI-LIPPI Ines, s.

53323/4	54045
53327/8	054013
053021/2	

CLÉMENT Edmond, t.   2-054098

COATES John, t.   052219
                         052223

CODOLINI Amelia, ms.

53208	54327
54320	054119-22
54323	

COJONINI, t.   052013

COLAZZA Luigi, t.

52889/90	2-52575/6
2-52415/6	54060
2-52424	54255
2-52428	54259-61

Colazza, Luigi (contd.)

54263	054097
54323	054107-9
054046/7	054115
054049	054130

COLIVA Giovannina, s.   53304-6

COLOMBATI Virginia, s.   54004
                           54006

COMANDINI Prof., t.   54760/1
                        54771

COMIDA M., s.   54447

CONFORTI   054381

CONSTANTINO Florencio, t.
                        2-52403-10
                        054164

CONTI Gino, t.

54437-9	054301/2
54461/2	054307-10
54468	

CORRADETTI Ferruccio, b.

52202	52543
52204-6	52547
52209	52550
52212	52553
52214/5	52563
52218/9	52572
52221/2	52575/6
52224	52817
52227	52833/4
52228	052043
52230/1	052046
52237	052049
52239	54000
52242-4	54003-7
52247	54049/50
52256	54070
52301-5	54095-7
52310	54100-5
52312	54114
52314	54119-21
52318	54123
52320	54125/6
52325	54137
52327	54144
	54515
	54525

CORTIS Antonio, t.   7-52308/9

DA 757

COSENTINO **Orazio**, t.	054463/4	DAVI G., t.	54443
	054473		054260
			054287
COTOGNI Antonio, b.	54373		
		DAVID Cecilia, s.	
CRESTANI Lucia, s.	53408-11	053159	054178/9
	053066	053173	054183/4
CROMBERG Leopoldo, bs.	53698-700	DAVIDOV Alexander, t.	2-52643-6
CROSSLEY Ada, c.	53361	DAVIES Ben, t.	52329
CUCINI Alice, ms .		D'AVIGNY Olimpia	
53500-3	54332	53119	54022-4
053079-80	054085/6	53126/7	54069
053119-24		53142-4	54073
		53146	54080-2
CUNEGO Egidio, t.		53249/50	54131-6
2-52732-4	54444	53253	54139
2-52736	54467	53288/9	54141-3
2-52745	054268-70		
2-52751.2-52777	054274	DEL BOSCO Giovanni	7-52230/1
2-52786	054277		
052280	054292/3	DELLA TORRE Nestore, b.	
052287	054350/1	2-52697	052266
54413	054362	052226/7	054214
54415	054379	052241-3	054219
54424			
54432		DEMHARTER Irma, s.	54057
.....		DESTINN Emmy, s.	
		53532/3	2-053199
DADDI Francesco, t.		7-53022	7-54000
52271-3	7-52187/8	053171	7-54005
52901-5	7-52190	053240	7-54007
2-52491-502	054205	2-053052-4	2-054019/20
7-52184		2-053101	2-054023
		2-053104	2-054053
DADO Augusto, bs.	054099	2-053111/2	2-054062/3
		2-053139-41	
DADO Signor	54780		
		DE ANGELIS Angela, s.	54265
DA GRADI L., t.			54322
2-52764	054290		054057
54418	054294		
		DE CASAS Bianca Lavin, s.	
D'ALESSIO Robert, t.	7-54028	53382	54423/4
		53386-90	054045
DAL MONTE Toti, s.	7-53084/5	53528-31	054196/7
	2-053219/20	53559-61	054267
	2-053238-43	53601	054271-4
		053168/9	054276-8
DALMORES Charles, t.	052261	053203-7	054296
		053242	
D'ARCO Tina	53546	54412	
	54377		

DE CISNEROS Eleonòra, ms.

053043

DE FRATE Ines, s.

53552-4	54391
053191/2	054213
54374	054231-4
54389	054236-8

DE GOGORZA Emilio, b.

52687	7-52214
52715	052177
52720	052212
7-52015	052215/6
7-52020	052260
7-52074	2-052109
7-52105	2-052159-62
7-52137	054071/2
	2-054104

DE GREGORIO F., t.

2-52706	052398-400
2-52741	54416/7
2-52744	54426
2-52746-9	54435/6
2-52752	54460
2-52754	54473
2-52756	54481
2-52758	054281-4
2-52761-3	054303/4
2-52775/6	054418/9
2-52784	054424
2-52790	054433
2-52792	054442
2-52795-7	054446/7
2-52806	054481/2
2-52835	
052301	

DE LAURENTIIS Giuseppe 7-52314/5
7-52323
7-54033

DE LUCA Giuseppe, b.

52420-6	2-052155/6
52444	2-052183
52773	2-052210
7-52095/6	2-052250
7-52098/9	54021
7-52160	54048
7-52177	7-54011/2
7-52199	054039
7-52203	2-054066/7
7-52235	2-054089
7-52273/4	2-054092/3
2-052116	2-054099
2-052118	2-054117
2-052127	2-054120/1
2-052130	2-054130

DE LUCIA Fernando, t.

52077-84	052111
52410-6	052129
52427	052184/5
52435-8	052239
52650-2	052250
2-52472-5	54293
2-52518-20	54357
2-52607/8	54384
2-52660/1	054043
2-52666/7	054080-4
2-52676	054171-3
2-52698-701	054175
2-52722-4	054215
2-52772-4	054217
052078	

DE LUNA Giuseppe Torres, bs.

2-52412	54260
2-52429	54298
052096	054046/7
54064	054087/8

DE MICHALSKA Stanislawa, s.

53313	054001
53316	054005
54042	

DE' MURO Bernardo, t.

7-52153/4	054346/7
052338-40	054477-9
052341-3	2-054056/7
052429-31	2-054070
2-052119-23	2-054072/3
2-052148	2-054076/7
2-052174	2-054088
2-052176	2-054126-9
2-052237	2-054134/5
7-54023	
7-54026/7	

DE NUNZIO A.   7-54025

DE NUNZIO Coppia   7-54024

DE PASQUALI Bernice, s. 53247
54010

DE PASQUALI Pietro, t.   54010

DE SEGUROLA Andres Perello, bs.

52633/4	2-52684
52637-40	052152
52643	052195-8
2-52567/8	052203-5
2-52571	052236
2-52582-4	54018/9
2-52633-5	54030/1
2-52665	54040

COSENTINO Orazio, t. 054463/4
 054473

COTOGNI Antonio, b. 54373

CRESTANI Lucia, s. 53408-11
 053066

CROMBERG Leopoldo, bs. 53698-700

CROSSLEY Ada, c. 53361

CUCINI Alice, ms .
 53500-3 54332
 053079-80 054085/6
 053119-24

CUNEGO Egidio, t.
 2-52732-4 54444
 2-52736 54467
 2-52745 054268-70
 2-52751.2-52777 054274
 2-52786 054277
 052280 054292/3
 052287 054350/1
 54413 054362
 54415 054379
 54424
 54432

  .....

DADDI Francesco, t.
 52271-3 7-52187/8
 52901-5 7-52190
 2-52491-502 054205
 7-52184

DADO Augusto, bs. 054099

DADO Signor 54780

DA GRADI L., t.
 2-52764 054290
 54418 054294

D'ALESSIO Robert, t. 7-54028

DAL MONTE Toti, s. 7-53084/5
 2-053219/20
 2-053238-43

DALMORES Charles, t. 052261

D'ARCO Tina 53546
 54377

DAVI G., t. 54443
 054260
 054287

DAVID Cecilia, s.
 053159 054178/9
 053173 054183/4

DAVIDOV Alexander, t. 2-52643-6

DAVIES Ben, t. 52329

D'AVIGNY Olimpia
 53119 54022-4
 53126/7 54069
 53142-4 54073
 53146 54080-2
 53249/50 54131-6
 53253 54139
 53288/9 54141-3

DEL BOSCO Giovanni 7-52230/1

DELLA TORRE Nestore, b.
 2-52697 052266
 052226/7 054214
 052241-3 054219

DEMHARTER Irma, s. 54057

DESTINN Emmy, s.
 53532/3 2-053199
 7-53022 7-54000
 053171 7-54005
 053240 7-54007
 2-053052-4 2-054019/20
 2-053101 2-054023
 2-053104 2-054053
 2-053111/2 2-054062/3
 2-053139-41

DE ANGELIS Angela, s. 54265
 54322
 054057

DE CASAS Bianca Lavin, s.
 53382 54423/4
 53386-90 054045
 53528-31 054196/7
 53559-61 054267
 53601 054271-4
 053168/9 054276-8
 053203-7 054296
 053242
 54412

DE CISNEROS Eleonora, ms.

	053043

DE FRATE Ines, s.

53552-4	54391
053191/2	054213
54374	054231-4
54389	054236-8

DE GOGORZA Emilio, b.

52687	7-52214
52715	052177
52720	052212
7-52015	052215/6
7-52020	052260
7-52074	2-052109
7-52105	2-052159-62
7-52137	054071/2
	2-054104

DE GREGORIO F., t.

2-52706	052398-400
2-52741	54416/7
2-52744	54426
2-52746-9	54435/6
2-52752	54460
2-52754	54473
2-52756	54481
2-52758	054281-4
2-52761-3	054303/4
2-52775/6	054418/9
2-52784	054424
2-52790	054433
2-52792	054442
2-52795-7	054446/7
2-52806	054481/2
2-52835	
052301	

DE LAURENTIIS Giuseppe

	7-52314/5
	7-52323
	7-54033

DE LUCA Giuseppe, b.

52420-6	2-052155/6
52444	2-052183
52773	2-052210
7-52095/6	2-052250
7-52098/9	54021
7-52160	54048
7-52177	7-54011/2
7-52199	054039
7-52203	2-054066/7
7-52235	2-054089
7-52273/4	2-054092/3
2-052116	2-054099
2-052118	2-054117
2-052127	2-054120/1
2-052130	2-054130

DE LUCIA Fernando, t.

52077-84	052111
52410-6	052129
52427	052184/5
52435-8	052239
52650-2	052250
2-52472-5	54293
2-52518-20	54357
2-52607/8	54384
2-52660/1	054043
2-52666/7	054080-4
2-52676	054171-3
2-52698-701	054175
2-52722-4	054215
2-52772-4	054217
052078	

DE LUNA Giuseppe Torres, bs.

2-52412	54260
2-52429	54298
052096	054046/7
54064	054087/8

DE MICHALSKA Stanislawa, s.

53313	054001
53316	054005
54042	

DE' MURO Bernardo, t.

7-52153/4	054346/7
052338-40	054477-9
052341-3	2-054056/7
052429-31	2-054070
2-052119-23	2-054072/3
2-052148	2-054076/7
2-052174	2-054088
2-052176	2-054126-9
2-052237	2-054134/5
7-54023	
7-54026/7	

DE NUNZIO A. 7-54025

DE NUNZIO Coppia 7-54024

DE PASQUALI Bernice, s. 53247

	54010

DE PASQUALI Pietro, t. 54010

DE SEGUROLA Andres Perello, bs.

52633/4	2-52684
52637-40	052152
52643	052195-8
2-52567/8	052203-5
2-52571	052236
2-52582-4	54018/9
2-52633-5	54030/1
2-52665	54040

De Segurola, Andres Perello (contd.)

54318/9	054184
54331	054195
54360	054262
54370/1	2-054050
054097	2-054052

DE SOUZA Marquis Francisco, b.
	52649

DE TURA Gennaro, t.
2-52593/4	54375
2-52601-4	54385
2-52639/40	54398/9
2-52670/1	54408
2-52695/6	7-54014
052206/7	054141-4
052256	054169
052265	054195
052295	054241-3
54334	054265
54341-4	

DE WITT, s.   2-054118/9

DIAZ M.   53544/5

DIDUR Ademo, bs.
52027	052028-30
052024	

DI ANNA, s.   054359

DI BERNARDO G., t.
	052348
	054376/7

DI LANDA Anita   53453-63

DOMAR Dora, s.
53587	054248/9
54400	054253
54428	

DONALDA Pauline, s.
	53520
	53537
	053104

DONES Paolo, t.
	7-52313
	7-52321

DRAGONI Matteo, b.
7-52209-12	2-054080
7-52218	2-054082
2-052132-6	2-054111-3
2-052189	2-054116
2-052221/2	2-054122

DRISTORA, s.   53303

DUCHÈNE Marie, s.   2-054050

. . . . .

EAMES Emma, s.
053058	054200
053091/2	2-054100
054071/2	

EDVINA Marie Louise, s. 2-053150

EGENER Minnie, c.   2-054067

EKMAN Ida, s.   053053

ESPOSITO Clotilde, c.
53403	54263
54250	054048
54259	

. . . . .

FABBRI Guerrina, c.
53318	053009
53321/2	053015
053006/7	053041

FABRIS Giulia, s.
	053251/2
53576	54425
53584	054285

FANTONI Signor
52381-5	52581
52549	52606-12
52551/2	52614
52557	54011-7
52574	

FARELLI Tina, s.
	53407
	54251/2
	054051/2

FARRAR Geraldine, s.
53343-5	2-053069
53363/4	2-053081/2
53425	54311
53430	7-54012
53469	054126
7-53001-4	054201-4
7-53025	054206
7-53040	2-054000-4
053176/7	2-054035
053215	2-054039
2-053009/10	2-054044
2-053037	2-054098

FASSIO Ida, s.   53400-2

FAVI   54379

FEDERICI Francesco, b.
  2-52702   054222/3
  2-52760   054227
  2-52801   054234
  2-52804/5   054263/4
  052246   054287
  052282-4   054289
  54431   54390
  54433

FELIX Benedikt, b.   52363

FERRABINI Ester, s.   53438

FERRANI Cesira, s.
  53147   54033
  53149/50   54035
  53281-7

FERRETTI Corrado, b.
  52213   54483
  52250-2   054420
  52254   054447
  54475

FINZI-MAGRINI Giuseppina, s.
  53377-80   54055
  53383   054045
          054396

FLETA Miguel, t.
  7-52236/7   7-52292
  7-52262   2-052215/6
  7-52270   2-054131-3

FOERSTER Gusti, s.   53435

FOSCA Titta, s.   53523/4
          54359

FRANCHI Nazzareno, bs.
  52223   52592-8
  52315   52618
  52323   54070
  52460   54106/7
  52479/80   54118
  52526-9   54122/3

FRANCILLO-KAUFMANN Hedwig, s.
          53555
          053219/20

FRASCANI Nini, ms.
  53362   053300/1
  053048   054376

FREZZI, s.   54419-21

FROSINI Ottavio, t.   52279-81
          52632

.....

GADSKI Johanna, s.
  053214   2-054005/6
  2-053144-8   2-054045/6
  054456   2-054101/2

GALAN Ramona, ms.
  53168-70   54108-12
  53172-6   54122
  53180-90   54124
  53366/7   54127
  54098/9

GALASSI Maria, ms.   54112/3

GALBIERO Gerolamo, t.
  2-52739/40   2-52757
  2-52742   54425

GALLI Amleto, bs.
  52408/9   54441/2
  2-52820   054302
  052299   054345

GALLI-CURCI Amelita, s.
  7-53023   2-053198
  7-53029/30   2-053208
  7-53044   2-053211
  7-53047   2-053214
  7-53050/1   2-053217
  7-53056   2-053230
  2-053126   2-053233-6
  2-053128   7-54011
  2-053130   7-54034/5
  2-053133-5   2-054066/7
  2-053137   2-054089
  2-053142   2-054099
  2-053161   2-054151/2
  2-053183
  2-053186

GALPERNI Adamo, b.   52149
          52153/4

GALVANY Maria, s.
  53293-7   053180-2
  53307   053193
  53482-5   053200
  53526/7   54315/6
  53549-51   54370/1
  53558   54384
  053162-5   054100/1

Galvany, Maria (contd.)
054110-2   054215
054180/1   054217
054208/9

GARBIN Edoardo, t.   52428-34
                       052010

GARGIULO, s.   2-054113

GARRISON Mabel, s.   2-053149
                       7-54015

GAY Maria, ms.
53516   2-053011
053140   2-053016-8

GENNARI Oreste, t.   054039

GENTILE M.   7-54025

GHELARDINI A., t.   2-52719
                       54430

GIACOMELLI Ida, s.
53429   54323
53497   054054/5
53504/5   054058-60
053102   054065
54146   054067-9
54152   054075
54268   054115
54274   054133
54284   054140
54290

GIANNINI Diege
52459   52504-9
52502   52523

GIGLI Beniamino, t.
7-52109-15   7-52329/30
7-52150/1   2-052140-3
7-52170/1   2-052175
7-52176   2-052197
7-52180   2-052214
7-52195   2-052219
7-52198   2-052233
7-52200/1   2-052235
7-52219/20   2-052244
7-52223   2-052290/1
7-52257   2-054083-6
7-52286/7   2-054105-9
7-52295/6   2-054114

GILBERTI A., t.
052331   54459   054326
54446   054313/4   054340

GILIBERT Charles, b.   054128

GILLY Dinh, b.
7-52244/5   7-54007
7-54000   2-054062
7-54005   2-054140/1

GIORGINI Aristodemo, t.
52168   052208
52170   052228
52173-8   052232
52194/5   052240
52197   052244
52199   052257
2-52421-3   052286
2-52564-6   54429
2-52664   7-54036
2-52677   054110-2
2-52691/2   054196/7
052083-5   054250
052105/6   054289
052149

GIOVANELLI Gino, t.
2-52708/9   054353/4
052247   054356
54400   054359
54428   054361
54431   054363
54445   054366
054221   054368
054253   054371
054264   054373

GIRALDONI Eugenio, b. 52401-6

GIRARDI Alexander, t. 52267
                       52270
                       52366

GIRAUD Fiorello, t.
52046-9   052067
7-52081-6   052069
7-52088-91   052070/1
7-52132/3

GIUDICE Franco lo, t. 2-052272/3

GIUSTI Giuseppe, b.   52758/9
                       52765
                       52768-71

GLUCK Alma, s.
7-53008/9   2-053089-91
7-53021   7-54006
7-53027   2-054069
2-053066   2-054103

GOETZEN V.De, b.

052333	054326
54446	054328-31
54451	054333
054314/5	054337
054322	

GRAMAGNA A., ms.

53616	054342/3
053284	054345
54441/2	2-054126
54469	2-054128

GRANADOS Francisco, t.

2-52688	54392-6
54388	054234-6
54390	054239

GRANFORTE Apollo, b. 7-52337/8
2-052286-9

GRASSOT Isabel, s. 53277/8
54030/1

GRAVINA Giovanni, bs. 52342/3
52367

GRIPPA Antonietta, s. 53156-9
53205
54084/5

GRISI Maria, s.

53473	54317-9
53487	54321
53495	54331
54291/2	054077-9
54302/3	054089

GROSSI Adalgisa, ms. 53160-2
54140

GUERRIERI G., t. 7-52319/20

. . . . .

HAYES Lulu, s. 7-54018

HELDER Ruby (The Lady Tenor)
7-53007

HELENA Edith, s. 53151
53334
53358-60

HEMPEL Frieda, s.

7-53012	053260-3
7-53026	053265
7-53083	053289/90

Hempel, Frieda (contd.)

053326/7	2-053184
053329	2-054050
2-053098-100	2-054052
2-053151/2	2-054060

HISLOP Joseph, t.

7-52252/3	2-052248/9
2-052200	2-052268/9
2-052232	2-054140/1

HOMER Louise, c.

7-53005	054456
7-53028	2-054015-7
2-053138	2-054044
2-053153-7	2-054069
054117	2-054094
054126	2-054097
054198	2-054101-3

HUGUET Giuseppina, s.

53138-41		54296
53260-71		54298
53274-6		54302
53308-10		54306/7
53452		54309/10
53474/5		54314
53480		54338/9
53510-3		54341
53563		54346-8
53566	54350/1	054076
53569	54356	054081-4
53589	54380	054087/8
53613	54399	054095/6
053001	54445	054099
053072-4		054146-52
053081/2		054154/5
053085/6		054157/8
053090		054162
053130		054165-7
053132		054171-3
053136		054175
053236		054250
54018/9		054264/5
54025-9		
54040		

. . . . .

IMPALLOMENI, s. 2-054116

ISALBERTI Silvano, t.

52140	52863
52161	54057
52169	

ISCHIERDO Emanuele, t.
2-52638   052193/4   54353

Ischierdo, Emanuele (contd.)
54355   054165
54359   054170
054098   054182/3
054102

.....

JACOBY Josephine, c.
2-054004   2-054037
2-054030-2   2-054061
2-054034

JADLOWKER Hermann, t.
2-52831   052437
2-52857   052440/1
052374/5   2-052070/1
052385/6   2-054035
052426
052428

JANNI Attilia, b.   054317
                          054477
                          2-054056/7

JERITZA Maria, s.   7-53058
                          7-53067/8
                          2-053212

JOANNA Clara, s.
053129   054142/3
053133   054159
54334-7   054165
54340   054168
54349

JOHNSON Edward, t.   7-52149
                          7-52156
                          7-52158

JÖRN Karl, t.   54311

JOURNET Marcel, bs.
2-52515/6   2-052270
7-52093   2-052274/5
7-52138/9   054135
7-52306   054205
7-52328   2-054010
052093   2-054029-34
052214   2-054037/8
2-052039   2-054067/8
2-052163-7

.....

KAMIONSKY Oscar, b.   52023-5
                          052064

KASCHMANN Giuseppe, b. 052031/2
                          052036-8

KOENEN Tilly, ms.   53514

KURZ Selma, s.   053179
53431   053254
53479   053273-80
53486   053283
53491   2-053077-80
53494
53496
53535
53564/5
53570

.....

LANZIROTTI Carmelo, t.
2-52522   054096
54151   054099
54309/10

LA PUMA Giuseppe, b.
52003   52831
52787   52837
52825/6   52842
        2-052042
        2-052044

LARA Pietro, t.
52906   54298
2-52514   54300
2-52525   54303
2-52547   54312/3
2-52549   54317
2-52738   54419-21
2-52767/8   54434
052124/5   054077
54295/6

LASHANSKA Ulda, s.   7-53063/4

LAZARO Hippolyte, t.   2-052045-7
                          2-052049/50

LEBRUN G., s.   054350
                          054362

LICETTE Miriam, s.   2-053122/3

LINDEN Julia, s.   53292

LIPKOWSKAYA Lydia, s.   053307/8

LJUNGBERG Göta, s.   2-054144/5

LLOPART M., s.	054463/4	MALATESTA Pompilio, bs.54366/7	
	054474/5		
		MALDACEA Nicola	2-52503-12
LONGHI Emma, ms.			
53314	054003	MALESCI Giorgio, t.	
53317	054005	52141-5	52530-3
53319/20	054007	52158-60	52538
53330	054011	52162	52688
53335-8	054014-8	52350-3	52864
053023	054020	52355	54500
54044	054022		
54046	054032	MAMELI Ida, ms.	53442
			054061
LOPEZ-NUNEZ Eugenia, c.			
53579	054279-82	MANGINI Bianca, s.	
53590-2	054291	53617	054321-3
054230		53626	054325
		053270/1	054328
LOTTI F., s.		54450	054336
053281	054303	54457	054344
54437	054305/6		
54461/2	054308-10	MANSUETO Gaudio, bs.	
54469	054342/3	052202	54440
054301	054387	052237	054185
		54400	054248/9
LUFRANO G., s.	53607	54408	
	53611		
	053259	MANURITTA Giovanni, t. 2-054149	
LULLI, b.	7-54029	MARAK Ottokar, t.	2-52652-4
			2-52656-9
LUNN Louise Kirkby, c.			
2-053000/1	2-054020	MARCEL Lucille, s.	053257
2-053067/8	2-054023		
2-053074/5	2-054040/1	MARCHESI Blanche, s.	53439-41
2-053121			
		MARCHETTI Silvia	
LUSSARDI G., b.		53543	54378
2-52821	054363	053198/9	054220
2-52823	054368	54376	
054353	054371		
054359	054373	MARCHINI Elisa, s.	
054361	054461/2	054349	054363
		054353	054373
LYCKSETH-SCHJERVEN Magna, s.			
	53391	MARDONES José, bs.	2-052239
			2-052247
.....			2-054130
MACNEZ Umberto, t.	2-52726-8	MARCONI Francesco, t.	
	052274-7	52016/7	052200
		52788	052221
MAGGI Giuseppe, b.		2-52631/2	052233/4
2-52800	054256/7	2-52662/3	54373
54443	054419	2-52672/3	054186-90
54462	054422	052054-8	054208
054246/7	054442	052065	054214

MARIANI, b.   054363
    054361   054371

MARINELLA Anna, s.   7-53093

MARISTANY José, t. 54019. 54025-9

MARSH Lucy Isabelle, s.2-054059

MARTINELLI Giovanni, t.

7-52051-3	2-052115
7-52056	2-052124
7-52060	2-052128
7-52065-7	2-052152
7-52076-9	2-052168
7-52087	2-052196
7-52100	2-052213
7-52107	2-052236
7-52141	2-052238
7-52215	2-054063
7-52303/4	2-054068
2-052085	2-054091
2-052099/100	2-054117
2-052102	2-054123
2-052105	2-054130

MARSH Lucy Isabelle, s.2-054059

MARTINENGO G., ms.   53633/4
                          54470
                          054402/3

MARTINEZ-PATTI Gino, t.

52022	54250-2
52035-9	54254
52085-7	54256/7
52794	54267/8
52884	54274
52898	54278
52900	54283/4
2-52413	54287/8
2-52427	054048
2-52488	054051-5
052077	054059/60
53427	054065-8
54065	054075
54068	

MARTIN Riccardo, t.   7-52009

MARTORANO, t.   2-054146

MATROIANI Mario, t.   54055
                         054045

MATZENAUER Margarethe, ms.
                         054401

MAURI Aurelio, t.   52391/2
                         52397

MAZZARA   52524

McCORMACK John, t.

7-52016	2-052169
7-52032-4	7-54003
7-52041	2-054011
7-52044	2-054018/9
7-52047	2-054021/2
7-52061	2-054025
7-52075	2-054040/1
7-52275/6	2-054055
2-052021---8	2-054059
2-052110/1	2-054061

MECHERINI Coppia   52704-7
                         52802/3
                         54036-9

MELBA Nellie, s.

053106-15	2-053263/4
053211/2	054128/9
2-053019-29	2-054025
2-053083	

MELIS Carmen, s.   53506-8
                         54333
                         054136-9

MELIUS, s.   7-53091/2

MELLERIO Laura, s.

53583	053255/6
53593-8	54405/6
053249	054242

MILANO Giuseppe, t., b.7-52189
                          7-52197
                          7-52325/6

MILERI Lina, ms.

53400	54295
53413	54297
53420/1	54300
53477/8	54321
053064	054055
053084	054058
54146	054063
54150	054068
54290	054090

MILILOTTI Bice, s.   054186-90

MINOLFI Renzo, b.
    2-52485   2-52554
    2-52517   2-52556

Minolfi, Renzo (contd.)

2-52577/8	54333
2-52586	54335/6
2-52592	54345
052126	54380
052134	054061
052150	054069
54147	054090
54271	054095
54285	054099
54297	054108
54306-8	054118
54324	054145

MOLINARI Enrico, b.

2-52735	54422
2-52750	54426
2-52759	54436
2-52766	54444
2-52802	

MONTECUCCHI Luigi, t.

52225	54002/3
52232-5	54009
52245	54075
52328	54077

MOREO Enrico, b.

52478	52599-605
52544-6	52613
52548	52616/7
52554-6	54085
52559-62	54098/9
52573	54124
52579	54508

MORESCHI Prof.Alessandro, castrato

54764	54773-7
54766	54780
54770	

MOSCISCA Maria, s. — 054389/90, 054392/3, 054395

MUMMERY Browning, t. — 2-054144/5

MURINO A.Rossi, s.
(see ROSSI-MURINO)

MURPHY Lambert, t. — 7-54004, 2-054051

MURRAY-DAVEY M., bs. — 2-052114

MUSSINI A., s. 53582 54422

MUZIO Claudia, s. — 053264

. . . . .

NEUMARKER A., b. — 054350, 054362, 054370

NICCOLINI Alessandro, bs. — 54308

NICOLETTI, bs.

52564	52571
52569	52580

NICOLICCHIA S., bs. — 54400, 54402/3, 54429

NIELSEN Alice, s. — 053137, 054164

NOTO Giuseppe, b. — 7-54037

NULLI N., s. — 54416

NUVOLERI, t. — 54403

. . . . .

ODDO Ignazio, t.

52286-8	52843
52290	52845
52800	52849/50
52809/10	

OFFERS Martje, c.

2-053226/7	2-054137/8
2-053244	2-054146

OLITZKA Rosa, c. — 53291

OLTRABELLA Augusta, s. — 7-54026/7, 2-054134

OTTAVIANI Lazzaro, t. — 52393, 52396

OTTOBONI Libero, t. — 54291/2, 54302, 054079

OXILIA Giuseppe, t.

52246	52321	52360/1
52255	52324	52445
52274/5	52330-4	
52317	52356-8	

PACINI Giuseppe, b.   2-054109

PAGNONI Gualtiero, b. 52387
52390
52395

PALET José, t.
7-52101   2-052125
7-52103   5-052000/1

PALLISER Esther, s.   53248

PALUMBO F.   52477
52498
52500/1

PANDOLFINI Angelica, s.
53333   053037/8
53340   053044

PAOLI Antonio, t.
2-52595-8   052332
2-52710-2   052335-7
2-52721   54340
2-52783   54407
2-52808/9   54451
2-52811   054156-62
2-52813-5   054174
2-52817   054262
052166-73   054330/1
052271/2   054337
052297   054399
052328-30

PARETO Graziella, s.
53521/2   054228/9
053151-7   2-054079-82
053208   2-054149/50
2-053172-9

PARNIS   2-054140

PAROLA A., t.   052413
054457
054459/60

PASSERI Maria, ms.
53525   054174
53605   054182
54281/2   054191
54361/2   054216
54364/5   054288
54368/9   054299
54375   054316
54382/3   054339/40
54459/60

PAVONI Rinalda, s.
54454   054326
54459   054332-4
054315   054473

PENZA Florigio   52521

PEREA Emilio, t.
52179-81   54253
52184-6   54270
52188-90   54272/3
2-52400   54279
2-52418/9 054050
052094   054063
052112

PEREIRA Malvina, s.
053314   054422
54481/2   054442

PERINI, c.   2-054066

PEZZUTI E., t.   2-52794
2-52827
054307

PICCOLETTI Giuseppina, s.
53424   54344
53428   054064
53449/50   054169
053070/1 054219
053209

PIETRACEWSKA Carolina, c.
53548   54410/1
053184   054210-2
053194   054218
053201/2 054258
053218   054263
053238

PIGNATARO Enrico, b.
52896   54283
2-52470/1 54286
2-52477   054056
54268

PINI-CORSI Antonio, bs.-b.
52774   052201
2-52526/7 052235
2-52557   052263
2-52637   052288/9
2-52703   54279-82
2-52717/8 54286
052099   54293
052130   54299
052135   54301
052182   54329/30

Pini-Corsi, Antonio (contd.)
54349-51	054094
54363-7	054125
054080	054191-3
054083	054216
054091	

PINI-CORSI Gaetano, t.
2-52610	54391
2-52627	54412
54329	054039
54338/9	054151-8
54350-2	054167/8
54369	054227
54382/3	054239

PINTO Amelia, s.   53232-4
                   53238-40

PINTUCCI Angelo, t.
52257	54007
52326	54049/50
52817	54144
54004	

PINZA Ezio, bs.
7-52241-3	7-54036
7-52289/90	2-054136
2-052240-3	2-054139
2-052278-80	2-054146
7-54028	

PLANÇON Pol, bs.
52070	052117
2-52585	052217/8
052090	

POLESE Giovanni, b.   54280

POLI-RANDACIO Tina, s.
7-53038	2-053190-2
7-53053	2-053205
2-053162	2-053218
2-053164	2-054137-9

POLISSENI Angelo, t.   52098-109

POLLINI Amelia, s.   53396/7
                     53399
                     54059

PONSELLE Rosa, s.
7-53074/5	2-053231/2
2-053216	2-053247
2-053222/3	

PONZANO A., c.   053328
                 054457-60

POPOVICI Honoria, s.   54407
                       54443
                       054287

POWER Stella, s.   2-053167/8

POZZI-CAMOLLA Vittorio, b.
                   054039

PREVE Cesare, bs.
2-52444-6	54278
2-52468	54285-9
2-52484	054056
2-52486/7	054061
052097	054063
54145	054066/7
54147	054069
54274	

PRINCIPE T., ms.
054348-53	054370
054362	054386

• • • • •

QUARANTA, t.   7-52191

QUERCIA Tullio, b.
52389	054004/5
54043	054009
054002	

QUINZI-TAPERGI Giuseppe, bs.
052262	054240
54387	054260
54389-91	054263
54431	2-054135
054233-5	

• • • • •

RADFORD Robert, bs.   2-052040

RAKOWSKY, s.   54409

RAMBELLI Nina, c.   54337
                    054141
                    054145

REICH Carl, bs.   2-52490

RICCARDI Papa   7-52281-3
                7-54033

RICCIO Agostino
52150	52874-83
52865-72	52887

RICCOBONO Ferdinando, t.052183

RIGUZZI Emilio, bs.   52742
                          52749
                          52760-3
                          52814/5

RIMONDINI G., b.   2-52737
                          052285
                          052352

RIZZINI Adele, s.   53427
                          54269-73
                          54289

RIZZO F., b.
      54423   054278
      054267   054296

ROCCHI A., s.   53606
                    53630

ROSALIN Jole   53541/2

ROSALIN Olga   53539/40

ROSCI Giuseppe, b.   054153
                         054156
                         054165

ROSELLI Ida, s.   53436/7

ROSSI Giulio, bs.   2-52521
                         054085

ROSSI-MURINO Adalgisa, s.
      53588   054282
      053245-7   054286
      54415   054291
      054279/80

ROTA Aristide, t.
      52051-8   52124-6
      52068   52133-7
      52093-7   52151/2
      52110-7

ROTHIER Leon, bs.   2-054050
                        2-054052

RUBINO Clothilde, s.
      53574/5   053248
      53577   053258
      53585/6   053266
      053244

RUFFO Titta, b.
      2-52528/9   2-52685-7
      2-52555   2-52828/9
      2-52621-5   7-52029-31
      2-52678-80   7-52035-7

Ruffo, Titta (contd.)
      7-52040   2-052075
      7-52048-50   2-052088
      7-52054   2-052090
      7-52062/3   2-052096
      7-52070-2   2-052103/4
      7-52143   2-052170
      7-52168   2-052181
      7-52173   2-052184-7
      7-52224-6   2-052190
      7-52258   2-052199
      7-52260   2-052225/6
      7-52263   54315/6
      7-52332   54359/60
      052132/3   054100-2
      052188-92   054180/1
      052248/9   054228/9
      052251   054396
      052376   2-054049
      052378-83

RUGGERO M., s.   054478/9
                        2-054070
                        2-054076

RUIS Adolfo, t.   52647

RUSS Giannina, s.
      53342   054019
      053008   054022
      053025   054024/5
      54046   054029
      054008   054032/3
      054015/6

RUSZKOWSKA Elena, s.
      53568   054254-7
      053237   054260/1
      053243   054268-74
      053250   054276
      54413

                    . . . . .

SABATANO Salvatore
      52701   52800/1
      52710   52804

SADERO Edoardo, t   7-52333/4

SAINESCU   054451

SALA Giuseppe, t.
      52899   54653
      54145   054079
      54291   054329/30
      54416   054370

SALVADOR Ines, c.
      053135   54334/5   54337

<table>
<tr><td colspan="2"><u>Salvador, Ines (contd.)</u></td></tr>
<tr><td>54353/4</td><td>054162</td></tr>
<tr><td>54356</td><td>054170</td></tr>
</table>

SALVATI S., t.

2-52838	054311/2
2-52840/1	054324
052396	054328-30
54449	054336
54451	054339
54455	054344
54457	054421
54475	

SALMARCO Mario, b.

52011	2-052033
52371-5	2-052041-4
52782	2-052072-4
7-52028	2-052171
052020	054026
052025-7	054028
052033/4	2-054011/2
052039-41	2-054018
052063	2-054021/2
2-052009-18	2-054025
2-052031	

SANCOVY Fortunio, t.	2-52606
	54332

SANGIORGI Remo, t.

052151	54322
54150	054078/9
54291	054089

SANIPOLI, s.	53602
	54434
	054299

SANTA-MARINA, s.	054292/3

SANTELIA Gina, s.	7-53094

SANTLEY Charles, b.	052000

SANTOLIVA-VILLANI M., s.

	053302
	054379/80

SANTORO A., s.

54388	054237
54391-3	054251
54429	054253

SARAH F., s.	53637
	054457-60

SCALA Coppia Les	7-54008/9

SCALFARO S., s.

54483	054433
054420/1	054444

SCAMPINI Augusto, t.

2-52611-6	052264
2-52689/90	054178/9
052186/7	054211
052245	054240
052258/9	

SCATTOLA Carlo, bs.	52388
	52399/400
	7-52111

SCHIAVAZZI Pietro, t.	52019

SCHIPA Tito, t.

7-52122/4	7-52305
7-52125	052421/2
7-52204/5	2-052150
7-52216/7	2-052281/2
7-52228	2-052292/3
7-52254/5	7-54020
7-52284/5	7-54034/5
7-52300	2-054151/2

SCHRODTER Fritz, t.	52377

SCHUMANN-HEINK Ernestine, c.

053103	2-053158/9
053158	2-054042
2-053014	

SCIPIONI Augusto, bs.	54329/30
	054125

SCOTTI Antonio, b.

52059	052225
52061	2-052000-4
52067	2-052007
2-52433-5	054070
2-52481-3	054074
7-52000/1	054117
7-52019	054127
7-52144	054199
052091/2	054202-6
052107-10	2-054000-3
052112-6	2-054013/4
052123	2-054043
052128	2-054095/6
052139	
052160/1	

SCOTTI Luisella	53192
	53195/6

SEMBRICH Marcella, s.
  53394   053216/7
  053054-7   2-053160
  053075-8   054074
  053096-100   054199-200
  053166   054205
  053170   2-054012
  053174   2-054100
  053213

SETTI Giulio, t.   2-054026

SEVERINA Gina, ms.   054199
                 054205

SIEBANECH Lina, s.   54342/3

SIGNORINI Francesco, t.
  2-52668/9   54386
  052229-31   054210
  052253-5   054213
  54374   054231/2

SILLICH Aristodemo, bs.
  2-52570   054105
  2-52572   054107
  2-52574   054114
  54152   054119-23
  54320   054133
  54326/7   054161
  54347   054168
  54352

SIMONETTA-RANCONI Luigi, t.
  7-52106   7-52126-30
  7-52120/1   2-052151

SMIRNOV Dimitri, t.
  2-52826   052296
  7-52172   052372/3
  7-52174/5   052410
  7-52179   052417
  052293   2-052192-4

SOBINOFF Leonid, t.   2-52655

SOBRINO Luisa, s.   053000

SOLARI Francesca, s.   053332
                 054480-2

SOLLOHUB I., s.   54471
              054409

SORGI Giuseppe, bs.   054009

STOPPA, b. 53427 54256 54258

STORCHIO Rosina, s.   53331/2
                 54048
                 054027

SUTTER Anna, s.   53547

SVICHER Isabella, s.   53444-7
      .....

TACCANI Giuseppe, t.   2-52587-91
                 054136-40
                 2-054118

TAMAGNO Francesco, t.
  52673-85   052068
  7-52277   052100-3

TAMINI, t.   2-52682

TANI G.   54378
                 54687

TASINI Colombo, b.   2-52819

TEBRO Ernestina, s.
  53130/1   53230/1
  53134   53235-7
  53221   54005

TEDESCHI Alfredo, t.   52138
                 52171/2
                 54054

TEGANI Riccardo, b.   054224
                 054227

TESSARI Gino, b.
  52447   54376
  52456/7   54378
  52629   54381
  52653   054220
  2-52674/5

TETRAZZINI Luisa, s.
  053141-8   2-053064/5
  053150   2-053070-3
  053195-7   2-053084-7
  053222-30   2-053092-4
  2-053012/3   2-053096
  2-053031   2-053114-8
  2-053033-6   2-053207
  2-053038   2-054034
  2-053040-50   2-054038
  2-053055-62

THEODORINI Elena, s.   53298-302

THORNTON Edna, c.

053128	2-054025
2-053051	2-054132

TISCI-RUBINI Giuseppe, bs.

52631	54470
52655	054019
52657	054024
52661	054402
2-52834	054404
052018	054407/8
54047	054410

TOMMASINI G., t.

2-52812	054332
54454	054334
054316	054450

TONINELLO   2-054135

TORRE Eugenio, t.

7-52181-3	54269
7-52185/6	7-54019

TRENTINI Emma, s.

53152-5	54065/6
53368-71	54253/4
53395	54256-8
54054	54262
54061/2	054050

TROMBEN Elisa, s.

54385	054221-3
054212	054227

TURCHETTI Anna Maria, s.
                        2-054136

TURIGLIA, s.   2-054122

.....

VAITE Mario, b.   52511

VALENTE Alessandro (VALLO) t.
                        7-52064

VALERO Fernando, t.   52716-9

VALLS Giovanni, t.

52146-8	2-52476
52897	54056
2-52426	054044
2-52430	

VAN BRANDT, s.   053125

VAN HOOSE Ellison, t.   2-054104

VASQUEZ Countess Italia, s.
                        53244

VENTURA Elvino, t.

52006	52859
52008	052003
52012	052006
52723-9	052014
52731/2	052021
52736-41	054001-6
52744-7	054008-13
52750	054015-17
52752	054019/20
52754-6	054025
52778/9	054029/30
52784	054033/4
52819	54042-4
52821	54046
52832	

VERLET Alice, s.   7-53000
                         2-053002/3

VIAFORA Gina, s.   054204

VIALE Aurelio, b.

52476	52537
52496/7	52539
52510	54086-94
52534/5	

VIGANO Ines, s.   7-54023
                         2-054127-9

VIGNAS Francisco, t.

52735	052007/8
052001/2	052013
052004/5	

VINCENT Ruth, s.   2-053124

VITTI Primo, t.   54757/8
                         54763

VOCCIA Coppia   7-54022

VOLTA   054220

VON RAPPÉ Signe, s.   053221

.....

WEDEKIND Erika, s.   53464
                         53538

WERRENRATH Reinald, b.
    7-54004   2-054051
    7-54015   2-054061

WOODMAN Flora, s.   2-053125
                     2-053127

.....

ZACCARI Ivo, t.   052118
                     54289
                     054064

ZACCARIA Emma, c.
    53414   53498
    53422/3   053087
    53488-90   54151
    53493   054096

ZAMBONI Maria, s.   2-054105/6
                     2-054114

ZANELLI Renato, b.
    7-52145-8   7-52238
    7-52161   2-052178
    7-52166   2-052182
    7-52202

ZANI, b.   2-054084

ZENATELLO Giovanni, t.
    52702/3   52764
    52711-3   52775
    52718   054027

ZEROLA Nicola, t.
    7-52005-8   2-052029/30
    7-52011   54410
    2-052019

ZIZOLFI Ida, ms.
    053315   54478
    053320   054438
    54474   054444

. . . . .

7" records : GREEN LABEL

1337 ROBERTI L'altalena

10690 SOTTOLANA Era di maggio "Costa"
10691 SOTTOLANA Fenesta che lucive (Bellini)
10771 MIELI Santa Lucia

10" records : GREEN LABEL

51084	TRILUSSA	Il museo meccanico (91101)	1/09
51085	TRILUSSA	Fifi...Er ventriloquio (91102)	1/09
51086	TRILUSSA	Er venditore di pianeti (91103)	1/09
51087	TRILUSSA	Er porco "Le feste de beneficenza" (91104)	1/09
51088	TRILUSSA	La nomina dei cavajere ..."L'istinto" (91105)	1/09
51089	TRILUSSA	L'amore der gatto "Carità cristiana" (91106)	1/09
51090	TRILUSSA	La gallina lavoratora "La pulce anarchica" (91107)	1/09
51091	TRILUSSA	Parla Maria la serva (91108)	1/09
51092	TRILUSSA	La donna barbuta "La donna gigante" (91109)	1/09
51093	TRILUSSA	Il coccodrillo vivente "L'assassino moderno" (91110)	1/09
51096	RUFFO	Essere o non essere "Amleto" (Shakespeare)	1914/5
51097	RUFFO	Apparizione dello spettro "Amleto" (Shakespeare)	1914/5

91036	DELLA ROSSA	Arringa dell'avvocato Tartaglia - I."'O Scarfaglietto"	
91037	DELLA ROSSA	do. do. - II. do.	
91039	E.SCARPETTA/V.SCARPETTA	Atto I. Scena IV. "No criatura sperduta"	
91040	E.SCARPETTA	Prologo I. "Il figlio d'Jorio"	
91041	E.SCARPETTA	Prologo II. do. do.	
91062	TOMMASINO	Pasquino maestro di ballo francese - I.	1910
91063	TOMMASINO	do. do. do. do. - II.	1910
91066	TOMMASINO	Dopo il matrimonio "Pasquino marito geloso"	1910
91067	TOMMASINO	Scena del soldato do.	1910
91070	TOMMASINO	Incontro di Paolo e Francesca "Parodia Francesca da Rimini"	
			(1910
91071	TOMMASINO	Scena d'amore "Parodia Francesca da Rimini"	1910
91074	TOMMASINO	Scena comica "Pasquino e l'imbroglione"	1910
91075	TOMMASINO	Scena comica "Pasquino incaricato di bastonare sè stesso" '10	
91078	TOMMASINO	Scena del dottore "Pasquino avvelenato"	1910
91079	TOMMASINO	Scena della gelosia "Pasquino avvelenato"	1910
91080	TOMMASINO	Testamento di Pasquino "Pasquino avvelenato"	1910
91081	TOMMASINO	Scena comica "Pasquino e l'oste nemico"	1910
91082	TOMMASINO	Scena col trattore "I due Pasquini gemelli"	1910
91083	TOMMASINO	Scena comica "Pasquino tutore burlato"	1910
91084	TOMMASINO	"Le astuzie di Pasquino con un maggiordomo indiscreto" 1910	
91085	TOMMASINO	"Pasquino risuscitatore di morti e volatore di Palloni" 1910	
91086	TOMMASINO	Dichiarazione d'amore "I mafiusi della Vicaria"	1910
91087	TOMMASINO	Scena comica "Il voto di zitellenza di Pasquino"	1910
91088	TOMMASINO	Mia Moglie nel pozzo "Pasquino marito geloso"	1910
91089	TOMMASINO	Equivoco della Giamberga "I due Pasquini gemelli"	1910
91092	TOMMASINO	Scena comica "Pasquino innamorato"	1910
91093	TOMMASINO	Scena comica "Pasquino facchino di cantina"	1910
91094	TOMMASINO	Cacciata dei ministri "Parodia Ruy Blas"	1910
91095	TOMMASINO	Romanza di Pasquino "Parodia Ruy Blas"	1910
91096	TOMMASINO	Duello Don Guritan e Pasquino "Parodia Ruy Blas"	1910
91097	TOMMASINO	Scena d'amore Pasquino e Ninetta "Parodia Traviata" 1910	
91098	GUASTI	Due parole - I. (Guasti)	
91099	GUASTI	Due parole - II.(Guasti)	
91110	E.SCARPETTA	Finale Atto II. "Miseria e nobilità"	

7" & 10" records : GREEN LABEL
x denotes 10" records

92006	DE PAOLI	La luna		1910
92030	DE ROSA	Marechiare		
92093	DADDI	Uocchie c' arragiunate (Falvo)		
92103	? (t)	Ribelle chi mi chiama "L'Africana" (Meyerbeer)		
92105	? (b)	All'erta marinar "L'Africana" (Meyerbeer)		
x 92145	CANTALAMESSA	Il fischio (D'Avigny-Cantalamessa)		1/10
x 92147	DADDI	Comme te voglio amà (Valente)		
x 92148	DADDI	Margarita (Fassone)		
x 92149	DADDI	Funiculì, Funiculà (Denza)		1910
x 92153	DADDI	Addio Napoli		
x 92154	DADDI	O' core mio (Fredi)		
x 92155	DADDI	Mattinata (Leoncavallo)		
x 92156	DADDI	Ndringhete ndra (De Gregorio)		
x 92157	DADDI	Vocca addirosa (Nutile)		
x 92158	DADDI	Che buò fa (Valente)		
x 92159	DADDI	Nun saccio (Fonzo)		
x 92160	DADDI	Uocchie mariuole (Valente)		
x 92161	DADDI	Rosa rusella (Di Chiara)		
x 92162	DADDI	Carcioffolà (Di Capua)		
x 92163	DADDI	'A simpaticona (Falvo)		
x 92164	DADDI	E' rose gelose (Ricciardi)		
x 92165	DADDI	Scètate		12/09
x 92166	DADDI	O sole mio		12/09
x 92167	DADDI	Ucchiuzzulle mariuncelle (Valente)		
x 92168	DADDI	Santa Lucia		
x 92170	DADDI	Musica proibita (Gastaldon)		1910
x 92173	DADDI	'O core d'e femmene		12/09
x 92174	DADDI	Voce 'e notte		12/09
x 92184	MALDACEA	La risata (Cantalamessa)		1/10
x 92185	MALDACEA	Echi del mondo		1/10
x 92204	VILLANI	Le donne di tutto il mondo (Falvo)		
x 92205	VILLANI	L'Arca di Noè (Villani)		
x 92206	VILLANI	La guida al Foro romano (De Gregorio)		
x 92207	VILLANI	L'attendente (Capolongo)		
x 92208	VILLANI	Serenata a Luisella (Fonzo)		
x 92210	VILLANI	La femme		
x 92211	VILLANI	Il damerino		
x 92212	VILLANI	Il professor Quattrocchi (Cataldo)		
x 92216	PASQUARIELLO	Chiarina mia (Segré)		1910
x 92218	PASQUARIELLO	Palomma 'e notte (Buongiovanni)		
x 92219	PASQUARIELLO	Viato a me (Falvo)		
x 92220	PASQUARIELLO	Comme 'o zuccaro (Fonzo)		
x 92221	PASQUARIELLO	'A gelosia (Nutile)		
x 92222	PASQUARIELLO	Firulì firulà		
x 92223	PASQUARIELLO	A fforza t'aggi'amà (Fonzo)		
x 92225	FIGLI DI CIRO	Palomma 'e notte (Buongiovanni)		
x 92226	FIGLI DI CIRO	Fenesta ntussecosa (Ricciardi)		
x 92227	FIGLI DI CIRO	'E Felinie (Fonzo)		
x 92231	FIGLI DI CIRO	Balla ba'		
x 92232	FIGLI DI CIRO	O marenare voga voga		12/09
x 92233	FIGLI DI CIRO	'A Surrentina nova		12/09
x 92234	FIGLI DI CIRO	'A calamita (Ricciardi)		
x 92235	FIGLI DI CIRO	Ndringhete ndra (De Gregorio)		
x 92236	FIGLI DI CIRO	Aprite la finestra (Cimino)		

x 92237 FIGLI DI CIRO Cicirenella
x 92242 POLISSENI Dall'ago al milione (Dall'Argine)
x 92243 POLISSENI È ver che amai Claretta "La Figlia di Madama Angot"(Lecocq)
x 92244 GRANIERI Pastorale "Orfeo all' Inferno" (Offenbach)
x 92245 GRANIERI Omaggio a Giove   do.   do.
x 92246 POLISSENI Romanza Atto III. "Il Viaggio di Susetta" (Asseur)
x 92247 POLISSENI Mozzo novello "Le Campane di Corneville" (Planquette)
x 92248 POLISSENI Valzer Atto III.   do.   do.
x 92249 C.BARBETTI Il mondo inter girai tre fiate   do. do.   do.
x 92250 V.SCARPETTA Imitazioni di FREGOLI "Vieni sul mar"
x 92251 V.SCARPETTA Imitazioni della Fougère "Le quartier en balade"
x 92252 V.SCARPETTA Imitazioni della " 'O Farenella"
x 92263 VILLANI Lo scioperante
x 92264 VILLANI La guardia travestita
x 92265 VILLANI Il quaresimalista
x 92266 VILLANI Il consigliere moderno
x 92267 VILLANI Tarantella ciociara
x 92268 VILLANI Il piffero di montagna
x 92269 VILLANI Il comico di Provincia
x 92270 VILLANI La mia preghiera
x 92271 VILLANI La mano
x 92272 VILLANI Il nipote dell'arciprete
x 92273 PASQUARIELLO 'O sciopero d'e nnammurate (De Gregorio)
x 92274 PASQUARIELLO Comme 'a luna (Nutile)
x 92275 PASQUARIELLO Tarantelluccia (Falvo)
x 92276 PASQUARIELLO Suonne sunnate (Capolongo)
x 92277 PASQUARIELLO Ammore che gira (Buongiovanni)
x 92278 PASQUARIELLO Manella mia (Valente)
x 92279 PASQUARIELLO Margarita (Fassone)
x 92280 PASQUARIELLO I baci (Di Chiara)
x 92281 PASQUARIELLO Villanova (Fonzo)
x 92282 PASQUARIELLO Maria bella (Nutile)
x 92283 PASQUARIELLO Tiempo perduto (Nardella)
x 92284 PASQUARIELLO Però però (Buongiovanni)
x 92285 PASQUARIELLO Na' palumella janca (Nutile)
x 92286 PASQUARIELLO Così com'è (Buongiovanni)
x 92287 PASQUARIELLO 'A gelusia (Buongiovanni)
x 92288 PASQUARIELLO Bella figlio (Chiarolanza)
x 92289 PASQUARIELLO L'aprile (Fonzo)
x 92290 PASQUARIELLO l'po 'si v'o ddico (Valente)
x 92291 COPPIA CORBETTA La cismoina   1910
x 92295 FIGLI DI CIRO Suonno 'e fantasia (Capolongo)
x 92296 FIGLI DI CIRO O core 'e Catarina (Capolongo)
x 92297 FIGLI DI CIRO T'arracumanno (Ricciardi)
x 92298 FIGLI DI CIRO 'A napulitana (Falvo)
x 92299 FIGLI DI CIRO Maria bella (Nutile)
x 92300 FIGLI DI CIRO Serenata a Luisella (Fonzo)
x 92301 FIGLI DI CIRO A Margellina (Segré)
x 92302 FIGLI DI CIRO O Sciampagnone (Buongiovanni)
x 92303 FIGLI DI CIRO Così com'è   (Buongiovanni)
x 92304 FIGLI DI CIRO Marenarella (Nutile)
x 92307 FIGLI DI CIRO Quanno 'a femmena vo' filà (Falvo)
x 92308 FIGLI DI CIRO Tarantelluccia (Falvo)
x 92309 FIGLI DI CIRO 'A speranza d'o surdato (Fonzo)
x 92310 FIGLI DI CIRO l'po' si vo' dico (Valente)
x 92311 FIGLI DI CIRO Chi sa Marì... (Fonzo)
x 92312 FIGLI DI CIRO Villanova (Fonzo)
x 92313 FIGLI DI CIRO Nun saccio spiegà (Fonzo)

```
x 92314 FIGLI DI CIRO   'A fforza t'aggi'amà (Fonzo)
x 92315 FIGLI DI CIRO   'A gelusia (Buongiovanni)
x 92316 FIGLI DI CIRO   Menella mia (Valente)
x 92319 FIGLI DI CIRO   Uocchie c'arragiuente (Falvo)
x 92320 FIGLI DI CIRO   Amore che ggira (Buongiovanni)
x 92322 FIGLI DI CIRO   Napule nà (Longone)                                    1910
x 92325 FIGLI DI CIRO   La risata (Cantalamessa)
x 92326 FIGLI DI CIRO   Teniteme presente (Di Chiara)
x 92327 FIGLI DI CIRO   Oj luna janca (Ricciardi)
x 92328 FIGLI DI CIRO   Caruli, Caruli (Nardiela)
x 92329 FIGLI DI CIRO   'A gelusia (Nutile)
x 92330 FIGLI DI CIRO   'A canzone 'e marechiaro (De Gregorio)
x 92331 POLISSENI       Finale Atto I. - I. "Il Mulino delle Rose" (Desormes)
x 92333 POLISSENI         do.    ) II.          do.          do.
x 92334 BORGHINI        Fortunato te Genesio            do.          do.
x 92335 MARESCA, L.     Oh! sfortunati fior            do.          do.
x 92336 POLISSENI       Bel sogno fu soltanto          do.          do.
x 92337 POMPEI          Io son politico                do.          do.
x 92338 POLISSENI       Per l'affar  che m'interessa "La Femme a Papà" (Hervé)
x 92339 BARBETTI, C.    Couplet di Florestano                do.          do.
x 92340 BARBETTI, C.    Quando al mattino                    do.          do.
x 92341 POLISSENI       Sta qui certo il mio papà            do.          do.
x 92342 POLISSENI       O giusto ciel                        do.          do.
x 92343 POLISSENI       Addio alla patria                    do.          do.
x 92344 VINCI           Occhietti belli (Luzzi)
x 92345 VINCI           L'insogno (Luzzi)
x 92346 VINCI           Fiore d'aprile (Luzzi)
x 92347 VINCI           Svejete amore santo (Luzzi)
x 92348 VINCI           Primavera (Luzzi)
x 92349 VINCI           Se fosse amore (Luzzi)
x 92350 ROMAGNOLI       Dolce visione (Luzzi)
x 92351 ROMAGNOLI       Eternamente (Luzzi)
x 92352 VINCI           Gelsomino gentile (Luzzi)
x 92353 ROMAGNOLI       Un guardo solo (Luzzi)
x 92354 SAVETTIERE      Campanedda d'oru (Gentile)
x 92355 SAVETTIERE      Ucchiuzzi niuri (Gentile)
x 92356 SAVETTIERE      Vurissi (L'Ustricana) (Gentile)
x 92357 SAVETTIERE      Rusignolu d'amuri (Gentile)
x 92358 VOLTA  Il duca d'amor incostante  "La Cicala e la Formica" (Audran) 1910
x 92359 TESSARI  Io soffio ognor              do.               do.       1910
x 92360 VOLTA    La ragion la guiderà         do.               do.       1910
x 92404 SHEPARD   Risata
x 92405 DELLA ROSA  Parodia (strofe di Don Cy)  "Geisha" (Jones)
x 92406 E.SCARPETTA  Parodia (Finale)  "Geisha" (Jones)
x 92416 PADRE CANCIELLO  Parola quinta (Mercadante)
x 92417 PADRE CANCIELLO  Ave Maria (Mercadante)
x 92418 PADRE CANCIELLO  Stabat Mater
x 92419 PADRE CANCIELLO  Salutaris Ostia
x 92433 FIGLI DI CIRO    La Spagnola (Di Chiara)                            1/10
x 92434 FIGLI DI CIRO    Pusilleco addiruso                                 1/10
x 92435 FIGLI DI CIRO    Comme facette mammete                              1/10
x 92436 FIGLI DI CIRO    Terra luntana                                      1/10
x 92437 FIGLI DI CIRO    Che te ne'importa 'e me                            1/10
x 92438 TESSARI          Dormi pure                                         1/10
x 92439 TESSARI          La paloma                                          1/10
x 92440 CANTALAMESSA     Guì, guì
x 92442 FIGLI DI CIRO    Frisio bello (Falvo)                               1/10
x 92443 FIGLI DI CIRO    Fronn' 'e rose (Ricciardi)                         1/10
```

x 92444 FIGLI DI CIRO	Mamma mia che vo' sapè (Nutile)		1/10
x 92445 FIGLI DI CIRO	Dint' 'a varca (Buongiovanni)		1/10
x 92446 FIGLI DI CIRO	Ma pecchè (Nardella)		1/10
x 92447 FIGLI DI CIRO	Sona organetto (Roessinger)		1/10
x 92448 FIGLI DI CIRO	Comm' 'a ll'acqua (Giannelli)		1/10
x 92449 FIGLI DI CIRO	Suspiranno (Spagnuolo)		1/10
x 92450 FIGLI DI CIRO	Chitarra nera (Nardella)		1/10
x 92451 FIGLI DI CIRO	Canzuncella amara (Spagnuolo)		1/10
x 92452 FIGLI DI CIRO	Bella ca duorme (Nardella)		1/10
x 92453 FIGLI DI CIRO	Io nun 'o ccredo (Buongiovanni)		1/10
x 92454 FIGLI DI CIRO	Canzone 'e Capemonte (Ricciardi)		1/10
x 92455 FIGLI DI CIRO	Tre figliole (Fonzo)		1/10
x 92456 FIGLI DI CIRO	Luce mia (Fonzo)		1/10
x 92457 FIGLI DI CIRO	N'ata cosa (Bellini)		1/10
x 92458 FIGLI DI CIRO	Carofano schiavone (Ricciardi)		1/10
x 92459 FIGLI DI CIRO	'E tre catene (Bellini)		1/10
x 92460 FIGLI DI CIRO	Luntan 'a te! (Bellini)		1/10
x 92461 FIGLI DI CIRO	Ojè Gnese, Gnese (Bellini)		1/10
x 92462 FIGLI DI CIRO	Catena 'e vase (Ricciardi)		1/10
x 92463 FIGLI DI CIRO	'A femmena è accussì (Fonzo)		1/10
x 92464 FIGLI DI CIRO	Sconosciuta (Fonzo)		1/10
x 92465 FIGLI DI CIRO	Core n' campagna (Ricciardi)		1/10
x 92466 FIGLI DI CIRO	Tarantella d' 'e suspire (Criscuolo)		1/10
x 92467 FIGLI DI CIRO	'I canto p' 'o mare (Ricciardi)		1/10
x 92468 FIGLI DI CIRO	'O mare 'e Santa Lucia (De Gregorio)		1/10
x 92469 FIGLI DI CIRO	Canzon' 'a Carmela (Bellini)		1/10
x 92470 FIGLI DI CIRO	'E stelle (Bellini)		1/10
x 92471 FIGLI DI CIRO	'E vviole (Fonzo)		1/10
x 92472 FIGLI DI CIRO	Mbraccia a mmè (Di Chiara)		1/10
x 92473 FIGLI DI CIRO	Angelarosa (Cannio)		1/10
x 92475 FIGLI DI CIRO	Nanninella (Di Chiara)		1/10
x 92476 FIGLI DI CIRO	Lily Kangy (Gambardella)		1/10
x 92477 FIGLI DI CIRO	Voce 'e notte (De Curtis)		1/10
x 92478 FIGLI DI CIRO	'O marenare mio (Di Capua)		1/10
x 92479 FIGLI DI CIRO	I'penzo sempe a te (Cannio)		1/10
x 92480 FIGLI DI CIRO	'A luntananza d' 'o surdato (Cannio)		1/10
x 92481 FIGLI DI CIRO	'A serenata d' 'o surdato (Cannio)		1/10
x 92482 FIGLI DI CIRO	Comm' 'o sole (Fassone)		1/10
x 92483 FIGLI DI CIRO	Ngiulinè (Di Chiara)		1/10
x 92484 FIGLI DI CIRO	Italia bella (Di Capua)		1/10
x 92485 FIGLI DI CIRO	Rosa 'e Maggio (Di Capua)		1/10
x 92486 FIGLI DI CIRO	Palummella (Di Chiara)		1/10
x 92487 FIGLI DI CIRO	'A cchiù bella è Napule (De Curtis)		1/10
x 92488 FIGLI DI CIRO	Pane e cepolle (De Curtis)		1/10
x 92489 FIGLI DI CIRO	Bella mia (Di Chiara)		1/10
x 92490 FIGLI DI CIRO	Nuttata 'e sentimento (Capolongo)		1/10
x 92491 FIGLI DI CIRO	Campagnò (Capolongo)		1/10
x 92492 FIGLI DI CIRO	Sì sta chitarra (Nardella)		1/10
x 92493 FIGLI DI CIRO	Ruotulo d'oro (Capolongo)		1/10
x 92494 FIGLI DI CIRO	'E femmene brutte (Falvo)		1/10
x 92495 FIGLI DI CIRO	Castigliana (Magliani)		1/10
x 92496 FIGLI DI CIRO	Bolero d'amore (Falvo)		1/10
x 92497 FIGLI DI CIRO	'A stessa d' 'a canzone (Capolongo)		1/10
x 92498 FIGLI DI CIRO	Bella Napulitana (Cavaliere)		1/10
x 92499 FIGLI DI CIRO	Vocca 'e granato (Falvo)		1/10
x 92500 FIGLI DI CIRO	Vi vorrei baciare (Di Chiara)		1/10
x 92501 FIGLI DI CIRO	L'arte d' 'o sole (Gambardella)		1/10
x 92502 FIGLI DI CIRO	Core cuntento (Buongiovanni)		1/10

x 92503 FIGLI DI CIRO	Ammore 'e femmene (Nardella)		1/10
x 92504 FIGLI DI CIRO	Chesta 'è 'a vita (Buongiovanni)		1/10
x 92505 FIGLI DI CIRO	Ohè, Ohè (Nutile)		1/10
x 92506 GIGLIO	Stornelli montagnoli		1910
x 92507 GIGLIO	L'ammore è comm' a ll'acqua (Giannelli)		1910
x 92508 GIGLIO	'O gira sole (Gambardella)		1910
x 92509 GIGLIO	Teresina Teresì		1910
x 92510 GIGLIO	Gira lo munno (Nardella)		1910
x 92511 GIGLIO	Tarantella surrentina		1910
x 92512 GIGLIO	Vide 'e vulà		1910
x 92513 LARA	Ma! (Bossi)		1910
x 93067 DI LANDA	La Mattchiche		
x 93068 DI LANDA	'A Vennegna		12/09
x 93069 DI LANDA	La ciociara		
x 93070 DI LANDA	Canadà		
x 93071 DI LANDA	'O Sciammeria (Capolongo)		
x 93072 DI LANDA	Cinematografo		
x 93073 DI LANDA	L'orticello		12/09
x 93074 DI LANDA	La zampognara (De Leva)		
x 93075 DI LANDA	Tarantella d'e vase		12/09
x 93077 DI LANDA	E gira gì		12/09
x 93083 DI LANDA	'E ragazze		12/09
x 93084 DI LANDA	Cinematografì - Cinematografà		12/09
x 93085 DI LANDA	Stornelli romani		
x 93086 DI LANDA	La virtù punita (Caucci)		
x 93087 DI LANDA	Sciuldezza bella		12/09
x 93088 DI LANDA	Nce vulesse (Segrè)		
x 93089 DI LANDA	Na cammerella (Falvo)		
x 93090 DI LANDA	Napolitana (Falvo)		
x 93091 DI LANDA	Graziella (Brunetti)		
x 93092 DI LANDA	Maggio (Fonzo)		
x 93093 DI LANDA	La capinera (Coronato)		
x 93094 DI LANDA	Carezze e baci (De Gregori)		
x 93095 DI LANDA	La mousmè (Perigozzo)		
x 93096 DI LANDA	Canadà		
x 93097 DI LANDA	La regina del mercà (Brunetti)		
x 93098 DI LANDA	La montanina (Carosio)		
x 93101 PERRELLA	Canzone della lavandaia		
x 93108 MARESCA, E.	Canzone dell'usignolo		
x 93109 V.BARBETTI	E finito il maritaggio "Il Mulino delle Rose" (Desormes)		
x 93110 MARESCA, E.	Gentil inver	do.	do.
x 93111 V.BARBETTI	Sortita di Pepita	do.	do.
x 93112 DI LANDA	Tarantelluccia (Falvo)		
x 93113 DI LANDA	So' turnato		
x 93114 DI LANDA	La chitarra		
x 93115 DI LANDA	Pas sour la bouche		
x 93116 DI LANDA	Nord America		
x 93117 DI LANDA	O' rumano		
x 93118 DI LANDA	Mattinata rusticana (Brunetti)		
x 93119 DI LANDA	Turin Cavouret (Brunetti)		
x 93120 DI LANDA	Capemonte (Giannelli)		
x 93121 DI LANDA	Tu nun me vuo chiu' bbene (Falvo)		
x 93122 DI LANDA	Comme 'o zuccaro (Fonzo)		
x 93123 DI LANDA	'A fforza t'agg'i amà (Fonzo)		
x 93124 MARESCA, E.	Le cocorite "La Femme a Papà" (Hervé)		
x 93125 MARESCA, E.	Le donne tutte son regine	do.	do.
x 93126 MARESCA, E.	Vestivo un abito severo	do.	do.

x93127	E.MARESCA	Tambour, clairon "La Femme a Papà" (Hervé)		
x93128	E.MARESCA	Se la mamma mi vedesse	do.	do.
x93129	VITALI	Quando di dice alla gonnella	do.	do.
x93130	E.MARESCA	Grandi gli occhi "Il viaggio di Susetta" (Asseur)		
x93131	V.BARBETTI	Bolero di Paquita	do.	do.
x93132	E.MARESCA	O liquor che scintilli	do.	do.
x93133	E.MARESCA	Nel folto bosco	do.	do.
x93139	MARCHETTI	Un dì Margot "La Cicala e la Formica" (Audran) 1910		
x93140	WALDES	Amo più il nostro asilo	do.	do.1910
x93141	MARCHETTI	Couplet di Teresa	do.	do.1910
x93142	WALDES	Lesti lavoriamo	do.	do.1910
x93190	DI LANDA	La Spagnuolo		1/10
x93191	DI LANDA	'A campagnola		1/10
x93192	LAMY	Fripponette		12/09
x93193	LAMY	La mode		12/09
x93194	LAMY	Giuochi d'amore		12/09
x93195	LAMY	La pipa		12/09
x93196	LAMY	Zizi pam pam		12/09
x93197	LAMY	È naturale (Capolongo)		12/09
x94031	COPPIA CORBETTA	Il ruscelletto (Brunetti)		1910
x94032	COPPIA CORBETTA	Ciribiribin (Pestalozza)		1910
x94033	COPPIA CORBETTA	Graziella (Brunetti)		1910
x94034	COPPIA CORBETTA	Follia (Brunetti)		1910
x94035	COPPIA CORBETTA	L'altalena (Selesi)		1910
x94036	COPPIA CORBETTA	Parodia Trovatore		1910
x94037	COPPIA CORBETTA	Serenata pout-pourri (Corbetta)		1910
x94044	E.MARESCA/POLISSENI	Dall'ago al milione (Dall'Argine)		
x94045	E.MARESCA/POLISSENI	Questa grazia "La Figlia di Madama Angot"(Lecocq)		
x94046	E.MARESCA/POLISSENI	Duetto Atto II."Il viaggio di Susetta" (Asseur)		
x94047	E.MARESCA/POLISSENI	Io ti chiamo "Lombardo" (Alda)		
x94048	E.MARESCA/POLISSENI	O bell'angiol di mia vita "Lombardo" (Alda)		
x94049	COPPIA CAPPELLI	Ncopp'u Scanno (canz. nap.)		
x94050	E.SCARPETTA/BIANCHE	Duetto Atto I. "Na Santarella" (con acc.di armonium)		
x94051	E.SCARPETTA/V.SCARPETTA	Duetto Atto I. "Nina Bone"		
x94060	COPPIA CORBETTA	La bella ortolanina (Franselva)		
x94061	COPPIA CORBETTA	La primavera (Corbetta)		
x94062	COPPIA CORBETTA	I due gemelli (Chiarolanza)		
x94063	COPPIA CORBETTA	Biondinella (Chiarolanza)		
x94064	COPPIA CORBETTA	Tu non me vuo' cchiù bene (Falvo)		
x94065	COPPIA CORBETTA	A bella guaglicna (Chiarolanza)		
x94067	V.BARBETTI/L.MARESCA	Questa notte in pace "Il Mulino delle Rose"		
x94068	V.BARBETTI/L.MARESCA	do. do. - II. do. (Desormes)		
x94069	E.MARESCA/POLISSENI	Duetto Principessa e Fabrizio - I. do. do.		
x94070	E.MARESCA/V.BARBETTI/POLISSENI/L.MARESCA	Fuggiamo... do. do.		
x94071	INES E TAKI	Il Vulcano		
x94072	INES E TAKI	Prete Giacomo		
x94073	INES E TAKI	Serenata d'amore		
x94074	INES E TAKI	Sul margine d'un rio		
x94075	INES E TAKI	La Bearnaise		
x94076	INES E TAKI	La Barchetta bruna		
x94077	E.MARESCA/POLISSENI	Questi occhiali perchè portate "La Femme a Papà" (Hervé)		
x94079	V.& C.BARBETTI	Dite su signor Giraflor "Il viaggio di Susetta"(Asseur)		
x94080	MARCHETTI/TESSARI	Parlate orsù "La Cicala e la Formica"(Audran)1910		
x94081	MARCHETTI/WALDES	Con gran mister Natal Divino	do. do. 1910	
x94082	MARCHETTI/WALDES/TESSARI/PONTANA	Quartetto	do. do. 1910	

252157	MASSA	Desiderio 'e tte (Ricciardi)	1914/5
252158	MASSA	Primm 'ammore (Di Jorio)	1914/5
252159	SARDELLA	Mamma (Feola)	1914/5
252160	BALSAMO	Stornelli dispettosi (Nicolò)	1914/5
252161	SARDELLA	Tu solo oj mare (Medina)	1914/5
252162	MASSA	Scetate oj bella (Ciociano)	1914/5
252163	BALSAMO	Quann 'uno è guaglione (Lama)	1914/5
252164	BALSAMO	Sponta 'a luna (Mario)	1914/5
252165	SARDELLA	Canta Abbrile (Mario)	1914/5
252166	SARDELLA	La campana della valle (Mario)	1914/5
252167	MASSA	Io na chitarra e' a luna (Mario)	1914/5
252168	MASSA	'O maremariello (Gambardella)	1914/5
252169	MASSA	Aria fresca (Nardella)	1914/5
252170	MASSA	Vocche desiderose (Nardella)	1914/5
252171	GILL	Al tramonto (Lanzetta)	1914/5
252172	GILL	Stornelli proibiti (Gill)	1914/5
252173	SARDELLA	In miesse 'o grano (Nardella)	1914/5
252174	SARDELLA	Suenno 'e felicità (Ciociano)	1914/5
252175	GILL	Addio chitarra (Magliani)	1914/5
252176	GILL	Canti passani (Magliani)	1914/5
252177	GILL	È tutto l'amore (Lama)	1914/5
252178	BALSAMO	Canzone napoletana (Mario)	1914/5
252180	RONCONI	Canzone perduta (Napolitano)	1914/5
252181	BALSAMO	Quann 'ammore vò fa ammore (Lama)	1914/5
252182	GILL	Ingenuità campestre (Mazzucchi)	1914/5
252183	SARDELLA	Oj barcunciello (Jorio)	1914/5
252184	RONCONI	Luna curtese (Valente)	1914/5
252185	RONCONI	Me diciste (Pennino) acc.mandolini e chitarre	1914/5
252186	MARCARELLA	Pecchè? (Pennino)	1914/5
252187	GILL	Mosiù, mosiù (Giannelli)	1914/5
252188	MARCARELLA	Rumanzetta capricciusa (Ricciardi)	1914/5
252189	MARCARELLA	Senza 'e tte (Pennino)	1914/5
252190	MASSA	Sturnellata napoletana (Capolongo)	1914/5
252191	MARCARELLA	Turnarrà (Lama)	1914/5
252192	GILL	Uno, due e tre (Gill)	1914/5
252193	GILL	Zampugnaro 'nnamurato (Gill)	1914/5
253001	ANGELELLI	Fra gente amica "Donna Juanita" (Suppé)	1910
253004	DI LANDA	L'amor non ha stagione (Brunetti)	1910
253014	DI LANDA	Vieni tesoro (Carosio)	1910
253015	DI LANDA	Ammore che ggira (Buongiovanni)	1910
253016	DI LANDA	Tarantella 'ntussecosa (Ricciardi)	1910
253017	DI LANDA	Sole dispettuso...(Ricciardi)	1910
253018	DI LANDA	Luna cortese (Valente)	1910
253019	DI LANDA	Stornelli spagnoli (Magliani)	1910
253020	DI LANDA	L'Americana (Cuccnato)	1910
253025	DE FLEURIEL	Il menestrello (Mirelli)	1911
253026	DE FLEURIEL	La regina del contado (Bossi)	1911
253027	ONORFUL	'A bella gioventù (Nutile)	1911
253028	ONORFUL	Amore castigliano (Mazzucchi)	1911
253029	ONORFUL	'A nnamurata d' 'o bersagliere (Fassone)	1911
253030	ONORFUL	Mare, mare mio! (Gambardella)	1911
253031	DE FLEURIEL	E girala la rota (Carocci)	1912
253033	ONORFUL	Hermosa la betta! (Cangiullo)	1911
253034	DE FLEURIEL	La mia rosa (Mirelli)	1911
253035	DE FLEURIEL	Il cestino rotto	1911
253036	DE FLEURIEL	La borsetta (Borù)	1911
253037	DE FLEURIEL	Lauretta (Caucci)	1911

253038	DE FLEURIEL	L'ortolanina (Brunetti)	1911
253039	ANGELELLI	Guardate un pò di qua e di là "Le Campane di Corneville"	
253048	MANGINI	'A frangesa (Costa) 1911	(Planquette)
253049	DE SAVIGNÉ	La jupe culotte (Mignone)	1911
253074	DE NARDIS	A Tripoli (Arona)	1914/5
253075	DE NARDIS	Frin-Frin Tobruk	1914/5
253076	DE NARDIS	A Tripoli (Arona)	1914/5
253109	DE CHARNY	'A Cardenia (Falvo)	1914/5
253117	GARELLI	Tutte le feste "Rigoletto" (Verdi)	1914
253119	BARBIERI	Ma dall'arido stelo "Un Ballo in Maschera" (Verdi)	1914
253121	ROCCHI	Voi lo sapete o mamma "Cavalleria Rusticana"(Mascagni)1914	
253122	LUFRANO	Tutto tramonta.. "Fedora" (Giordano)	1914
253124	BALDINI	Già l'odio m'abbandona "L'Africana" (Meyerbeer)	1914
253125	BALDINI	Su bianca nuvoletta "L'Africana" (Meyerbeer)	1914
253126	SOLARI	L'altra notte in fondo al mare "Mefistofele"(Boito)	1914
253127	SOLARI	Notte cupa "Mefistofele" (Boito)	1914
253128	BALDINI	D'amor sull'ali rosee "Il Trovatore" (Verdi)	1914
253129	SOLARI	Immenso Fthà "Aida" (Verdi)	1914
253130	SOLARI	Ancor son io tutta attonita "Manon" (Massenet)	1914
253131	BEINAT	Re dell'abisso "Un Ballo in Maschera" (Verdi)	1914
253132	BEINAT	È lui nei palpiti "Un Ballo in Maschera" (Verdi)	1914
253133	MUSETTE	Marianna (Mattiello)	1914/5
253134	MUSETTE	Son bella a gli occhi vostri (Mattiello)	1914/5
253135	BIJOÙ	Biricchina (canzonetta internazionale)	1914/5
253136	BIJOÙ	Io conosco un biondino (canz. internazionale)	1914/5
253137	CARPI	Er sor capanna (Caucci)	1914/5
253138	CARPI	Stornelli romani (Caucci)	1914/5
253139	DONNARUMMA	Ammore giovane (Mario)	1914/5
253140	DONNARUMMA	Canta Abbrile (Mario)	1914/5
253141	BIJOÙ	A la Martinique	
253142	BIJOÙ	La canzone del Missouri (canz.americana)	1914/5
253143	DONNARUMMA	A canzone 'e Santa Lucia (Mario)	1914/5
253144	DONNARUMMA	L'amor mio non muore	1914/5
253145	DONNARUMMA	'A fidanzata (Mario)	1914/5
253146	MUSETTE	Core a core (Mario)	1914/5
253147	DONNARUMMA	Tutti così (Capolongo)	1914/5
253148	BIJOÙ	Indostan (canz.internazionale)	1914/5
253149	BIJOÙ	Tango argentino do. do.	1914/5
253150	DONNARUMMA	Mamma (Feola)	1914/5
253151	DONNARUMMA	Un sierve 'o Re (Nardella)	1914/5
253152	BIJOÙ	Margarita (canz.italiana)	1914/5
253153	BIJOÙ	Pompilia (canz.internazionale)	1914/5
253154	MUSETTE	Tango (Silvestre)	1914/5

254010	PALAZZI/DE GREGORIO	Come di rose un cespo "La Vedova Allegra" (Lehàr)	
254015	MARCHETTI/TESSARI	Duetto dei baci "Geisha" (Jones)	1911
254016	CIOTTI/TESSARI	Quand'ero bambinella "Geisha" (Jones)	1911
254017	ASCENZI/FAVI	Vendita all'asta di Mimosa "Geisha" (Jones)	1911
254018	DIAZ/D'ARCO/ASCENZI	Di Molly qual fia la sorte "Geisha" (Jones) 1911	
254019	D'ARCO/TANI	Ogni uom nei lacci d'amor "Geisha" (Jones)	1911
254020	MARCHETTI/TESSARI/TANI/FAVI	Al vedere tal sorpresa "Geisha"(Jones)1911	
254021	PALAZZI/DE GREGORIO	Coi bambin' fa mestieri "Donna Juanita"(Suppé)	
254024	DE NARDIS/CAVANNA	La parigina che si fa ammirar "Eva" (Lehàr) 1913/4	
254025	DE NARDIS/RIGHINI	Lascia adunque parlare il cuor! "Eva" (Lehàr) 1913/4	
254037	CAVANNA/RIGHINI	Con amor guarda e me! "Conte di Lussemburgo" (Lehàr)'13/4	
254039	ELLENA/PETRONI	D'ogni salotto ero il lion do. do.	1913/4
254040	PERRETTI/LANZI	Haja, vieni un po' a guardare "La Vedova Allegra" (Lehàr) 1913/4	

254041 ARGENTI/GIOVANELLI Sei tu, felicità "Conte di Lussemburgo" (Lehàr)
254042 ARGENTI/GIOVANELLI D'astri al chiaror "Sogno di un Valzer" (Strauss)
254047 GIOVANELLI Colle donne...come agir ? "La Vedova Allegra" (Lehàr)
254055 DE GREGORIO/SCALFARO In tramway (Darewsky)   1913/4
254058 SPINELLI/CANALI La polenta (Denza)   1914/5
254059 GARELLI/SCHIPA Libiam ne' lieti calici "La Traviata" (Verdi)1914
254060 GARELLI/SCHIPA Un dì felice aterea "La Traviata" (Verdi) 1914
254061 BARBIERI/LUSSARDI Rivedrai le foreste "Aida" (Verdi)   1914
254062 CASINI/MAGGI Morrò! la mia memoria "La Traviata" (Verdi) 1914
254063 MUZIO/TOMMASINI Amami Alfredo   do.   do.   1914
254064 CASTELLANI/BETTONI La rivedrò nell'estasi "Un Ballo in Maschera"
                                               (Verdi) 1914
254065 CASTELLANI/BARBIERI Non sei tu "Un Ballo in Maschera" (Verdi) 1914
254066 SOLARI/DE GREGORIO Manon! Tu piangi? "Manon" (Massenet) 1914
254067 SOLARI/DE GREGORIO Sì, maledico ed impreco do. do.   1914
254068 SOLARI/DE GREGORIO Oh sogne incantator!   do. do.   1914
254069 SOLARI/DE GREGORIO La mia non è la mano   do. do.   1914
254070 BEINAT/GARCIA Perigliarti ancor languente "Il Trovatore"(Verdi) 1914
254071 SOLARI/JANNI Turiddu, mi tolse "Cavalleria Rusticana" (Mascagni)1914
254072 SOLARI/JANNI Ad essi non perdono   do.   do.   do 1914
254073 DUETTO ROSSETTI Le petit objet (canz.italiana)   1914/5
254074 DUETTO ROSSETTI Stornello del mietitore (Vagnetti)   1914/5

259259 "I promessi sposi" - Dal romanzo di Manzoni. Predica di
                  PADRE AGOSTINO DA MONTEFELTRO   1911

7-251024 "Amore del prossimo" : Predica di PADRE AGOSTINO DA MONTEFELTRO 7/20
7-251025 "L'uomo"   do.   do.   do.   7/20
7-251044 TESTONI "La Sgnera Cattareina" in viaggio per il pellerinazzio
                  a Roma (I sonetti della "La Sgnera Cattareina")10/19
7-251045 TESTONI "La Sgnera Cattareina" nei ricordi di Roma   10/19
7-251046 TESTONI   do. do. e la guerra   10/19
7-251047 TESTONI   do. do. e i monumenti di Roma   10/19
7-251048 TESTONI   do. do. e il matrimonio   10/19
7-251049 TESTONI   do. do. in automobili   10/19
7-251050 TESTONI   do. do. affittacamere   10/19
7-251051 TESTONI   do. do. ultime chiacchiere   10/19
7-251097 MARINETTI (Dische Futuristi) Decl. dell'autore :
                  Bombardamento di Adrianopoli (Marinetti)   9/24
7-251098 MARINETTI Definizione del futurismo (Marinetti)   9/24
7-251099 MARINETTI Quattro piani di sensualità in uno stabilimento
                  di bagni (Marinetti)   9/24
7-251100 R. DE ANGELIS Brano del manifesto dul teatro di Varietà
                  con violino e piano   9/24
7-251129 PASTONCHE La Preghiera alla Vergine "Divina Commedia" (Dante) 5/26
7-251130 PASTONCHE Buonconte e la Pia   do.   do. 5/26
7-251131 PASTONCHE La beffa ai diavoli   do.   do. 5/26
7-251132 PASTONCHE Episodio di Ulisse   do.   do. 5/26
7-251133 PASTONCHE (a) L'Infinito (Leopardi) (b) Alla sera (Foscolo) 5/26
7-251134 PASTONCHE (a) Il soldato (Pastonche) (b) Aprile (Pastonche)5/26
7-251135 PASTONCHE (a) I grandi alberghi (b) Povere vecchie nonne 5/26
7-251136 PASTONCHE Le mani italiche   5/26
7-251137 PASTONCHE La vergine cuccia (Parini)   5/26
7-251138 PASTONCHE Le pastorelle montanine (Sacchetti)   5/26
7-251112 SPILOTROS Predica di Monsignor Del-le-pine (Recit.comica) 12/25

7-252000	FORTEZZA	Ch'agg'i 'a fa? (Criscuolo)	1914/5
7-252001	FORTEZZA	Facitece fa 'a pace (Cosentino)	1914/5
7-252002	DE ANGELIS (t)	Casa 'e campagna (Mario)	1914/5
7-252003	DE ANGELIS (t)	Rumenzetta militare (Tagliaferri)	1914/5
7-252004	FORTEZZA	Serenata sulitaria (Del Vecchio)	1914/5
7-252005	FORTEZZA	Il vostro cuore (Del Vecchio)	1914/5
7-252006	FORTEZZA	Tre lacrime (Cosentino)	1914/5
7-252007	FORTEZZA	L'amore e delizioso (Fortezza)	1914/5
7-252008	FORTEZZA	Nenna nce può venì (Cosentino)	1914/5
7-252009	FORTEZZA	Me diciste (Pennino)	1914/5
7-252010	FORTEZZA	Pecchè? (Pennino)	1914/5
7-252011	MEDINA	Sempe tu! (Medina)	1914/5
7-252012	MEDINA	Si vo' turna (Di Jorio)	1914/5
7-252013	VALLO	A Trieste (Carosio)	1914/5
7-252014	ASCOLI	Canzone garibaldina (Falvo)	1914/5
7-252015	ASCOLI	La Brabantese (Campenhout)	1914/5
7-252016	ASCOLI	Marcia italica (Balladori)	1914/5
7-252017	MIELI	Va bel militar "I Saltimbanchi" (Ganne)	1914/5
7-252018	PERNA	Il cavallo scalpita "Cavalleria Rusticana" (Mascagni)	1914
7-252019	DUFRANNE	La Brabançonne (Campenhout)	1914/5
7-252020	DUFRANNE	La Marseillaise (in Francese)	1914/5
7-252021	ASCOLI	Le campane di S.Giusto (Arona)	1915/6
7-252022	ASCOLI	O gioventù d'Italia	1915/6
7-252023	ASCOLI	Il canto della Vittoria (Carosio)	1915/6
7-252024	ASCOLI	Le campane di Trento e Trieste (Giannelli)	1915/6
7-252025	ASCOLI	Il soldatino (Spingi, spingi!) (Giannelli)	1915/6
7-252026	ASCOLI	Stornelli patriottici (Giannelli)	1915/6
7-252027	ASCOLI	Stornelli di guerra (Montefiore)	1915/6
7-252030	ASCOLI	Sai chiagnere tu? (Nardella)	1915/6
7-252031	ASCOLI	Te si scurdato 'e Napule (Nardella)	1915/6
7-252032	ASCOLI	So 'ncatenato a te! (Pennino)	1915/6
7-252033	ASCOLI	Tiempo passato (Cosentino)	1915/6
7-252034	ASCOLI	'E sunature 'e manduline (Ciociano)	1915/6
7-252035	MASSA	Nun si tu (Medina)	1915/6
7-252036	ASCOLI	Canzone di trincea (Mario)	1915/6
7-252037	ASCOLI	Serenata all'Imperatore (Mario)	1915/6
7-252038	SALVI,U.	Amore e patria (Valente)	1915/6
7-252039	SALVI,U.	Savoja urrah! (Valente)	1915/6
7-252040	SALVI,U.	La canzone dell'Adriatico (Mario)	1915/6
7-252041	ASCOLI	A Trieste (Carosio)	1915/6
7-252042	ASCOLI	Inno a Trieste (Parrocchia)	1915/6
7-252043	ASCOLI	'A canzone 'e Pusilleco (Fonzo)	1915/6
7-252044	ASCOLI	Mandulinata a mare (Buongiovanni)	1915/6
7-252045	SALVI,U.	Bruna mia (Feola)	1915/6
7-252046	SALVI,U.	Canzone della Bohème (Lama)	1915/6
7-252047	ASCOLI	Chi canta e chi dorme (Mario)	1915/6
7-252048	ASCOLI	L'arte p'annamurà (Mario)	1915/6
7-252049	SALVI,U.	La bella Tina (Feola)	1915/6
7-252050	SALVI,U.	Il vostro odore (Feola)	1915/6
7-252051	ASCOLI	Bella ca pe' tte moro (Fassone)	1917
7-252053	ASCOLI	Catena (Valente)	1915/6
7-252054	ASCOLI	'O marenaro (Valente)	1915/6
7-252055	ASCOLI	'E richiamate (Fonzo)	1915/6
7-252056	ASCOLI	'O surdate allero (Buongiovanni)	1915/6
7-252057	ASCOLI	Mamma carnale (Mario)	1915/6
7-252058	ASCOLI	Torna a cantà (Magliani)	1915/6
7-252059	ASCOLI	Marcia 'e notte (Mario)	1915/6
7-252060	ASCOLI	Strofe neutro-attive (Magliani)	1915/6

```
7-252061 ASCOLI     Quanno cantave tu (Nardella)                              1915/6
7-252062 ASCOLI     Quanno 'o destino vo' (Nardella)                          1915/6
7-252065 SALVI,U.Nuova Italia (Cannio)                                        1915/6
7-252066 SALVI,U.Ma l'amor mio non muore (Rambaldo)                           1915/6
7-252067 ASCOLI     Stornellata futurista (Nardella)                          1915/6
7-252068 ASCOLI     Addio, Signorina! (Berniaux)                              1917
7-252069 ASCOLI     Piccoli baci (Mario)                                      1917
7-252070 ASCOLI     Cuor felice (Mario)                                       1917
7-252071 ASCOLI     La piccola amica (Magliani)                               1917
7-252072 ASCOLI     Napule canta (Tagliaferri)                                1917
7-252073 ASCOLI     Tra le siepi (Lama)                                       1917
7-252074 ASCOLI     Ho detto al sole (Capaldo)                                1917
7-252075 ASCOLI     Amor di donna (Mazzucchi)                                 1917
7-252076 ASCOLI     'O surdato nnamurato (Cannio)                             1917
7-252077 ASCOLI     Fa così l'amor (Silvestri)                                1917
7-252078 ASCOLI     Ronda d'amore (Mazzucchi)                                 1917
7-252079 ASCOLI     Passa la gioventù (Cataldo)                               1917
7-252080 ASCOLI     Te ride 'o cielo...(Ciociano)                             1917
7-252081 ASCOLI     Serenata (Amadei)                                         1917
7-252082 ASCOLI     Amammoce in silenzio (Medina)                             1917
7-252083 ASCOLI     Sempre tu! (Medina)                                       1917
7-252084 ASCOLI     L'addio del bersagliere (Lama)                            1917
7-252085 MIELI      Nella sala degli antenati  "Le Campane di Corneville"
                                                       (Planquette)           1917
7-252086 BROCCARDI  Ella mi fu rapita "Rigoletto" (Verdi)(6452ae)             1917
7-252087 BROCCARDI  Parmi veder le lagrime "Rigoletto" (Verdi)(6453ae)1917
7-252088 BROCCARDI  Scorrendo uniti "Rigoletto" (Verdi)(6455ae)               1917
7-252097 PRAT       Serenata d'Arlecchino "Pagliacci" (Leoncavallo)           1917
7-252098 BOLIS      Recondita armonia "Tosca" (Puccini)                       1917
7-252099 BOLIS      E lucevan le stelle "Tosca" (Puccini)                     1917
7-252100 PEZZUTI    Guardate, pazzo son "Manon Lescaut" (Puccini)             2/19
7-252101 PEZZUTI    Tra voi belle "Manon Lescaut" (Puccini)                   2/19
7-252102 ASCOLI     Canti nuovi (Gill)                                        3/19
7-252103 ASCOLI     Torna a Surriento (Di Capua)                              3/19
7-252104 ASCOLI     La petite Dame (Darewsky)                                 3/19
7-252105 ASCOLI     L'amour (Christiné)                                       3/19
7-252112 BADINI     Pescatore, affonda l'esca "La Gioconda" (Ponchielli)7/19
7-252113 BADINI     Oh, dei verd'anni miei "Ernani" (Verdi)                   7/19
7-252114 MICHELUZZI La serenata del saltimbanco (Giannelli)                   7/19
7-252115 MICHELUZZI Strimpellata di Pierrot (Nutile)                          7/19
7-252116 PLINIO  Serenata del Torero "Dall'Ago al Milione" (Dall'Argine)8/19
7-252117 MICHELUZZI Barcarola del Marinaio    do.         do.                 8/19
7-252118 MICHELUZZI Leggenda "La Mascotte" (Audran)                           8/19
7-252119 BETTONI    Ah! finalmente! "Tosca" (Puccini)                         4/19
7-252120 ZANI       Buona Zazà "Zazà" (Leoncavallo)                           11/19
7-252121 ZANI       Zazà, piccola zingara "Zazà" (Leoncavallo)                11/19
7-252122 BERGAMINI  Dai campi, dai prati "Mefistofele" (Boito)                11/19
7-252123 BERGAMINI  Giunto sul passo estremo "Mefistofele" (Boito) 11/19
7-252124 TACCI      È quella! (Moleti)                                        9/19
7-252125 BOSSI      Sotto i ponti di Parigi (Scotto)                          9/19
7-252126 TACCI      La piccola fioraia (Giuliana)                             9/19
7-252127 MARI       Chi siete? (Cosentino)                                    9/19
7-252128 MARI       Stornelli d'autunno (Ricciardi)                           9/19
7-252129 MOLINARI   Le mani delle donne (Molinari)                            9/19
7-252130 MOLINARI   Non andartene gattina (Molinari)                          9/19
7-252131 PASQUALILLO Il giorno tre (Cinque)                                   9/19
7-252132 MOLINARI   Le mandorle più belle (Molinari)                          9/19
7-252133 MOLINARI   Cirano moderno (Molinari)                                 9/19
```

```
7-252134 TACCI      La chiamavano Cosetta (Bixio)                          9/19
7-252135 TACCI      La serenata del paggio (Bixio)                         9/19
7-252136 GIANNINI   'O mare 'e Surriento (Falvo)                           9/19
7-252137 GIANNINI   'E napulitane (Falvo)                                  9/19
7-252138 MARI       Mmiezzo' ó grano (Nardella)                            9/19
7-252139 BERTI ,G.  Guardann' á luna (De Crescenzo)                        9/19
7-252141 TACCI      Il giardino dell'anima (Moleti)                        9/19
7-252142 BERTI,G.   Bionda sirena (Pugliese)                               9/19
7-252143 BERTI,G.   Canti notturni (Mazzucchi)                             9/19
7-252144 BOSSI      Bambina (Bixio)                                        9/19
7-252145 GIANNINI   Torna al tuo paesello (Giuliani)                       9/19
7-252146 TACCI      Bionda sirena (Giuliani)                               9/19
7-252147 TACCI      Amore senza baci (Palone)                              9/19
7-252148 TACCI      Bacio morto (Rusconi)                                  9/19
7-252149 GIANNINI   Luna cortese (Gervise)                                 9/19
7-252150 GIANNINI   Torna Palomma (Bixio)                                  9/19
7-252151 GIANNINI   'A chiù bella canzona (Valente)                        9/19
7-252152 GIANNINI   Prigioniero d'amore                                    9/19
7-252153 GIANNINI   Fronne (d'Annibale)                                    9/19
7-252154 GIANNINI   Pupatella mia (d'Annibale)                             9/19
7-252155 GIANNINI   'O Marenariello (Gambardella)                          9/19
7-252156 GIANNINI   Pusillecu addiruso (Gambardella)                       9/19
7-252157 MARI       Vase 'e femmena (Capolongo)                            9/19
7-252158 GIANNINI   Nun saccio spiegà (Fonzo)                              9/19
7-252159 PASQUALILLO Come l'ombra (Mazzucchi)              .               9/19
7-252160 BERTI,G.   Passa la gioventù (Cataldo)                            9/19
7-252161 BERTI,G.   Boccuccia d'oro (Cataldo)                              9/19
7-252162 BERTI,G.   Baci d'amore (Cataldo)                                 9/19
7-252163 MARI       Cuor felice (Pugliese)                                 9/19
7-252164 MARI       Chi te'ncatena (Bossi)                                 9/19
7-252165 MARI       Diversità (Capolongo)                                  9/19
7-252166 GIANNINI   Cantammo p'o mare (Valente)                            9/19
7-252167 GIANNINI   Tu a chi vuò fa murì (Valente)                         9/19
7-252168 PASQUALILLO Soldatino (Bellini)                                   9/19
7-252169 PASQUALILLO Senza cielo (Bellini)                                 9/19
7-252170 BROCCARDI  Ch'ella mi creda libero "La Fanciulla del West"(Puccini)
                                                                          11/19
7-252171 TALIANI    Beppino rubacuori (Pieraccini)                        11/19
7-252172 TALIANI    Fior di mortella (Pieraccini)                         11/19
7-252173 TALIANI    E lo mio demo (Pieraccini)                            11/19
7-252174 TALIANI    Chi tardi arriva (Pieraccini)                         11/19
7-252176 TALIANI    E uno, e due, e tre (Pieraccini) con pno.             11/19
7-252177 TALIANI    V'insegnerò (Pieraccini)              do.             11/19
7-252178 TALIANI    In casa mia non ci non stato (Pieraccini) con pno.    11/19
7-252179 TALIANI    Ci vuol altro (Pieraccini) con pno.                   11/19
7-252180 TALIANI    Quando cammini (Pieraccini)                           11/19
7-252181 TALIANI    Macina pur mugnaio (Pieraccini)                       11/19
7-252184 BADINI     Un dì m'era di gioia "Andrea Chenier" (Giordano)       1/20
7-252185 BROCCARDI  Vedi, io piango "Fedora" (Giordano)                    1/20
7-252186 BROCCARDI  Amor ti vieta "Fedora" (Giordano)                      1/20
7-252194 PAPACCIO   Capinera (Giuliani)                                    4/20
7-252196 PAPACCIO   Femmena amata (Nardella)                               4/20
7-252197 PAPACCIO   Passa una donna (Cattedra)                             4/20
7-252198 PAPACCIO   'Nu rampicante (Nardella)                              4/20
7-252199 GIANNINI   Napule 'e notte (Bixio)                                4/20
7-252200 GIANNINI   Bella Triestina! (Bixio)                               4/20
7-252201 PAPACCIO   Mandulinata 'e notte (Di Capua)                        5/20
7-252202 PAPACCIO   Signorina (Giuliani)                                   5/20
```

7-252203 PAPACCIO	Voglio la mamma (Giuliani)	5/20
7-252206 MARI	'A legge (Mario)	1/21
7-252207 MARI	'O festino (Mario)	1/21
7-252208 MARI	Buongiorno a Maria (Mario)	1/21
7-252209 MARI	Santa Lucia luntana (Mario)	1/21
7-252210 GIANNINI	Canzona 'e Pusilleco (Leone)	1/21
7-252211 GIANNINI	Canzona semplice (Mario)	1/21
7-252212 MARI	Colei che sa baciare (Mario)	1/21
7-252213 MARI	Biondo fantasma (Mario)	1/21
7-252214 GIANNINI	Cummedia (Mario)	1/21
7-252215 MARI	Marionette (Manzi)	1/21
7-252216 MARI	Dubbio (Mario)	1/21
7-252217 MARI	Vipera (Mario)	1/21
7-252218 PAPACCIO	E sbocciano le rose (Mario)	1/21
7-252219 GIANNINI	Le rose rosse (Mario)	1/21
7-252220 GIANNINI	L'eredità (Mario)	1/21
7-252221 GIANNINI	Tarantella masculina (Mario)	1/21
7-252222 MARI	La leggenda del Piave (Mario)	1/21
7-252223 PAPACCIO	Madonnina blù (Mario)	1/21
7-252224 FERNANDEZ	Ah! Finalmente "Tosca" (Puccini)	2/21
7-252225 MARI	Piccole mani (Mario)	1/21
7-252240 MASSA	Estasi d'amore (Fragna)	1/21
7-252241 MASSA	Pulcinella non ride! (Albano)	1/21
7-252242 GABRÉ	Filava...filava! (Bixio)	1/21
7-252243 GABRÉ	La canzone della soffitta (Bixio)	1/21
7-252244 MASSA	Serenata perduta (Bixio)	1/21
7-252245 MASSA	Vicino a ttè (De-Luca)	1/21
7-252246 MASSA	Chiaro...cu'mme' (Albano)	1/21
7-252247 MASSA	Mandulinata napulitana (Albano)	1/21
7-252248 MASSA	Si t'affaccia tu! (Albano)	1/21
7-252249 MASSA	Tu faie pe' mme! (Fragna)	1/21
7-252250 GABRÉ	'A ricetta... (Bixio)	1/21
7-252251 MASSA	Odio (Bixio)	1/21
7-252252 GABRÉ	E l'edera sei tu... (Mario)	1/21
7-252253 GABRÉ	Mille baci (Manzi)	1/21
7-252254 GABRÉ	Mondo piccino (Rulli)	1/21
7-252255 GABRÉ	Gelsomino (Mario)	1/21
7-252256 PAPACCIO	Lontananza (Moleti)	1/21
7-252257 GABRÉ	Sogna la gioventù (Rulli)	1/21
7-252258 PAPACCIO	Làsseme e và.. (Medina)	1/21
7-252259 PAPACCIO	Napule mio...(Mario)	1/21
7-252260 GABRÉ	Serenatona (Mario)	1/21
7-252261 PAPACCIO	Fanfarra' e maggio (Ingenito)	1/21
7-252262 GIANNINI	Accussì vò Pusilleco (Ciociano)	1/21
7-252263 GIANNINI	'A scatulella (Ciociano)	1/21
7-252264 GIANNINI	Ciardeniello suspiruso (Di Jorio)	1/21
7-252265 GIANNINI	Mandulinata mia (Di Jorio)	1/21
7-252266 PAPACCIO	Matenata (Nardella)	1/21
7-252267 GIANNINI	Matenata 'e vase (Ciociano)	1/21
7-252268 GIANNINI	Nun m'a fà sunnà! (Ciociano)	1/21
7-252269 GIANNINI	P'ò mare 'e Surriento (Ciociano)	1/21
7-252270 GIANNINI	Velivoll, velivolà (Ciociano)	1/21
7-252271 GIANNINI	Vi' che gran felicità (Buongiovanni)	1/21
7-252272 GABRÉ	Canti del mare (Medina)	1/21
7-252273 GIANNINI	Cara compagna (Ciociano)	1/21
7-252274 GIANNINI	Sole 'ncantato (Ciociano)	1/21
7-252275 PAPACCIO	Sulo 'a chitarra mia (Barbieri)	1/21
7-252276 GIANNINI	Buscie 'e femmena (Nardella)	1/21

7-252277	GIANNINI	Faie tu pure accussi! (Colonnese)	1/21
7-252278	GIANNINI	'Nu desiderio' e che? (Nardella)	1/21
7-252279	GIANNINI	Ullero, Ullero...ca nun è overo (Colonnese)	1/21
7-252280	GIANNINI	Si è guappo o no! (Giannelli)	1/21
7-252281	GIANNINI	'Sti ccose nun se fanno! (Spagnolo)	1/21
7-252282	R.DE ANGELIS	Arlecchino innamorato (Staffelli)	1/21
7-252283	R.DE ANGELIS	Cuore vagabondo (Bellini)	1/21
7-252284	R.DE ANGELIS	Ingenuamente! (Staffelli)	1/21
7-252285	R.DE ANGELIS	Manca la corrente... (Staffelli)	1/21
7-252286	R.DE ANGELIS	Lasciamoci così! (Criscuolo)	1/21
7-252287	R.DE ANGELIS	Un' avventura al Canadà (Staffelli)	1/21
7-252288	GIANNINI	Che bella cosa oinè (Capolongo)	1/21
7-252289	GIANNINI	Femmena amata (Nardella)	1/21
7-252290	GABRÈ	Donna! (Giuliani)	1/21
7-252291	GABRÈ	La storiella della nonna (Giuliani)	1/21
7-252292	GABRÈ	Gira 'o munno (Valente)	1/21
7-252293	GABRÈ	Trovatella (Cattedra)	1/21
7-252294	MASSA	L'ingrata (Cosentino)	1/21
7-252295	MASSA	Signora...o Signorina? (Cosentino)	1/21
7-252299	MONTI	Santa Lucia luntana (Mario)	1922
7-252300	MONTI	Serenata (Mario)	1922
7-252303	PESSINA	Ciondolo d'oro (Guglielmetti)	1/22
7-252304	PAPACCIO	Chitarra malinconica (N.N.)	1/22
7-252305	SERRA	Soldato ignoto (Mario)	1/22
7-252306	POLISSENI	Signor, non fu mai in America "Donne Viennesi" (Lehàr)	2/22
7-252307	POLISSENI	O viennesi do. do.	2/22
7-252308	POLISSENI	A mezzanotte "Phi-Phi" (Christiné)	2/22
7-252309	POLISSENI	L'arte passatista do. do.	2/22
7-252310	POLISSENI	Tutte le bambine "La Ragazza Olandese" (Kalmàn)	4/22
7-252312	TUMINELLO	Mimì (Rulli)	5/22
7-252313	TUMINELLO	Mondana (Rulli)	5/22
7-252314	TUMINELLO	Ninnolo (Rulli)	5/22
7-252315	TUMINELLO	Come una coppia di "Champagne" (Borella e Rampoldi)	5/22
7-252316	TUMINELLO	Sotto l'ombrello (Marì)	5/22
7-252317	TUMINELLO	Calze di seta (Marì)	5/22
7-252318	TALIANI	Fiorin, fiorello! "L'Acqua Cheta" (Pietri) acc.chitarra e mand.	6/22
7-252319	TALIANI	Di chez Maxim l'ambito tron "Il Re di Chez Maxim" (Costa)	6/22
7-252320	TALIANI	Romanza di Max do. do.	6/22
7-252321	TUMINELLO	Ronda di viveurs (Corona)	6/22
7-252322	TUMINELLO	Troppo fox-trot! (De Bosi)	6/22
7-252323	TUMINELLO	"Cocottina" (Ripp)	6/22
7-252324	TUMINELLO	Frai Bantù (Mignone)	6/22
7-252325	TALIANI	Canzone di Giuliano "La Mazurka Blù" (Lehàr)	7/22
7-252326	SERRA	La leggenda del Piave (Mario)	11/24
7-252328	TUMINELLO	Marion (Cortopassi)	4/23
7-252329	DALUMI	Yvonne (Rulli)	4/23
7-252330	SERRA	Ninna, Nanna (Spadaro)	4/23
7-252331	SERRA	Follia (Borella-Rampoldi)	4/23
7-252332	TUMINELLO	Séparé (Bixio)	4/23
7-252333	TUMINELLO	Danza come sai danzare tu (Bixio)	4/23
7-252334	DALUMI	Sotto il raggio della luna (Ripp)	4/23
7-252335	DALUMI	Bimbe, uscite pure di sera..(Guglielmetti)	4/23
7-252336	NICHINI	Fiamme nere (Ferretti)	4/23
7-252337	DALUMI	La mezzanotte (Del Genovese)	4/23
7-252338	TUMINELLO	T'ho sempre amato! (Ferradini)	5/23
7-252339	SERRA	Mentre tu sogni (Brumalto)	5/23
7-252340	DALUMI	Amore bancario (Cosentino)	5/23

```
7-252341 DALUMI     Mai più (Ripp)                                      5/23
7-252342 DALUMI     Pardon (Rulli)                                      5/23
7-252343 DALUMI     L'orologio (Mario)                                  5/23
7-252344 DALUMI     Moglie regina (Mario)                               5/23
7-252345 TUMINELLO  Codda o suli (Volpes-Fardella)                      6/23
7-252346 TUMINELLO  Risisti, o cori (Volpes-Fardella)                   6/23
7-252347 TUMINELLO  La Piscicani (Volpes-Fardella)                      6/23
7-252348 TUMINELLO  M'ammazzasti (Volpes-Fardella)                      6/23
7-252349 SERRA      Il Fox-trot della nostalgia (Vitaliani)             8/23
7-252350 MARESCOTTI O Bajadera "La Bajadera" (Kalmán)                   9/23
7-252351 SERRA      Così piange Pierrot (Bixio)                        10/23
7-252352 SERRA      Come la bambola (Bixio)                            10/23
7-252353 SERRA      Danzomania (Bixio)                                 10/23
7-252354 SERRA      Stornelli amari (Bixio)                            10/23
7-252355 SERRA      Danzan i campagnoli! (Rusconi)                     10/23
7-252356 SERRA      Ombre e campane (Berra)                            10/23
7-252357 SERRA      Ständchen (Heykens)                                10/23
7-252358 SERRA      'E Napule (Bixio)                                  10/23
7-252359 DALUMI     Tabarin (Stolz)                                    11/23
7-252360 DALUMI     Serenata montana (Blanc)                           11/23
7-252361 DALUMI     Fiocca la neve (Cimara)                            11/23
7-252362 DALUMI     Stornello (Cimara)                                 11/23
7-252363 DALUMI     Lanterna giapponese (Kreutzler)                    11/23
7-252364 DALUMI     Fior d'Andalusia (Abbati)                          11/23
7-252365 DALUMI     Inno Nazionale Antiblasfemo (Magri)                11/23
7-252366 DALUMI     'A Baxadonna (Barbieri)                            11/23
7-252367 MARESCOTTI Buongiorno a Maria (Mario)                          1/24
7-252368 ASCOLI     Ladra...(Mario)                                     1/24
7-252369 MARESCOTTI Mandulinata a Surriento (Mario)                     2/24
7-252370 MARESCOTTI Torna a Marechiare (Mario)                          2/24
7-252371 DALUMI     Cavaliere di grazia "La Gran Via" (Valverde)        3/24
7-252372 SERRA      Il capriccio (Rulli)                                1/24
7-252373 SERRA      Lampadina blù (Abbati)                              1/24
7-252374 SERRA      Color sincerità (Mario)                             1/24
7-252375 DALUMI     La gavotta dei nonni (Criscuolo-Doria)              2/24
7-252376 SERRA      Il paese della civiltà (Guglielmetti)               2/24
7-252377 SERRA      Chissà come si chiama in Giapponese!? (Borella)     2/24
7-252378 SERRA      La canzone del mattino (Rulli)                      2/24
7-252379 SERRA      Ballate, bembine...(Benech)                         2/24
7-252380 SERRA      Mandulinata e il' emigrante (Ciaravolo)             2/24
7-252381 SERRA      Farfalla bianca (Mario)                             2/24
7-252382 SERRA      È questo l'amore (Guglielmetti)                     3/24
7-252383 SERRA      E canta Italia (Ustrumillo)                         3/24
7-252384 SERRA      Occhi verdi (Bixio)                                 3/24
7-252385 SERRA      'E canzone (Bixio)                                  3/24
7-252386 SERRA      Vieni al Tabarin (Colonnese)                        3/24
7-252387 SERRA      Come Manon (Rampaldi)                               3/24
7-252389 RICCIOLI   A Torino (La Torinese) "Bacco in Toscana" (Brogi)   5/24
7-252390 SERRA      Non ridere Chiffon (Caleffa)                        6/24
7-252391 SERRA      Colombina innamorata (Piovano)                      6/24
7-252392 SERRA      Simplicità (Staffelli)                              6/24
7-252393 SERRA      Leggenda marina (De Domenico)                       6/24
7-252394 SERRA      Si chiamava Pi-ci-ci (Rulli)                        6/24
7-252395 SERRA      Io vi adoro (Mercier)                               6/24
7-252396 PASQUARIELLO Giuocettolo (Colonnese)                           7/24
7-252397 PASQUARIELLO Il salotto Liberty (Bellini)                      7/24
7-252398 PASQUARIELLO Core furastiero (Mario)                           7/24
7-252399 PASQUARIELLO Canzona appassiunate (Mario)                      7/24
7-252400 PASQUARIELLO Sulla Riviera (Mario)                             7/24
```

7-252401	PASQUARIELLO	Cara Signora Italia (Mario)	7/24
7-252404	SERRA	Biondo corsaro (Del Pelo)	11/24
7-252405	SERRA	Scampolo (Raimondi)	11/24
7-252406	SERRA	Il fox-trot degli studenti (Spadaro)	11/24
7-252407	SERRA	L'ultimo Arlecchino (Bixio)	11/24
7-252408	SERRA	Johnson (Rulli)	11/24
7-252409	SERRA	Il paese del Ka-Kao (Rulli)	11/24
7-252410	SERRA	Il treno va (Rusconi)	11/24
7-252411	SERRA	Rosita (Fagiolari)	11/24
7-252412	SERRA	Bocca d'oro (Jaffe)	12/24
7-252413	SERRA	Non ritornate rondini (Billi)	12/24
7-252414	SERRA	Signori, io son Douglas (Di Lazzaro)	12/24
7-252415	SERRA	La protesta degli scimpanzè (Abbati)	12/24
7-252416	SERRA	L'età dei sogni (Rulli)	12/24
7-252417	SERRA	Io cerco Titina "Mdlle.Tobogan" (Daniderff)	12/24
7-252418	SERRA	Morenita (Abbati)	12/24
7-252419	SERRA	Donne sincere (Mignone)	12/24
7-252420	SERRA	Notti Giapponesi (Beneck)	12/24
7-252421	SERRA	Gingillo (Rulli)	12/24
7-252422	ETTI	Scettico blues (Rulli)	2/25
7-252423	ETTI	Sentinella (Guglielmetti)	2/25
7-252424	ETTI	Rusticanella (Cortopassi)	2/25
7-252425	ETTI	Leggimi il destino (Bixio)	2/25
7-252426	AGNOLETTI	Tu che di Vienna "Contessa Maritza" (Kalmán)	3/25
7-252427	AGNOLETTI	Vieni, tzigano do. do. do.	3/25
7-252428	DE EGUILEOR	O Padre mio "L'uomo che ride" (Pedrollo)	6/25
7-252429	DE EGUILEOR	È finita do. do.	6/25
7-252430	DE EGUILEOR	Astro d'amor do. do.	6/25
7-252431	SERRA	Donna e stagione (Mignone)	9/25
7-252432	SERRA	Maggio, e parlale d'amor (Mignone)	9/25
7-252433	SERRA	La leggenda del Corno d'oro (Tartarini)	9/25
7-252434	SERRA	Mamma, non l'amo più (Bixio)	9/25
7-252435	SERRA	Oh! Baby! (Donaldson)	9/25
7-252436	SERRA	"Le Ukulele" (Conrad)	9/25
7-252437	SERRA	Mamma! (Billi)	10/25
7-252438	SERRA	Patria lontana (Piovano)	10/25
7-252439	SERRA	La Java del villaggio (Fragna)	10/25
7-252440	SERRA	Pian...pianin,,,(Hermite)	10/25
7-252445	GIORGINI	Tu che a Dio "Lucia di Lammermoor" (Donizetti)	10/25
7-252446	GIORGINI	Chi son? Sono un poeta "La Bohème" (Puccini)	10/25
7-252447	GIORGINI	Questa donna conoscete? "La Traviata" (Verdi)	10/25
7-252448	SERRA	Criollita (Sentis)	11/25
7-252449	SERRA	Ma la mia sartina (Borella)	11/25
7-252450	SERRA	Foxtrot della notte (Mignone)	11/25
7-252451	SERRA	I veri apâches (Bixio)	11/25
7-252452	GIORGINI	Questa o quella "Rigoletto" (Verdi)	11/25
7-252453	GIORGINI	La donna è mobile "Rigoletto" (Verdi)	11/25
7-252454	GIORGINI	Cielo e mar "La Gioconda" (Ponchielli)	11/25
7-252455	GIORGINI	A te, o cara "I Puritani" (Bellini)	11/25
7-252456	MANFRINI	Vi ravviso "La Sonnambula" (Bellini)	3/26
7-252457	GIORGINI	Mi par d'udir "I Pescatori di Perle" (Bizet)	4/26
7-252458	GIORGINI	Della mia vita do. do. do.	4/26
7-252459	GIORGINI	Quanto è bella "L'Elisir d'amore" (Donizetti)	4/26
7-252460	GIORGINI	Una furtiva lagrima do. do. do.	4/26
7-252461	BOLIS	Romanza del fiore "Carmen" (Bizet)	4/26
7-252462	SPILOTROS	Stornelli Baresi	12/25
7-252463	SPILOTROS	Quadriglia Barese - I.	12/25
7-252464	SPILOTROS	do. do. - II.	12/25

7-252465	BERTI,R.	La canzone del blues (Vigevani)	11/25
7-252466	BERTI,R.	In terra lontana (De Serra)	11/25
7-252467	BERTI,R.	La danza delle bambole (Vigevani)	12/25
7-252468	BERTI,R.	Maliarda (Padovani)	12/25
7-252469	BERTI,R.	La canzone di Marga (Marrone)	12/25
7-252470	BERTI,R.	Il moro e il caffè (Vigevani)	12/25
7-252471	SERRA	In terra lontana (De Serra)	1/26
7-252472	SERRA	Bimba...addio! (Giordano)	1/26
7-252473	SERRA	Nella Jungla nera (Ripp)	1/26
7-252474	SERRA	India (Ripp)	1/26
7-252475	SERRA	In fondo al mare (Ripp)	1/26
7-252476	SERRA	Ah! se parlasse il pianerottolo! (Ripp)	1/26
7-252477	SERRA	La Scimmilandia (Ripp)	1/26
7-252478	SERRA	Creola - Canzone tango (Ripp)	1/26
7-252479	SERRA	Fior del Turkestan (Piovano)	1/26
7-252480	SERRA	Fiocchi di neve (Giordano)	1/26
7-252481	SERRA	Teodoro (Oneglio)	1/26
7-252482	GABRÉ	Finestrella d'oro (Mignone)	2/26
7-252483	GABRÉ	Fior di loto (Arnaldi)	2/26
7-252484	GABRÉ	Nuvola (Bixio)	2/26
7-252485	GABRÉ	Leggenda rossa (Bixio)	2/26
7-252486	GABRÉ	Amanti (Simi)	2/26
7-252487	GABRÉ	Suona, fanfara! (Simi)	2/26
7-252488	GABRÉ	Donna che sai mentire (Simi)	2/26
7-252489	GABRÉ	Addio, signora! (Simi)	2/26
7-252490	GABRÉ	Canta Pierrot (Bixio)	3/26
7-252491	GABRÉ	Lo stornello delle fragole (Staffelli)	3/26
7-252492	GABRÉ	Sfinge! (Bonavolontà)	3/26
7-252493	GABRÉ	Lo shimmy delle stelle (Nardella)	3/26
7-252494	GABRÉ	Lagreme Napulitane (Buongiovanni)	3/26
7-252495	GABRÉ	'O paese d'o sole (d'Annibale)	3/26
7-252496	SPADARO	Papà, mammà e tutta la famiglia (Spadaro)	4/26
7-252497	SPADARO	È il tuo Antonio (Bernard-Valsien)	4/26
7-252498	SPADARO	Il monte e il piano (Spadaro)	4/26
7-252499	SPADARO	Casentino e Mugello (Spadaro)	4/26
7-252500	SPADARO	È il tuo papà (Spadaro)	4/26
7-252501	SPADARO	Il ritorno al paesello (Da una vecchia canzone)	4/26
7-252502	SPADARO	Vieni a Dixie-land (Spadaro)	4/26
7-252503	SPADARO	New York (Spadaro)	4/26
7-252504	SPADARO	Jazz band in famiglia (Spadaro)	4/26
7-252505	SPADARO	Petit béguin (Spadaro) in italiano e francese	4/26
7-252506	BERTI,R.	Suona la mezzanotte (Rusconi)	6/26
7-252507	BERTI,R.	E' l'ultimo shimmy (Fragna)	6/26
7-252508	BERTI,R.	Madre! (Silvestri)	6/26
7-252509	BERTI,R.	Amor tzigano (Dragonetti)	6/26
7-252510	BERTI,R.	Lo stornello del marinaro (Albano)	6/26
7-252511	BERTI,R.	Musica d'orni dì (Bernard)	6/26
7-252512	BERTI,R.	L'isola dei pappagalli (Vanner)	6/26
7-252513	BERTI,R.	Scusi, ha dimenticato niente? (Abbati)	6/26
7-252514	"MISCEL"	È lei quella biondina? (Bixio)	5/26
7-252515	"MISCEL"	Stella del mare (Del Pelo)	5/26
7-252516	"MISCEL"	Piccola Pompadour (Abbati)	5/26
7-252517	"MISCEL"	Quartiere latino (Abbati)	5/26
7-252518	"MISCEL"	Mezzanotte (Bonavolontà)	5/26
7-252519	"MISCEL"	Turbine (Grimaldi)	5/26
7-252520	"MISCEL"	Reginella - "Olì, Olì, Olà" (Raimondi)	5/26
7-252521	"MISCEL"	Fantaccino biondo (Raimondi)	5/26
7-252522	"MISCEL"	È tornato Pierrot (Rulli)	5/26

7-252523	"MISCEL"	Malisrda (Rulli)	5/26
7-252532	SERRA	Conosci quel paese? (Mendes)	9/26
7-252533	SERRA	Italia bella (Cortopassi)	9/26
7-252534	SERRA	Passano gli studenti (Simi)	9/26
7-252535	SERRA	Il fox-trot delle piume (Simi)	9/26
7-252536	PETROLINI	Fortunello (Petrolini)	9/26
7-252537	PETROLINI	Roba seria (Petrolini)	9/26
7-252538	PETROLINI	Canzone a Nina (Gaudiosi)	10/26
7-252539	PETROLINI	Serenata pedestre (Petrolini)	10/26
7-253000	MUSETTE	Alice (Del Vecchio)	1914/5
7-253001	MUSETTE	Chiamateme 'o furiere (Consentino)	1914/5
7-253002	MUSETTE	Brilla l'amore (Criscuolo)	1914/5
7-253003	CONFORTI	L'amore per te (Del Vecchio)	1914/5
7-253004	MUSETTE	Cor felice (Mario)	1914/5
7-253005	MUSETTE	Ritornello proibito (Di Chiara)	1914/5
7-253006	MUSETTE	Facciatustella (Cosentino)	1914/5
7-253008	GOLETTI	La ragazza neutrale (Colombino)	1914/5
7-253009	AICARDI	Canzone garibaldina (Falvo)	1914/5
7-253010	DURVILLE	Speranza 'e gioventù (Moleti)	1914/5
7-253011	DURVILLE	Vieni sul mar (Moleti)	1914/5
7-253012	DURVILLE	Canti d'Ottobre (Brunetti)	1914/5
7-253013	DURVILLE	La Baya (Christiné)	1914/5
7-253014	ERMOLLI	Andate, o mamma "Cavalleria Rusticana" (Mascagni)	1915
7-253015	DURVILLE	Marietta (Sterny Courquin)	1915/6
7-253016	DURVILLE	Serenatella (Medina)	1915/6
7-253017	DURVILLE	Le campane del villaggio (Allegri)	1915/6
7-253018	DURVILLE	Vieni (Denza)	1915/6
7-253019	BEVIGNANI	È strano! "La Traviata" (Verdi)	1917
7-253020	MÉNIER	È la fanciulla in gran pensier "La Signorina del Cinematografo" (Lombardo)	1915/6
7-253021	MÉNIER	Marcia Latina (Mario)	1915/6
7-253022	RAVELLI	La montanara (Valente)	1915/6
7-253023	BALDINI	Ma dall'arido stelo "Un Ballo in Maschera" (Verdi)	1917
7-253024	BALDINI	Mezzanotte, e che vegg'io do. do. do.	1917
7-253025	GIOANA	Romanza di Germana "Le Campane di Corneville" (Planquette)	1917
7-253031	ANNITA	Pagliaccio, mio marito "Pagliacci" (Leoncavallo)	1917
7-253032	DOMAR (s)	Frou Frou del Tabarin "La Duchessa del Bal Tabarin" (Leon Bard)	1917
7-253034	BOSINI	Sa dirmi, scusi "La Boheme" (Puccini)	6/19
7-253035	GOTTARDI	Ritorna vincitor "Aida" (Verdi)	2/19
7-253036	GOTTARDI	I sacri nomi do. do.	2/19
7-253037	PIERRETTE	La demoiselle du Journal (Christine)	3/19
7-253038	PIERRETTE	Le rêve passe (Helmer & Krier)	3/19
7-253039	PIERRETTE	La ronde des baisers (Jardin)	3/19
7-253040	PIERRETTE	Valse d'un jour (Christiné)	3/19
7-253041	DOMAR(s)	Valzer dei campanelli "La Duchessa del Bal Tabarin" (Leon Bard)	
7-253042	DOMAR(s)	Entrata di Chiffon "La Regina del Fonografo" (Léon Bard)	10/19
			7/19
7-253043	BURCHI	Suicidio! "La Gioconda" (Ponchielli)	7/19
7-253044	BOSINI	Aria del pesciolino. "Geisha" (Jones)	8/19
7-253045	BOSINI	Cion-China "Geisha" (Jones)	8/19
7-253046	BOSINI	Canzone della Vilja "La Vedova Allegra" (Lehàr)	8/19
7-253047	REMONDINI	Vissi d'arte "Tosca" (Puccini)	4/19
7-253048	DARCLÉE	La figlia della strada (Giuliani)	9/19
7-253049	DE GIOIA	'O sole mio (Di Capua)	9/19
7-253050	DE GIOIA	Santa Lucia	9/19

```
7-253051 CAVALIERI   Donnine del Giappone (Silvestri)                          9/19
7-253052 DARCLÉE     Bambola (Valente)                                         9/19
7-253053 BIJOÙ       Joujou (Valente)                                          9/19
7-253055 DE GIOIA    Voce 'e notte (De Curtis)                                 9/19
7-253056 DE GIOIA    Torna a Surriento (De Curtis)                             9/19
7-253057 DE GIOIA    La gondola nera (Rotoli)                                  9/19
7-253058 AILEMA      Capinera (Giuliani)                                       9/19
7-253059 AILEMA      Perchè fò l'amore (Giuliani)                              9/19
7-253061 DE GIOIA    Marechiare (Tosti)                                        9/19
7-253062 DE GIOIA    Bambola infranta (Tati)                                   9/19
7-253063 BIJOÙ       La musique americaine (Ignoto)                            9/19
7-253064 BIJOÙ       Addio Brunetta (Bixio)                                    9/19
7-253065 AILEMA      Comm'aggi a fa (Liberato)                                 9/19
7-253066 AILEMA      Ammore'n campagna (Capolongo)                             9/19
7-253067 AILEMA      Sta passanno 'a giuventù (Liberato)                       9/19
7-253068 DE GIOIA    Mare! Mare! (Perla)                                       9/19
7-253069 DARCLÉE     Rondine (Liberato)                                        9/19
7-253070 BARTOLOMASI Laggiù nel Soledad  "La Fanciulla del West" (Puccini)11/1
7-253073 DARCLÉE     Peccato (Giuliani)                                        4/20
7-253074 AILEMA      Giovinezza (Bixio)                                        4/20
7-253075 AILEMA      La Signorina del Magazzino (Bixio)                        4/20
7-253076 DARCLÉE     Mai più (d'Annibale)                                      1/21
7-253077 AILEMA      Piererotta (Bixio)                                        1/21
7-253078 DARCLÉE     Pentimento (Dramis)                                       4/20
7-253079 DARCLÉE     Ridi, perchè? (d'Annibale)                                4/20
7-253080 AILEMA      Pazzarella (d'Annibale)                                   4/20
7-253081 AILEMA      Bionda o Bruna (Giuliani)                                 5/20
7-253082 AILEMA      Per te (Giuliani)                                         5/20
7-253083 DARCLÉE     Mamma, mammina (Cattedra)                                 5/20
7-253085 AILEMA      Tarantellona (Mario)                                      1/21
7-253086 DARCLÉE     Farfalla (Mario)                                          1/21
7-253087 AILEMA      Gioia mia! (Mario)                                        1/21
7-253088 BARTOLOMASI Vissi d'arte  "Tosca" (Puccini)                           2/21
7-253089 BARTOLOMASI Immenso Fthà  "Aida" (Verdi)                              11/20
7-253090 PAGANI      Chi mai fra gl'anni   do.  do.                            11/20
7-253091 PAGANI      Danza dei giovani schiavi mori  do.  do.                  11/20
7-253092 BARTOLOMASI Qui Radamès verrà            do.  do.                     11/20
7-253093 PAGANI      L'aborrita rivale           do.  do.                      11/20
7-253094 DE MARY     Apaches (Rulli)                                           1/22
7-253095 DE MARY     L'amore grigio-verde (Christiné)                          1/22
7-253096 DARCLÉE     Povera mamma (Giuliani)                                   1/22
7-253097 DE MARY     Nel paese dei Zulù (Ripp)                                 1/22
7-253098 DE MARY     La canzone del Sénégal (Rusconi)                          1/22
7-253099 DE SIMONI   Hajà! Hajà! "Principessa della Czarda" (Kalmán)           2/22
7-253100 DE SIMONI   Perchè cercar la gioia   do.  do.  do.                    4/22
7-253101 DE SIMONI   La fanciulla del pescatore "La Ragazza Olandese" (Kalman)
                                                                               4/22
7-253102 DE SIMONI   Quando sento risonar          do. do. do.                 4/22
7-253104 SANIPOLI    Fogli vergati sotto un incanto  "Sì" (Mascagni)           8/22
7-253105 SANIPOLI    Poche rose languenti       do.    do.                     8/22
7-253106 ROSSI       Sono una donna (Staffelli)                                5/23
7-253107 GARGIULO    Perduti abbiam padroni "Le Campane di Corneville"
                                                 (Planquette)                  3/24
7-253108 JUANITA     La Violetera (Padilla)                                    1/24
7-253109 JUANITA     La Java (Yvain)                                           1/24
7-253110 PRIMAVERA   Tenentin, caro amore  "Casta Diva" (Bellini)              5/24
7-253111 LIDELBA     Vien tu, vien gentil mio Cavalier!  "La Bajadera"
                                            .        (Kalmán)                  6/24
```

```
7-253112 LIDELBA    Siviglia, ai meraviglia! "Fior di Siviglia" (Cuscinà) 6/24
7-253113 LIDELBA    Miranda son, Fior di Siviglia        do. do. do.        6/24
7-253114 PRIMAVERA  Solo uno sguardo al passato "La Donna Perduta"(Pietri)2/25
7-253115 PRIMAVERA  Luna, luna                           do. do. do.        2/25
7-253117 ARMAGNI-GENNARI   (a) Ave Maria di Lourdes (in italiano)
                           (b) Ave Maris Stella (in latino)               4/25
7-253118 ARMAGNI-GENNARI   Cristo Risusciti. Trascr. di una melodia
                                Pasquale del Sec.XII.                     4/25
7-253119 ARMAGNI-GENNARI   (a) Nel Ciel (Preghiera del mattino) do.       4/25
                           (b) L'Angelus (Preghiera della sera) do.       4/25
7-253120 ARMAGNI-GENNARI   (a) Dove sei stato, mio bell'Alpino? do.       4/25
                           (b) O Dio del Cielo                  do.       4/25
7-253121 ARMAGNI-GENNARI   (a) Il testamento del maresciallo   do.        4/25
                           (b) Sul cappello (Trascr. di canti di soldati 1915-8)
                                                                          4/25
7-253122 ARMAGNI-GENNARI   (a) Il risveglio di primavera
                           (b) Girotondo
                           (c) O pallina pazzerella                       4/25
7-253123 ARMAGNI-GENNARI   (a) O pescator dell'onda
                           (b) Cincirinella
                           (c) Il musicante girovago                      4/25
                           (Trascr. di canti popolari del Mo.Schinelli)
7-253124 ARMAGNI-GENNARI   (a) L'Orfano (Pascoli-Sincero)
                           (b) I bimbi vanno a nanna (Schumann)           4/25
7-253125 ARMAGNI-GENNARI   Alpes (Bossi) Canto ginnastico                 4/25
7-253126 ARMAGNI-GENNARI   La Canzone del Grappa (Meneghetti)             4/25
7-253127 ARMAGNI-GENNARI   (a) La fanfara dei Bersaglieri
                           (b) La bandiera tricolore                      4/25
7-253128 ARMAGNI-GENNARI   (a) Preghiera (Giacchetti)
                           (b) Le manine (Visonà)                         4/25
7-253131 SALVI      Spargi d'amaro pianto "Lucia di Lammermoor" (Donizetti) 10/25
7-253132 FELLA      Mi chiamano Mimì "La Bohème" (Puccini)                10/25
7-253147 COBELLI    Suicidio! "La Gioconda" (Ponchielli)                  11/25
7-253148 ABBRESCIA  Habanera  "Carmen" (Bizet)                           4/26


7-254000 GIOANA/MIELI/BERARDI  Vent'anni ancor non ho "I Saltimbanchi" (Ganne)
                                                                          1914/5
7-254001 GIOANA/MIELI          E l'amor                       do. do.     1914/5
7-254002 GIOANA/MIELI/BERARDI  Senza pensieri                 do. do.     1914/5
7-254003 ERMOLLI/TUMINELLO  Tu qui, Santuzza? "Cavalleria Rusticana"(Mascagni)
                                                                          1915
7-254004 ERMOLLI/PERNA   Turiddu mi tolse l'onore       do. do. do.       1915
7-254005 ERMOLLI/PERNA   Comare Santa, allor            do. do. do.       1915
7-254006 COPPIA TAKINES  Affacciati alla finestra (Dellacasa)             1915/6
7-254007 COPPIA TAKINES  La Pifferara (Dellacasa)                         1915/6
7-254008 COPPIA TAKINES  Avanti...! Marcia (Dellacasa)                    1915/6
7-254009 COPPIA TAKINES  Voce di Patria (Dellacasa)                       1915/6
7-254010 COPPIA TAKINES  Rondinella d'amor (Dellacasa)                    1915/6
7-254011 COPPIA TAKINES  Serenata eccentrica (Dellacasa)                  1915/6
7-254012 BEVIGNANI/TUMINELLO  Che è cio? "La Traviata" (Verdi)            1917
7-254013 BEVIGNANI/TUMINELLO  Un dì felice eterea   do.    do.            1917
7-254014 BEVIGNANI/BADINI  Pura siccome un angelo do.     do.             1917
7-254015 BEVIGNANI/BADINI  Bella voi siete        do.     do.             1917
7-254016 TUMINELLO/BADINI  Di sprezzo degno        do.     do.            1917
7-254017 BEVIGNANI/TUMINELLO  Ah, non più! a un tempio  do. do.           1917
7-254018 MENIER/U.SALVI  O bianca Mizzi "La Signorina del Cinematografo"
                                                      (Leon Bard) 1915/6
```

7-254019 MÉNIER/U.SALVI La mia vetturina
"La Signorina del Cinematografo" (Leon Bard)   1917
7-254020 SPINELLI/PESSI La vita non è che un valzer   do. do. do.   1915/6
7-254021 MÉNIER/U.SALVI Stendiamoci allor la man   do. do. do.   1915/6
7-254022 SPINELLI/PESSI Spargete di rose il suo cammin do. do. do.   1915/6
7-254023 BROCCARDI/SALA/DANISE/BETTONI/LIMONTA Gran nuova! gran nuova!
(6454ae)"Rigoletto" (Verdi)   1917
7-254024 ZERNI/DANISE   Figlia! mio padre (6448ae) do.   do.   1917
7-254025 ZERNI/DANISE/GARRONE/BROCCARDI Già de tre lune   do.do.(6463ae)1917
7-254026 ZERNI/DANISE/GARRONE/BROCCARDI Veglia o donna   do.do.(6462ae)1917
7-254027 ZERNI/GARRONE/BROCCARDI Giovanna, ho dei rimorsi do.do.(6457ae)1917
7-254028 ZERNI/GARRONE/BROCCARDI Addio! addio!   do.do.(6474ae)1917
7-254029 ZERNI/SALA/BETTONI/LIMONTA Caro nome   do.do.   1917
7-254030 ZERNI/BROCCARDI/DANISE/BETTONI E l'ami ?   do.do.(6459ae)1917
7-254031 BROCCARDI/DANISE/BETTONI La donna è mobile   do.do.(6450ae)1917
7-254032 ZERNI/BROCCARDI/GARRONE/DANISE
Un dì, mi ben rammentomi   do.do.(6449ae)1917
7-254033 ZERNI/BROCCARDI/GARRONE/BETTONI M'odi,ritorna o casa do.do. 1917
7-254034 ZERNI/BROCCARDI/GARRONE/BETTONI Povero giovin   do.do.(6465ae)1917
7-254042 MONTANELLI/CONTI È dessa   "Pagliacci" (Leoncavallo)1917
7-254043 PRAT/CONTI Duettino Arlecchino-Colombina   do.do.   1917
7-254044 DOMAR (s)/MICHELUZZI Ah! Ah! come si sta bene
"La Duchessa del Bal Tabarin" (Leon Bard)1917
7-254045 DOMAR (s)/MICHELUZZI Bacia, bacia sempre più   do.do.   1917
7-254046 DOMAR (s) Valzer dei campanelli   do.do.   1917
7-254047 SPINELLI/GARUFFI A un' altra hai donata"Addio Giovinezza"(Pietri)7/19
7-254048 SPINELLI/GARUFFI Va, va, non ti posso creder   do.do.   7/19
7-254049 DOMAR(s)/MICHELUZZI Budubu, Budubu "Il Marito Decorativo"(Bossi)7/19
7-254050 DOMAR(s)/MICHELUZZI Oh! piacer! una pioggia di baci do.do.   7/19
7-254051 DOMAR(s)/MICHELUZZI Duetto delle campane
"La Duchessa delle Campane" (Leon Bard) 10/19
7-254052 DOMAR(s)/MICHELUZZI Duetto del boudoir
"La Regina del Fonografo" (Leon Bard)   7/19
7-254053 DOMAR(s)/MICHELUZZI Valzer Pierrot   do.do.   7/19
7-254054 DOMAR(s)/MICHELUZZI Ah! Chiffon   do.do.   7/19
7-254055 DOMAR(s)/MICHELUZZI E gira, e rulla   do.do.   7/19
7-254056 DOMAR(s)/MICHELUZZI Duetto delle rose   do.do.   7/19
7-254057 DOMAR(s)/MICHELUZZI La vita non è che un valzer
"La Signorina del Cinematografo"(Leon Bard)7/19
7-254058 DOMAR(s)/MICHELUZZI O bianca Mizzi   do.do.   7/19
7-254059 DOMAR(s)/MICHELUZZI La vetturina   do.do.   7/19
7-254060 DOMAR(s)/MICHELUZZI Napoleone   do.do.   7/19
7-254061 BURCHI/FEZZUTI/BADINI O sommo Carlo "Ernani" (Verdi)   7/19
7-254062 PLINIO/TURRONI Duetto comico "L'Ave Maria" (Bettinelli)   8/19
7-254063 STERNY/PLINIO Two-step   do.   do.   8/19
7-254064 BOSINI/MICHELUZZI Tace il labbro "La Vedova Allegra" (Lehàr) 8/19
7-254065 TURRONI Duetto dei piccioni "La Mascotte" (Audran)   8/19
7-254066 REMONDINI/BROCCARDI Dilla ancora la parola "Tosca" (Puccini) 4/19
7-254067 FREGOSI/CARNEVALI Fu grave sbaglio "Tosca" (Puccini)   4/19
7-254068 ZANI/BROCCARDI/REMONDINI/PLINIO Vi è noto che un prigione do. 4/19
7-254069 ZANI/BROCCARDI/REMONDINI/PLINIO Dov' è dunque Angelotti? do. 4/19
7-254070 BROCCARDI/N.N.(bs) Mario Cavaradossi a voi!   do. do. 4/19
7-254071 REMONDINI/BROCCARDI E non giungono   do. do. 4/19
7-254072 FESTA/BADINI Gente indiscreta "Il Barbiere di Siviglia"(Rossini)6/20
7-254073 DI LELIO/CARNEVALI/BADINI/PEREIRA Ah! che ne dite? do. do. 6/20
7-254074 CARNEVALI/PEREIRA Ora mi sento meglio   do. do. 6/20
7-254075 CARNEVALI/TALIANI/PEREIRA Insomma,mio signore   do. do. 6/20
7-254076 ONORI/BETTONI Leggiadre rondinelle "Mignon" (Thomas)   1/20

```
7-254077 ONORI/BETTONI   Sofferto hai tu?                    "Mignon" (Thomas)  1/20
7-254081 SALVANESCHI  Dilla ancora la parola  "Tosca" (Puccini)                 2/21
7-254082 PACINI/CECCARELLI  Fu grave sbaglio    do.      do.                    2/21
7-254083 PACINI/SALVANESCHI/MAZZANTI/BARTOLOMASI  V'è noto che un prigione
                                                  "Tosca" (Puccini)             2/21
7-254084 PACINI/SALVANESCHI/MAZZANTI  Dov'è dunque Angelotti?  do. do.          2/21
7-254085 SALVANESCHI/FERNANDEZ  Mario Cavaradossi?            do. do.           2/21
7-254086 SALVANESCHI/BARTOLOMASI/FERNANDEZ  E non giungono!   do. do.           2/21
7-254087 BARTOLOMASI/PAGANI/TRENTINI  Ohimè! di guerra fremere  "Aida"(Verdi)
                                                                               11/20
7-254088 FERNANDEZ/PAGANI/BRILLI  O Re! pei sacri Numi   "Aida" (Verdi) 11/20
7-254089 DE SIMONI/POLISSENI  Spesso il cuore s'innamora
                              "La Principessa della Czarda" (Kalmán)     2/22
7-254090 CASTAGNETTA/POLISSENI  Il gran prodigio fa ch'io goda!  do.do.  2/22
7-254091 DE SIMONI/POLISSENI  Strette ardenti              do.do.        2/22
7-254092 CASTAGNETTA/VEZZANI  Cadere innanzi al peplo  "Phi-Phi"(Christiné)2/22
7-254093 CASTAGNETTA/VEZZANI  Mio bel Pireo            do.      do.       2/22
7-254094 CASTAGNETTA/VEZZANI  Nuova York ci lancia  "Sì" (Mascagni)      2/22
7-254095 CASTAGNETTA/VEZZANI  E' proprio una sciocchezza  do. do.        2/22
7-254096 CASTAGNETTA/VEZZANI  Donne mie "La Principessa della Czarda"(Kalmán)
                                                                         4/22
7-254097 CASTAGNETTA/VEZZANI  Quando il suon! "La Ragazza Olandese" (Kalmán)
7-254098 DE SIMONI/POLISSENI  Io t'amo già       do. do. do. 4/22   (4/22
7-254099 CASTAGNETTA/VEZZANI  Amsterdam, Rotterdam  do. do. do.          4/22
7-254100 DE SIMONI/POLISSENI  Mia sarai          do. do. do.             4/22
7-254101 CASTAGNETTA/VEZZANI  Non potevo immaginar  do. do. do.          4/22
7-254110 TALIANI/SANIPOLI  Signore, no! Nella gentil casetta
                           "L'Acqua Cheta" (Pietri)                      6/22
7-254111 TALIANI/SANIPOLI  Walzer delle violette "E arrivato L'Ambasciatore"
7-254112 TALIANI/SANIPOLI  Questo bel visin              (Bellini)       6/22
                           "È arrivato l'Ambasciatore" (Bellini)         6/22
7-254113 TALIANI/SANIPOLI  Verso un ciel più sereno
                           "Il Re di Chez Maxim" (Costa)                 8/22
7-254114 TALIANI/SANIPOLI  In un cheto asil    do.      do.              8/22
7-254115 TALIANI/SANIPOLI  Da che il mondo  "La Mazurka Blù" (Lehàr)     7/22
7-254116 TALIANI/SANIPOLI  Grullo, grullo...ci dobbiam sposar  do. do.   7/22
7-254117 TALIANI/SANIPOLI  Il Polacco dansar vuol          do. do.       7/22
7-254118 TALIANI/SANIPOLI  No, tacer non posso
                           "È arrivato l'Ambasciatore" (Bellini)        10/22
7-254119 TALIANI/SANIPOLI  Voi meditate, interpretate  do. do. do.     10/22
7-254120 ARGENTI/GIOVANELLI  Con amor guarda a me!
                           "Il Conte di Lussemburgo" (Lehàr)             1/23
7-254122 DALUMI/GARGIULO  Odette  "La Ragazza della Penombra" (Rulli)    8/23
7-254123 LIDELBA/MARESCOTTI  Quando in cielo  "La Badajera" (Kalmán)     9/23
7-254124 LIDELBA/MARESCOTTI  Il piccolo Bar     do. do.      do.         9/23
7-254125 LIDELBA/MARESCOTTI  L'uomo che tiene    do. do.     do.         9/23
7-254126 DALUMI/GARGIULO  Oggi il mondo s'è cambiato
                           "La Ragazza della Penombra" (Rulli)          12/23
7-254127 DALUMI/GARGIULO  Troppi adorator  do. do.           do.        12/23
7-254128 DALUMI/GARGIULO  Ogni ragazza  "Selvaggia" (Bellini)           12/23
7-254129 DALUMI/GARGIULO  Appena spunta il sol  do. do.                 12/23
7-254130 BENEDETTI/GARGIULO  Dell'Università la luce siam noi tre
                           "Don Gil dalle calze verdi" (Carabella)       3/24
7-254131 BENEDETTI/DALUMI  Io son gentil, fanciulla  do. do. do.        3/24
7-254132 RICCIOLI/PRIMAVERA  Oh, che piacer "Bacco in Toscana" (Brogi)   5/24
7-254133 RICCIOLI/PRIMAVERA  E piribiribì...e piribiribò  do.do.do.      5/24
7-254134 D'ARY/DOMAR  Fiorin d'erbetta "Bacco in Toscana" (Brogi)        5/24
7-254135 DOMAR/PRIMAVERA  Quando tra i monti   do. do. do.               5/24
```

```
7-254136  RICCIOLI/PRIMAVERA   Duetto Genovetta e Fridolino "Casta Diva"(Bellini)
                                                                          5/24
7-254137  RICCIOLI/PRIMAVERA   Ah! se qui fosse il mio tesor    do. do. do.5/24
7-254138  DOMAR/PRIMAVERA/RICCIOLI  One step dei pazzi          do. do. do.5/24
7-254139  RICCIOLI/PRIMAVERA   Quando siam di carnevale         do. do. do.5/24
7-254140  DOMAR/PRIMAVERA      Piccin séparé                    do. do. do.5/24
7-254141  LIDELBA/AGNOLETTI    Occhi fondi e neri! "La Bajadera" (Kalmán)  6/24
7-254142  LIDELBA/AGNOLETTI    Mia bella signorina  "Bambù" (Carabella)    6/24
7-254143  LIDELBA/AGNOLETTI    Bambù, Bambù, che cosa cerchi tu?  do. do.  6/24
7-254144  LIDELBA/AGNOLETTI    Siam persone molto chic                     7/24
                               "La Bambola della Prateria" (Lombardo-Zerkovitz)
7-254145  LIDELBA/AGNOLETTI    Dite, non so ben capire          do. do. do.  7/24
7-254146  LIDELBA/AGNOLETTI    Un cow-boy non sa                do. do. do.  7/24
7-254147  LIDELBA/AGNOLETTI    Come un gattin perfetto          do. do. do.  7/24
7-254148  RICCIOLI/PRIMAVERA   Un uom potete...                              7/24
                               "La Ragazza d'Oltremare" (Ballig e Capellan)
7-254149  RICCIOLI/PRIMAVERA   Quando un ballo risuona susdente  do.do. do.7/24
7-254150  RICCIOLI/PRIMAVERA   Sull'albero tra i rami "La Donna Perduta"(Petri)
                                                                          2/25
7-254151  DOMAR/PRIMAVERA      D'esser la tua sposina           do.do.do.   2/25
7-254152  RICCIOLI/PRIMAVERA   La donna di diamanti             do.do.do.   2/25
7-254153  RICCIOLI/PRIMAVERA   Casetta bella, bella padroncina  do.do.      2/25
7-254154  RICCIOLI/PRIMAVERA   Se vieni a Varasdin "Contessa Mariza"(Kalmán)3/25
7-254155  RICCIOLI/PRIMAVERA   Vorrei sognare di te             do.do.do.   3/25
7-254156  RICCIOLI/PRIMAVERA   Ti guardi il Ciel                do.do.do.   3/25
7-254157  RICCIOLI/PRIMAVERA   Bruna bimba d'Ungheraa           do.do.do.   3/25
7-254158  RICCIOLI/PRIMAVERA   Chi può dir che sia  "Grand Hotel" (Caucci)  4/25
7-254159  RICCIOLI/PRIMAVERA   Mica so' micco - Tango           do.do.do.   4/25
7-254160  RICCIOLI/PRIMAVERA   Glielo dico schietto "Il Ventaglio"(Cuscinà)4/25
7-254161  RICCIOLI/PRIMAVERA   Ciabattino e Ciabattina          do.do.do.   4/25
7-254162  RICCIOLI/PRIMAVERA   E lui e lei, e lei e lui
                               "La Bella Mammina" (Eysler)                   6/25
7-254163  RICCIOLI/PRIMAVERA   C'è ai Cielo...dentro il vin  do.do.do.       6/25
7-254164  RICCIOLI/PRIMAVERA   Pierrot e Pierrette
                               "La Maschera danzante" (Benatzky)            5/25
7-254165  RICCIOLI/PRIMAVERA   Suona, bel zingarello            do.do.do.   5/25
7-254167  GIORGINI/FELLA       Libiam nei lieti calici  "La Traviata" (Verdi) 10/25
7-254168  MANFRINI/NOTO        Suoni la tromba  "I Puritani" (Bellini)     11/25
7-254169  GIORGINI/SALVI       D'un pensiero  "La Sonnambula" (Bellini)     3/26
7-254170  GIORGINI/SALVI       Un dì felice eterea  "La Traviata" (Verdi)   3/26
7-254171  GIORGINI/SALVI       Parigi o cara             do.              do.    3/26
7-254180  RICCIOLI/PRIMAVERA   Oh, com'è bello giudare i cavalli!
                               "L'Acqua Cheta" (Pietri)                     7/26
7-254181  DOMAR/PRIMAVERA      Dal dì che t'ho veduta           do.do.do.   7/26
7-254182  DOMAR/PRIMAVERA/RICCIOLI  Belle siam contadinette  do.do.do.     7/26
7-254183  RICCIOLI/DOMAR       Meglio è un bicchier             do.do.do.   7/26
7-254184  RICCIOLI/PRIMAVERA/DOMAR  Felicità, felicità!
                               "È arrivata l'Ambasciatore" (Bellini)  6/26
7-254185  RICCIOLI/PRIMAVERA   Nel tren non si riposa ben       do.do.do.   6/26
7-254186  RICCIOLI/PRIMAVERA/DOMAR  Leone qua! Leone là!
                               "Addio Giovinezza" (Petri)                   6/26
7-254187  RICCIOLI/PRIMAVERA   Cioccolatin, Cioccolatin         do.do.do.   6/26
7-254190  SERRA/SUARDÒ         Carità d'amore (Ripp)                        1/26
7-254191  SERRA/SUARDÒ         Nilo blù (Ripp)                              1/26
7-254192  SERRA/SUARDÒ         Uno strano fior (Ripp)                       1/26
7-254193  SERRA/SUARDÒ         Sfoglia la margherita (Ripp)                 1/26
7-254194  SERRA/SUARDÒ         Cina! (Ripp)                                 1/26
```

```
7-254516 ANDREINI/BADINI/BETTONI/BARACCHI/CECCARELLI
                    Pranzar in casa  "La Bohème" (Puccini)           6/19
7-254517 GIANA      Ohè, là! le guardie! Aprite        do.do.do.    6/19
7-254518 ANDREINI/BADINI/BETTONI/BARACCHI/CECCARELLI
                    Ha visto ?                          do.do.do.    6/19
7-254519 BOSINI/ANDREINI/BADINI  Marcello finalmente   do.do.do.    6/19
```

12" records :: GREEN LABEL

```
0252000 LANZINI  Uno check sulla Banca Rothschild
                    "Il Conte di Lussemburgo" (Lehàr)       1913-1914/5
0252001 DE GREGORIO  A qual gloir divin  "Racconti d'Hoffmann"(Offenbach)
                                                            1913-1914/5

0253000 MARCHETTI  Orsù dal marchese si vada  "Geisha" (Jones)      1911
0253001 MARCHETTI  La nostra vita è di piacer   do.   do.           1911?
0253002 LUFRANO   Dolce notte i rei d'amor "Racconti d'Hoffmann" (Offenbach)
                                                                    1913/4
0254000 MARCHETTI/TESSARI/VOLTA  O mia Mimosa  "Geisha" (Jones)     1911
0254001 LANZINI/POMPEI/PETRONI  Colle donne...come agir?
                    "La Vedova Allegra" (Lehàr)                     1913/4
```

```
2-0252000 TUMINELLO   O Lola  "Cavalleria Rusticana" (Mascagni)      1915
2-0252001 TUMINELLO   Brindisi        do.       do.                  1915
2-0252002 TUMINELLO/RAVELLI  Mamma, quel vino è generoso  do.do.     1915
2-0252003 TUMINELLO   Dei miei bollenti spiriti "La Traviata" (Verdi) 1917
2-0252004 DANISE      Cortigiani, vil razza  "Rigoletto" (Verdi) (346af) 1917
2-0252005 DANISE      Pari siamo             do.         do.(348af)  1917
2-0252006 MONTANELLI  Si può? Prologo I.  "Pagliacci" (Leoncavallo)  1917
2-0252007 MONTANELLI  Un nido  do. II.       do.        do.          1917
2-0252008 BOLIS       Che gelida manina  "La Bohème" (Puccini)       6/19
2-0252009 BETTONI     La calunnia "Il Barbiere di Siviglia" (Rossini) 2/19
2-0252010 ZANI/N.N.(bs)  Tosca è buon falco  "Tosca" (Puccini)       4/19
2-0252011 BROCCARDI   E lucevan le stelle     do.       do.          4/19
2-0252012 BETTONI     Ite sul colle  "Norma" (Bellini)               12/19
2-0252013 TALIANI     Ecco ridente  "Il Barbiere di Siviglia"(Rossini) 6/20
2-0252014 BADINI      Largo al factotum       do.       do.          6/20
2-0252015 DI LELIO    La calunnia             do.       do.          6/20
2-0252016 PACINI/FERNANDEZ  Tosca è buon falco  "Tosca" (Puccini)    2/21
2-0252017 SALVANESCHI  E lucevan le stelle    do.       do.          2/21
2-0252018 TRENTINI    Celeste Aida           "Aida" (Verdi)          11/20
2-0252021 TALIANI     Firenze è come un albero fiorito "Gianni Schicchi"
                                                         (Puccini)   12/20
2-0252022 ROMAGNOLI   No, interrogo invan  "Faust" (Gounod)          4/21
2-0252023 ROMAGNOLI   Ah! vieni, estremo de' miei dì  do. do.        4/21
2-0252024 LIMONTA     Su, da ber (Kermesse)              do. do.     4/21
2-0252025 PACINI      Dio possente                       do. do.     4/21
2-0252026 PACINI      S'hai tu poter di demon             do. do.    4/21
2-0252027 ROMAGNOLI   Salve dimora                        do. do.    4/21
2-0252028 PACINI      Morte di Valentino                  do. do.    4/21
2-0252029 LUPATO      Improvviso "Andrea Chenier" (Giordano)         7/21
2-0252030 PACINI      Lagrime e sangue  do.       do.                7/21
2-0252031 PACINI      Un dì m'era di gioia  do.   do.                7/21
2-0252032 LUPATO      Si fui soldato        do.   do.                7/21
2-0252035 SERRA       Nulla...nullina (Borella)
                                                                     1/24
```

```
2-0252036 SERRA       Estero...mania (Abbati)                                  1/24
2-0252037 GIORGINI    In povertà mia lieta  "La Bohème" (Puccini)              4/25
                      Ch'ella mi creda libero "La Fanciulla del West"(Puccini)
                      O dolci baci  "Tosca" (Puccini)                          4/25
2-0252038 BERGAMINI   Ma come dopo il nembo  "Werther" (Massenet)             8/25
2-0252039 BALLIN      Tu m'hai salvato  "La Wally" (Catalani)                  8/25


2-0253001 ERMOLLI     Preghiera  Sc.III.Pt.II."Cavalleria Rusticana"(Mascagni)
                                                                             1915
2-0253002 BEVIGNANI   È strano              "La Traviata" (Verdi)            1917
2-0253003 BEVIGNANI   Addio del passato        do.      do.                 1917
2-0253004 ANNITA      Qual fiamma avea      "Pagliacci" (Leoncavallo)       1917
2-0253005 BENEDETTI   Aria di Anna "Loreley" (Catalani)                     1917
2-0253006 BOSINI      Mi chiamano Mimì  "La Bohème" (Puccini)               6/19
2-0253007 BENEDETTI   Una voce poco fa "Il Barbiere di Siviglia"(Rossini)2/19
2-0253008 N.N. (s)    Io de' sospiri  "Tosca" (Puccini)                     4/19
2-0253009 BURCHI      Casta diva  "Norma" (Bellini)                        12/19
2-0253010 BARTOLOMASI Ernani involami  "Ernani" (Verdi)                    11/19
2-0253011 BARTOLOMASI Madre pietosa vergine  "La Forza del Destino"(Verdi)
                                                                           11/19
2-0253012 BARTOLOMASI Pace, pace, mio Dio        do.      do.              11/19
2-0253013 AGOSTINI    Un bel dì vedremo "Madama Butterfly" (Puccini)       11/19
2-0253014 PEREIRA     Una voce poco fa "Il Barbiere di Siviglia"(Rossini)6/20
2-0253015 PEREIRA     Io sono docile        do.     do.     do.            6/20
2-0253016 MOMETTI     Che vecchio sospettoso!  do.     do.     do.         6/20
2-0253017 BARTOLOMASI/MAZZANTI/FERNANDEZ  Com'è lunga l'attesa
                                          "Tosca" (Puccini)                2/21
2-0253018 BARTOLOMASI Ritorna vincitor    "Aida" (Verdi)                  11/20
2-0253019 BARTOLOMASI I sacri nomi            do.     do.                 11/20
2-0253020 BARTOLOMASI O cieli azzurri         do.     do.                 11/20
2-0253021 PAGANI      Ohimè!..morir mi sento   do.     do.                11/20
2-0253028 PALADINI    O mio babbino caro  "Gianni Schicchi" (Puccini)     12/20
2-0253029 PALADINI    Senza mamma, bimbo  "Suor Angelica" (Puccini)       12/20
2-0253030 TIMITZ      Le parlate d'amor  "Faust" (Gounod)                  4/21
2-0253031 BOSINI      I gran Signori        do.     do.                    4/21
2-0253032 BOSINI      Aria di gioielli      do.     do.                    4/21
2-0253033 BARTOLOMASI La mamma morta "Andrea Chenier" (Giordano)           7/21
2-0253036 CARUGATI    Sì, mi chiamano Mimì  "La Bohème" (Puccini)          4/25
                      Un bel dì vedremo "Madama Butterfly" (Puccini)
                      Ah, in quelle trine morbide "Manon Lescaut"(Puccini)
2-0253037 VOLTOLINA   Aurette a cui si spesso  "Lohengrin" (Wagner)        8/25


2-0254000 ERMOLLI/RAVELLI  Dite, mamma Lucia  "Cavalleria Rusticana"(Mascagni)
                                                                          1915
2-0254001 ERMOLLI/TUMINELLO  No, no, Turiddu rimani  do.      do.         1915
2-0254002 BEVIGNANI/TUMINELLO  Dell'invito trascorsa è già l'ora
                                          "La Traviata" (Verdi)           1917
2-0254003 BEVIGNANI/TUMINELLO  Libiam nei lieti calici  do.  do.         1917
2-0254004 BEVIGNANI/TUMINELLO  Si ridesta in ciel l'aurora    do.        1917
2-0254005 BEVIGNANI/TUMINELLO  Sempre libera         do.                 1917
2-0254006 BEVIGNANI/BADINI     Alfredo? Per Parigi    do.                 1917
2-0254007 BEVIGNANI/BADINI     Dite alla giovane      do.                 1917
2-0254008 BEVIGNANI/BADINI     Imponete               do.                 1917
2-0254009 BEVIGNANI/TUMINELLO  Amami Alfredo          do.                 1917
2-0254010 BADINI/TUMINELLO     Di Provenza il mar     do.                 1917
2-0254011 BEVIGNANI/TUMINELLO  Alfredo! Voi?          do.                 1917
```

2-0254012 BEVIGNANI/TUMINELLO Scena della Borsa   "La Traviata" (Verdi) 1917
2-0254013 BEVIGNANI/TUMINELLO Parigi o cara   do.   do.   1917
2-0254014 BROCCARDI/SALA Questa o quella "Rigoletto" (Verdi) (352af) 1917
2-0254015 BROCCARDI/SALA/DANISE/GARRONE Minuetto e seguito do. (354af)1917
2-0254016 BROCCARDI/SALA/DANISE/BETTONI/LIMONTA Ch'io gli parli!do.(355af)1917
2-0254017 DANISE/BETTONI Signor! va...   do.   do. (347af)1917
2-0254018 ZERNI/BROCCARDI È il sol dell'anima   do.   do. (369af)1917
2-0254019 ZERNI Caro nome   do.   do. (372cf)1917
2-0254020 ZERNI/DANISE Piangi, fanciulla   do.   do.(373af) 1917
2-0254021 ZERNI/DANISE/BETTONI/LIMONTA Si, vendetta do.   do.(362af) 1917
2-0254022 SIMZIS/BADINI Deh,non parlare al misero   do.   do.(3160c) 1917
2-0254023 BADINI/PEZZATI La-rà, la-rà, la-rà   do.   do.(3165c) 1917
2-0254024 SIMZIS/BADINI Mio padre!..Dio!   do.   do.(3164c) 1917
2-0254025 SIMZIS/PEZZATI/BROCCARDI/BADINI Bella figlia dell'amore (3163c)1917
2-0254026 ZERNI/GARRONE/BETTONI Somiglia un Apollo (366af) do.   do. 1917
2-0254027 BROCCARDI/BADINI/FERNANDEZ Della vendetta (3167c) do.   do. 1917
2-0254028 SIMZIS/BADINI Lassù in ciel   (3161c) do.   do. 1917
2-0254029 BOLIS/MONTANELLI M'accordan di parlare? "Pagliacci" (Leoncavallo)
                                                                        1917
2-0254030 CONTI/BOLIS Un tal gioco   do.   do.   1917
2-0254031 CONTI/MONTANELLI Sei là? Credea   do.   do.   1917
2-0254032 CONTI/BADINI Silvio, a quest'ora   do.   do.   1917
2-0254033 CONTI/BADINI/MONTANELLI No, più non m'ami do.   do.   1917
2-0254034 CONTI/BADINI/MONTANELLI/BOLIS Cammina adagio do.   1917
2-0254035 MONTANELLI/BOLIS Io la sorveglio   do.   do.   1917
2-0254036 MONTANELLI/BOLIS/CONTI Nome di Dio   do.   do.   1917
2-0254037 MONTANELLI/BOLIS/BADINI/PRAT Sperai (Finale) do.   do.   1917
2-0254038 ANDREINI/BADINI/BETTONI Questo Mar Rosso "La Bohème" (Puccini)6/19
2-0254039 ANDREINI/BADINI/BETTONI/BARACCHI Ho pagato il trimestre do. 6/19
2-0254040 ANDREINI/BADINI/BETTONI Pensier profondo   do.   do.   6/19
2-0254041 BOSINI/ANDREINI Non sono in vena   do.   do.   6/19
2-0254042 BOSINI/ANDREINI/BADINI/BARACCHI/BETTONI Ehi! Rodolfo! do.   6/19
2-0254043 BOSINI/ANDREINI/BADINI/BARACCHI/BETTONI Aranci, datteri do. 6/19
2-0254044 BOSINI/ANDREINI/BADINI/BARACCHI Che guardi?   do. do. 6/19
2-0254045 BOSINI/GIANA/ANDREINI/BADINI/BETTONI/BARACCHI/CECCARELLI
                    Ch'io beva del tossico   do.   do.   6/19
2-0254046 BOSINI/ANDREINI/BADINI/BARACCHI/BETTONI/MAESTRI
                    Parpignol! Parpignol!   do.   do.   6/19
2-0254047 BOSINI/GIANA/ANDREINI/BADINI/BETTONI/BARACCHI/CECCARELLI
                    Quando m'en vo soletta   do.   do.   6/19
2-0254048 BOSINI/GIANA/ANDREINI/BADINI/BETTONI/BARACCHI
                    Marcello! Sirena!   do.   do.   6/19
2-0254049 BOSINI/BADINI Mimì? Son io   do.   do.   6/19
2-0254050 BOSINI/ANDREINI Addio! Che! Vai?   do.   do.   6/19
2-0254051 ANDREINI/BADINI O Mimì, tu più   do.   do.   6/19
2-0254052 BOSINI/GIANA/ANDREINI/BADINI Addio dolce svegliare do. do. 6/19
2-0254053 TISCI-RUBINI/ZANI/BARACCHI Che ora sia   do.   do.   6/19
2-0254054 ANDREINI/BADINI/BARACCHI/BETTONI Gavotta! Minuetto do. do. 6/19
2-0254055 BOSINI/GIANA/ANDREINI/BETTONI/BADINI/BARACCHI Vecchia zimarra 6/19
                                           "La Bohème" (Puccini)
2-0254056 BOSINI/GIANA/ANDREINI/BADINI/BETTONI/BARACCHI
                    Musetta! C'è Mimì   do. do.   6/19
2-0254057 BOSINI/ANDREINI Tornò al nido   do. do.   6/19
2-0254058 BOSINI/ANDREINI Sono andati?   do. do.   6/19
2-0254059 BOSINI/GIANA/ANDREINI/BADINI/BETTONI/BARACCHI
                    Che ha detto il medico?   do. do.   6/19
2-0254060 BOSINI/BETTONI Signor concesso sia   "Faust" (Gounod)   3/19
2-0254061 BOSINI/BETTONI Ciel! che voce odo mai?   do.   do.   3/19

Printed in the USA
CPSIA information can be obtained
at www.ICGtesting.com
LVHW022238041023
760187LV00035B/827